Market Structure and Competition Policy

Market Structure and Competition Policy applies modern advances in game-theory to the analysis of competition policy and develops some of the theoretical and policy concerns associated with the pioneering work of Louis Phlips. Containing contributions by leading scholars from Europe and North America, this book observes a common theme in the relationship between the regulatory regime and market structure. Since the inception of the new industrial organisation, economists have developed a better understanding of how real-world markets operate. These results have particular relevance to the design and application of anti-trust policy. Analyses indicate that picking the most competitive framework in the short run may be detrimental to competition and welfare in the long run, concentrating the attention of policy makers on the impact on the long-run market structure. This book provides essential reading for graduate students of industrial and managerial economics as well as researchers and policy makers.

GEORGE NORMAN is the holder of the Cummings Family Chair in Entrepreneurship and Business Economics at Tufts University and is the Director of the Graduate Program in Economics. His publications include *Economies of Scale, Transport Costs, and Location, The Economics of Imperfect Competition: A Spatial Approach,* and *Industrial Organization: Contemporary Theory and Practice* (with D. Richards and L. Pepall).

JACQUES-FRANÇOIS THISSE is Professor of Economics in the Center for Operations Research and Econometrics at the Université Catholique de Louvain. He is the author of *Does Economic Space Matter?* and *Discrete Choice Theory of Product Differentiation.*

Professor Louis Phlips

Market Structure and Competition Policy

Game-Theoretic Approaches

Edited by

GEORGE NORMAN

and

JACQUES-FRANÇOIS THISSE

CAMBRIDGE
UNIVERSITY PRESS

PUBLISHED BY THE PRESS SYNDICATE OF THE UNIVERSITY OF CAMBRIDGE
The Pitt Building, Trumpington Street, Cambridge CB2 1RP, United Kingdom

CAMBRIDGE UNIVERSITY PRESS
The Edinburgh Building, Cambridge CB2 2RU, UK   http://www.cup.cam.ac.uk
40 West 20th Street, New York, NY 10011-4211, USA   http://www.cup.org
10 Stamford Road, Oakleigh, Melbourne 3166, Australia
Ruiz do Alarcón 13, 28014 Madrid, Spain

© First published 2000

Typeface Times 10/12 pt.   *System* 3b2 [ADVENT]

A catalogue record for this book is available from the British Library

Library of Congress Cataloguing-in-Publication Data

Market structure and competition policy: game theoretic approaches/edited by
George Norman and Jacques-François Thisse.
      p.   cm.
A collection of 12 papers by European and North American scholars which develops
some of the theroretical and policy concerns associated with the pioneering work of
Louis Phlips.
ISBN 0-521-78333-X
      1. Competition–Government policy–Mathematical models. 2. Industrial
policy–Mathematical models. 3. Game theory. 4. Phlips, Louis. I. Norman, George,
1946– II. Thisse, Jacques-François. III. Phlips, Louis.
HB238.M37 2000
338.6ı048–dc21   00-028960

ISBN 0521 78333 X Hardback

Transferred to digital printing 2004

Contents

Figures

Tables

Contributors

Claude d'Aspremont *Université Catholique de Louvain, Belgium*
Gianni De Fraja *University of York, England*
André de Palma *Université de Cergy-Pontoise, France*
David Encaoua *Université Paris I, France*
James W. Friedman *University of North Carolina, USA*
Robert J. Gary-Bobo *Université de Cergy-Pontoise, France*
Jonathan H. Hamilton *University of Florida, USA*
Stephen Martin *University of Copenhagen, Denmark*
Massimo Motta *European University Institute, Italy*
Damien J. Neven *Université de Lausanne, Switzerland*
George Norman *Tufts University, Massachusetts, USA*
Jean-Pierre Ponssard *Laboratoire d' Econométrie de l'Ecole Polytechnique, France*
P.K. Mathew Tharakan *Faculteit Toegepaste Economisch Wetenschappen, Belgium*
Jacques-François Thisse *Université Catholique de Louvain, Belgium*
Xavier Wauthy *Facultés Universitaires Saint-Louis, Belgium*
Yves Zenou *Ecole Nationale des Ponts et Chaussées, France*

Louis Phlips: a brief biography

Louis Phlips was born in 1933 in Brussels. He received a doctorate in economics at the Université Catholique de Louvain and a doctorate in law at the Katholieke Universiteit Leuven. After teaching for four years at Fribourg University (Switzerland), he returned to his *alma mater* from 1966 until 1989. He then joined the European University Institute in Florence (Italy) until 1997, when he retired from Academia. He now spends his time playing the piano and drawing.

During his 23 years at the Université Catholique de Louvain, Louis was first director of the Economic Analysis Unit (ANEC) and then a member of CORE (Center for Operations Research and Econometrics). Before Switzerland, he visited Nuffield College to work with P.S.W. Andrews on industrial pricing. Between Switzerland and Louvain, he visited the University of Chicago (Fall and Winter 1965) and Harvard University (Spring and Summer 1966) to work with Henk Houthakker on his econometric utility tree. He wanted to find out which empirical commodity groupings correspond to the theoretical concept (if any) of an 'industry'.

Already in those early days, Louis' research interests had clearly taken shape: use price theory to better understand observed business practices. It all goes back to his 1961 doctoral thesis *De l'intégration des marchés* that asked (and answered) the question: what will happen to the cartels (that were in operation in most European industries) once the Common Market authorities start reinforcing an anti-trust policy? Since there were no statistical industry data available for Europe, Louis volunteered to compute concentration ratios from the new industrial census. They form the bulk of his North-Holland monograph *Effects of Industrial Concentration: A Cross-Section Analysis for the Common Market* (1971).

His Ph D thesis had a yellow cover. It was followed by the green North-Holland cover. Having chosen blue for his elementary time series analysis (*Analyse chronologique*), the next cover couldn't but be red. Louis used to say: 'Mao has his red book, why shouldn't I have one too?' *Applied Consumption Analysis* (1974, enlarged 1983) was the result. Its exercises made a full generation of doctoral students suffer and grumble, but at the end of the day they had learned how to bridge the gap between demand theory and econometrics.

After 10 years of applied econometric work, Louis felt relieved to return to his old love, industrial economics. His 1983 Cambridge University Press book of *The Economics of Price Discrimination* was his answer to a remark (made by a so-called 'pure' theorist) that price discrimination is a market failure. Louis made the point that if price discrimination is a failure, then everything business men do is a failure too: price discrimination is indeed present everywhere, in pricing over the space and time domain as well as over the quality and income domain.

Being surrounded by world-famous theorists, Louis had to try his hand at applying some (elementary) game-theory to his favourite topics. Hence his *Economics of Imperfect Information* (1988) which got a policy flavour in *Competition Policy: A Game-Theoretic Perspective* (1995), both from Cambridge University Press.

The final bouquet was – at the request of Cambridge University Press – a selection of published articles which he found worth turning into required reading on *Applied Industrial Economics* (1998).

Louis was a visiting professor at the Universities of Montréal, Pennsylvania, Cornell, Leuven and Bielefeld. One of the founders of the European Economic Association, he was its Secretary until 1989 and its President for 1995. He is a member of the Academia Europaea and a fellow of the Econometric Society.

Introduction

George Norman and Jacques-François Thisse

In his doctoral thesis published in 1962, Louis Phlips argued that European firms in the cement industry attempted to coordinate their actions by using basing-point pricing systems and more or less formal agreements about geographical markets. At the time that Louis was formulating his ideas, European competition policy was still in its infancy. It is perhaps no surprise that those who were formulating policies at that time paid little attention to the work of a doctoral student. It is somewhat ironic that these have come to centre stage at the end of Louis' distinguished academic career. It is also amusing to note that after a long and productive detour through consumption analysis, applied econometrics and industrial economics, Louis himself has chosen to return to his original love as shown by his *Competition Policy: A Game-Theoretic Perspective.*

Game-theoretic methods are now indispensable in the design, formulation and testing of competition policy in Europe and anti-trust policy in the United States. Until very recently, the connection was from market structure through market behaviour, as explained by game-theoretic tools, to competition policy. We can see this timeline, for example, in the formulation of merger policy and policies with respect to cartels. What is new is the realisation that this is a two-way street. Just as market structure affects competition policy, competition policy equally affects market structure. As European competition policy is becoming more active, it has become increasingly endogenised in the strategic decisions of the firms whose behaviour the policy is intended to affect. It is dangerous for policy makers to ignore this change in behaviour. For example, we are now aware that in some circumstances making a market more competitive is not necessarily beneficial to consumers. Rather, the additional competition may increase market concentration and may facilitate tacit or even explicit coordination among the surviving firms. This connection from competition policy to market structure and the welfare effects of policy is a recurrent theme of this book.

1

Louis' early interest in basing-point pricing extended to spatial price policy when he wrote a report for the European Commission in 1976. This culminated in his book on *The Economics of Price Discrimination* that had a significant influence on scholars and policy makers alike. An essential preliminary to any discussion of price discrimination is that we should be able to define what we mean by 'discriminatory prices'. The conventional definition prior to Louis' analysis was that price discrimination exists when the same product is sold to different consumers at different prices but this is unsatisfactory, for at least two reasons. First, such a definition might lead us to conclude that price discrimination exists when a company sells its product in two different cities – say, New York and London – at different prices. Clearly this conclusion would be wrong since it ignores the different costs of supplying these two cities. Secondly, we might conclude that there is no price discrimination if the firm sells its product in London and New York at the *same* prices. This is equally wrong since the prices now do *not* reflect the different costs of supplying these two cities. Louis was able to circumvent these problems by providing us with the following definition:

Price discrimination should be defined as implying that two varieties of a commodity are sold (by the same seller) to two buyers at different *net* prices, the net price being the price (paid by the buyer) corrected for the cost associated with the product differentiation. (Phlips, 1983, p. 6, emphasis in the original)

Applying this to our example, price discrimination exists if the difference between the London and the New York prices is not equal to the difference in the seller's marginal costs of supplying London and New York.

Starting from this definition, Louis was one of the first to point out that price discrimination is a pervasive marketing practice that survives despite the attempts by regulators to limit or eliminate its use. This might come as no surprise if we were to consider only situations where firms are able to exercise considerable market power since price discrimination provides the firm with a remarkably efficient means by which consumer surplus can be converted into profit. What was more surprising and influential was Louis' clear demonstration that price discrimination is widespread in oligopolistic and more generally imperfectly competitive markets. Moreover, he showed through both theory and evidence that the degree of price discrimination present in such markets is, if anything, *stronger* than would characterise a monopolist in the same markets. This analysis set an agenda that remains current and active today.

European cement manufacture provides a classic case study of many of Louis' ideas. The price and competition policies of the major manufacturers are under scrutiny by the European Commission. Chapter 1, by d'Aspremont, Encaoua and Ponssard shows how the questions that motivated Louis Phlips in his doctoral dissertation can be revisited using modern game-theoretic techniques. In particular, these authors discuss the relationship between spatial pricing policies and market behaviour and performance in an industry characterised by high transport costs. Their analysis provides an important illustration of the connection noted above between competition policy and market structure. Denying cement firms the use of, for example, basing-point pricing, has increased price competition but has also been associated with a dramatic increase in market concentration.

There is a related issue that also recurs in a number of chapters in this book: the role of *information*. d'Aspremont, Encaoua and Ponssard discuss the impact on prices of facilitating practices such as most-favoured customer clauses or meet-the-competition promises. Recent analyses suggest that this kind of information exchange between firms changes the resulting market equilibria from Bertrand to Cournot, with the surprising result that consumers lose out. These authors show that this is a short-run effect only that ignores the connection between the competitive environment and long-run market structure. The idea behind this is in fact very simple and general. If firms expect tough competition (e.g. *à la* Bertrand) we are likely to see greater industry concentration and higher prices than if they anticipate soft competition (e.g. *à la* Cournot).

Competition policy is still evolving in the European Union, perhaps because such a policy is relatively young in Europe by historical standards. This is in sharp contrast with the long history of anti-trust policy in the United States. Neven in chapter 2 correctly points out that European policy makers could benefit from applying some of the lessons that have been learned in the United States. There are some common elements. For example, on both sides of the Atlantic, the principle is emerging that the possession and exercise of market power is not of itself evidence of violation of competition or anti-trust rules. Rather the appropriate courts have to find evidence of explicit coordination when there are several firms involved, or evidence of attempts to extend market power when the market is effectively monopolised. Microsoft was not being investigated because it has an effective monopoly of operating systems. It *was* being investigated to see whether it has tried to use its operating system monopoly to extend its market power into browser markets. By contrast, there are some sharp distinctions between United States and European policies. Neven points to two of these. First, it is reasonably common practice in the United States to take the existence of market power as an indication of the possibility that there is coordination between firms. Secondly, the United States anti-trust authorities tend to take the existence of facilitating practices as a presumption of coordination. Neither principle is yet established in Europe.

There is a major difficulty confronting the Commission in its pursuit of coordinating practices that is well articulated by Friedman in his insightful discussion of the Folk Theorem in chapter 3. This can be simply stated. Once firms recognise that they interact repeatedly, then it is possible for them to settle on a non-cooperative dynamic equilibrium that looks very like a market outcome that would emerge from explicit coordination. This is an example of what Louis Phlips has referred to as the 'indistinguishability problem'. The theory of repeated games suggests that firms can form non-cooperative strategies that support collusive outcomes. These strategies always involve some credible threats to punish deviations. It is difficult to see how these threats can be made credible without their being communicated between the relevant firms since in principle they are never actually observed. The act of communication is in violation of competition policy, but is remarkably difficult to observe.

An equally difficult issue facing both the Commission and the international trading community is the design and implementation of effective anti-dumping (AD) legislation. These problems are eloquently addressed by Tharakan in chapter 4 and draw together two important themes of Louis' work: price discrimination and the design of competition policy, in this case at the supra-national level. A particularly interesting feature of the use of AD measures is the dramatic proliferation in the number of countries initiating such measures. In 1990 four groups launched around 82 per cent of AD investigations: Australia, Canada, the European Union and the United States. By 1997 this proportion had fallen to less than 49 per cent with AD actions being actively used by a number of developing and Newly Industrialising Countries (NICs). There is a danger that the strategic use of AD measures will seriously undermine movement towards multilateral trade liberalisation. Indeed, there is the real-risk that these measures will lead to the escalation of protectionism under the guise of measures purported to ensure some kind of 'level playing field' in international trade.

Tharakan points out that the welfare effects of AD legislation are at best ambiguous – a conclusion that applies equally to legislation intended to prevent price discrimination. Indeed, most of the analysis that has been conducted has concluded that AD legislation actually imposes large welfare losses on both the exporting country *and* the importing country that initiates the AD investigation. The solution that is suggested to correct the detrimental strategic and welfare consequences of AD actions is to change the regulations developed by the World Trade Organisation (WTO) and individual nation states on AD legislation, restricting their application to cases of predatory price dumping. This type of dumping does have detrimental welfare effects and needs to be corrected. Identifying such dumping suffers from many of the same problems that confront the anti-trust authorities in trying to prove predatory pricing *within* a country: another application of Louis' 'indistinguishability problem'. Tharakan points out, however, that a number of new methods have been developed for detecting attempted predation. One particularly useful such test involves a 'two-tier approach'. First, assess the market power of the supposed predator: only if such power exists is predatory power either feasible or likely. For those cases that 'pass' the first test, consider price–cost and other factors. It is a relatively simple matter to extend this type of test to the international arena. If this had been done, Tharakan notes that its impact would have been to reduce significantly the number of AD complaints that reach the second-tier test.

We noted above that there is an important link from competition policy to market structure that has been neglected by policy makers, both in Europe and in the United States. The next group of chapters focuses on this link from different perspectives. Norman and Thisse in chapter 5 argue that the naive application of the idea that competition is always and everywhere desirable may have unforeseen and harmful effects. Policies that create too tough a competitive environment may be detrimental to consumers and social welfare through their impact on firms' medium- and long-run decisions. The stronger are the structural effects of competition policy, the more likely is it that blind adherence by the anti-trust authorities to the benefits of competition is misguided. In particular, these authors show that consumers are likely to lose from price deregulation in markets characterised before deregulation by high levels of concentration. This suggests a role for regulators that has not been considered, despite the fact that it lies at the heart of the Folk Theorem of repeated games: the regulator should impose a minimum period of time over which prices cannot be changed. Such a slowing in the speed of response undermines the effectiveness of the punishment that supports the tacitly collusive outcome.

The same trade-off between tough competition and concentrated market is also at the centre of d'Aspremont and Motta's work and concerned Phlips in the introduction to *Applied Industrial Economics*. In chapter 6, they develop a similar set of policy conclusions, using a different setting. Specifically, they consider a situation in which anti-trust authorities attempt to break down price coordination to create an environment in which prices are set competitively. In so doing, the variety of products is reduced, prices are increased and consumers are worse off.

Hamilton in chapter 7 considers a related but somewhat different set of ideas. In the United States, the Federal Trade Commission (FTC) regulates advertising. In particular, it has developed policies to prevent the use of 'bait-and switch' tactics. If a firm advertises a low price, it must also be able to show that it has sufficient inventory to meet anticipated demand. This can be a significant constraint on the firm but it can be circumvented if the firm offers a 'raincheck'. This is a promise to supply at the sale price once new inventory has been received. What Hamilton shows is that the requirement that rainchecks be offered deters vigorous competition. Again, a policy designed to protect consumers may actually harm them.

The idea that competition policy may drastically affect market structure is illustrated in chapter 8 by Martin in a yet different context. Suppose that firms can undertake R&D that leads to process innovations. The firms may also collude and the competition authorities take market performance as a signal of the potential existence of collusion. Martin shows that a stronger competition policy reduces both pre-innovation and post-innovation profits, but the latter relatively less than the former. Consequently, tougher competition policy induces additional R&D spending. The additional R&D, by reducing costs, also reduces the probability of investigation by the authorities. This is not necessarily beneficial to the collectivity. There is an inverted U-shaped relationship between competition policy and expected net welfare. Once again, a moderately strict competition policy improves welfare; excessively strict competition does not.

Regulation remains one major dimension of competition policy, particularly in its application to the behaviour of previously state-owned monopolies that have been privatised, or the creation of new natural monopolies such as cable television. The interesting issues are, first, the design of regulatory policy itself and, secondly, whether it is possible to create a competitive environment in some industries. De Fraja in chapter 9 discusses some of the main issues that arise in the design of regulatory regimes. Recent analyses have discussed how competition and regulation affect industry performance and how the interaction between the regulator and the regulated affects industry structure in ways that are determined by the regulatory rules. What De Fraja shows is that a wide variety of outcomes can arise, leading to the need for a case-by-case approach to the modelling of the interplay between the regulator and the regulated.

The final three chapters of this book open new avenues for research in which competition policy, while not yet developed, will undoubtedly have an important role to play. It is fair to say that time is at best implicit in many game-theoretic contributions to the design of competition policy. Yet, entry and exit of firms arise in real-time and seems to exhibit some robust stylised facts: (1) entry is frequent and relatively easy; (2) entry tends to be associated with innovation; (3) entrants suffer a high failure rate and (4) exit follows successful entry. Ponssard in chapter 10 develops a dynamic model of competition that has the potential of exhibiting many of these features. The main message to be drawn from his analysis is that the outcome of the entry/exit dynamics will be determined by the interplay between competitive advantage that tends to favour entrants and mobility barriers that tend to favour incumbents.

The banking industry has often been considered as a prototype of a competitive market. However, the large number of mergers observed in recent years suggests that it is now more appropriate to see these markets as being oligopolistic. Although the banking sector has been and is still very regulated, very little attention has been paid to the process of competition between banks. In order to develop appropriate tools in competition policy, one must develop a better understanding of the future working of this sector because of its new more concentrated structure. In this perspective, de Palma and Gary-Bobo in chapter 11 present one of the first modellings of oligopolistic competition of the banking sector. They show that the behaviour of banks is potentially unstable in that a small change in the underlying parameters can induce a sharp change in equilibria – for example, from safe to risky. Their contribution thus sheds light on the importance of determining the role of the central bank as a regulator of competition in this sector.

The spirit of chapter 12 by Wauthy and Zenou is similar in that it invites us to think of other institutions as possible actors in the design of competition policy. It draws our attention toward the interaction between the product and labour markets. By affecting the product market, the anti-trust authorities may influence the choice of technologies and, therefore, the need for skilled or unskilled workers. One is not accustomed to think in these terms but their contribution leads us to think of the possible implications for workers of competition policy as well as of the connections between competition policy and training.

1 Competition policy and game-theory: reflections based on the cement industry case

Claude d'Aspremont, David Encaoua and
Jean-Pierre Ponssard

1 Introduction

Is the main objective of competition policy the *maintenance of competition per se* or the *promotion of economic efficiency*? These two goals do not necessarily have the same basis or the same implications.[1] The goal of maintaining competition *per se* can be justified morally, politically and legally by the wish to protect individual freedom and rights, and by limiting the power of agents. This faith in the democratic virtues of interacting competitive forces is grounded in a political philosophy which sees regulatory mechanisms resulting from *impersonal* market forces as a guarantee against the arbitrariness of authority, whether public or private. In this sense, competition is a right which warrants protection. Economically, competition is not considered as an end in itself but rather as a mechanism for allocating resources which in many, if not all cases, promotes economic efficiency. The question the economist has then to answer is whether or not, depending on the circumstances, competition promotes the reduction of costs, the selection of the most efficient businesses, the welfare of consumers, the creation of new products, the entry of new enterprises, the development of technological progress and innovation and so on.

To what extent do these two goals of competition policy overlap? Before setting out our framework to formulate an answer to this question, let us introduce the basic issues.

Clearly, if competition policy adopted an exclusively normative approach, consisting of the decentralised inducement of an efficient

An initial version of this chapter was presented at the conference 'Economic Analysis and Antitrust Issues in Concentrated Sectors: The Case of the Cement Industry', Paris, Carré des Sciences (15 January 1996). We wish to thank Louis Phlips, Hervé Tanguy, Jacques-François Thisse and the other participants at the conference for their comments and suggestions.

[1] See, for example, Jenny (1993); Encaoua (1997).

allocation of resources, based on the perfectly competitive behaviour of firms, the convergence between the above two goals would be total, according to the First Welfare Theorem. Such an approach means, however, that each business would be obliged to comply with the rule of maximising profits by taking the environment in which it operates as fixed – an outrageous requirement. We know that that is not how competition policy functions. Rather than decreeing rules *a priori*, free competition limits itself to prohibiting certain types of behaviour judged to be reprehensible in so far as they hinder the free play of market forces. However, the interpretation of this notion is tricky since no precise system of reference exists for judging deviant behaviour.

Thus, in many oligopolistic sectors the reference to 'perfect competition' is totally unrealistic. Market forces are not impersonal and the limited number of actors naturally leads firms to adopt strategic behaviour in which they anticipate their competitors' reactions. We have thus to ascertain which rules would need to prevail on these markets in order to ensure that the discrepancy was not too great between the principle of maintaining rivalry, implicit in the free play of market forces, on the one hand, and the concern to enhance economic efficiency and the social optimum, on the other.

The independent behaviour of the different actors is one of the guiding principles of all competition policies; they defend this rule by opposing anything which may indirectly facilitate collusion between firms (agreements or information exchange concerning prices, quantities produced or capacities, etc.). However, this type of approach is soon limited without an appropriate conceptual model to analyse imperfect competition as such. It results, for example, in only explicit agreements being condemned while tacit collusion becomes acceptable, the latter being seen as an expression of rational behaviour between independent agents with a common perception of their environment.[2]

With the formalisation of imperfect competition by means of game-theory, another step forward can be taken. The ambiguous notion of parallel behaviour is replaced by the more precise one of non-cooperative equilibrium. It then becomes possible to reflect on the interaction between

---

[2] Wood pulp is a case in point. The alignment of prices among about 50 wood pulp producers was judged by the European Commission to be an expression of a concerted practice. The European Court of Justice (ECJ), however, regarded wood pulp to be an homogeneous product for which the market is perfectly transparent. It considered that the firms may have reacted identically to modifications in their environment without any formal agreement. For the European Commission decision (19 December 1984), see the *Official Journal of the European Communities*, L851, and for the ECJ judgement in the appeal case (31 March 1993), see *Recueil de la Jurisprudence de la Cour de Justice et du Tribunal de Première Instance*, I, 1993, 3. For a case study, see Phlips (1995, pp. 131–6).

certain rules of the game and the degree of economic inefficiency of the non-cooperative equilibrium which may result from it. Some rules may then appear to be less effective than others and be condemned as such, whereas others will be encouraged. This approach thus provides a more powerful frame for examining competition policy.

The present chapter develops this type of analysis in relation to the cement industry. It considers several rules concerning price policy, the exchange of information and external growth operations (mergers and acquisitions), with particular reference to models derived from game-theory.

The cement industry is a typical example of an oligopolistic sector. Cement is an homogeneous good for which the price elasticity of demand is weak, production requires heavy investments and distribution involves high transport costs. Consequently, there are often few local competitors. They are, however, subject to competitive pressure from the outside, from distant firms which try to sell at marginal costs.

The sector has a rich history of anti-trust cases in the United States, Europe and Japan, which have provided subject-matter for an extensive literature on the various standpoints taken. In the present chapter we draw essentially on the cases referenced in the historical analysis by Dumez and Jeunemaître (2000). In some of these cases there is clear proof of agreement while in many others the questions concern practices with far less obvious effects – e.g. the choice of price regulation (the use of points of parity, for instance), the role of information exchange between competitors and the choice of the relevant market for analysing concentration.

We shall consider these questions of principle in the light of several theoretical developments which are particularly relevant to a study of the cement industry.

First, what is the impact of a *pricing system*, in relation to its degree of discrimination, in a context of horizontal differentiation? Numerous studies have focused on this question since the first articles by Spence (1976) and Salop (1979). Most reached the classical conclusion that more competitive pricing had a positive impact on welfare (Phlips, 1983). Norman and Thisse (1996) examined the same question by considering the role of the irreversibility of investments. They show that highly competitive pricing may lead to greater market concentration and ultimately to a loss of welfare for the economy as a whole.

The second question concerns *information exchange* – or, more generally, trade practices which shape competition. How are they justified and what is their impact? Information exchange usually concerns commitments to align prices on advance notification. But there are other facilitating practices. Holt and Scheffman (1987) showed that such practices could influence the intensity of competition – for example, by causing it to change from Bertrand to Cournot competition. This conclusion is used by d'Aspremont and Motta (2000) in a context of horizontal differentiation. They show that more intense competition may lead to greater concentration.

These theories, in terms of both pricing and facilitating practices, provide arguments in favour of the maintenance of rules tending to moderate competition in the short term and thereby limit concentration in the sector. Of course, in these models it is always assumed that firms' behaviour remains non-cooperative. The question of whether a particular rule promotes agreements between firms remains relevant. However, empirical studies by Sutton (1991) reinforce the general assumption that the intensity of competitive pricing can have a retroactive effect on concentration. The value of theoretical analyses is then to specify the mechanisms which may favour this retroaction to a greater or lesser degree.

Lastly, we examine a point which has received relatively little attention in the literature but is directly relevant to the empirical analysis of the cement industry. When we study this sector over periods of about 10 years, we are struck by the considerable importance of the buying and selling of assets – production units, here – for purposes of restructuring (Tanguy, 1987). The indivisibility of investments, the stagnation of demand in most developed countries and the increase in the minimal economic size of production investments are all factors which make competition in the cement business resemble a *game of Go*. In this game, some positions which are still profitable do not seem viable in the long term; the company then tries to sell them at a profit to a rival in a better position who has anticipated the situation more accurately. This process of restructuring the industry, favoured by a degree of financial concentration, seems to play a major part in the strategy of cement firms (Collomb and Ponssard, 1984). From a theoretical point of view, we are then led to question the relationship between short-term competition rules and firms' capacities to engage in this process of long-term efficiency.

A natural starting point for the study of this question is the modelling of competition in a dynamic context with free entry. Now, it has already been shown that in this type of context strong potential competition which facilitates entry does not necessarily lead to greater economic efficiency but may, on the contrary, lead to a waste of capital (Eaton and Lipsey, 1980; Maskin and Tirole, 1988). This results from the fact that incumbent firms may be induced to create entry barriers artificially by means of defensive measures involving heavy costs (advertising, vertical integration, renewal of assets before this is due, etc.) rather than lowering their prices. This analysis, developed in the absence of competitive advantages between firms, has been completed so as to take into account possibilities of asymmetry (Gromb, Ponssard and Sevy, 1997). The authors show that an effective process of selection will be initiated, in which a more efficient entrant will replace a less efficient incumbent. However, this selection depends on a mechanism of rational expectations which presumes that firms are able to assess their respective structural positions.

The rest of this chapter is organised as follows. In section 2 the characteristics of the cement industry are analysed in detail. Section 3 develops theoretical considerations and explains the results mentioned above. In the conclusion (section 4) we summarise the lessons drawn from the proposed approach and suggest some general ideas in terms of competition policy for an oligopolistic sector such as the cement industry.

2   Characteristics of the cement industry

In this section we present the basic economic characteristics of the cement industry by following the classical approach which consists of successively examining demand, supply and market structure. On the basis of these characteristics we are then able to define the main economic stakes in the sector. Our presentation concerns the industrialised countries and, more specifically, Europe. We have drawn upon the French case for many of our examples.

Demand

Demand in the cement industry is typically that of an activity which is mature, cyclical and with low price elasticity. It is also characterised by a high degree of horizontal differentiation in terms of location and a low degree of vertical differentiation in terms of quality.

Let us look at each of these points. Cement is an homogeneous product. Most of its sales concern about half a dozen commercial varieties, of which Portland cement is by far the leader. No brand name exists, so that one supplier's products can easily be substituted for another. Cement is, however, an experience good; its quality is guaranteed by standards with which the supplier has to comply. These standards are often national but in most cases the products of one country can easily be approved in neighbouring countries. Standards therefore do not constitute trade barriers as such, even if they may hinder trade.

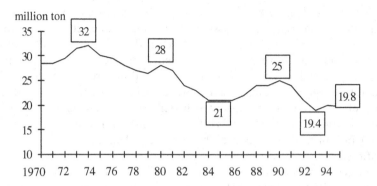

Figure 1.1   Cement consumption, 1970–1994, million tons

Although cement is one of the main ingredients used in the construction industry, it accounts for only 2 per cent of the costs. The price of cement therefore has little impact on final demand which is essentially the result of macroeconomic conditions (economic growth rate, interest rates, policy of infrastructure development, etc.). By contrast, intermediaries such as producers of precast concrete or prefabricated material are strongly affected by prices, with the result that pressure is constantly exerted on suppliers to lower prices. This pressure will be particularly strong when the sector is concentrated downstream.

Figure 1.1 represents the consumption of cement in France over the period 1970–95 (trade syndicate data). This demand, typical of industrialised countries, appears to be cyclical with a downward trend after peaking in 1974 (this peak occurred a little earlier in the United Kingdom and Germany and more recently in Spain and Italy). This demand curve does not encourage the entry of new competitors.

Let us now consider horizontal differentiation in this sector. The demand for cement is geographically widely dispersed and corresponds roughly to population density. Although cement is an upstream industry, it differs from other basic industries such as aluminium, steel or glass, for which demand is concentrated both geographically and in terms of the number of customers. In the cement industry demand is, by contrast, dispersed in multiple zones of consumption, each of which comprises numerous customers. Geographical factors thus determine the structure of the market. For example, in areas with high levels of consumption, accessible by waterway (such as London, Marseilles or Barcelona) the market stakes differ from those of more isolated areas (such as Berne, Grenoble or Madrid).

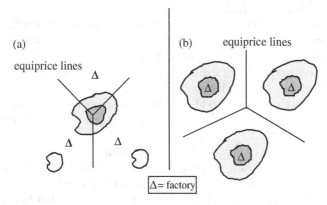

Figure 1.2   Maritime and land models of market structure. (a) Maritime model
(b) Land model

Figure 1.2, adapted from Tanguy (1987), illustrates this phenomenon.
On the left, producers compete on a major market; on the right, each
producer is relatively isolated on its natural market. These two extreme
cases – called the *maritime* and the *land* model, respectively, by Dumez
and Jeunemaître (2000), as well as all the possible intermediate forms,
constitute the *playing field* of the cement industry. The traditional playing
field is the land model, but the maritime model takes over when communication over vast distances becomes possible (the Great Lakes and
Mississippi networks in the United States, the North Sea network, the
Euro–Mediterranean network, and so on).

Supply

Two economic considerations are important *a priori* in structuring supply
in a market characterised by strong horizontal differentiation:

- The trade-off between fixed costs and transport costs which, depending on the economic size of the factories, gives an initial idea of the
  density of the network of production units covering the territory, in
  relation to the density of demand
- The level of investment costs and the life-span of facilities which
  determine the rigidity and the duration of the network.

We shall begin our discussion of supply by giving a rough idea of the
main expense items and the profitability factors of a production unit, and
by simplifying the transport question.

Factory costs and key factors of profitability
The following data (table 1.1), drawn from interviews with professionals in the sector in France, give a breakdown of expenses for a production unit which has a capacity of 1 million tons per year and costs 1 billion francs in investments. This size is representative both of current technical capacities and of the economic stakes in most industrialised countries. For high-growth urban markets or for *on-shore* plants intended for an essentially maritime environment, larger dimensions would be more appropriate.

The main items in table 1.1 may be grouped together as *variable* expenses, which change in proportion to production, and as *fixed* expenses which are reduced to the ton but remain constant, irrespective of production. (By contrast, fixed costs may vary in relation to capacity; we shall return to this point below.) With regard to variable expenses, the item 'market access' represents transport costs for an average geographical dispersion. For a production of 1 million ton/year, variable expenses are 150 Fr/ton and fixed expenses are 180 Fr/ton, a total cost (excluding economic depreciation) of 330 Fr/ton.

In 1995 in France the average customer price including transport was roughly 450 Fr/ton. This type of factory therefore has a profit before tax of 450 − 330 = 120, or 80 Fr/ton after tax (for a tax rate of 33.3 per cent).

To evaluate the operating profit after depreciation and taxes, one has to subtract the capital charges for investment (taken here to be equal to

Table 1.1   *Cost/profit structure for a production unit with a capacity of 1 million tons per year, running at full capacity*

Capacity: 1 million ton/year	Fr/ton (F/T)	Total	
Material	30		
Energy	70		
Market access	50	150	Variable costs
Factory fixed costs	100		
Maintenance	40		
Overhead	40	180	Fixed costs
(commercial, administrative)			
Selling price	450		
Earnings before tax	120		
Taxes	40		
Econ. depreciation	76		
Econ. rent	4		

8 per cent), taking into account the delayed deductibility of this expense owing to tax depreciation. By considering a life-span of about 20 years while tax depreciation is over a shorter time period, one can obtain a rough estimate in proceeding as follows. First compute the tax shield associated with depreciation (given local fiscal rules, in our example this amount would be 250 Fr/ton); secondly, after subtracting this amount from the investment cost (to obtain $1000 - 250 = 750$ Fr/ton), compute the economic depreciation associated with this capital investment of 750 Fr/ton on 20 years. With a unit capital cost of 8 per cent per year that gives approximately 76 Fr/ton in our case. The economic rent generated by this production unit would then be 4 Fr/ton. This cost structure implies that the economic rent is quite sensitive to price variation and to utilisation rate. This sensitivity is typical of a capital-intensive process industry in which the fixed costs (after tax) together account for over 65 per cent of the total cost.

It is generally considered that fixed factory costs and investments are largely determined by capacity. When the latter increases from 800 k ton/year to 1,500 k ton/year, they may be reduced by a factor of about 35 per cent. This calculation makes it possible to determine the part of fixed costs which is *truly fixed*. The corresponding economy explains why it may be advantageous to build large plants, provided that transport costs to the market are not too high.

The preponderance of transport costs
Transport costs depend on several factors: the means of transport used, the quantity transported and the distance covered. The three main means of transport are: road for short distances (less than 200 km), rail for longer distances (200–600 km) and finally water, essentially maritime. In the latter case, the cost is generally not considered to depend on the distance.

Each means of transport is economical not only for certain distances but also in relation to a minimum quantity which ranges from 25 ton for a lorry to 1,300 ton for a train and about 10,000 ton for a boat or ship. This is explained primarily by the loading and unloading costs involved. Boats are usually loaded directly from an on-shore plant whereas unloading costs require expensive facilities.

It is therefore possible to draw up a comparative table of transport costs (see table 1.2). All the corresponding data are drawn from interviews with professionals in the industry.

In an analysis of competition transport costs, which may easily amount to 100–150 Fr/ton, rapidly account for a significant fraction of the factory cost. Greater efficiency in production costs is thus soon lost in relation to

Table 1.2 *Estimation of transport costs*

Transportation mode	Road (0–200 km)	Railway (200–600 km)	Sea ex: Greece–USA
Loading	18 Fr/ton	15 Fr/ton	—
Per km	0.35 Fr/ton × km	0.25 Fr/ton × km	70 Fr/ton
Unloading	—	20 Fr/ton	80 Fr/ton
Total/ton	18–88 Fr/ton	85–185 Fr/ton	150 Fr/ton
Standard quantity	25 ton	1300 ton	10000 ton

a competitor who may be better placed on the market. On the other hand, the discrepancy between the price and the variable cost clearly constitutes a strong incentive to marginal-cost selling. Given the destabilising nature of this type of selling, it is likely to develop over large distances to avoid possible retaliation. In such cases harbour areas will be structurally more vulnerable to imports than inland areas.

If we wanted to use managerial stylisation, we could say that favourable transport conditions will tend to multiply the areas of contact between a large number of competitors, since the market will resemble a commodity market. By contrast, the exclusive use of road transport in areas of moderate consumption will bring together only a small number of competitors since the market will resemble a juxtaposition of specialised activities. This is another way of distinguishing between a maritime and a land model.

The network and its rigidity
By taking the geographical distribution of demand, fixed factory costs and transport costs, it is possible to determine an effective networking of a given territory. Applied to the territory of France, and excluding all imports and exports of cement, we find about a dozen production units with capacities of between 800 k ton/year and several million ton/year. (We note, however, that a capacity of several million ton/year is not realistic because of competitive vulnerability.)

Although theoretical, this calculation helps us to locate the real network. In 1995 France had about 20 production sites, whereas there had been about 50 in the early 1980s for a market which, admittedly, was 50 per cent bigger. Thus, the size of the plants has increased, which has enabled them to benefit from economies of scale in a shrinking market.

This type of calculation is, however, too static and overlooks some important dimensions. The historical analysis in the French context illustrates the extremely rigid nature of cement production. For example, no new plant was built between 1980 and 1995. Three factors explain this phenomenon: first, the life-span of factories is very long – about 20–30 years; secondly, it is relatively more economical to renovate old factories than to build new ones; and, lastly, environmental constraints (notably for the opening of quarries) make the creation of new units more and more difficult. In a context of stagnating demand peculiar to industrialised countries, these three factors generate a very stable industrial structure.

These elements enable us to complete the description of the spatial playing field by introducing a time dimension, and then examine the strategies used by competitors on this time–space playing field.

Market structure and the implications of restructuring

The time–space playing field has to be analysed in light of the fact that the vast majority of firms in the sector have several plants. Many of them are part of major multinationals active in several countries. Surprisingly, in view of its regional character, the cement sector is highly internationalised.

In France, for example, there were about 30 factories in 1995 but only four rival firms (Holderbank, Lafarge, Ciments Français and Heidelberg). These firms were, moreover, well established in other European countries, North America and, in some cases, Latin America and Asia. Similarly, in the United Kingdom there are three dominant cement groups, and this type of concentration is also apparent in Spain and Germany, even if in those countries many independent single-plant firms remain operational. This highly concentrated multiplant structure results far more from a process of acquisitions than from one of internal development. The rigidity of supply explains why.

Concentration has two main objectives. The first is the wish to stabilise competition in a context of a tit-for-tat-type strategy. Numerous acquisitions in Europe thus followed the setting up of the Single Market and the rapid increase in *uncontrolled* exports. Several large companies acquired positions in Greece or Italy, for example, in an attempt to exert pressure on national manufacturers.

The second factor seems equally important. Financial concentration makes it possible to benefit from industrial rationalisation campaigns through the renovation and/or closure of several plants in the same area. On the one hand financial concentration enables firms to raise funds, which is essential in such a capital-intensive industry and, on the other, the existence of several plants close together makes it possible to reorganise flows without becoming involved in trade wars.

Let us consider two examples of this type of process concerning the border area between France and Belgium. In the early 1990s the company Ciments Français bought out the Belgian firm CCB. Following this acquisition, it closed down two of its own plants in the region. Conversely, Holderbank bought out the company Cedest and closed one of the newly acquired plants. Thus, within a few years a financial and industrial restructuring had taken place in an area which for a long time had had an overcapacity. This occurred without any price war for the selection of the best plants. The questions are: on what was the selection process based, and how effective was it?

We suggest the following interpretation. In the process of acquisition and restructuring, it was as if the firms practised a form of *indirect competition* on the physical assets market (either to acquire existing factories or to sell them) rather than on the product market. Consider a given playing field. Some production units seem to be doomed (e.g. problems of quarries being too small to warrant heavy but essential investments), although still able temporarily to defend a natural market. Moreover, for various reasons other more modern factories in the vicinity have an overcapacity. There thus exist opportunities for value creation derived from industrial restructuring. The firms will prepare this type of set up by means of purely financial acquisitions and/or overinvestments in existing sites to discourage investment in other sites. This amounts to a sort of *game of Go* in which the status of a production unit may switch from one side to another without this being immediately foreseeable. The fact that there are now four cement firms in France while in the 1960s there were close to 40 accounts for the size of the phenomenon of financial concentration and industrial restructuring.

The cost structure is at the origin of this process. It explains why a plant, even an old one which is less efficient as regards variable costs and fixed factory costs, yet no longer has depreciation charges, remains marginally profitable unless the selling price drops by at least 40 per cent. However, this type of price decrease would by nature be extremely costly for all the actors involved. In the cement industry, the selection process by price war is hardly credible and easily backfires on those who initiate it. A production unit is consequently a long-term strategic asset. It allows a firm either to acquire plants close by in order to improve the efficiency of the area, or to realise a capital gain on sales by trying to recover a significant part of the value derived by the acquirer from this enhanced efficiency.

3   Theoretical analysis of some relevant competition rules for the cement sector

In this section we examine the theoretical implications of the above characteristics of the competition process, as regards both the price regime and information exchange (or others facilitating practices).

When transport costs account for a significant proportion of all costs, competition must be analysed on two levels. The first is the establishment of the way in which transport costs are incorporated into prices. Multiple *pricing systems* are possible. At this level coordination between firms may already appear, in so far as they may agree on a particular pricing system for transport costs. The second is that of the establishment of *price levels* as such, incorporating transport costs in relation to the pricing system adopted at the first level. At this second level (which is the only one to consider when transport costs are not very high) coordination, or mutual understanding on the basis of information exchange between firms, plays an essential part in the establishment of a mode of competition.

The role of the pricing system

In a context of geographical differentiation, competition is extremely intense locally (although limited to a small number of neighbouring competitors). By nature it is scarcely affected by changes in distant areas. In these conditions, the direct threat regulating prices is the entry of a competitor. This may either be a direct entry through the construction of a new production unit or, more probably, in the cement sector, an entry linked to the construction of a terminal allowing for mass deliveries from an existing but distant plant. Entry on the market is thus a major strategic decision in which the reaction of local competitors cannot be overlooked.

One of the first articles to study this question was that of Eaton and Wooders (1985). The authors showed, in particular, that spatial competition is 'fierce' but 'local'. The same point is examined by MacLeod, Norman and Thisse (1988).

To study this question, two systems of pricing are usually chosen: the system of uniform *FOB pricing* (or *mill pricing*), and the system of non-uniform *discriminatory delivered pricing* (discriminatory pricing with absorption of transport costs). It is these two systems which are of interest to us here, although we cannot entirely overlook other pricing systems which have been used and analysed. For example, a system at the origin of many discussions is that of *points of parity*, where the delivered price is equal to a *base price* associated with a point in space (the point of parity, agreed in advance) to which are added (shadow) transport costs calculated from this point and not from the point where the seller is located (unless this corresponds to the point of parity). Phlips (1983) presents this pricing system in detail. It was prohibited in the United States, particularly in the case of cement (see Areeda and Kaplow, 1948). In Europe, in the case of steel, it was adopted by article 60 of the ECCS treaty. It was even considered during discussions (between 1981 and 1994) between the German, Belgian and Dutch cement industries and the European Commission. This system is generally considered to favour price collusion (all the producers agree on a single rate for transport) and to be globally inefficient in terms of location. Since transport costs paid by buyers do not correspond to real costs, cross-hauling will generally occur. Another price system, also used in the past by the cement industry in the Benelux countries, is that of *uniform delivered prices per zone*. This system poses similar problems when there is wide geographical dispersion; it is generally applied in areas with a strong concentration of buyers (in cities).

Let us revert to a theoretical comparison between the two most common price systems – *mill pricing* and *discriminatory pricing*.

For a long time most economists considered that non-uniform discriminatory pricing was preferable because it provided an incentive for more vigorous short-term competition for established firms. Moreover, under some symmetry assumptions, this regime results in collectively optimal locations. If buyers' *reservation prices* are high enough for demand to be covered completely, we then have an efficient solution. Yet this result also depends on an implicit assumption of relocation without costs, following an entry. When this assumption is not verified, as is the case in a sector such as the cement industry, it is possible to show that the absence of discrimination becomes socially preferable. The reason for this result derives from the fact that an entry penalises incumbent firms far more in a system of *mill pricing* and that they have therefore to protect themselves by a less concentrated market structure (more firms) and, finally, lower prices (Norman and Thisse, 1996).

The impact of information exchange on prices

In so far as it may lead to collusion, or to agreements between firms likely to limit competition, or to the abuse of a dominant position, the exchange of information on prices is one of the main targets of anti-trust authorities. The Sherman Act (1890) in the United States served above all to prohibit price collusion, as did the application, in Europe, of articles 85 and 86 of the Rome Treaty (1957). We note, however, that information of this nature is not always exchanged in the same way. It may be direct or indirect, organised through announcements or contracts. For example, it may be agreed that a competitor may make public advance announcements on price changes (which are not binding), which the other competitors may or may not follow.[3] Similarly, sales contracts may include particular clauses such as *the most-favoured customer*, which excludes discrimination between consumers, or *meet-or-release*, which guarantees the customer the best price compared to other competitors. It has been shown that such practices generate more coordination between firms, resulting in less competition. This reduction in competition depends to a large degree on the specific practices adopted. Thus, if all the practices just cited are adopted, and if adjustments as compared to announced prices are possible at the time of the sale (by granting discounts), then the solution observed should be a Cournot-type solution. The role of discounts is to enable firms to defend their territory (Holt and Scheffman, 1987).

Yet reduced competition and welfare losses, resulting from certain types of coordination, may be a short-term effect only. The long-term effect, if we take structural adjustment in the industry into account, may be positive for the collective welfare by allowing a less concentrated structure to be maintained.

The following example (inspired by the Hotelling model), described in figure 1.3, illustrates this possibility (d'Aspremont and Motta, 2000).

We presume that the consumers are uniformly distributed in a straight line. Each of them buys a unit of the good if, and only if, the price is less than a given price (the *reservation price*, presumed to be the same for everyone). There are three possible (equidistant) locations and a fixed set-up cost for three potential producers. In the first stage, the producers decide whether or not to set up. The transport pricing scheme is presumed to be that of FOB prices where the customer must pay the factory price plus the transport cost, with the latter taken to be proportional to the distance. In the second stage no producer may increase its profits by unilaterally changing its price. If competition is of the Cournot type (more coordinated), this change is envisaged by considering that the competitors will adjust their factory prices to retain their customers. If competition is of the Bertrand type (less coordinated), competitors are supposed to maintain their factory price at a fixed level. *Ex ante*, a producer sets up only if it anticipates a positive profit after set-up costs.

---

[3] This is standard practice in the cement industry. In the United States the industry was sued on this point by the anti-trust authorities but won its cases (cf. Dumez and Jeunemaître, 2000).

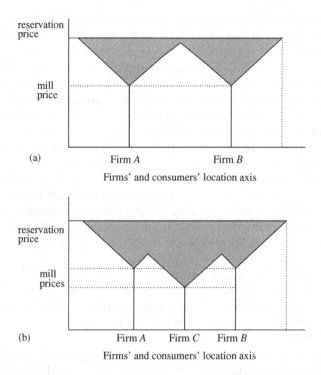

Figure 1.3 The effect of competition on pricing: Cournot and Bertrand examples. (a) Bertrand (b) Cournot

In the example (figure 1.3), two producers will set up if competition is of the Bertrand type (figure 1.3a) and three will set up if it is of the Cournot type (figure 1.3b). Moreover, the consumer surplus, measured by the difference between the purchase price and the reservation price (the shaded area on both figures), is greater in the Cournot than in the Bertrand case (owing to the presence of an additional competitor). The same relationship is verified for the total surplus (consumer surplus plus sum of profits).

More short-term competition but greater concentration in the long run

The general ideal conveyed by the above results is that it may be preferable to have a less concentrated structure (more firms) with less intense price competition, rather than more intense price competition resulting in a more concentrated structure (with fewer firms). The trade-off between the level of short-term competition and the level of concentration may then become an issue. Now, it is accepted that a high level of concentration often goes hand in hand with the exercise of increased monopoly. This idea is corroborated by the empirical studies of Sutton (1991) in the agri-food sector.

As far as the cement industry is concerned, we can certainly interpret the construction of the European Union as a period of intensified competition in the short term, challenging national oligopolies. The extent of mergers and acquisitions in Europe can then be considered as the natural consequence of this intensification of competition.

The basic question is whether this increase in concentration will not eventually result in less intense competition. We may also wonder whether a policy limiting competition in the short term by allowing anti-dumping within the Union, for example, would not have had the effect of limiting purely defensive acquisitions, without hindering the restructuring process.

In order to consider the terms of this question in more depth, we need a frame of analysis enabling us to understand the possible forms of the acquisition–restructuring process, and to investigate corresponding gains and the impact of the competition dynamics in the materialisation of such gains.

Dynamic efficiency and selection process in the long run

Let us assume that potential competitors are constantly trying to enter a market on which only a limited number of firms can make a sustainable profit. Let us consider two questions. Does the entry/exit process select the most efficient firms? Does potential competition generate efficiency in the incumbent firms? The first question concerns productive efficiency while the second concerns allocative efficiency.

Intuitively it may seem that the less rigid the market, the closer to perfect competition the competitive process, the more the answers to the above questions are likely to be affirmative. This idea is more particularly linked to the notion of contestable markets (Baumol, Panzar and Willig, 1982). It is then advisable to encourage everything which may promote market flexibility by eliminating all forms of rigidity. However, this type of reasoning is particularly misleading, for two reasons.

First, this reasoning is theoretically inaccurate because strong potential competition can lead to high levels of *waste*. This point was initially demonstrated by Eaton and Lipsey (1980), who were also the first to propose a formalisation of dynamic competition with free entry. In their model, firms use their capital investments as entry barriers. Once paid for, a facility has a definite life-span known to all, and its use involves zero marginal costs. It is therefore in an incumbent firm's interests to renew its capital well before the facility reaches the end of its life, so that a price war in the event of a competitor's entry will be credible. Even if the incumbent's profits are whittled away by competitive pressure, the consumer does not benefit from this pressure which is merely a waste of capital. Maskin and Tirole (1988) considered this question by looking at the role of capacity as a barrier to entry. They show that potential competition not only disciplines the incumbent firm but also induces it to act efficiently. Steinmetz (1998) shows that when firms can choose between anticipated renewal resulting in wasted capital on the one hand and reduced prices on the other, it is in their interests to choose wastage. These different approaches show that any judgement of productive efficiency will strongly depend on the form of competition.

Let us illustrate this type of wastage in the cement industry. If we compare the market zones in which a given factory delivers, we notice that these areas vary considerably from one country to the next – for example, they are geographically limited in France but spread out in the United States. As an explanation we may imagine that efforts towards extreme flexibility, required by strong short-term competition in the United States, may lead to overinvestment in logistics, including in numerous terminals. Steinmetz' results suggest that this form of capital waste in the United States is favoured by firms, to the detriment of price reductions, whereas in France weaker short-term competition results in greater logistic efficiency.

Let us now consider the second reason for which a policy aimed at maximal contestability may be illusory. The underlying reasoning may be ill-suited to reality, for the concrete nature of rigidity may be partly structural and its elimination is not always possible. In these conditions, it is certainly preferable to develop a theory of imperfect competition which takes into account the existence of *mobility barriers* limiting entries and exits on a market. By simplifying, we could then imagine that the strategy of incumbent firms consists of acting on these barriers in order to choose between immediate profits, of whatever size, on the one hand and risks of entry, of whatever degree, on the other. As for potential competitors, one may imagine that their strategies consist of seeking a competitive advantage (innovation, enhanced efficiency, etc.) enabling them to enter at a lower cost and with greater chances of success.[4] It is then worthwhile to explore those factors which favour the substitution of more efficient firms for less efficient ones and, finally, promote technical progress.

---

[4] Scherer (1992) and Geroski (1995) provide a large number of empirical studies to justify this formulation of the problem.

In order to understand the theoretical conditions in which this selection process may be initiated, we can start with the following. Consider the case of two firms: an entrant and an incumbent. In this context the level of the entry barrier resulting from the incumbent's strategy must be greater than or equal to the rent expected by the potential competitor in the event of it replacing the incumbent. Suppose that the least efficient firm is able to retain its position on the market for a fairly long period. We are going to show that a contradiction will result as the end of the game becomes more distant. This is because the rent of the least efficient firm is certainly lower than that of the most efficient one. This difference between rents will increase as the horizon becomes more distant (assuming that the discount rate is not too high). Consequently, to remain on an horizon that is more and more distant, the least efficient firm must raise the level of its entry barrier (and thus decrease its current profit). This reasoning leads to an *avalanche effect* which widens the gap between the rents. As soon as the horizon goes beyond a certain stage the least effective firm will have a negative total rent owing to its efforts to bar the entry of a more efficient competitor. It is then in its interests not to bar the entry and rather to adopt a strategy of exiting in the most profitable way possible.

This intuition may be formalised (Gromb, Ponssard and Sevy, 1997; Ponssard, 2000) but the reasoning behind it is admittedly based on rational expectations. This property of positive selection may, for example, be contrasted with other well established results on the *effect of reputation*. In the models integrating this effect, a little uncertainty always enables an incumbent monopoly, even an inefficient one, to protect itself in the long run against efficient entrants by *acting strong* (Kreps and Wilson, 1982).

The mechanism through which inefficient firms are replaced by more efficient ones naturally makes one think of the merger/acquisition and restructuring process as analysed earlier for the cement industry. The theoretical analysis then suggests that a degree of transparency of information will certainly be necessary if the corresponding expectations are to be developed. By highlighting the non-necessity of price wars in a successful process of selection, this analysis also invites us to grant a significant role to gains derived from mergers, even if these also increase the monopoly power resulting inherently from the spatial differentiation of the sector.

In the Schumpeterian view, characterising the present competitive dynamic, these monopoly powers would be challenged by sources of innovation. In other words, it is the very existence of monopoly power which encourages firms to strive for greater efficiency and to want to take advantage of it elsewhere. Even if we need to be careful in this interpretation, we may consider that such a mechanism is not totally unrelated to the fact that the biggest cement firms are European corporations, whereas American firms remain, on the whole, regional (before being bought out by European firms). It is noteworthy that American firms were hardly able to enjoy the efficiency gains which attend mergers and acquisitions, primarily because the anti-trust authorities have an extremely limited view of the notion of a relevant market.

4 Conclusion

This chapter has attempted to illustrate some of the contributions of game-theory to competition policy, by analysing the case of the cement industry.

These contributions have been focused on elements of doctrine such as questions of pricing systems, information exchange and other facilitating practices; questions which were debated at length in the anti-trust cases in which the cement industry was involved. On these subjects, the analysis suggests that a reinforcement of short-term competition must logically be accompanied by greater financial concentration in the industry. This hypothesis is confirmed in the European cement industry by a large number of mergers and acquisitions throughout the Union. It naturally leads to questions on the anti-trust regulations which need to be established.

To answer such questions, it is necessary to have a thorough understanding of the part played by financial concentration in industrial restructuring typical of a capital-intensive sector. The theoretical analysis of the selection process in an industry characterised by rigidity provides several benchmarks on the subject. Because of this rigidity, price wars in processes of selection are relatively ineffective; some other form of selection must then be encouraged. Systematic efforts towards greater fluidity, contrary to widespread belief, does not necessarily constitute a favourable context for this selection. This approach (which relies on a simplistic interpretation of the notion of contestability) may have the unintended effect of wasting resources in an attempt to preserve established positions at all costs[5] without this resulting in an effective selection and without the consumer necessarily benefiting (in terms of price and quality of service). By contrast, a certain transparency of information may contribute to this process of selection by 'revealing' winning and losing positions in

---

[5] In the cement industry, this corresponds to inefficient choices in relation to production capacity, multiplication of terminals, high transport costs, etc.

the long term. By highlighting the structural conditions of the sector, this transparency[6] may also facilitate the analysis of a competition authority by enabling it to distinguish between efficient and inefficient areas, independently of the stability or instability of short-term competition in those areas.

Finally, when considering a highly oligopolistic sector, this theoretical analysis allows one to diverge fairly systematically from an approach which merely applies the principles of perfect competition (maximising short-term competition, absence of information exchange, as much fluidity as possible, total independence in the behaviour of firms, etc.). It is not, however, a question of looking for general rules in game-theory, in so far as this theory is merely an instrument of analysis. The approach which we believe to be the most fruitful consists of starting by analysing the economic characteristics of the sector concerned, and then applying game-theory to clarify the impact of a particular mode of organising competition in the sector. This chapter also indicates how this type of approach may indirectly contribute to new theoretical developments.

Bibliography

Areeda, P. and L. Kaplow (1948) *Antitrust Analysis*, Boston: Little Brown & Co.
d'Aspremont, C. and M. Motta (2000) Tougher price competition or lower concentration: a tradeoff for anti-trust authorities?, chapter 6 in this volume
Baumol, W.J., J. Panzar and R.D. Willig (1982) *Contestable Markets and the Theory of Natural Monopoly*, New York: Harcourt Brace Foranorich
Collomb, B. and J.-P. Ponssard (1984) Creative management in mature capital intensive industries: the case of cement, in A. Charnes and W.W. Cooper (eds.), *Creative and Innovative Management*, Cambridge, Mass.: Ballinger
Dumez, H. and A. Jeunemaître (2000) *Understanding and Regulating the Market at a Time of Globalization: The Case of the Cement Industry*, London: Macmillan
Eaton, B.C. and R. Lipsey (1980) Exit barriers are entry barriers: the durability of capital as a barrier to entry, *Bell Journal of Economics*, 10, pp. 721–9
Eaton, B.C. and M.H. Wooders (1985) Sophisticated entry in a model of spatial competition, *Rand Journal of Economics*, 16, pp. 282–7
Encaoua, D. (1997) Les politiques communautaires de la concurrence, in H. Brochier *et al.*, *L'Economie Normative*, Paris: Economica
FTC *v.* Cement Institute, 333 US 683, pp. 355–60
Geroski, P.A. (1995) What do we know about entry?, *International Journal of Industrial Organization*, 13, pp. 421–40

---

[6] In the cement industry this consists of knowing the utilisation rate of capacities, the age and technical characteristics of the facilities, the level of prices, etc. in a given geographical area.

Gromb, D., J.-P. Ponssard and D. Sevy (1997) Selection in dynamic entry games, *Games and Economic Behavior*, 21, pp. 62–84

Holt, C.A. and D.T. Scheffman (1987) Facilitating practices: the effects of advanced notice and best-price policies, *Rand Journal of Economics*, 18(2), pp. 187–97

Jenny, F. (1993) Competition and efficiency, chapter 10 in B. Hawk (ed.), *1993 Fordham Corporate Law Institute*: Transnational Juris Publications

Kreps, D. and R. Wilson (1982) Reputation and incomplete information, *Journal of Economic Theory*, 27, pp. 253–79

MacLeod, W.B., G. Norman and J.-F. Thisse (1988) Price discrimination and equilibrium in monopolistic competition, *International Journal of Industrial Organization*, 6, pp. 429–46

Maskin, E. and J. Tirole (1988) A theory of dynamic oligopoly, part I: overview and quantity competition with large fixed costs, *Econometrica*, 56(3), pp. 549–69

Norman, G. and J.-F. Thisse (1996) Product variety and welfare under tough and soft pricing regimes, *Economic Journal*, 106, pp. 76–91

Phlips, L. (1983) *The Economics of Price Discrimination*, Cambridge: Cambridge University Press

(1995) *Competition Policy: A Game Theoretic Perspective*, Cambridge: Cambridge University Press

Ponssard, J.-P. (2000) Modelling the entry and exit process in dynamic competition: an introduction to repeated-commitment models (Chapter 10 in this volume)

Salop, S.C. (1979) Monopolistic competition with outside goods, *Bell Journal of Economics*, 10, pp. 141–56

Scherer, F.M. (1992) *International High-Technology Competition*, Cambridge, Mass.: Harvard University Press

Spence, M. (1976) Product selection, fixed costs, and monopolistic competition, *Review of Economic Studies*, 43, pp. 217–35

Steinmetz, S. (1998) Spatial preemptions with finitely lived equipments, *International Journal of Industrial Organization*, 16, pp. 253–70

Sutton, J. (1991) *Sunk Costs and Market Structure: Price Competition, Advertising and the Evolution of Concentration*, Cambridge, Mass.: MIT Press

Tanguy, H. (1987) L'instrumentation des choix stratégiques, chapter 2, thèse de doctorat, Paris: Ecole Polytechnique

2 Legal standards and economic analysis of collusion in EC competition policy

Damien J. Neven

1 Introduction

In his presidential address to the European Economic Association (Phlips, 1996), Louis Phlips noted that the legal framework towards collusion in the European Union drew an interesting distinction between agreements and concerted practice. He further conjectured that the latter concept might cover what economists would refer to as 'tacit collusion', or 'implicit coordination'. This conjecture, which I found intriguing, is further investigated in this chapter. Its objective is thus to evaluate the legal standard and underlying economic analysis applied in the European Community towards collusion.

For a long time, collusion was not considered as a serious concern for policy makers. Throughout the 1950s and 1960s, the view was indeed widely held among economists that firms could not exercise market power collectively without some form of explicit coordination. They pointed out that if firms selling substitutes often had a collective interest in raising price above marginal cost, such a move was not compatible with individual incentives. Firms would thus attempt to cheat and secretly expand sales, thereby taking advantage of the output restriction undertaken by their competitors. As a consequence, informal cartels were considered to be inherently unstable in the absence of explicit enforcement mechanisms and accordingly were not seen as a major concern for anti-trust policy (see Stigler, 1956, for a vivid exposition of this view).

In this context, anti-trust policy could focus on the detection of more explicit arrangements between firms; indeed, one could expect firms to try and undertake some explicit coordination in order to design and implement enforcement mechanisms which would protect their collective

I would like to thank Massimo Motta and Thomas von Ungern for useful comments on a previous version of this chapter.

exercise of market power against opportunistic behaviour by individual participants. Such coordination would with reasonable likelihood leave some material traces on which a conviction could be brought. Accordingly, a policy which banned explicit coordination arrangements between firms was seen as a sufficient instrument against collusion.

The theory of repeated games has cast some doubt on this approach. According to these theoretical developments, if firms interact with each other repeatedly, the pursuit of individual interest may be consistent with the collective exercise of substantial market power.[1] Firms which contemplate deviating from an outcome involving substantial aggregate market power will trade-off the resulting short-term gains against the long-term consequences of foregoing the cooperation of their competitors. This outcome may thus be supported as a non-cooperative equilibrium. Collusion may not be unstable as originally anticipated and stable arrangements may require little coordination between firms, and possibly none at all.

This raises a dilemma for the design of a policy towards collusion: on the one hand, if the legal standard focuses on explicit coordination between firms and requires evidence of such coordination, a potentially large number of collusive outcomes will fall outside the prohibition. Yet, if the legal standard tries to cover instances of collusion without explicit coordination, it will prohibit non-cooperative practices.

This dilemma has been widely discussed by economists, lawyers and practitioners in the United States (see, for instance, the 1992 special issue of the *Antitrust Bulletin*). Legal standards applied in the United States have also changed over time and currently place less emphasis on evidence of explicit coordination between firms.

The objective of this chapter is to analyse the approach followed by the European Commission and the European Court of Justice (ECJ). We will review landmark decisions as well as more recent case law and try to evaluate both legal standards and the underlying economic analysis.

The chapter is organised as follows. Section 2 considers a simple framework for the design of policy rules towards collusion. Section 3 analyses the legal standard which arises from the case law. Section 4 considers

---

[1] The idea that firms might resist taking advantage of competitors in the short term because by doing so they would risk jeopardising a profitable arrangement in the long term has been discussed informally for some time in both the economics and the management literature (see for instance, Scherer, 1980 and Porter, 1985, respectively). The important contribution from the repeated-game-literature has been to confirm that this intuition is sound, as well as being robust to the introduction of some reasonable restrictions. Following Friedman's original contribution (1971), there is now a large literature on the subject. See, for instance, Rees (1993) for a survey.

the economic analysis presented in some decisions. Section 5 concludes and offers some policy recommendations.

2 A framework for designing policy rules

As indicated above, the design of a policy towards collusion faces a dilemma such that on the one hand, if the legal standard focuses on explicit coordination between firms and requires evidence of such coordination, a potentially large number of collusive outcomes will fall outside the prohibition. On the other hand, if the legal standard tries to cover instances of collusion without explicit coordination, it will prohibit non-cooperative practices.[2]

One can wonder at the outset whether the first part of this dilemma is in practice a serious concern: in other words, can firms realistically exercise market power collectively without coordination? The insights from the theory of repeated games are ambiguous in this respect. To the extent that many outcomes involving substantial market power can be supported as non-cooperative equilibria, it is unclear how firms will make sure that they focus on a particular one. This question has by and large not been treated formally[3] so far, and it is not clear whether the selection of a particular outcome can be undertaken simply through market interactions. Schelling (1960) proposed a theory of focal points which does not require direct coordination between firms; according to this view, firms will select outcomes, or at least behavioural rules, which are 'self-evident', and firms may want to try and affect the perception of particular outcomes, or particular rules, as self-evident. For instance, a prior announcement of a well defined price increase (say, a given percentage) may be sufficient to establish a self-evident way to behave. Short of theoretical backing or empirical evidence, it is still difficult to assess how much weight should be given to these conjectures. At the very least, it seems that selecting a particular outcome through market interactions, if feasible, will be a highly imperfect process. Firms trying to improve on the selection of the outcome may have to resort to explicit coordination.

In order to analyse the case law and evaluate current legal standards, it is useful to distinguish between two different (albeit not mutually exclusive) approaches for the design of a policy towards collusion. On the one

---

[2] This distinction is meaningful only if market interactions through which firms may progressively select an outcome as focal points and support it are not considered as explicit coordination.

[3] Harrington (1989) has combined a non-cooperative repeated game with a cooperative selection of a particular outcome (modelled as a Nash bargaining game).

hand, the prohibition can be formulated in terms of coordination (where unlawful coordinations can be specified further or left general). The evidence required for establishing the existence of unlawful coordination then includes either direct material evidence (memos, minutes of meetings) or evidence on firm behaviour in the market which is consistent only with the existence of coordination.

On the other hand, the prohibition could be formulated in terms of a benchmark of market power (in the spirit of the EC merger regulation). Evidence required to establish a prohibition could then rely on two types of evidence – namely, evidence on aggregate outcomes and evidence on those types of firm behaviour that are consistent only with the collective exercise of market power.

We consider both approaches in turn. Consider first an approach based on market power. The main drawback of this approach is associated with the cost of type I errors. This would involve the conviction of firms which are not attempting to exercise market power collectively and are doing no more than 'simply' maximising profits. Competition policy might thereby discourage the pursuit of profitable activity that is a central motive behind the operation of a market economy. In this context, type I errors will have to be minimised. To the extent that the trade-off between type I and type II errors is severe, type II errors may become large and the policy will be rather ineffective. As discussed in Neven, Papandropoulos and Seabright (1998), the evaluation of market power (either directly or through the observation of firm behaviour) often involves a serious trade-off between type I and type II errors. This arises because market power is hard to measure directly (cost being endogenous) and because *ex post* strategies such as parallel behaviour can often be explained in different ways and suffer a pro-competitive interpretation.

Second, consider an approach based on a legal standard of coordination. The cost of type I errors in this context is likely to be substantially smaller. Firms may be discouraged from undertaking some innocent forms of coordination but there is hardly a presumption that coordination between firms is welfare-improving[4] (at least regarding behaviour in the final output market between firms selling substitute products). Accordingly, a reasonably relaxed attitude towards type I errors could

---

[4] In some instances, coordination between firms may be necessary because competition may fail to bring about an equilibrium (namely, when the core is empty); coordination between firms may then be seen as an attempt to establish a stable outcome in an otherwise chaotic environment. A legal prohibition of coordination would prevent this reasonable attempt to maintain stability. As indicated by Sjostrom (1989), highly unstable outcomes can indeed arise when entry is costless and when firms operate with large capacities relative to demand or in the presence of a large fall in demand.

be adopted, which in turn will reduce the magnitude of type II errors (in this context, the trade-off between type I and type II errors is also rather steep – see Neven, Papandropoulos and Seabright (1998) for a discussion of this issue).

Overall, there is therefore a presumption in favour of a legal standard which prohibits coordination rather the exercise of market power itself. We now turn to the statute and case law of the European Community and try to evaluate what standard has been applied.

3   The legal standard in the European Community

Article 81(1) (previously 85(1)) of the Rome Treaty (1957) stipulates that agreements or concerted practices between firms which distort competition are prohibited. What is meant by 'agreements' and 'concerted practices' is not further specified in the treaty and we have to turn to the case law to delineate these concepts further. It is of course tempting to associate an agreement with a formal understanding between firms and to associate a concerted practice with the implicit collusion which arises in equilibrium of non-cooperative repeated games. This would imply that the legal standard of the European Community includes both a prohibition of coordination (to the extent than an agreement requires a coordination) and a prohibition in terms of a benchmark of market power.

The early case law established a couple of principles in this respect.

Some coordination is unlawful

The early decision on *Zuiker Unie*[5] by the ECJ considers explicitly the coordination between firms:

The degree of 'co-ordination' and 'co-operation'... must be understood in the light of the concept inherent in the provision of the Treaty relating to competition that each economic operator must determine independently the policy which he intends to adopt on the common market ... Although it is correct to say that this requirement of independence does not deprive economic operators of the right to adapt themselves intelligently to the existing and anticipated conduct of their competitor, it does however strictly preclude any direct or indirect contact between such operators, the object or effect whereof is either to influence the conduct on the market of an actual or potential competitor or to disclose to such a competitor the course of conduct which they themselves have decided to adopt or contemplate adopting in the market.

---

[5] 1976, 1 *CMLR* 295.

This statement established two important principles. First, it makes clear that *interdependent decision making* by firms is in itself legitimate. From the economist's point of view, the recognition that strategic interdependence is not only a fact in most industries but is also an integral part of competition, is clearly welcome.[6]

The second principle established by the decision is one of prohibition: coordination between firms which involves direct or indirect contact between them to *influence each other's behaviour* (or that of a third party), is not legitimate. This decision thus provides a first definition of coordination and has established that it is unlawful.

Unfortunately, this definition leaves an important ambiguity. It is not clear from this formulation whether some forms of market interaction between firms (which may be aimed at establishing a focal point for coordination or simply at the initiation of a punishment phase) can be seen as a form of indirect contact between firms.

'Agreements' are associated with coordination

Throughout the case law, the definition of an 'unlawful agreement' has been relatively uncontroversial and has been clearly associated with a process of coordination between firms, for which there is material proof. The central element in an agreement seems to be an exchange of undertakings. For instance, the fact that firms may have expressed their joint intention to conduct themselves in the market in a specific way is sufficient to constitute an agreement.[7] It is also clear for the Court that the binding and rule making character of an agreement is not due to legal factors[8] and that it does not have to be set down in writing.

Unsurprisingly, what is meant by a 'concerted practice' has proved much more controversial and the concept has evolved a great deal over time. Two important steps can be distinguished.

---

[6] Indeed, the United States anti-trust authorities have not also shown the same wisdom; the United States case law regarding the application of para. 1 of the Sherman Act (1890) tends to draw a distinction between independent behaviour and a joint action. 'Independent behaviour' is defined in a very strict fashion and excludes the type of strategic interdependence envisaged by the *Zuiker Unie* decision (see for instance Yao and DeSanti, 1993). By contrast, a 'joint action' is supposed to entail a conscious commitment to a common scheme. The problem with this distinction is, of course, that it does not allow for a complete typology to the extent that an action that is not independent is not necessarily a joint action. By including some strategic interactions as legitimate behaviour, the *Zuiker Unie* decision avoids this pitfall.

[7] See for instance, the *Chemiefarma* case, *ECR* 661.

[8] Indeed, prohibited agreements are legally void under para. 2 of article 85.

Concerted practices and individual behaviour

In the early decisions, the concept of 'restrictive practices' was meant to cover circumstances where there is no material evidence of explicit coordination.[9] Concerted practices were associated with firms' behaviour indicative of a *common policy* being pursued. This was expressed, for instance, by AG Mayras in the *Dyestuff*[10] decision:

It is my opinion that the authors of the Treaty intended to avoid the possibility of the prohibitions of article 85 concerning anti-competitive acts being evaded by undertakings which, while following a common policy, act in such a way as to leave no trace of any written document which could be described as an agreement

and

... such an interpretation ... is of obvious interest as to the proof of the existence of a concerted practice which, even implying a certain manifestation of will of the participating undertakings, cannot be sought in the same circumstances as the proof of an express agreement.

But there is need, first, for an objective element, essential to the concept of concerted practice: the *actual* common conduct of the participating undertakings ... However, the simple finding of a common conduct, parallel or concordant, of undertakings on the market clearly cannot suffice to establish a concerted practice within the meaning of article 85(1). It is still necessary for that conduct not to be the consequence, or at least *the main consequence*, of the structure and the economic conditions of the market. There should be added a certain will of the parties to act in common ... but this common will may, according to circumstances, be deduced from all the informational data gathered on the conduct of the undertakings.

This passage suggests that a concerted practice is indeed associated with evidence that firms follow a common policy, which results from a hidden process of coordination. Rightly, the AG also suggests that a solid analysis of counterfactuals should form part of the evidence on behaviour. However, the AG also insists on evidence that parties have a certain will to act in common (and hence have coordinated their behaviour) while accepting fairly loose standards of proof (in particular, that intention can be presumed from the outcomes).

---

[9] The particular distinction between 'agreement' and 'concerted practices' referred to here, which was established early on in the case law, has certainly meant that the Commission and the Court did not have to extend to the concept of an agreement beyond common usage. The wisdom of this approach is apparent if it is compared with the United States approach in which agreements are supposed to catch all forms of coordination. As a consequence, the United States case law had to extend the meaning of an agreement as far as considering that indirect means of communications may constitute an agreement (see, e.g., Kovacic, 1993).

[10] 1972, *CMLR* 60, p. 571.

In terms of the typology discussed above, this evidence therefore suggests that a concerted practice effectively corresponds to coordination which is established from evidence about firms' individual behaviour (whereas an agreement is a form of coordination which is established from direct evidence[11]) – but this correspondence is not quite accurate, because some evidence about intentions is also required. Importantly, this interpretation would seem to imply that the prohibition associated with concerted practices is not one of market power; in other words, the pursuit of a firm's own interest, even if it leads to market power, seems to be excluded from the prohibition provided it is undertaken without coordination.

In the decision on *Zuiker Unie*,[12] the ECJ has however moved closer to a prohibition of market power. In that decision, the court has expressed the condition of a 'common will' differently by requiring that firms should be aware of the cooperative logic behind their behaviour. A concerted practice was defined as:

a form of co-ordination between undertakings which, without having been taken to the stage where an agreement properly so called has been concluded, *knowingly*, substitute for the risk of competition, practical co-operation between them which leads to conditions of competition which do not correspond to the normal conditions of competition of the market.

The definition provides a minimal condition for a coordination to occur – namely, that firms should realise what they are doing! Indeed, at the non-cooperative equilibrium of a repeated game, firms need to understand the (cooperative) logic of their behaviour. According to this definition, non-cooperative equilibria in a repeated game could thus arguably be considered as 'concerted practices' and prohibited.

This definition has, however, not been confirmed by additional case law. On the contrary, a narrower definition of intent (common will) has been used and evidence of such intent has been required. This practice is also consistent with the perception (explicit in the passages above) that type I errors would be unacceptably frequent if concerted practices could be established solely on the basis of behaviour. It is indeed one of the fixed

---

[11] There is a direct consequence of this distinction between agreements and concerted practices (as noted by AG Mayras): to the extent that concerted practices will be established by outcomes, it is not necessary to further establish that a concerted practice has the effect of restricting competition. This is an integral part of the proof that there is a concerted practice in the first place. By contrast, where agreements are concerned, it is necessary to prove that they have the object or effect of restricting competition. This additional requirement has, however, not proved to be a major hurdle in the case law (see Guerrin and Kyriazis, 1992).

[12] 1976, *CMLR* 295.

points in the case law since the *Dyestuff* decision that the ECJ has refused to consider evidence on outcomes and economic counterfactuals as sufficient.[13]

This approach is not altogether very different from that found in the United States, where additional factors are required in addition to parallel behaviour in order to find a conviction. Among those factors, evidence of anti-competitive intent behind the parallel conduct[14] and the absence of a credible explanation for the conduct in the absence of detailed communication or coordination are given heavy weight (see Baker, 1993).

The concept of concerted practice that emerges from these decisions would still be greatly clarified if it were stated explicitly how the economic counterfactual (the 'normal conditions of the market') should be treated. So far little has been said (except in *Polypropylène*,[15] where it was established that evidence on behaviour need not be limited to parallel behaviour but could include any conspicuous behaviour which could not be explained in terms of 'normal competitive conditions'). As a result, there has been some confusion in the case law (see below). Effectively, what the Commission has to do is to show that observed behaviour could not reasonably be explained without some form of coordination. This ought to be explicitly acknowledged. It should also be clarified, in particular, that behaviour which can be explained as the pursuit of a firm's own interest in the absence of coordination will not be taken as evidence for the existence of a 'concerted practice'.

Concerted practices – weak direct evidence of coordination

Decisions by the Commission and subsequent reviews by the ECJ have extended the concept of 'concerted practices'. In *Polypropylène*[16] as well as in later decisions such as *Flat Glass*[17] or *LEDP*,[18] the Commission argued that evidence on behaviour was not really necessary to establish the presence of a concerted practice. It sought to extend the concept to

---

[13] The same attitude can be found in the United States, where the requirement of the Sherman Act that an agreement should be proved has never been stretched to the point that evidence on outcomes was sufficient to deduce the existence of an agreement. Even under article 5 of the FTC act, which does not require proof that an agreement exists, evidence on outcomes has not so far been considered sufficient (see Kovacic, 1993).

[14] Indeed, the very notion of an 'agreement' under United States law, defined as a conscious commitment to a common scheme, requires some intent (see Kovacic, 1993).

[15] 1992, *CMLR* 84.

[16] 1992, *CMLR* 84, 1986 and *OJ L* 230/1, 1986.

[17] *OJ L* 33/44, 1989.

[18] *OJ L* 74/21, 1989.

situations where the factual evidence on direct coordination between firms was insufficient to support the conclusion that there has been an agreement (for instance, no clear exchange of undertakings), but where there was still abundant evidence of communication between firms regarding anti-competitive actions. The Commission has thus perceived a hole in the coverage of the legal concepts, between situations that can qualify as concerted practices because of evidence on behaviour and situations that can qualify as agreements because of abundant factual evidence. It has tried to extend the concept of 'concerted practice' in order to cover this hole. This reaction is presumably a consequence of the considerable frustration that the Commission must have felt in dealing with counterfactual behaviour in order to establish the existence of concerted practices (in its original definition).

For instance, in the *Polypropylène* decision, the Commission stated in article 87 that:

toute prise de contact direct ou indirecte entre elles ayant pour objet ou pour effet, soit d'influencer le comportement sur le marché d'un concurrent actuel ou poten- tiel, soit de dévoiler à un tel concurrent le comportement que l'on est décidé, ou que l'on envisage soit même sur la marché...peut tomber sous le coup de l'article 85 paragraphe 1 en tant que pratique concertée. [All points of direct or indirect contact between them which have for their object or their effect either to influence market behaviour in relation to actual or potential competition or to unveil such competitive behaviour or what is envisaged on the market, shall fall under article 85, para. 1 as concerted practices.]

The companies involved challenged the interpretation of the Commission during the administrative procedure by stating (article 88 of the decision) that 'la notion de pratique concertée suppose des actes manifestés sur le marché' [the concept of concerted practice presupposes demonstrable action on the market]. In their view, the Commission should have shown that companies had tried to put into effect what was allegedly concerted. The case was brought to Court essentially on this ground (in addition to procedural issues).

The ECJ firmly rejected the argument of the Commission that con- certation (i.e. exchange of information and opinions between firms which can be used as a vehicle to outline common views) could be taken as evidence of a concerted practice *per se*. However, it has suggested that when there is evidence of concertation, the effects on the market could be presumed. As stated by AG Versterdrof:

It can therefore be maintained that in principle concertation will automatically trigger subsequent action on the market which will be determined by the con- certation, whether the undertakings do one thing or another with regard to their market policy, that is to say regardless of whether they subsequently behave in a more or less uniform way in the market.

Effectively what this ruling has done is to declare that the Commission was wrong on principles but right in its practice. There is still a subtle difference between the Commission's argument that coordination is *per se* a concerted practice and the ECJ ruling that when there is evidence of concertation, behaviour can be presumed; in the latter case, it is still possible for a firm to overturn the presumption – namely, to argue that the content of the concertation has not affected its behaviour: for instance, because it has put in place commitment mechanisms to prevent the use of the knowledge gained in the concertation (such as firing the executives concerned).

Legal standards: some conclusions

The main conclusion which emerges from our review of these legal concepts is that the current legal standard is on the whole (if one excludes some ambiguous statements in *Zuiker Unie*) one of coordination and not one of market power. In particular, it does not seem that firms which collectively exercise market power in repeated market interactions can be considered to have engaged in a concerted practice. In addition, it seems that the legal norm of coordination is quite general and covers many different forms. There is no form of coordination which has been explicitly excluded from the prohibition.

There is one clear implication from the observation that legal standards are solely defined in terms of coordination – namely, that behaviour which is consistent with the collective exercise of market power by firms which act independently is irrelevant to establishing the presence of unlawful practices. This issue is discussed further in section 4.

The concept of 'concerted practices' has evolved a great deal in recent years. A concerted practice can currently be found on two different grounds: first, by evidence on the conduct of firms (which includes parallel conduct but also any suspicious conduct which cannot be credibly explained in terms of 'normal' competitive behaviour) supplemented by evidence on intent; secondly, by evidence on concertation (regarding practices which can have anti-competitive effects) from which conduct in the market can be presumed.

Because of this evolution, one can wonder whether the distinction between agreements and concerted practices is still very meaningful. Both can be established from direct evidence of coordination and the only difference is that evidence may be weaker for concerted practices. Hence, it seems that any agreement is *a fortiori* a concerted practice.

In this context, it would clarify matters a great deal if the Commission or the ECJ were to state explicitly that the legal standard is indeed one of coordination, and furthermore that coordination can be established either by direct evidence or by evidence on market behaviour for which coordination is the only reasonable explanation.

If the legal rule which emerges seems relatively clear, the analysis of firms' behaviour and the standards that economic counterfactuals should meet have remained rather vague ('the normal conditions of competition'). It is therefore important to evaluate how this analysis has been undertaken in practice. This is the objective of section 4.

4   Economic counterfactuals in case law

In cases[19] where the Commission is trying to establish a concerted practice on the basis of behaviour, the analysis of the counterfactual will be essential. What the Commission has to show is that the behaviour of firms cannot be explained without resorting to some form of coordination. Importantly, therefore, it is not enough for the Commission to establish that the behaviour of firms is consistent with some prior form of coordination: it has to show that the observed behaviour cannot be explained in terms of alternative competitive processes which do not involve coordination. The ECJ has indeed firmly established that in case of litigation, the burden of proof falls on the Commission (see Guerrin and Kyriazis, 1992).

The next subsections consider some flaws in the Commission's reasoning that appear in a number of decisions.

Alternative explanations not involving coordination

The Commission has on a number of occasions failed to consider whether the observed behaviour might be explained without appeal to coordination. First, the evidence on behaviour brought forward by the Commission sometimes almost reads like a textbook description of non-cooperative strategies in repeated games. Such evidence is of course not indicative of coordination and, as suggested above, is effectively irrelevant to the prosecution if the legal rule is one based on coordination.

---

[19] Many decisions by the Commission in the area of secret horizontal agreement and concerted practices are appealed in Court. We reviewed all decisions by the Commission in the period 1989–95 (whether or not they were appealed in Court) as well as all the important ECJ decisions in the same period, together with the original Commission decisions relating to those cases (which may accordingly have been taken prior to 1989). In what follows, we will focus on the analysis of economic counterfactuals. A more complete analysis can be found in Neven, Papandropoulos and Seabright (1998).

The *Welded Steel*[20] case serves as an illustration of such unconvincing arguments (admittedly, the factual evidence of concertation was so strong in this case that the Commission did not have to rely much on interpreting the behaviour). In particular, the case contains a detailed account of what economists would refer to as the 'trigger of a price war'. For instance in paragraphs starting at 38, the Commission describes first an exchange of information between French and Italian producers. At some stage, official statistics are published with a significant discrepancy from the declaration of Italian producers. Suspicion then arises, which is confirmed when a Belgian producer warns its French competitors that is has found, by chance, evidence of substantial sales at low prices by an Italian producer through a small company in Briançon (France). This triggers a price war, in which French producers ('nous sommes en guerre') reduce price by 15 per cent. After a few months, prices have returned to their original level.[21] Of course, all this evidence is consistent with the view that firms were acting without coordination. Reporting this evidence has, in our view, weakened rather than strengthened the case.

In other cases, the Commission has indeed considered whether observed behaviour could not be explained without coordination. But the analysis is sometimes unconvincing.

In *Wood Pulp*,[22] the Commission also argued that the sequence of price announcements, as well as the level of prices, could not be explained in a more competitive framework. Regarding the sequence of price announcements, the Commission noted that the first price to be announced was almost always met by subsequent ones. The Commission claimed that such pattern could not arise in a competitive environment because firms

[20] Producers of welded steel throughout Europe coordinated sales in a number of national markets (Italy, the Benelux, Germany and France) between 1980 and 1985. Part of the incentive to coordinate arose because a crisis cartel was established in Germany and allowed by the Bundeskartellamt. In order to make it effective, imports had to be restricted. The Commission found ample factual evidence of coordination and 14 companies were fined, with fines ranging from 20,000 to 1,375,000 ECU (*JO L* 260, 1989).

[21] A similar incident occurred a couple of years later where, in line with the principles discussed above, there is also evidence of prices creeping up to their original level (rather than adjusting abruptly).

[22] Producers of wood pulp from the United States (organised as an export cartel exempter under the Webb–Pomerene Act), Canada, the Scandinavian countries and several member states were found by the Commission to have coordinated prices between 1975 and 1981. There was evidence of numerous contacts between firms but little factual evidence of coordination. Much of the decision turned on the interpretation of 'parallel behaviour', in particular pre-announcement of prices. As many as 36 companies were fined, with amounts ranging from 50,000 to 500,000 ECU. The decision was appealed on several grounds. The question of Community competence was settled in the first Court decision (27 September 1988) in favour of the Commission. The second Court ruling (31 March 1993) annulled most of the Commission decision, except regarding the United States export cartel (*JO L* 85/1, 1985).

would normally experiment with different prices before converging to some equilibrium level. The suggestion that independent firms would normally experiment with different prices seems intuitively appealing, at least for transaction prices; but pre-announced prices carry little commitment and serve mostly to establish a maximum price for consumers. In this context, after a first announcement has been made, the best strategy of an independent firm may be to quote the same price: it certainly has no incentive to quote a higher maximum price as customers would turn to the firm having made the first announcement. Quoting a lower price may also be unattractive, as firms would foreclose the option of reaching agreement on an intermediate price (in between the original announcement and its lower reply). By meeting the first announcement, subsequent firms may not foreclose any option and thus keep open the possibility of providing rebates later. Altogether, it is far from clear that the sequence of prices could not be explained in terms of competitive interactions.

The Commission also considered evidence regarding price levels, arguing that uniform prices should not be expected in a competitive environment, given wide differences in the location of customers, in the cost structure of firms and large changes in the exchange rates. According to the Commission, these factors should have led firms to quote different prices. However, the argument is puzzling: first, it is clear that in a competitive environment, different suppliers will end up quoting the same price for a given delivery (say, for a given product, at a given place and time); low-cost suppliers will make some profit but will not charge lower prices. In this respect, the uniformity of prices, as quoted by suppliers, is thus perfectly consistent with a very competitive environment. Second, the Commission seems to argue that the variation of prices across different types of products and across space is low and that more variation would be observed if firms did effectively compete. Yet, some degree of discrimination across products and space is consistent both with competition and some form of prior coordination. It is unclear whether coordination will always lead to more discrimination. At the very least, the Commission should have argued its case in more detail.

In *Flat Glass*,[23] the Commission considered a somewhat unusual form of parallel behaviour which could prove useful in other cases. The

---

[23] Three Italian producers of float glass were found to have violated both article 85 and 86. Regarding article 85, the Commission held that the three producers had coordinated prices and commercial policies in both the automotive and non-automotive markets. The Commission brought material evidence of coordination and of parallel behaviour. The companies were fined between 1,700,000 and 7,000,000 ECU. They appealed and the Court of First Instance annulled most of the decision (*CMLR* 302, 1992) because of insufficient legal standards of proof. It also reduced the fines (cancelling the fine altogether for one firm and reducing them by as much as six-sevenths for the other two). (*JO L* 33/44, 1989).

Commission suggested that firms had classified their main customers in a number of different categories in order to define appropriate rebates. The Commission argued that such common classification was the result of an explicit coordination because they did not respect the specificity of the relationship between each firm and its main customers (for instance, customers were given rebates proportional to total purchases addressed to the firms in the coordination, rather than proportional to the purchases addressed to individual firms). In principle, the argument seems convincing. However, the Court rejected the evidence brought forward by the Commission as insufficient (and indeed, the factual claim by the Commission was weak).

The distinction between coordination itself and resulting behaviour

This distinction has sometimes been far from clear. For example, there is a puzzling analysis of coordination in *Wood Pulp*. First, the Commission considered the pre-announcement of prices that firms undertook before each quarter, emphasising the simultaneity of the announcements (within a few days of each other), the similarity of price levels that were announced and the fact that the first-price announcement was almost always met by subsequent ones. However, the Commission adopted a very ambiguous interpretation of this evidence: effectively, the Commission could not decide whether these announcements were the result of a previous process of coordination, and should be seen as an outcome, or whether these announcements should be seen as a process of coordination in itself. The ambivalence of the Commission is most apparent in the following excerpts from the decision (paras. 107–8):

Les annonces de prix en succession rapide ou même simultanément auraient été impossibles sans un flux constant d'information entre les entreprises visées. [Price announcements in rapid succession or even simultaneously will be impossible without a continual flow of information between the enterprises.]

Le système des annonces trimestrielles, que les entreprises ont choisi volontairement, constituait à tout le moins en soi un échange indirect d'information quant à leur comportement futur sur le marché. [The system of three-monthly announcements which firms have chosen voluntarily constitutes an indirect exchange of information concerning their future conduct on the market.]

Following the logic that price announcements were a process of coordination rather than the outcome of such a process, the Commission even went as far as to argue that 'prior information exchanges, should be seen as a separate infringement of article 85 (1)'. This confusion was not lost on the defendants and the Court of First Instance. For instance, AG Darmon states (paras. 242–3 of his opinion):

> Is the 'common price' the result of the concertation between the undertakings prior to the announcement themselves . . .? Or does the system of price announcements constitute the machinery of concertation for fixing that common price? The lack of clarity in the Commission's position is unfortunate . . . The Commission's position in this case has the consistency of mercury. Just as one is about to grasp it, it eludes one, only to assume an unexpected shape.

In theory, the argument that the system of price announcements should be seen as a process of coordination seems more appropriate. As emphasised by Kühn and Vives (1994), the prices that are announced by firms carry little commitment value. Indeed, the actual prices in *Wood Pulp* sometimes differed from the announced prices[24] (even though the Commission tried to argue that discrepancies were small). Accordingly, announced prices could hardly be seen as the decision resulting from a prior process of coordination. These prices should rather be seen as a form of what game theorists call 'cheap talk'. Accordingly, the firms' announcements can be interpreted as an attempt to establish some focal point (whether this should be seen a sufficient evidence of coordination will be discussed in the next subsection). This interpretation was considered by the AG in his opinion; he accepted the view that such indirect information exchanges could be seen as unlawful, but rejected the argument in the case at hand because of insufficient reasoning.

Acceptance of weak reasoning by the defendants

In some cases the Commission could have dismissed more strongly arguments advanced by the defendants. An example is the argument by Solvay and ICI in *Soda-Ash*,[25] that market sharing could be explained as the

---

[24] However, the combination of pre-announcements with most-favoured customer clauses can act as a facilitating practice (see Holt and Scheffman, 1987). In the present case, there is evidence of contracts using most-favoured customer clauses.

[25] Whereas Solvay has concentrated its sales of soda-ash on the continent, where it holds a large market share (> 60 per cent), ICI has a near-monopoly in the United Kingdom and has never penetrated the continent. An agreement, known as 'page 1000', was struck between the companies in 1945 to maintain the actual market-sharing arrangements which prevailed at the time. The agreement was formally suspended by the time the United Kingdom joined the Community. The Commission held that the companies had continued to coordinate their behaviour to maintain the market-sharing thereafter. The Commission had evidence of sustained contacts between the companies but not factual evidence of coordination. The interpretation of 'parallel behaviour' – namely, whether market-sharing could arise in a competitive condition – was essential. Fines of 7,000,000 ECU were imposed on each company. They appealed and the decision was annulled by the Court of First Instance, on procedural grounds (*JO C* 341, 19 December 1995–*JO L* 152/1, 1991).

equilibrium of a Cournot game. The firms argued that 'Cournot is characterised by the expectation of undertakings in an industry that other undertakings will maintain output whatever the individual does'. According to the expert witness, producers in the soda-ash industry could thus be expected to concentrate on their home market and refrain from competition with one another. The Commission dismissed the expert witness because she proved (in the administrative hearings) to be unaware of the documentary evidence attached to the statement of objections. Being ill informed, the Commission argued, she could not reach a relevant conclusion.

Such a dismissal avoided confronting directly the arguments of the firm. These arguments could nevertheless have been seriously questioned by the Commission. For instance, the reference to Cournot in the firm's submission is clearly a misrepresentation. The firms seem to imply that because Cournot firms take rival output as given, any output configuration can be seen as the outcome of a Cournot game. This implication is clearly incorrect and misses the equilibrium condition – namely, that firms' outputs have to be mutual best replies. The Commission could have argued further that most models of international trade which assume Cournot behaviour predict significant cross-hauling (bilateral exports). The absence of market-sharing has actually been considered as a major attraction of the Cournot framework in international trade, such that it can account for (widely observed) intra-industry trade. It takes extremely large barriers to trade to obtain an outcome where firms stay in their home markets.[26]

Inconsistency of burden of proof

In some cases, the arguments of the Commission regarding firm behaviour do not seem to be consistent with the allocation of the burden of proof. *Soda-Ash* is a case in point. The defendants argued that they did not penetrate each other's market (with ICI holding close to a monopoly in the United Kingdom and Solvay holding more than 60 per cent of continental Europe), simply out of fear of retaliation. Indeed, the defendants could have argued that when firms potentially meet in several markets at the same time, a successful non-cooperative exercise of market power will typically involve market-sharing.[27] This is more likely to occur when domestic firms have a cost advantage at home, which certainly

---

[26] See for instance, Neven and Phlips (1985) and Smith and Venables (1988).
[27] See Bernheim and Whinston (1990). Admittedly, the Commission decision was published less than two years after the relevant academic paper was published.

holds in the present case, given the evidence being provided on transport cost.

The Commission argued that this behaviour could also be seen as the outcome of explicit coordination:

the possibility of retaliation which Solvay and ICI claim as the reason for their respective abstention from each other's home market in no way excludes the existence of an understanding ... retaliation was the normal sanction for any breach of the home market principles: the threat of retaliation thus served to encourage continued cooperation.

The point is well taken but it would help the prosecution only if it were for the firm to show that its behaviour could not be seen as the outcome of coordination.

5 Conclusions

The first conclusion to emerge from our analysis is that the current legal standard is one of coordination and not one of market power. Firms which collectively exercise market power in repeated market interactions cannot be considered to have engaged in a concerted practice. In addition, the recent case law suggests that many forms of coordination are presumed unlawful; neither the Commission nor the Court has ever considered that some form of coordination might be useful or necessary.

Secondly, the concept of a 'concerted practice' has evolved in such a way that the distinction between agreements and concerted practices may no longer have much point. In our view, it would clarify matters a great deal if the Court were to state explicitly that the concepts are equivalent (recent decisions in any case suggest the Commission no longer attaches any importance to the distinction).

Thirdly, the analysis of firms' behaviour which has been undertaken by the Commission in recent cases often appears unconvincing, or even misguided. In the context of a coordination rule, what the Commission has to show is that firms' behaviour cannot be explained without some underlying process of coordination. The Commission often overlooks alternative and plausible explanations behind firm behaviour, which do not involve a process of coordination. In particular, the main insights from the repeated-game-literature (which imply that no coordination may be needed for the exercise of some market power) have not been fully absorbed into the Commission's thinking.

Commission decisions are also interesting in terms of the arguments that they overlook. In particular, the Commission does not try to argue that circumstances were favourable to the development of some collective exercise of market power so that attention is warranted or that concertation was likely. Such arguments (known as economic plausibility factors) are however used routinely in United States case law (see Ginsburg, 1993 and references therein) and could serve at least to establish a first-presumption.

Finally, the Commission has rarely appealed to the existence of facilitating practices in order to establish a presumption, a practice which is also common in United States case law, particularly when it can be shown that the facilitating practice has been established by the defendants. The most common facilitating practice that appears in recent cases is the establishment of a research and information centre on the industry (see *Wood Pulp, Polypropylène, LEDP, PVC, Welded Steel*). Invariably, these research and information centres have gathered information about firms' behaviour in addition to aggregate statistics and have organised or even hosted meetings between competitors. The Commission could have taken a stronger line against such institutions and counted their mere existence a serious presumption of coordination.

Bibliography

Baker, J.B. (1993) Two Sherman Act section 1 dilemmas: parallel pricing, the oligopoly problem, and contemporary economic theory, *The Antitrust Bulletin*, Spring, pp. 143–219

Bernheim, B.D. and M.D. Whinston (1990) Multimarket contact and collusive behaviour, *Rand Journal of Economics*, 21(1), pp. 1–25

Friedman, J. (1971) A non-cooperative equilibrium for supergames, *Review of Economic Studies*, 38(1), pp. 1–12

Ginsburg, D.H. (1993) Non price competition, *The Antitrust Bulletin*, Spring, pp. 83–111

Guerrin, M. and G. Kyriazis (1992) Cartels: proofs and procedural issues, *1992 Fordham Corporate Law Institute*

Harrington, J.E., Jr (1989) Collusion among asymmetric firms: the case of different discount factors, *International Journal of Industrial Organisation*, 7, pp. 289–307

Holt, C. and D. Scheffman (1987) Facilitating practices: the effects of advance notice and best-price policies, *Rand Journal of Economics*, 18(2), pp. 187–97

Kovacic, W.E. (1993) The identification and proof of horizontal agreements under the antitrust laws, *The Antitrust Bulletin*, Spring, pp. 5–81

Kühn, K.-U. and X. Vives (1994) Information exchange among firms and their impact on competition, Report to DG IV

Neven, D. and L. Phlips (1985) Discriminating oligopolists and common markets, *The Journal of Industrial Economics*, 34(2), pp. 133–50

50   Damien J. Neven

Neven, D., P. Papandropoulos and P. Seabright (1998) *European Competition Policy and Agreements between Undertakings: Article 85 in Theory and Practice*, London: CEPR

Phlips, L. (1996) On the detection of collusion and predation, *European Economic Review*, Papers and Proceedings, 40(3–5), pp. 495–510

Porter, M. (1985) *Competitive Advantage: Creating and Sustaining Superior Performance*, New York: Free Press

Rees, R. (1993) Tacit collusion, *Oxford Review of Economic Policy*, 9(2), pp. 27–40

Schelling, T. (1960) *The Strategy of Conflicts*, Cambridge, Mass: Harvard University Press

Scherer, F.M. (1980) *Industrial Market Structure and Industrial Performance*, Chicago: Rand McNally

Sjostrom, W. (1989) Collusion in ocean shipping: a test of monopoly and empty core models, *Journal of Political Economy*, 97(5), pp. 1160–79

Smith, A. and T. Venables (1988) Completing the internal market in the European Community, *European Economic Review*, 32(7)

Stigler, G. (1964) A theory of oligopoly, *Journal of Political Economy*, 72(1), pp. 44–61

Yao, D.A. and S.S. DeSanti (1993) Game theory and the legal analysis of tacit collusion, *The Antitrust Bulletin*, Spring, pp. 113–41

3 A guided tour of the Folk Theorem

James W. Friedman

1 Introduction

The *Folk Theorem* suggests the possibility of cooperation through a self-enforcing agreement. The phrase '*Folk Theorem for repeated games*' refers strictly to a theorem stating that a certain large class of single-shot game payoffs can be obtained as Nash equilibrium payoffs if the game is repeated infinitely many times and the players do not discount their payoffs (Aumann, 1960). It refers more broadly to similar results, supported by subgame perfect equilibria (SPEs), for games that are finitely repeated and infinitely repeated games in which players may discount payoffs. Perhaps the most striking implication of these results is the possibility of apparently cooperative outcomes in non-cooperative games when these games are knowingly played many times by a fixed collection of players.

I have been aware of, and impressed by, the work of Louis Phlips for about a quarter of a century. His work on competition policy is meticulous and distinguished. The topic of my contribution bears on competition policy, because the Folk Theorem literature spells out means by which firms can attain outcomes that appear collusive without, necessarily, engaging in overt collusion – or, indeed, even discussing together what to do.

Infinite horizon oligopoly is a well known example of a repeated game. The Cournot model is the most widely taught example and it is typical in that the Cournot equilibrium (i.e. the Nash equilibrium of the single-shot Cournot market) generally results in a payoff profile that lies inside the payoff possibility frontier. However, if the Cournot market is infinitely repeated, then it may be possible to achieve virtually any payoff profile on

I thank Scott Baker, Jacques-François Thisse, Olivier Compte and an anonymous referee for helpful comments, but absolve them of any responsibility.

the frontier. This result is a two-edged sword. On one hand, it provides a theoretically well grounded foundation for cooperative payoffs when binding agreements are impossible – that is, it shows how firms can collude by means of self-enforcing agreements. On the other hand, it shows that almost any payoff outcome is a theoretical possibility, which robs the model of predictive power.

My purpose in this chapter is to review the meaning and significance of the Folk Theorem in both the narrow and the broad senses. To do this I will refer to a number of models and theorems, relate them to each other and relate them to the commonsense interests of economists in their roles as scholars and policy advisors. The coverage will vary in comprehensiveness; the main purpose of this chapter is to provide sufficient introduction to the Folk Theorem literature to give a good intuitive sense of some of the main results and to provide further readings. In section 2 a model will be specified that should orient the reader and provide helpful tools for understanding the rest of the chapter. Section 3 discusses the Folk Theorem in the narrow sense and notes various questions and objections that the original Folk Theorem raises. A prominent objection is that the result is flawed because the equilibrium strategies seem to rely on unbelievable threats. This is discussed in section 4 where results are reviewed that solve this difficulty. Section 5 considers whether the predictive power can be sharpened, whether the results critically depend on the discontinuous nature of the equilibrium strategies used in proofs, and whether single-shot games can be brought within the scope of the theorems. While single-shot games cannot come within the purview of the Folk Theorems, it is seen in section 6 that some finite horizon games can be covered. The general nature of the Folk Theorem equilibria is that players are expected to behave in a particular way and, when some player does not choose as expected, she is punished. Clearly this requires that players have some ability to monitor other players' choices. In section 7 the extent of that ability is examined. Section 8 examines Folk Theorem results for games that go beyond the repeated-game-framework by permitting the payoff function of time period t to depend on the past choices of the players – that is, there are state variables in the model. Finally, in section 9, some concluding remarks are offered.

2   Some basics

The basic framework of repeated games is presented below. First, a conventional strategic game (the single-shot game) is described. This chapter is concerned mainly with repeated games in which this single-shot game is repeated at regular intervals, either infinitely, or for a known, fixed number of times.[1] A striking aspect of the Folk Theorem is that equilibria are possible in which a player may obtain in each play of the single-shot game a payoff that is distinctly below the payoff associated with any Nash equilibrium of the single-shot game itself. The greatest lower bound on this payoff is called the player's *minmax payoff*. Following the specification of the single-shot game, the repeated game is characterised for discounted infinitely repeated games and for finitely repeated games. Given that payoffs in the single-shot game Γ are bounded, the payoffs in these two classes of repeated games are clearly bounded. The specification of the repeated game must be derived in a natural way from the underlying single-shot game, the information that will be obtained by players over time and the time preferences of the players.

Imagine a standard strategic game that is specified by the triple $\Gamma = \langle N, S, P \rangle$ where (i) $N = \{1, \ldots, n\}$ is the finite set of players, (ii) $S = \times_{i \in N} S_i$ is the strategy space of the game with $S_i \subset \Re^m$ being the strategy set of player i and (iii) $P = (P_1, \ldots, P_n)$ is the profile of payoff functions with $P_i : S \to \Re$ being the payoff function of player i. For each player i in a game Γ certain payoffs are called *individually rational*; these are payoffs that exceed the lowest payoff v_i to which player i can be forced by the other players. That is

$$v_i = \min_{s_{-i} \in S_{-i}} \max_{s_i \in S_i} P_i(s_{-i}, s_i)$$

Let $v = (v_1, \ldots, v_n)$. For any Nash equilibrium payoff profile x in the game Γ, the relationship $v \leq x$ must hold. This is easily illustrated by a Cournot duopoly game in which inverse demand is given by $p = \max\{0, 61 - q_1 - q_2\}$, each firm has a marginal cost of one, fixed cost is zero and the output of each firm must be between zero and 60. Thus $N = \{1, 2\}$, $S_i = [0, 60]$ and $P_i(q_1, q_2) = q_i \max\{0, 61 - q_1 - q_2\} - q_i$. It is easily verified that the Nash equilibrium is uniquely $(20, 20)$ with associated payoffs of 400 for each player. The minmax payoff profile is $v = (0, 0)$. To see this, note that the strategy profile $(0, 60)$ forces player 1 to a payoff of zero; if player 2 chooses $q_2 = 60$ then player 1 maximises her payoff by choosing $q_1 = 0$ and achieving a payoff of zero. Similarly, the choice of 60 by player 1 will force player 2 down to a payoff of, at most, zero.

A repeated game occurs when, typically, the set N of players will play the game Γ repeatedly at fixed time intervals that we may denote $t = 0, 1, 2, \ldots,$ $T - 1$ with each player i knowing, before choosing $s_{it} \in S_i$ at time t, the actual history of choices $h_t \equiv (s_0, s_1, \ldots, s_{t-1}) \in S^t$ made by everyone in the past.

---

[1] In section 8 the possibility of playing a fixed, varying sequence of games is discussed and also the possibility of playing a sequence of games in which the game at any period depends on past choices.

For finite T the repeated game is called Γ^T, indicating that Γ will be played T times and the infinitely repeated game is called Γ^∞. The condition that at time t each player knows h_t, is called *perfect monitoring*.

Complete specification of Γ^T, for either finite or infinite T, requires that (i) the repeated-game-strategy sets of the players be derived from the single-shot strategy sets S_i and the information conditions of the repeated game, (ii) discount parameters $\delta = (\delta_1, \ldots, \delta_n)$ must be specified and (iii) the repeated-game-payoff functions be specified as functions of the repeated-game-strategy profiles. That is, $\Gamma^T = \langle N, \mathfrak{S}^T, \delta, \mathfrak{P} \rangle$ needs to be defined where $\mathfrak{S}_i^T$ is the repeated-game-strategy set of player i, $\delta_i \in (0, 1]$ is the discount parameter of player i and $\mathfrak{P}_i : \mathfrak{S}^T \to \mathfrak{R}$ is the repeated-game-pay-off function of player i. It will help to avoid confusion if elements of S_i are called *moves*, because they are naturally regarded as moves in the repeated game, and the word *strategy* is reserved for repeated-game strategies.

Let $H \equiv \{(s_0, s_1, \ldots, s_{t-1}) \in S^t | t = 1, \ldots, T\}$ denote the *set of histories of the game* Γ^T. It is understood that the null history $\emptyset \in H$. Thus the set of histories associated with time t is S^t, the t-fold product of S with itself, and H can also be written as $\{\emptyset\} \times_{t=1}^T S^t$. If T is finite, Γ^T is a *finitely repeated game*. The set of histories can be partitioned into the set Z of terminal histories and the set $H \backslash Z$ of non-terminal histories. At each non-terminal history each player i must choose a move from S_i while, at a terminal history, the game ends. For infinitely repeated games, all finite histories in H are non-terminal and all infinite histories are terminal. A strategy for player i in the repeated game Γ^T is a function $\sigma_i : H \backslash Z \to S_i$ – that is, a strategy for player i is a function that associates with each possible non-terminal history a specific move in S_i. $\mathfrak{S}_i^T = \{\sigma_i | \sigma_i(h) \in S_i, h \in H \backslash Z\}$ is the set of repeated-game strategies and $\mathfrak{S}^T = \times_{i \in N} \mathfrak{S}_i^T$ is the set of repeated-game-strategy profiles.

Except as occasionally and specifically noted below, I will take the sets S_i to be compact and convex, and will assume that players always choose pure strategies and that there are no other sources of randomness in the game. Thus a specific strategy profile $\sigma = (\sigma_1, \ldots, \sigma_n) \in \mathfrak{S}^T$ will clearly cause a specific terminal history, denoted $h^\sigma = (s_0^\sigma, s_1^\sigma, \ldots, s_{T-1}^\sigma)$, to be played where $s_t^\sigma \in S$, for each player i and time $t \geq 0$, $s_{it}^\sigma = \sigma_i(s_0^\sigma, s_1^\sigma, \ldots, s_{t-1}^\sigma)$ and $s_{i0}^\sigma = \sigma_i(\emptyset)$. The payoff of player i associated with the single-shot game at time t is, given the strategy profile σ, $P_i(s_t^\sigma)$. If player i discounts using the discount parameter $\delta_i \in (0, 1)$, then the repeated-game-payoff function of player i is defined as

$$\mathfrak{P}_i(\sigma) = \sum_{t=0}^{T} \delta^t P_i(s_t^\sigma)$$

Letting $\mathfrak{P} = (\mathfrak{P}_1, \ldots, \mathfrak{P}_n)$ and $\delta = (\delta_1, \ldots, \delta_n)$, we may write $\Gamma^T = \langle N, \mathfrak{S}^T, \delta, \mathfrak{P} \rangle$. If the game is infinitely repeated it may be denoted Γ^∞ and if payoffs are not discounted, with a slight abuse of notation, the game is denoted $\Gamma^T = \langle N, \mathfrak{S}^T, 1, \mathfrak{P} \rangle$ to signify that $\delta = (1, \ldots, 1)$.

Sections 3 and 4 review the most basic Folk Theorem material. The results in section 3 are apparently due to Aumann (1960). Aumann's theorem permits equilibrium behaviour that can be interpreted as non-believable threats. This behaviour is eliminated by the further results in section 4, which are due to Rubinstein (1979) for infinitely repeated games without discounting and Fudenberg and Maskin (1986) for infinitely repeated games with discounting.

3 The (original) Folk Theorem

Apparently during the 1950s various people became aware that the Nash equilibrium payoff profiles of infinitely repeated games without discounting went far beyond the payoff profiles generated by the repeated play of single-shot Nash equilibria. Some early writings of Aumann (e.g. 1960) bear on this as does Luce and Raiffa's (1957, section 5.5) discussion of the repeated prisoners' dilemma. Theorem 1 is the original Folk Theorem, the result that was known in some game-theory circles many years ago.[2] In the theorem the *overtaking criterion* is used to evaluate infinite sums. One infinite sequence of payoffs $\{x^t\}_{t=0}^\infty$ is preferred to a second sequence $\{y^t\}_{t=0}^\infty$ according to the overtaking criterion if, after some finite time T^*, the sum of payoffs under the first sequence is always larger than the sum under the latter – that is, $\sum_{t=0}^T x^t > \sum_{t=0}^T y^t$ for all $T > T^*$.

Theorem 1: *Let $\Gamma^\infty = \langle N, \mathfrak{S}^\infty, 1, \mathfrak{P} \rangle$ be an infinitely repeated game without discounting, based on the single-shot game $\Gamma = \langle N, S, P \rangle$, and let $x \in \Re^n$ be an achievable payoff profile in Γ (i.e. there exists some $s' \in S$ such that $P(s') = x$). Then if $x \gg v$ there exists a strategy profile $\sigma' \in \mathfrak{S}^\infty$ that is a Nash equilibrium of Γ^∞ for which the payoff profile in every period of play is x.*

Proof: Denote by $s' \in S$ the single-shot strategy profile that achieves x, let $z_i = \max_{s_i \in S_i} P_i(s'_{-i}, s_i)$ be the largest possible payoff player i could achieve in a single period by maximising against s'_{-i} and let $u^i \in S$ be a single-shot strategy profile that achieves the minmax payoff of player i. (That is, $P_i(u^i) = \min_{s_{-i} \in S_{-i}} \max_{s_i \in S_i} P_i(s_{-i}, s_i) = v_i$.) Define the strategy profile σ' as follows: (i) $\sigma'_i(\emptyset) = s'_i$, (ii) for any non-terminal $h \in H$

---

[2] To my knowledge, the first formal, published statement of theorem 1 is in Aumann (1960).

such that $h = (s', \ldots, s')$, $\sigma'_i(h) = s'_i$, (iii) for any other non-terminal $h = (s_0, \ldots, s_t)$ find the earliest time τ for which $s_\tau \neq s'$ and the player with the lowest index j for which $s_{j\tau} \neq s'_j$, and then set $\sigma'_i(h) = u^j_i$ for each player $i \in N$. Clearly, the payoff sequence $(x_i, \ldots, x_i, z_i, v_i, \ldots)$ is overtaken by $(x_i, \ldots, x_i, x_i, x_i, \ldots)$. ∎

What drives this proof is exceedingly clear: if a player i deviates from σ'_i at some time t this deviation is immediately known before the next round of choices is made, permitting the other players to punish player i in perpetuity by driving her payoff to v_i ever afterward. The maximum gain that player i can obtain is finite – namely, $z_i - x_i$ – and the subsequent loss is $x_i - v_i$ which, when carried out forever, is unbounded. In effect, the infinite repetition of the game permits the players to make a non-binding agreement to select some s' in each repetition of Γ and to punish deviators from this agreement in a fashion consistent with Nash equilibrium. Apparently, an agreement might be self-enforcing if present actions are subject, when needed, to later discipline.

Very few proofs will be found below; however, the proof above is useful to present because it is simple, it makes clear precisely what causes the result to be true and it is typical of the proofs of many of the theorems that will be discussed below. Later proofs will either be omitted or briefly sketched. Like the proof above, the proofs of theorems below are typically based on constructing a strategy profile that satisfies the conditions of the theorem.

Two major implications flow directly from this theorem and some perplexing questions are also raised by it. The first implication is that virtually any payoff profile x for a single-shot game Γ that is a cooperative game-solution can, according to theorem 1, be supported as a Nash equilibrium payoff in each period of the repeated game. To take a prominent cooperative game-solution concept, the core is a subset of the payoff profiles that weakly dominate v and is also a subset of the payoff profiles on the payoff possibility frontier. Thus an attainable payoff profile x such that $x \geq v$ with $x_i = v_i$ for at least one player i would not be sustainable under the conditions of theorem 1, but could be in the core; however, any core payoff profile satisfying $x \gg v$ would be in the core. Similarly, the Shapley value and its non-transferable utility generalisations would be sustainable under the conditions of the theorem for nearly all games as would the Nash bargaining solution and other two-person bargaining solutions such as that of Kalai and Smorodinsky. The second implication is that the Folk Theorem is lacking in predictive power: that any feasible, individually rational payoff profile of Γ can be supported means that anything vaguely reasonable can be supported.

Questions raised by theorem 1 include: (i) Are these equilibria based on punishments that players can be expected to carry out? (ii) Is there a natural way to reduce the set of payoff profiles that can be supported in equilibrium in order to provide more predictive power? (iii) Is the infinite repetition of the game absolutely necessary? (iv) Do the results require the discontinuous behaviour embodied in the strategy profile σ' that is used in the proof of the theorem? (v) Must the intertemporal game be a strictly repeated single-shot game – that is, could the intertemporal game be either a sequence of varying single-shot games or be a sequence of single-shot games in which the exact nature of the game at time t depends on the earlier behaviour of the players? (vi) Will the results change if players, at time t, have inexact or partial information about the earlier choices of other players? (vii) Is anything fundamentally different if the single-shot game Γ is finite so that $\sigma_i(h)$ is a probability distribution over the (finite) set of single-shot game pure strategies of player i? Each of these questions will, to some extent, be addressed in subsequent sections.

4   Credibility of theorem 1

A moment's thought will make clear that it is not in a player's interest to punish a defector forever, because such behaviour is not, in general, a best reply to the strategies of the other players. The missing element is that the punishment that players carry out against a defector must be in the interest of the punishers to carry out; otherwise it is not credible. We will see below that credibility is implied by subgame perfection – that is, by the requirement that the strategy profile be a Nash equilibrium when restricted to any subgame of the original game, whether or not that subgame would be encountered along the path of play generated by the strategy profile from the beginning of the game.[3] In particular, this must hold even for subgames that will never be encountered when the players stick to their equilibrium strategies from the start. Theorem 2 of Rubinstein (1979) shows that the Folk Theorem can be restated with the substitution of 'subgame perfect equilibrium' (SPE) in place of 'Nash equilibrium'. Following that, a parallel result, due to Fudenberg and Maskin (1986), is stated that extends these results to infinitely repeated games with discounting.

Consider the duopoly game mentioned above. For player 2 to punish player 1, player 2 must choose $q_2 = 60$ and receive a payoff of -60 forever. Player 2 would be better off choosing $q_2 = 0$ and it is natural

---

[3] The point of subgame perfection is to impose optimal (Nash equilibrium) play on parts of the game that are not encountered along the equilibrium path.

to believe that player 1 would understand this. That is, following the equilibrium strategy profile, the players will experience the history $h^{\sigma'} = (s', s', \ldots)$, punishment is called for if some other history occurs (i.e. if some player i deviates from s'_i); if player 1 deviates in the duopoly game, then a subgame occurs within which player 2 is not selecting a best reply to the behaviour of player 1. Player 2 incurs a punishment cost that is too high to be in his interest. It would make more sense if the punishment meted out by player 2 had a finite duration after which higher payoffs were received by player 2 and if, given the defection of player 1, carrying out the prescribed punishment would benefit player 2 more than failing to carry it out. That is, the threats and punishments would be credible if σ' were an SPE. Then, following any physically possible history at time t (i.e. following any $h \in S^t$), the strategy profile σ' would induce a Nash equilibrium on the subgame commencing at history h and no player could profitably shirk from any prescribed punishment that he was supposed to carry out under σ'. This credibility problem was recognised and solved in Rubinstein (1979) by the following theorem.

Theorem 2:   *Let $\Gamma^\infty = \langle N, \mathfrak{S}^\infty, 1, \mathfrak{P} \rangle$ be an infinitely repeated game without discounting, based on the single-shot game $\Gamma = \langle N, S, P \rangle$, and let $x \in \mathfrak{R}^n$ be an achievable payoff profile in Γ (i.e. there exists some $s' \in S$ such that $P(s') = x$). Then if $x \gg v$ there exists a strategy profile $\sigma' \in \mathfrak{S}^\infty$ that is an SPE of Γ^∞ for which the payoff profile in every period of play is x.*

The proof of this theorem differs from that of theorem 1 by constructing a somewhat different strategy profile σ' under which deviations from equilibrium behaviour are followed by a two-phase response from the other players. The first, called the *punishment phase*, punishes the defector and the second, called the *reversion phase*, restores play to s'. This two-phase design is crafted so that a punishing player will be better off carrying out the prescribed punishment. To be more precise, when a player i deviates from the behaviour prescribed by σ'_i then that player is forced to her minmax payoff v_i for a finite length of time that is long enough to render the deviation unprofitable; following that *punishment phase*, σ' directs that the players return to choosing s' (unless and until another deviation occurs). The strategy profile is also designed so that, if some player j among those charged with carrying out the punishment should deviate from the required punishing behaviour, then that player is punished by forcing him to his minmax payoff v_j for a long enough time to make his deviation unprofitable.

Discounting causes additional difficulties as compared with the no-discounting case. The problem is that, when a player deviates, the reward is immediate while any punishment in response to the deviation takes place starting in the future and extending further into the future. Consequently, a deviation that yields player i an extra payoff of 10 at time t cannot be rendered unprofitable by reducing that player's payoff by 2 for each of the next five periods. The gain is 10 while the loss is $2\delta_i(1 + \delta_i + \delta_i^2 + \delta_i^3 + \delta_i^4)$; indeed, if $\delta < 5/6$, taking away 2 units per period forever will not make the deviation unprofitable. Thus whether a particular individually rational payoff profile can be supported by an SPE strategy profile depends on the values of the players' discount parameters; however, if the discount parameters are large enough, then the required strategy profiles are constructed somewhat along the lines of those for theorem 2. The basic result is due to Fudenberg and Maskin (1986).

Theorem 3: *Let $\Gamma^\infty = \langle N, \mathfrak{S}^\infty, \delta, \mathfrak{P} \rangle$ be an infinitely repeated game with discounting, based on the single-shot game $\Gamma = \langle N, S, P \rangle$, and let $x \in \mathfrak{R}^n$ be an achievable, individually rational payoff profile in Γ. Then there is a profile of values $0 \ll \delta^* \ll 1$ of the discount parameters such that if $\delta \geq \delta^*$ there exists a strategy profile $\sigma' \in \mathfrak{S}^\infty$ that is an SPE of Γ^∞ for which the payoff profile in every period of play is x.*

A related result, due to Friedman (1971), is worth mentioning, partly because it appeared rather early in the development of this literature and partly because it deals with an interesting subset of possible equilibria. This result proves the existence of SPEs in models with discounting that support payoff profiles that strictly dominate some single-shot Nash equilibrium payoff profile using extremely simple strategies. The equilibrium strategies are similar to those in theorem 1 except that, in place of forcing a deviating player to her minmax payoff following a deviation, the players instead revert to choosing a single-shot Nash equilibrium profile. Such strategies are called *trigger strategies* owing to their characteristic of calling for one particular action profile s' and then, when any deviation occurs, triggering a change to some specific alternative profile s^c that is selected irrespective of who deviated, when the deviation occurred, or the size of the deviation. Because the reversion is to such a profile, the equilibrium is subgame perfect and the reversion can continue forever. This result, then, has the advantage of using equilibrium strategies with a very simple structure and has the disadvantage that fewer payoff profiles can be supported by such strategy profiles (only those profiles with payoffs above single-shot Nash payoffs rather than profiles with payoffs above v).

5 Scope and appeal of theorems 2 and 3

This section addresses items (ii), (iv) and (vii) from the discussion at the end of section 3 – that is, can the number of supported payoff profiles be reduced, is behaviour based on discontinuous decision rules a necessary condition of equilibrium and can the theory handle finite single-shot games? Taking the last question first, suppose for the moment that the sets S_j are finite and denote by Ψ_j the corresponding set of mixed strategies for player j in the single-shot game Γ.

The problem posed by finite games is that one player i cannot observe the probability distribution $\psi_j \in \Psi_j$ that player j uses. Player i observes only the realisation of ψ_j that player j implements; therefore, it is not clear that an arbitrary individually rational payoff profile $P(\psi) \gg v$ can be supported by a subgame perfect strategy profile in the infinitely repeated game. There are two ways to deal with this difficulty. One way is to assume it away; to assume that the probability distributions ψ are observable. A more acceptable solution is to show that $P(\psi)$ is within an arbitrarily small ε of a payoff profile that can be attained by a deterministic sequence of choices, $\{s^k\}_{k=1}^K \subset S$ for finite K. That is, the payoff profile $P(\psi)$ is a convex combination of several payoff profiles that are associated with pure strategy profiles. If the weights of the convex combination were all rational numbers, then $P(\psi)$ could be attained by a finite sequence of deterministic choices. If the weights are not rational, then the payoff can be approximately attained with a deterministic sequence of choices. Details may be found in Fudenberg and Maskin (1991).

Turning now to whether the set of supported payoff outcomes can be reduced, the results in section 4 make clear that bringing in subgame perfection has no effect. As there appears to be nothing inherently objectionable to any particular SPE, there may be no natural refinement to suggest. Friedman (1971) did suggest a selection rule for trigger strategy equilibria (i.e. equilibria for which the punishment is reversion to single-shot Nash equilibrium behaviour) which is called the *balanced temptation equilibrium*. Suppose the trigger strategy equilibrium is given by $\langle s', s^c \rangle$ where s' is the action profile the players expect prior to any deviation and s^c is a single-shot Nash equilibrium that will be implemented following any deviation. The defining feature of the balanced temptation equilibrium is that

$$\frac{\max_{s_i \in S_i} P_i(s'_{-i}, s_i) - P_i(s')}{P_i(s') - P_i(s^c)} = \frac{\max_{s_j \in S_j} P_j(s'_{-j}, s_j) - P_j(s')}{P_j(s') - P_j(s^c)} \quad (3.1)$$

for all players i and j. The numerator in (3.1) is the maximum one-shot gain to a player and the denominator is the reduced payoff per period that will ensue following a deviation. Thus the higher this ratio, the more appealing a deviation. If players were negotiating over some Pareto optimal payoff profile to support with trigger strategies, this criterion might stand out as an attractive candidate.

Another observation on this question is that we ought not to expect a highly abstract model to specify a unique equilibrium. The very generality of the model, its freedom from institutional and historical detail, make uniqueness appear unreasonable to expect. At the same time, when a model is specialised to deal with a particular applied situation, there may be institutional or historical facts that are relevant and that will serve to greatly reduce the set of believable equilibria.

Empirically observed behaviour in repeated games is hard to come by. The main source of which I am aware is the experimental laboratory; however, in an experiment the subjects are necessarily in a finite horizon game. The laboratory setting presents another difficulty; one can observe what players actually choose to do, but one cannot observe what they would do in situations that have not arisen. So, for example, if players consistently choose some s' that is not, itself, a single-shot Nash equilibrium, we cannot tell what a player might do in the event of a deviation from s'. There have been experiments in which subjects have behaved consistently with Folk Theorem equilibria; however, the underlying strategies giving rise to their choices is not entirely clear. The evidence is suggestive and encouraging, because it has involved such circumstances as oligopoly experiments with subjects choosing joint profit maximising outputs or prices and prisoners' dilemma games with subjects choosing to *not confess*.[4] These choices have frequently been followed until only a few periods before the end of the game at which time the players have reverted to single-shot Nash behaviour. In the oligopoly games the reversion would often be gradual, taking two or three periods to be completed.

Turning now to the necessity of discontinuous decision rules, there is something rather severe in meeting any deviation by player i, whether small or large, by the same response. This response is designed so that it can effectively punish the most profitable deviation; one size fits all. This is like having a criminal code that punishes all infractions from overtime parking to murder with lifetime imprisonment. Not only does common sense rebel, but it is implausible that people would actually be willing to carry out such policies despite their desirable theoretical properties. Of course,

---

[4] See, for example, Friedman (1967) and Rapoport and Chammah (1965). The former deals with repeated duopoly games in which much time is spent at the same point on the Pareto frontier with a breakdown of cooperation near the end. The latter is similar, but in a repeated prisoners' dilemma.

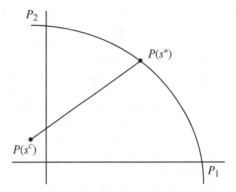

Figure 3.1   The continuous Folk Theorem

in the world of our complete information models with players who never make inadvertent errors, no player ever deviates and no punishments ever need to be carried out; however, it is appealing to have a variant to theorem 3 that shows that the equilibrium strategy profiles can employ continuous decision rules: that is, rules under which the smaller the deviation, the smaller the change in the behaviour of the players and, as the size of a deviation goes to zero, the change in the other players' choices goes to zero. This is done in Friedman and Samuelson (1990, 1994).

The (1990) paper deals with games in which the most severe punishment is to revert to single-shot Nash equilibrium and the (1994) paper proves a counterpart to theorem 3 for continuous strategies. The basic idea is more easily explained for (1990) with the help of figure 3.1. Suppose the payoff outcome to be supported is $P(s^*)$ and that $P(s^c)$ is a Nash equilibrium payoff of Γ. The repeated-game-equilibrium payoff profiles always call for choosing a point on the line connecting $P(s^*)$ and $P(s^c)$. At the beginning, the strategies call for choosing s^* and for continuing this choice until some player j defects. Suppose a defection occurs with player j choosing s_j^0. The size of the defection is measured by the amount $P_j(s_{-j}^*, s_j^0) - P_j(s^*)$ – that is, by the extra payoff the defector obtains in the period of defection. If $P_j(s_{-j}^*, s_j^0) - P_j(s^*) \leq 0$ the defector actually does not gain and no defection is deemed to have occurred. Otherwise, following the defection, the equilibrium strategy profile calls for choosing a point on the line segment connecting $P(s^*)$ and $P(s^c)$ whose distance from $P(s^*)$ is proportionate to $P_j(s_{-j}^*, s_j^0) - P_j(s^*)$ as long as the required movement does not go below $P(s^c)$. Thus a very small defection causes a very small punishment and, as the size of the defection goes to zero, the size of the punishment goes to zero. The most severe punishment will take the players to the single-shot Nash payoff profile but, in general, the size of the punishment will be in proportion to the size of the defection as measured by the short-term gain to the defector. The equilibrium strategies are also designed so that the level of punishment diminishes over time. Suppose that some player has defected at time t and then, at time $t+1$, all players adhere to the equilibrium strategy profile and choose actions that put them at the appropriate point between $P(s^*)$ and $P(s^c)$. Then, in subsequent periods, $t+2$, $t+3$, and so on, the equilibrium strategy profile directs the players to choose action profiles giving them ever-higher payoffs that converge to $P(s^*)$. In general, whenever the players are choosing on the line segment between $P(s^*)$ and $P(s^c)$ and are below $P(s^*)$, the strategies call for moving upward over time toward $P(s^*)$ and if a defection occurs from some point below $P(s^*)$, the strategies call for a downward movement relative to the point to which they would have gone had there been no defection. In this way the equilibrium strategy profiles are *forgiving*, in contrast to the grim trigger strategy profile.

The generalisation of Friedman and Samuelson (1990) that is carried out in (1994) requires more complicated strategies to mirror the need to tailor the punishment to the identity of the defector. Thus a defection calls for a move toward the minmax payoff of the defector and the exact upward movement of payoffs following a defection also depends on who defected. But the basic elements are the same: the size of punishment is proportionate to the profitability of the defection, the largest punishment puts a player at her minmax payoff and the equilibrium strategies are forgiving in the sense that they move toward higher payoffs over time after a punishment process is started.

6 Finite repetition

Finitely repeated games raise two questions. The first is whether the Folk Theorem results can be extended to finitely repeated games. The short answer, discussed on p. 64, is 'yes', as long as the single-shot game has multiple Nash equilibrium outcomes. This result leads to the second question: why do we observe cooperative play in laboratory experiments employing finite repetition and single-shot games having a unique Nash equilibrium? This will be discussed on p. 65.

The Folk Theorem in finitely repeated games

It is clear from the results reviewed thus far that, under SPE play, the ability to obtain payoff outcomes that differ from single-shot Nash payoffs depends critically on the ability to punish deviations at time t

after those deviations have occurred. When the time horizon is infinite, there is always a future time in which to do this; however, deviation at time $T-1$ in a T-period game cannot be punished: that is, players must choose a single-shot Nash action profile in the last period of a finitely repeated game. It follows immediately from this that, if the Nash equilibrium of Γ is unique, then any SPE of Γ^T must call for choosing this unique action profile in each play of Γ. The argument is by backward induction: in the final period, no matter what the history of the game, only the (unique) single-shot Nash action profile can be chosen; in the second to final period, there is no way to influence the final period through the current period choice, so that only the single-shot Nash action profile can be chosen; and so forth.

If the single-shot game has several Nash equilibria, the situation changes, because it may be possible to punish in period $T-1$ for a deviation at period $T-2$. Suppose that there are two single-shot Nash equilibria, s' and s'', such that $P(s') \gg P(s'')$. For a Nash reversion (i.e. trigger strategy) SPE, the repeated-game-strategy profile would call for choosing some s^* where $P(s^*) \gg P(s'')$ for periods $t = 0, \ldots, T-k$ or until a deviation occurs (whichever is first), and then choosing s' in periods $T-k+1, \ldots, T-1$. Suppose, for example, that the game is symmetric and, for each player, $P_i(s^*) = 10$, $P_i(s') = 5$, $P_i(s'') = 1$ and a deviation at any time would bring an increase in payoff of 7. Choose $k = 3$, assume no discounting and suppose a player deviates at time $t < T-2$. The deviator's payoff is $t \cdot 10 + 17 + 1 \cdot (T-t-3) + 1 \cdot 2$; her payoff if she had not deviated would have been $t \cdot 10 + 10 + 10 \cdot (T-t-3) + 5 \cdot 2$. The former minus the latter is $7 - 9(T-t-3) - 4 \cdot 2 < 0$. The immediate gain of 7 is offset by two periods at the end in which payoff drops by 4 per period. Deviation earlier that $t = T-3$ is even more costly. Deviation in periods $T-2$ or $T-1$ produces no gain in the period of deviation and, for deviation at $T-2$, a further loss of 4 in the final period.

An essential feature of the equilibrium strategy profile is that there are one or more periods at the end of the game when the players are choosing single-shot Nash action profiles. The length of this *endgame* phase depends on the difference between the payoff of each player when no deviations have occurred and when punishment is taking place. If the game is repeated sufficiently many times (more than two for the example above), then it is possible to have equilibrium strategy profiles that are like those in theorem 3 until the endgame phase where either a non-punishing or a punishing single-shot Nash action profile is chosen, depending on the history of the game to that point.

The proof of existence of SPEs in finite horizon repeated games that support any individually rational payoff profile is in Benoît and Krishna

(1985). A more limited result, applying to Nash reversion strategies and supporting only payoff profiles that give each player a payoff larger than the smallest single-shot Nash payoff that player could receive is Friedman (1985).

Theory clashes with experimental evidence

Rapoport and Chammah (1965) report considerable cooperative play in repeated, finite horizon prisoners' dilemma games played under complete information. This behaviour is persistent, it is not subgame perfect and others have reported similar behaviour (e.g. Friedman, 1963). I have often pondered what I would do as a subject in a finitely repeated game with a unique Nash equilibrium and have concluded that, if the number of repetitions were numerous (say, over 20), I would give cooperation a chance. If the other player would go along, both would have much to gain. I would cease the cooperative play late in the game or when the other player did so first. A few early trials of cooperative behaviour on my part would risk a small cost in return for possibly large gains.

In attempting cooperation, I would be gambling that the other player is not 'rational' (i.e. that the other player does not analyse the game in the conventional way and under the conventional assumptions). This is precisely the thrust of Kreps et al. (1982), who show that it is rational for a player to give cooperation a chance in a finitely repeated prisoners' dilemma if the player places sufficient probability on the other player being 'irrational' in a specific way. In their case, the irrationality is that the other player is dedicated to tit-for-tat (the other player chooses at time t whatever you chose at time $t - 1$).

7 Imperfect monitoring

To this point it has been assumed that, at any period t, each player knows what all players have chosen in all past periods. Such an assumption, called *perfect monitoring*, is likely to be violated in many circumstances and it is important to know whether its violation causes the demise of the Folk Theorem. At one extreme, where there is no monitoring, Kaneko (1982) has shown that the only possible SPEs are strategy profiles that call for single-shot Nash actions in all periods. By *no monitoring* is meant that, at any time t, a player has received absolutely no information indicating what other players have chosen in the past. In a game this will generally mean that a player does not even know what single-period payoffs she has achieved thus far. Kaneko's result is not surprising and, of course, there remains a large intermediate terrain between no monitoring and perfect monitoring. As far as I am aware, this terrain was first explored by Porter (1983) and Green and Porter (1984) and then was expanded importantly by Abreu, Pearce and Stacchetti (1986, 1990). Further work has been done; important results along with many references may be found in Fudenberg, Levine and Maskin (1994).

To see how the nature of monitoring can affect the set of possible equilibria, consider first a conventional Cournot oligopoly with n firms. Suppose that individual output levels cannot be observed, but that market price can be observed. Any deviation from a prescribed output level by a single firm will result in a change in market price; therefore, price will contain enough information for the firms to determine deviations. Now alter the model along the lines of Green and Porter (1984) so that demand has a stochastic component. When the market price is observed, a firm cannot tell with certainty whether there has been a deviation, because the price depends both on firms' output decisions and on the realisation of the random variable. The larger the difference between the observed price and the expected price contingent on no deviation, the more a deviation will be suspected by a firm. If firms triggered to single-shot Nash following any observed price that fell below the expected (collusive) price, the firms would be treating too many negative random variable realisations as if they were deviations; however, they would catch most deviations. As the price on which they trigger is lowered, they make fewer 'mistakes' by triggering when no one deviated, but they make small deviations more tempting, because small deviations are more likely to be treated like small negative random shocks.

8   Stationarity and structural time-dependence

Repeated games are precisely that: the finite or infinite repetition of a specific single-shot game. This class of games could be generalised in either of two ways. One would be to specify an infinite sequence of single-shot games $\{\Gamma_t\}$ where the game Γ_t is known to be played in period t. Another way would be to introduce *structural time-dependence* into the model – that is, the payoff functions for any time period t would depend on the past behaviour of the players. Neither of these generalisations stands in the way of the Folk Theorem.

Consider the former: a repeated game in which the single-shot game played at time t is Γ_t. Writing out the conditions that would characterise an SPE would be laborious, because the current gains and future losses to deviations by one player would be different in each time period; however, the basic principles used in theorems 2 and 3 could be brought to bear. The main reason one does not see this worked out in the literature is because this generalisation is conceptually easy to carry out, but is extremely cumbersome to write out.

Introducing state variables is less straightforward, because the manner in which the state variables enter into the present and future payoffs is very important. A general formulation appears very difficult. A special case has been considered in Friedman (1990), where the vector of state variables can be partitioned into n sets with each set 'belonging' to a specific player. The sense in which a state variable 'belongs' to a specific player i is that the value of that variable at time t depends on the previous actions of player i only, and not upon the actions of any other player. Furthermore, the transition mechanism is required to be concave in the states and actions. Under these conditions, the Folk Theorem can be generalised. An interesting example for which the desired conditions hold is oligopoly with the state variables being the capital stocks of the firms.

9   Conclusion

The Folk Theorem and related results raise and solve problems at the same time. In the oligopoly literature beginning with Cournot (1960 [1838]) and continuing through Bertrand (1883, English translation in Daughety, 1988) and Chamberlin (1956) there is an ongoing dispute concerning whether Cournot's equilibrium, in which firms are non-collusive, is the 'correct' solution to the 'oligopoly problem' or whether firms attain the joint profit maximum or some other payoff possibility frontier outcome through collusion and cartelisation. Until the Folk Theorem results were available, the analytical apparatus of economics favoured Cournot; on the other hand, there were those who believed that, one way or another, despite cartel agreements being illegal (and hence not enforceable in law courts), firms would somehow manage to collude successfully. Empirical evidence was scant. The Folk Theorem shows how collusive outcomes can be attained as (subgame perfect) non-cooperative equilibria. In a sense, this vindicates both Cournot and his critics.

This reconciliation and explanation is very heartening; at the same time, it greatly decreases the predictive power of oligopoly theory and of game-theory generally. Any individually rational payoff profile can be supported by an SPE. To my mind, this implies that other considerations must be brought into applications of the theory. In a sense, when a 'cooperative' outcome is being attained, there is an element of trust between the players because, at any time, another player can reap short-run gains by maximising her current payoff with respect to her current action. The investigation of the role of trust is long overdue.

In producing cooperative behaviour from a conventional non-cooperative equilibrium, the Folk Theorem blurs the distinction between explicit collusion, tacit collusion and unintentional cooperation. From the standpoint of intent, this makes anti-trust investigation rather delicate. In addition, it opens up consideration of partial collusion wherein players collude on certain choices (e.g. prices) and not on others (e.g. location) as in Friedman, Jéhiel and Thisse (1995).

In various sections above, elaborations and extensions of the Folk Theorem were sketched. These help to expand and refine the scope of this family of results. My presentation has not been complete, either in the sense of completely explaining those results that are mentioned or by even mentioning everything in the large literature. The particular things chosen for inclusion reflect the peculiarities of my own knowledge and interests and do not always reflect the inherent importance of the subject. I hope the reader will be encouraged to explore this area further.

Bibliography

Abreu, D., D. Pearce and E. Stacchetti (1986) Optimal cartel monitoring with imperfect information, *Journal of Economic Theory*, 39, pp. 251–69
(1990) Toward a theory of discounted repeated games with imperfect monitoring, *Econometrica*, 58, pp. 1041–63
Aumann, R.J. (1960) Acceptable points in games of perfect information, *Pacific Journal of Mathematics*, 10, pp. 381–417
Benoît, J.-P. and V. Krishna (1985) Finitely repeated games, *Econometrica*, 53, pp. 905–22
Bertrand, J. (1883) Review of Walras' *Théorie Mathématique de la Richesse Sociale* and Cournot's *Recherches sur les Principes Mathématiques de la Théorie des Richesses, Journal des Savants*, 68, pp. 499–508
Chamberlin, E.H. (1956) *The Theory of Monopolistic Competition*, 7th edn., Cambridge, Mass: Harvard University Press
Cournot, A. (1960 [1838]) *Researches into the Mathematical Principles of the Theory of Wealth*, trans. N.T. Bacon, 1897, New York: Kelley
Daughety, A.F. (ed.) (1988) *Cournot Oligopoly: Characterization and Applications*, New York: Cambridge University Press
Friedman, J.W. (1963) Individual behavior in oligopolistic markets: an experimental study, *Yale Economic Essays*, 3, pp. 359–417
(1967) An experimental study of cooperative duopoly, *Econometrica*, 35, pp. 379–97
(1971) A non-cooperative equilibrium for supergames, *Review of Economic Studies*, 38, pp. 1–12
(1985) Cooperative equilibria in finite horizon noncooperative supergames, *Journal of Economic Theory*, 35, pp. 390–8

(1990) A modification of the Folk Theorem to apply to time-dependent super-games, *Oxford Economic Papers*, 42, pp. 317–35.

Friedman, J.W., P. Jéhiel and J.-F. Thisse (1995) Collusion and anti-trust detection, *Japanese Economic Review*, 46, pp. 226–46

Friedman, J.W. and L. Samuelson (1990) Subgame perfect equilibrium with continuous reaction functions, *Games and Economic Behavior*, 2, pp. 304–24

(1994) An extension of the 'Folk Theorem' with continuous reaction functions, *Games and Economic Behavior*, 6, pp. 83–96

Fudenberg, D., D. Levine and E. Maskin (1994) The Folk Theorem with imperfect public information, *Econometrica*, 62, pp. 997–1039

Fudenberg, D. and E. Maskin (1986) The Folk Theorem in repeated games with discounting and with incomplete information, *Econometrica*, 54, pp. 533–54

(1991) On the dispensability of public randomization in discounted repeated games, *Journal of Economic Theory*, 53, pp. 428–38

Green, E.J. and R.H. Porter (1984) Noncooperative collusion under imperfect price information, *Econometrica*, 52, pp. 87–100

Kaneko, M. (1982) Some remarks on the Folk Theorem in game theory, *Mathematical Social Sciences*, 3, pp. 281–90

Kreps, D.M., P. Milgrom, J. Roberts and R. Wilson (1982) Rational cooperation in the finitely repeated prisoner's dilemma, *Journal of Economic Theory*, 27, pp. 245–52

Luce, R.D. and H. Raiffa (1957) *Games and Decisions*, New York: Wiley

Porter, R.H. (1983) Optimal cartel trigger price strategies, *Journal of Economic Theory*, 29, pp. 313–38

Rapoport, A. and A.M. Chammah (1965) *Prisoner's Dilemma*, Ann Arbor: University of Michigan Press

Rubinstein, A. (1979) Equilibrium in supergames with the overtaking criterion, *Journal of Economic Theory*, 21, pp. 1–9

4   Predatory pricing and anti-dumping

P.K. Mathew Tharakan

The law and economics of predatory pricing is something of a swamp. Fortunately, it is not necessary to enter that swamp to discuss contemporary anti-dumping policy. (Hindley, 1991, p. 29)

1   Introduction

Recent years have seen the widespread use of anti-dumping (AD) measures by World Trade Organisation (WTO) members. But the most striking development in this field is the swift proliferation of the users of such measures. By the late 1990s, the exclusiveness[1] of the club of traditional AD users[2] had become an anachronism. The developing countries are now initiating about half of the total number of AD cases.[3] As foreseen by Messerlin and Reed (1995) the realisation is beginning to dawn on the traditional users of AD measures that contingent protection is a game that any WTO member can play. This new development has given greater weight to the traditional concern that AD practice is a form of backdoor protectionism, which is eroding the hard-won gains of multilateral trade liberalisation.

Geoffrey Reed, Jacques-François Thisse and an anonymous referee carefully read earlier drafts of this chapter and made a number of useful suggestions. I am grateful to them.
[1] In this chapter I concentrate my attention on the AD, rather than the countervailing duty (CVD) system. According to the information supplied to me by the Rules Division of the WTO secretariat, the number of CVD investigations (action against subsidised exports) during 1980–97 was equal to 29.5 per cent of the AD cases investigated during the same period. Subsidies generally being the actions of governments themselves, CVD actions have a much higher diplomatic visibility (Jackson, 1990, pp. 3–4). But some authors (see Howell, Wolff and Ballantine, 1997, p. 4) argue that the preferential attention given to AD actions is unfair, because 'many types of subsidies are either not countervailable or are countervailable only at rates that do not offset the effect of subsidy'.
[2] The traditional users of AD measures are: Australia, Canada, the European Union, New Zealand and the United States.
[3] See Miranda, Torres and Ruiz (1998, p. 64).

70

Various factors have contributed to the above-mentioned concern. They are not limited to the fact that AD regulations (both at WTO and national level) and practices contain considerable ambiguity (see below). At the more fundamental level, the notion of 'dumping' as defined in the WTO, and the corresponding national regulations, are of questionable validity from an economic point of view. But economists do agree that certain types of dumping can indeed be welfare-reducing. The most important among them is predatory pricing.[4]

Curious as it might seem, both the critics and the advocates of AD actions often shy away from analysing the question of dumping within the framework of predatory pricing. In the case of the former, it is because predation is not at present a necessary legal condition for imposing AD measures, and secondly because they consider predation to be unlikely anyway (Hindley, 1991). Interestingly, the supporters of AD measures sometimes readily agree that predatory dumping as defined by economists probably occurs 'only in extraordinarily rare cases in the real world' (Howell, Wolff and Ballantine, 1997, p. 5). Nevertheless they argue for the continued use of AD measures on the ground that 'dumping' can lead to the erosion, and in some cases the disappearance, of domestic industries for reasons unrelated to their state of competitiveness.

Given the conceptual and operational problems connected with the use of the AD mechanism (see section 2), the first-best-solution would be to dismantle it. But there would be enormous amount of political economy pressures against such a move. While there is no unanimity of opinion among scholars as to whether the harmonisation of competition rules among trading countries is a necessary condition for the abolition of anti-dumping, in view of the spillover effects of anti-competitive practices and for political economy considerations, it would have been helpful if progress were made in this area. Although there is no lack of concrete proposals for action in this field,[5] progress at multilateral level is likely to remain slow.[6] In any case a severe disciplining of the AD mechanism is required. The first step in this direction could be to limit AD actions to cases of predatory dumping.

As important contributions by Louis Phlips (1995) and others[7] have shown, predatory attempts can indeed occur. Further, as competition (anti-trust) approach to predatory pricing has demonstrated (see section 3), legal measures can be devised to detect such attempts. The main thrust of

[4] See Viner (1923); Willig (1997).
[5] See for example, Scherer (1994); Jacquemin *et al.* (1998).
[6] See Lloyd (1998).
[7] See for example, Phlips and Moras (1993).

this chapter is to suggest that in the light of the above developments, the current WTO definition of 'dumping' could be reformulated so as to cover only predatory price dumping, and that the measures to detect and counteract such dumping could be patterned after those which are already being employed by the competition (anti-trust) authorities.

The plan of the chapter is as follows. In section 2 we explain the nature and the dimension of the problem of anti-dumping. Section 3 briefly surveys the competition policy approach to predatory pricing. Section 4 summarises the empirical evidence which has become available concerning the results that are likely to emerge if a competition policy-type of approach is applied to AD cases. Section 5 sums up the conclusions.

2   The nature and dimensions of the AD problem

Nature of the problem

At the conceptual level
According to article 2.1 of the WTO Anti-Dumping Agreement (1994):

a product is considered as being dumped, i.e. introduced into the commerce of another country at less than its normal value, if the export price of the product exported from one country to another is less than the comparable price, in the ordinary course of trade, for the like product when destined for consumption in the exporting country.

Article 2.2.1 specifies that home sales 'at prices below unit (fixed and variable) costs of production' will not be considered to represent 'normal value', except if they were made only for short periods and in small quantities. The wording of articles 2.1 and 2.2.1 has led to various types of transactions being considered as 'dumping'. Among them two categories dominate: (1) international price discrimination, and (2) sales below average cost.

National and international price discrimination is a phenomenon that is often observed and much analysed. It consists of the practice of charging two or more different prices for a like product, either within a single-segmented market, or between two or more separated markets.

In his well known book, *The Economics of Price Discrimination*, Phlips (1985)[8] explains with remarkable clarity the nature of price discrimination and sums up the conditions which are required for its occurrence. The latter include: the impossibility of resale of the commodity between sub-markets; differences in the intensity in consumers' demand and the

---

[8] The 1st edition of the book was published by Cambridge University Press in 1983. The references given in this chapter pertain to the 2nd edition published in 1985.

possibility of sorting out customers according to such differences; and some monopoly power on the part of the seller.[9]

As could be expected, the conditions necessary for international price discrimination ('dumping') to take place are almost the mirror image of the general case which Phlips (1995) states. Since the classic work of Viner (1923), an important stock of literature which deals with the economics of dumping has become available.[10] The following conditions are necessary for 'dumping' to occur: First, the firm concerned should be able to separate its home market from its foreign markets. If this is not the case, re-exports of the dumped product back to the home market will eliminate the price differential.[11] Another important requirement is that the firm which is dumping should have sufficient market power to influence the price. A third necessary condition is that the price elasticity of demand should be higher in the export market than in the home market of the firm that dumps. If the sources of supply are limited and the firm has the power to influence the prices in the home market there will be only a relatively small change in the quantity demanded for a given change in the price in that market, while this may not be the case in the foreign market. If these conditions are met, a monopolist, or a quasi-monopolist, might charge a lower price in the foreign market than at home in an attempt to maximise his profits. This 'dumping', as defined by article 2.1, can occur without any predatory intent.

In such a scenario, the negative impact on the aggregate economic welfare occurs mainly in the country of the firm which dumps. The consumers in that country will have to pay a price that is kept 'artificially' high. In contrast, their counterparts in the country into which the products are dumped will gain, especially if the process goes on permanently. But there will be also adverse effects such as the reduction of the producers' surplus, and the creation (increase) in unemployment in the importing country. The standard solution to that problem is to be found in the 'specificity rule' which states that the policy tools which have a direct impact on the sources of distortions separating private and social benefits and costs are more efficient than less specific measures. In the present context, this means that if international price discrimination leads to problems for specific groups in particular countries, it is better that public policy directly helps those who are adversely affected instead of using import protection that is harmful to the economy as a whole. Still, if we are concerned with the aggregate world welfare, the problem of

---

[9] See Phlips (1985), pp. 14–16.
[10] See for example, Deardorff (1990); Hindley (1991).
[11] In some cases, differences in the specification of the product demanded can make this difficult. Captive distribution systems can be another obstacle to international price arbitration.

protectionism and the monopoly power which makes dumping by firms in the exporting country possible will have to be dealt with. For this purpose, multilaterally negotiated reduction of protection and national enforcement of competition policy rules are better solutions than AD measures because the latter can be diverted for protectionist purposes.

As mentioned earlier, selling below average cost is another form of international transaction considered as dumping within the scope of article 2.2.1. But selling below average cost, when a portion of the costs are fixed, is a normal behaviour for a firm when prices are depressed. So long as the price which the firm (whether domestic or foreign) can obtain is above its marginal cost, it is rational to adjust the prices below average cost in the short run, in times of slack demand. But if the 'below-cost' inference of 'dumping' contained in article 2.1.1 is interpreted to include 'predatory pricing', then the picture changes substantially.

Predatory pricing is the most classical genre of dumping scenarios (Viner, 1923). While a detailed discussion of the concept (and possible identification of it) is reserved until later, essentially it amounts to 'attempted monopolisation', and its occurrence clearly raises problems for the state of competition in the importing country. Intuitively it is clear that given the negative effect of predatory dumping on aggregate national (and world) welfare, there is an economic rationale for counteracting such action. As we shall see later, very stringent conditions have to be met if predation is to take place. Nevertheless, the possibility of its occurrence cannot be ruled out. Further, competition policy authorities in some countries,[12] have developed and implemented methods for identifying predatory actions by firms.

At this point it should be stressed that the supporters of AD actions are not happy with this type of conceptual categorisation (see, for example, Stewart, 1991). They emphasise the imperfect nature of the market structure prevailing in 'foreign' countries and point out that this may include captive distribution systems which make effective competition from abroad practically impossible. The rent thus created can be used to price discriminate internationally. Distance and transaction costs can prevent price arbitrage. According to them, all this means that firms with authentic comparative advantage, operating in open markets with effective competition rules face injurious 'artificial' international competition.

Another strain of the pro-AD argument holds that economists ignore certain forms of unfair actions, such as 'disciplinary dumping' and 'cartel

---

[12] For a detailed description of enforcement mechanism used in various countries, see OECD (1989, pp. 49–79).

maintenance dumping' (Howell, Wolff and Ballantine, 1997). The former refers to the alleged practice by cartels of dumping or threatening to dump in order to enforce adherence to their price maintenance and market allocation arrangements. The latter is the practice by which surpluses are removed from the geographic zones that are the object of the cartel's market stabilisation activities, and sold at dumping prices. The objective is not predation but simply the maintenance of pre-agreed prices and the curbing of competition within a fixed geographic area.

But neither of the above arguments explain why multilateral trade liberalisation and enforcement of competition rules, rather than AD measures, cannot solve the problem.

At the operational level

The definition of dumping contained in article 2.1, and which basically means that the margin of dumping is obtained by deducting the export sales price from the home market sales price, raises a number of well known problems in practice.[13] The calculation of the home market price, and the adjustments which are necessary before it can be compared with the export sales price, is only part of the difficulty.

The investigating authorities may choose to 'construct' the normal value if the domestic sales are of 'low volume', if 'they are not in the ordinary course of sale', or for certain other reasons. Sales at prices below unit costs (fixed and variable) of production plus administrative selling and general costs may be treated as not being in the ordinary course of trade if the authorities determine that such sales are made within an extended period of time in substantial quantities. The export price itself may be 'constructed' in certain cases. The most common justification for such a procedure is the likelihood that there is an association or a compensatory arrangement between the exporter and the importer or a third party. In such cases, allowances are made for all costs incurred between importation and resale, including all duties and taxes in addition to a 'reasonable' profit margin.

It is clear that a procedure such as the one briefly described above can give rise to a number of problems, particularly for the respondents. 'Errors of judgement' on the part of the investigating authorities can turn out to be very costly for the firms being investigated. For example, erroneous dumping findings could be reached if any of the elements constituting the costs or profit margins are overestimated. Further, the discretion provided to the investigating authorities by the AD rules creates a fertile ground for protectionist pressures.

---

[13] They are summed up in Tharakan (1999).

An affirmative dumping finding alone is not enough for the imposition of AD duties. Injury to the 'like-product' domestic (complainants' country's) industry is the second necessary condition. In order to be operative for imposing AD duties, injury must be shown to have occurred (or there is a threat thereof); injury must be 'material'; it must be caused by the cited dumping; and there must be injury to the like-product industry. At the operational level, each one of these aspects can lead to erroneous findings. Above all, it is extremely difficult to disentangle the various causes of injury and ascribe accurately to 'dumping' that part which it might have caused. In addition, certain administrative practices such as 'cumulation', by which investigating authorities aggregate all 'like' imports from all countries under investigation and assess the combined impact upon the domestic industry[14] strikingly increase the probability of affirmative findings.[15] Further, work by Hansen and Prusa (1996) for the United States cases, and that of Tharakan, Greenaway and Tharakan (1998) shows that cumulation creates a 'super-additivity effect'. This means that for a given cumulated import market share, the greater the number of countries cumulated, the greater the probability of an affirmative finding on injury caused by dumping. Moreover, the method usually used for measuring injury margin – i.e. 'price undercutting', which consists of the comparison of adjusted weighted average resale prices of similar products with the prices of similar products in the domestic market – can lead to the finding of incorrect margins from an economic point of view. This measure might be simply an indicator of the economic inefficiency of the firms believed to have been injured or the distorted structure of the market in which they are operating.

Dimensions of the problem[16]

The proliferation of AD actions
Four contracting parties of the GATT – Australia, Canada, the European Union and the United States – accounted for most AD and CVD actions

---

[14] This controversial practice was legitimised by article 3.3 of the WTO Anti-Dumping Agreement (1994).

[15] For example, in the *Personal fax machines case*, against firms from Japan, Malaysia, South Korea, Singapore, Thailand, Taiwan, Hong Kong and China, the EC Commission cumulated the market share of all the defendants. The cumulated market share figure was close to 65 per cent, while the individual market share of some of the defendants was less than 5 per cent. As could be expected, an affirmative injury decision was reached by the Commission against all the defendants. Such an outcome would have been unlikely if cumulation had not been used (See Tharakan, Vermulst and Tharakan, 1998).

[16] This section is based on Tharakan (1999). Permission from Blackwell Publisher gratefully acknowledged.

Table 4.1   *AD investigations, by reporting country, 1987–97*

No.	Reporting country	Total no. of investigations launched, 1987–97	Per cent
1	United States	391	17.8
2	Australia	383	17.4
3	European Union	355	16.2
4	Canada	188	8.6
5	Mexico	188	8.6
6	Argentina	123	5.6
7	Brazil	97	4.4
8	South Africa	88	4.0
9	New Zealand	59	2.7
10	India	55	2.5
11	Korea	53	2.4
12	Turkey	32	1.5
13	Poland	25	1.1
14	Colombia	20	0.9
15	Israel	16	0.7
16	Peru	14	0.6
17	Finland	13	0.6
18	Indonesia	13	0.6
19	Malaysia	13	0.6
20	Venezuela	12	0.5
21	Philippines	11	0.5
22	Sweden	11	0.5
23	Austria	9	0.4
24	Chile	9	0.4
25	Thailand	6	0.3
26	Costa Rica	5	0.2
27	Japan	4	0.2
28	Singapore	2	0.1
29	Guatemala	1	0.0
	Total	2196	100.0

Source: WTO Secretariat, Rules Division, Anti-Dumping Measures Database.

during the 1980s. But as table 4.1 and figure 4.1 show, the picture has changed radically during more recent years. The most important fact that emerges is that the use of AD measures is no longer confined to a limited number of industrialised countries. In 1990, the above-mentioned 'gang of

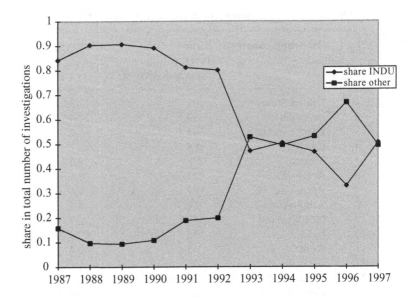

Figure 4.1   AD investigations, by reporting country, 1987–97, share in the total number of investigations
Note: INDU = Reporting Industrialised Countries (Australia, Austria, Canada, European Union, Finland, Japan, New Zealand, Sweden and United States); Other = All other reporting countries shown in table 4.1.
Source: WTO Secretariat, Rules Division, Anti-Dumping Mechanism Database.

four' accounted for 87.27 per cent of the total of AD investigations launched. By 1997, the corresponding figure had diminished to 48.49 per cent! A number of developing and newly industrialised countries (NICs) are now active users of the AD mechanism.

Figure 4.1 shows a 'scissors effect' in the pattern of the share of the industrial countries and the other reporting countries in the total number of AD investigations launched during the period 1987–97.[17] Until 1992, WTO members other than the nine industrialised 'countries' (Australia, Austria, Canada, European Union, Finland, Japan, New Zealand, Sweden and United States) taken into account in figure 4.1 accounted for only about 20 per cent of the total number of investigations. The year 1993 was a turning point, with the share of the other countries rising sharply and that of the industrialised countries declining. The former was caused mainly by the large number of investigations opened by Mexico,

[17] I am thankful to an anonymous referee for calling my attention to this fact and enquiring about the reasons behind it.

Brazil and Argentina.[18] The latter was caused by the fact that the traditional users of the AD system, such as the United States, filed fewer cases in 1993 compared to the previous year.[19] It could well be that the firms which came under increased competition from abroad owing to trade liberalisation in the NICs like Mexico stepped up their efforts for obtaining selective protection by filing more AD cases, and the government was willing to reassure them in this respect by agreeing to initiate the cases. The decline in the number of cases filed by the traditional users is more difficult to explain. It is possible that as more and more WTO (GATT) members started to enact AD legislations, and use them, the traditional users realised the importance of reining in. But it is not certain that this wise reaction will continue to prevail. As figure 4.1 shows, by 1997 the share of the traditional users was increasing again. But in spite of that, as figure 4.1 confirms, non-traditional users are now important players in the AD game.

Effects of AD actions
We have already referred (p. 73) to the standard international trade-theoretic view that AD actions will usually have a negative effect on the aggregate national welfare of the importing country.[20] But where the AD duty-imposing nation has monopsony power, and the necessary conditions for nationally optimal tariffs are met, it might obtain welfare gains, but at the risk of facing retaliation, possibly in other sectors. And even in the cases where nationally optimal tariffs can be used, the aggregate world welfare is likely to decrease from the imposition of AD duties. But it must be also noted that models based on certain specific assumptions and viewing AD legislation as the outcome of strategic interaction between governments have yielded interesting counterintuitive results for a generalised and strict enforcement of AD rules (see Anderson, Schmitt and Thisse, 1995).

Some of the earlier empirical work on anti-dumping measured the sector–country incidence of AD actions at a detailed level. Tharakan (1988) found a low import incidence of AD measures for the European Community, while Finger's (1981) results indicated the opposite for

[18] For example, the number of cases started by Mexico rose from 26 in 1992 to 70 in 1993. In the case of Brazil it rose from 9 to 34; and for Argentina, from 14 to 27 (see Tharakan, 1999, p. 203).
[19] In the case of the United States, the number of AD investigations reported decreased from 83 in 1992 to 32 in 1993; for Australia, from 71 to 59; for the European Union from 42 to 21; and for Canada from 46 to 25. Note that in the case of Australia and the European Union the number of cases filed had once again shown an increase by 1997 (Tharakan, 1999, p. 203).
[20] For a standard, textbook exposition of this view see Lindert (1991, pp. 164–70).

the United States. The calculations carried out by the Commission of the European Communities (1997, p. 4) indicate that the absolute value of the trade covered by definitive AD measures in 1996 was 2,919,000 euro, which was the equivalent of just 0.6 per cent of the total imports of the Union. But a low incidence of a given measure on imports might be simply due to the stringency, or the trade-diverting effect, of the measure itself. For example, if an AD measure halted all imports, the measured import incidence will be zero!

Some researchers have analysed the effect of AD actions on imports over a period of time. Messerlin's (1989) work showed that in the case of the European Community, imported quantities of the products affected by AD actions fell by 36 per cent in the third year after initiation and prices increased by 12 per cent in the fifth year. According to an ITC study (USITC, 1995), imported quantities declined by 73 per cent and unit values increased by 32.7 per cent for imports with high calculated dumping margins. Prusa (1997) found that in the case of the United States, imports subject to AD duty decline, but this effect is undermined by the simultaneous increase in the imports from the 'non-named countries'.

The effects of AD actions on the strategic behaviour of firms and governments, and their implications for profits, employment and welfare are now receiving increasing attention. Foreign direct investment (FDI) triggered by AD actions and its effect on employment creation have attracted particular interest. The theoretical analysis of Haaland and Wooton (1998) indicates that targeted firms would have an incentive to set up local production both in the case of unilateral AD action, and in the case of reciprocal anti-dumping. They also show that the improved domestic employment resulting from foreign firms setting up local production might be significant. But not surprisingly, they find that using AD policies for employment purposes is a 'beggar-thy-neighbour' policy and that if both (all) countries pursue such policies, the net employment effect will be minimal.

For understandable reasons, specific attention has been paid by some authors to the FDI responses of Japanese firms involved in AD investigations. As far as the employment results of such investments are concerned, the results seem to differ. Blonigen (1998) found that for the period 1980–90, the effect of AD actions on Japanese FDI in the United States was unimportant and the employment generated a small fraction (less then 5 per cent) of total United States affiliate employees by Japanese firms. But the findings of Belderbos (1997a, pp. 450–1) suggest that the effect is probably greater in the case of the European Union, at least in the electronics sector.

Not much work has been carried out to estimate the collective economic effect of the numerous active AD/CVD decisions. An exception to this – which we shall briefly describe – is the work of Gallaway, Blonigen and Flynn (1999) which uses a computable general equilibrium (CGE) model for this purpose. Their version of the CGE model makes it possible to simultaneously focus on the economic effects of narrowly targeted AD/CVD decisions in certain sectors (as with a partial equilibrium analysis), while at the same time estimating the combined economy-wide effects of all outstanding AD/CVD orders they apply to their model for AD/CVD decisions made by the United States.

The results of the Gallaway, Blonigen and Flynn exercise show that the United States AD/CVD actions led to welfare losses amounting to about $4 billion in 1993. This was second only to the Multifibre Agreement (MFA) among the welfare loss-generating protectionist instruments. Among the reasons which the authors put forward for such a high-welfare loss, the following are particularly interesting. The United States AD decisions provide an incentive for foreign firms to raise their United States price in order to reduce AD margins. In other words, the AD measures make it possible for the foreign firms to capture rents at the expense of the United States economy. Secondly, because a large number of AD/CVD affirmative decisions involve manufacturing sectors that are upstream to many significant United States production sectors, they result in larger welfare losses not only for United States consumers, but also for United States producers and exporters downstream to the sector concerned. On the basis of their findings the authors argue that the trade liberalisation achievements of GATT in the post-war period may turn out to be hollow if more countries begin to implement AD regimes – which, as we saw on pp. 76–9, is exactly what is happening.

But the most damaging effects of AD actions cannot be captured in figures alone. Frequent investigations, even when the complaints are finally rejected, amount to a form of harassment of the defendants because of the uncertainty and expenses such actions create. AD actions are sometimes used as a tactic to force foreign exporters to provide 'undertakings' to raise export prices. Such undertakings certainly played a very important role in the AD policy of the European Communities in the past (see Tharakan, 1991). According to Finger and Murray (1993), almost half of all AD actions in the United States are superseded by negotiated export restrictions before they come to a formal, legal end.

Some authors (for example, Miranda, Torres and Ruiz, 1998) hold the view that the use of AD measures might have helped some countries to navigate from a controlled to a liberalised trading regime. But the spread of the use of the AD mechanism means that it is now poised to become the most important trade-restricting device in the post-Uruguay Round World (Gallaway, Blonigen and Flynn, 1999). It has also increased the possibility of 'chain reactions' in the field of anti-dumping actions.

3   The competition policy approach to predatory pricing

The theory of predation: the swamp isn't what it used to be

There is no universally accepted definition of predatory pricing or of 'attempted monopolisation'. A useful working definition is as follows:

Predatory pricing behaviour involves a reduction of price in the short run so as to drive competing firms out of the market or to discourage entry of new firms to gain larger profits via higher prices in the long run than would have been earned if the price reduction had not occurred. (Joskow and Klevorick, 1979, p. 220).

Predatory pricing dumping is low-priced exporting with the intention of driving rivals out of business in order to obtain monopoly power in the importing market. The consequent welfare loss is not limited to the importing country alone. Increase in the prices subsequent to successful predation and the disappearance of competitive firms justifies some kind of public policy action against such attempts.

Predatory dumping is not the only form of 'monopolising dumping'. In so-called 'strategic dumping' if the exporters' home market is foreclosed to foreign rivals, and if each independent exporter's share of their home market is of significant size relative to their scale economies, the exporters will be able to have a significant cost advantage over foreign rivals (Willig, 1997, p.7). While strategic dumping does not require the exit of rivals or the subsequent increase of prices, it leads to the distortion of competition and the creation of profitable market power. But its applicability is limited. If protection is to create significant economies of scale, home markets must be sufficiently large relative to the rest of the relevant world's trading market. In fact, the very knowledge about the possibility of the use of strategic dumping would make it very difficult for any individual country to practice it. Hence we shall concentrate our attention on predatory price dumping.

Over recent decades, a sea change has taken place in our theoretical understanding of the phenomenon of predation. The various contributions which have helped to bring about this change are summarised in OECD (1989); Carlton and Perloff (1990, chapter 13); Phlips (1995); Tirole (1995, chapter 9), etc. and need no recapitulation here. In this subsection we shall concisely sum up those elements which have played a crucial role in bringing about a fundamental change in the policy treatment of predation within the framework of competition policy in some countries. The purpose is to search for the lessons which such developments might contain and which can help bring about a similar change in AD policy. Hence the overview given in this subsection is highly selective and arguably oversimplified.

A powerful school represented by McGee (1958), Bork (1978), Easterbrook (1981) and others holds the view that predation is unlikely to exist and, even in the rare cases that it does, cannot be of any importance. The essence of this well known argument is as follows: predation is more costly to the predator than to the intended prey. This is because the predator must meet all demands at the low price he sets, but an equally efficient rival is free to contract output in order to minimise its losses. In other words, the predation attempt which will increase the predator's market share will also increase his costs. At the same time, future monopoly profits are uncertain for various reasons. There is no way to rule out (re-)entry during the post-predation period. Even in industries where fixed costs are high, the predator who succeeds in forcing his rivals into bankruptcy must make sure that the assets of the latter come under his control, or are permanently withdrawn from the industry. Further, forcing an equally efficient rival to exit might prove to be an impossible task given access to smoothly functioning capital markets, financially strong backers, or loyal customers who are willing to enter into long-term contracts. To quote McGee's (1980, p. 297) memorable phrase: 'No one has yet demonstrated why predators could acquire the reserves they will need, while victims cannot.' In addition, a firm attempting predation has to discount to present value the future profits which in turn should cover both present losses and forgone present profits. It should also discount for the uncertainty about such monopoly profits becoming available at all. Given all such considerations, merger or acquisition will be clearly cheaper than predation, particularly if the predator and victim are operating in a single-market.

It can well be that the predatory attempt is a precursor to merger or acquisition. The objective here would be to weaken the rival, and then make a takeover/merger bid. Stated another way, pre-merger predatory behaviour can reduce the cost of acquisition to the predator. But competition policy regulations usually contain provisions that bar mergers that lead to significant increases in market power (which is of course necessary if the losses incurred in the predatory manoeuvre are to be recuperated).

The celebrated 'chain store paradox' (Selten, 1978) demonstrated, using game-theoretic analysis, how rational operators (players) could unravel threats of predation in multiple markets. If the threat of predation is not credible, it cannot be used as an effective signal to competitors and potential entrants in other markets not to enter or compete vigorously. Predatory signals can be unravelled because the would-be victims know that the threats cannot be implemented effectively. Nevertheless, the 'chain store paradox' and the debate which it triggered, clarified the strength *and* weaknesses of this line of reasoning. In a multiple market scenario, the impossibility of predation hinges on the assumption that each potential entrant knows what the outcome would be if predation is attempted. If the potential entrant is uncertain as to whether the incumbent's lowering of the price is the result of a predation attempt or a genuine cost advantage, the chain of reasoning breaks down. In fact *credibility* of the threat is central to the issue of successful predation. As Phlips (1995, p. 189) argues 'if under complete information predation is impossible ... then predation can occur only to the extent that the potential victim has doubts about the predatory nature of a price cut and that the predator manages to manipulate these doubts to its own advantage'. With information being imperfect, (potential) entrants will then have to base their expectations about future predation on past conduct. This in turn, gives the established firm an incentive to build a reputation as a predator (Milgrom and Roberts, 1982).

In the 'credible-behaviour' version of such models, the incumbent chooses, during period 1, his production strategy in such a way that the potential entrant is confronted with certain loss in the case of entry and hence abstains from entering during the second period. In order for this to happen, the potential rivals must not only have (at least) strong doubts about the prospects of post-entry profitability, but must not also know what the rival's costs are. If the rivals suspect that predator is trying to build up, and use, a reputation for irrational behaviour, why should they acquiesce by exiting or avoiding entry? It is in their interest to call the bluff of the predator. In fact, experienced observers suggest that the image of passive victims implicit in the above type of models has probably nothing much to do with the real-life situations where predation attempts are made and beaten off (OECD, 1989, p. 12).

Recent attempts to partially rehabilitate the 'long-purse theory' have not really succeeded in providing a satisfactory answer to McGee's celebrated question. As will be recalled, the 'long-purse theory' holds in essence that since (if) the predator has substantial resources, he can sustain losses for a longer period of time, and drive the weaker prey out of the market. For this argument to hold, the ability of the prey to raise the capital necessary to fight back must be limited by some upper bound (see Telser, 1966). But the creditors only stand to gain by lending to an efficient counter-attacker. If one wants to get around this difficulty and partially rehabilitate the long-purse theory, one has to introduce imperfections in the capital market. The potential victim may be located in a country with less well developed financial markets; the latter might make errors of judgement about the state of efficiency of the former, or may be overawed by the reputation of the predator. Further, it has to be assumed that outside financing is costlier than internal financing. The increasing role played by venture capitalists makes the argument rather unconvincing.

The issue of non-price predation has also received considerable scholarly attention. Non-price predation is often considered within the context of raising the rivals' costs. It is evident that if a firm can raise rivals' cost without increasing its own, then its profits can be increased at the expense of its rivals. The theoretical developments in this area have been surveyed by various authors, including, Baker (1989); OECD (1989, pp. 13–14); Carlton and Perloff (1990, pp. 417–23). What is relevant for the present analysis is the fact that those types of cost-raising actions which effectively lead to welfare loss usually require some market, or political power on the part of the firm initiating such action. But it is also true that certain types of strategic actions such as R&D investments by a dominant firm which can spread its costs over a larger output than its rivals (and thereby raise costs disproportionately for its rivals) may in fact lead to welfare gains in terms of better products and lower prices to the consumers.

To sum up: the possibility of successful price predation taking place depends on a set of crucial assumptions. The most important among them is that the predator has market power. This is often associated with the segmentation of the markets. Other important conditions include the credibility of the threat and imperfections in the financial markets. While *observed* cases of successful predation are rare, it does not mean that they are unimportant, or should be ignored. Predation attempts, whether of national or foreign origin need to be detected and countered, because successful predation leads to welfare loss. This realisation has, in turn, led to the development and use of certain well established methods by competition authorities in certain countries in order to evaluate complaints of predatory pricing. They are reviewed in the following subsection.

Identification of predatory pricing: lessons from competition policy

In the event of a major revision of the definition of dumping being accepted by the WTO members in the next round of multilateral trade negotiations, confining the phenomenon to predatory pricing, the national authorities who will have to implement the new regulations will be faced with the question of identifying predatory pricing dumping.

They will have the advantage of being able to pattern their procedure largely along the lines used by competition authorities in countries where competition law is well developed and actively applied.[21] We shall refer to only some of them here.[22]

In the United Kingdom certain competition agencies such as the Office of Fair Trading (OFT) and the Monopolies and Mergers Commission (MMC, now the Competition Commission) deal with complaints including those related to alleged predation. The OFT deals with the question whether the action is anti-competitive. In the case of an affirmative finding, the OFT has the power to refer the matter to the MMC. The latter judges not only whether the action is anti-competitive, but in addition whether it operates against the public interest. The OFT is known to have adopted a three-stage process in certain cases, in order to ascertain if predatory attempts took place.[23] The first step involves the decision as to whether predation was feasible in the market under investigation. The second stage considers the relationship between the incumbent's costs and revenue, and specifically whether the incumbent's actual profits were negative. If the incumbent did in fact incur losses in the market where predation was alleged, the third stage of investigation considers evidence of intent. Following Phlips' work (1987), Dodgson, Katsoulacos and Newton (1993) have proposed the 'Economic Modelling Approach' (EMA), which considers the opportunities available to both the incumbent and the entrant and the actions they take. They argue that although the results may be in some circumstances model-specific, the approach can be used to provide general insights into the process of identifying predatory behaviour and to investigate particular cases.

The evaluation of predatory pricing in the United States especially has been strongly influenced by scholarly work, particularly two highly influential articles. (Areeda and Turner, 1975; Joskow and Klevorick, 1979).[24] Interestingly, the influence of these two contributions, and others were concretised in an important Supreme Court decision resulting from an anti-dumping case (*Matsushita Elec. Indus. Co* v. *Zenith Radio Corp.*, 475

---

[21] It is useful to make a distinction here between competition policy and competition law. By 'competition policy' one means a set of measures employed by a government to ensure and enhance competition, with competition laws being one among such measures (see Djankov and Hoekman, 1998, p. 1109).

[22] For other examples, see OECD (1989, chapter VI).

[23] For example, the *Highland Scottish Omnibuses* (*HSO*) case.

[24] In the words of the two United States Federal Trade Commissioners (Miller and Pautler, 1985, p. 495), 'scholarly research has played a crucial role in bringing about a fundamental change' in the United States government's treatment of predation, in competition law cases. This is in stark contrast with the situation in AD law and practice where the influence of scholarly research, according to me, has been minimal.

US 574, 1986). The net result of these developments is the so-called 'two-tier approach'.[25]

The reasoning behind, and the substance of, the two-tier approach can be summarised as follows: the alleged predator must have market power in order to be successful. So in the first stage of the investigation of any complaint alleging predatory pricing behaviour, a clear market power standard must be applied. Only those cases in which an affirmative finding is made on this criterion should pass on to the second stage where appropriate price–cost comparisons and other relevant factors (such as the evidence concerning the intent of the respondents) could be taken into account. There is no reason why such an approach cannot be used, with the necessary adaptations for the international context, in AD cases, if the definition of (harmful) dumping is confined to the predatory kind.

Both stages of the 'two-tier' approach need some clarification. The starting point of the rationale underlying the market structure analysis (stage 1) is based on the notion of 'error costs'. Such costs could be of two kinds: the error that involves labelling a truly competitive price cut as predatory ('false positive error') and the error that involves the failure to identify a truly predatory price cut ('false negative error'). Many structural characteristics affect these error costs, and as Joskow and Klevorick (1979, p. 224) point out, one must look at the interaction of a variety of market characteristics 'to make reasonably sound empirical judgements about the relative magnitude of the two sets of error costs'.

The relevant structural characteristics can be grouped into three basic categories:

(1) factors indicative of short run monopoly power
(2) conditions of entry into the market
(3) the dynamic effects of competitors or entrants on the costs of production and quality of products offered to consumers.

Admittedly, the task of inferring unobservable long-run market outcomes from observable short-run market conditions is a difficult one. The assumption made under this type of reasoning is that the current market power of the alleged predator provides a lower bound to the power that would follow upon the execution of a successful predatory price cut. Short-run monopoly power can be measured by the predator's market share and the elasticity of the demand for its product. Conditions of entry have to be evaluated on the basis of factors such as capital requirements, consumer loyalties, learning curves, the sequence of entry and the quality

---

[25] For a description of the facts concerning this important case, see Belderbos (1997b, pp. 143–50).

of information about the risks of entry. The 'dynamics of the market' takes into account the trends in the market, the sources of innovation and technological progress and a set of other considerations concerning the relationship between prices and changes in supply or demand.[26] If the analysis concerning the market structure characteristics carried out in the first tier were to show that predation is unlikely the case would be dismissed. If this were not the case, a broad inquiry into the pricing practices of the respondent could be undertaken. Thus the important role played by the use of the two-tier approach is to eliminate 'harassment suits'.

There is no unanimity about the factors which should be taken into account in the 'second tier', although broad lines of agreement can be discerned. The need for some sort of cost-based test to evaluate claims of predatory pricing is not disputed. Areeda and Turner (1975) proposed a short-run average variable cost test as a surrogate marginal cost test. The reasoning here is that the marginal-cost pricing is the economically sound division between acceptable, competitive behaviour and 'below-cost' predation. But since the incremental cost of making and selling the last unit cannot readily be inferred from conventional business accounts, the more readily available variable cost is proposed as a proxy. Baumol (1996) has argued that there is no need to be apologetic about the use of some variant of average variable cost in a predation test. The main thrust of his argument is that the concept of 'average total cost' (ATC) violates all economic logic in the case of multiproduct firms which dominate the industrial scene. This is because all multiproduct firms have fixed costs incurred in common on behalf of two or more products and there is no economically defensible way of allocating such costs among the firm's various products. Thus the position is that any individual price that is not below average variable costs (or one of its variants) cannot be predatory.

In concluding this subsection it should be noted that in an important contribution, Phlips (1995) has proposed a 'rule-of-reason standard' to establish predation with all evidence at hand. The purpose here is to determine whether the behaviour of the alleged predation has changed what would have been a positive entry value under normal conditions into a negative one. The onus should be on the complainant to show this has happened. The respondent's best defence is to show that its post-entry price in the entrant's market does not imply immediately forgone profits that are compensated by larger profits in that or other markets, now or in the future.

---

[26] For a concrete summing up of these points see OECD (1989, p. 30–1).

4   And if the swamp were fertile ...

Economists, unlike science-fiction writers, have no time-machines at their disposal to observe the future. There is no accurate way of predicting the proportion of AD complaints which would be rejected if predatory pricing were to be made the necessary condition for imposing AD measures. But the results of some empirical work help us to make some useful inferences.

In order to review the results in the context of the analysis contained in the preceding sections, let us imagine the following scenario: the much-expected multilateral trade negotiations at WTO leads to a revision of the 1994 Anti-Dumping Agreement, stipulating that AD measures can be imposed only in those cases where predatory pricing by the respondent firm can be proved. Let us further assume that at the operational level, such a decision will be made on the basis of the criteria used in competition (anti-trust) cases, along the lines outlined on pp. 86–8. In addition, let us make such a decision retroactive.

The empirical studies mentioned below make use of a market power test similar to that of the first stage of the two-tier approach used in the anti-trust cases. They apply this test to the AD cases decided by the European Community, United States, Canada and Australia, during the 1980s. As mentioned earlier, these four GATT members accounted for the vast majority of all the AD cases initiated in 1990. In other words, the results of the empirical studies indicate what proportion of the AD cases decided in the past would have passed the first-tier test in a competition policy-type of regime.

Bourgeois and Messerlin (1997) analyse the likelihood of the existence of 'monopolising behaviour' in the EC AD cases initiated during the period 1980–89. A detailed 'screening process' is used for this purpose. The first screen aims at assessing the capacity of the respondents (foreign firms) involved in AD cases, to behave as predators. The crucial pre-condition required for this purpose is a 'dominant position' which, on the basis of the history of competition enforcement, is assumed to require an extrapolated (for the year following the AD decision taken) EC market share of 40 per cent or more. The second screen eliminates the AD cases terminated by a negative outcome. The third screen takes into account the number of countries involved in a given case. If a case involves four or more different countries, the possibility of joint predatory behaviour is considered rather low. The fourth screen takes into account the number of firms involved in a given AD case. The costs of colluding required by joint predatory behaviour involving eight or more firms, and the costs of maintaining a joint monopoly, appear to be too high in such circumstances. The fifth and final screen uses the information that is available concerning EC firms to make a judgement about the possibility of attempted predation.

Out of the 297 cases to which the above screening procedures were applied Bourgeois and Messerlin (1997) found only seven cases – i.e. about 2.4 per cent of the total, which could be considered, at most as mere possible candidates for a closer examination of predatory behaviour. Out of these seven cases, four involved exporters from non-market economies. None of the seven cases dealt with sophisticated manufactured products. On the basis of further analysis of the seven cases, Bourgeois and Messerlin conclude that only one case (concerning tungstic oxide and acid) appears to resemble an attempted predation.

A similar exercise was carried out by Hyun Ja Shin (1994) for AD cases decided by the United States authorities during the period 1979–89. Her sample included all 282 investigations with non-negative outcomes. Her screening criteria included the level of concentration among the United States producers in the industry concerned under the reasoning that injury caused by dumping might result in a significant increase in the market share held by the respondent in these industries. The second criterion took into account the level of concentrated shares among the respondent country's exporting firms. If such exports (to the United States) were diffused among many suppliers, predatory pricing would be relatively unlikely. The third element in the screening pertained, as in the case of the exercise for the EC mentioned above, to the cases where exports from several countries were simultaneously challenged. Further, the importance of the United States market shares of the respondents and the rapidity of the increase in such shares were examined. Finally, it was verified whether the alleged dumped imports were coming from markets with protection from potential competition by the existence of significant entry barriers.

Hyun Ja Shin's exercise showed that out of the initial sample of 282 United States AD cases with non-negative outcomes only 20 cases (about 7 per cent of the total) could be considered to be consistent with the hypothesis that they might pose a foreseeable threat to competition. She points out that this conclusion seems to be robust to reasonable alternations in the thresholds and criteria that were applied to the data.

Niels and ten Kate (1997) refer to the results obtained for Canada and Australia in studies contained in a report to the OECD (which also included Bourgeois and Messerlin's and Hyun Ja Shin's studies, and in which a similar approach was used). For the 155 Canadian AD cases initiated between 1980 and 1991, and the 20 Australian cases between

1988 and 1991 that resulted in AD actions, predatory pricing was found to be highly implausible.

The authors of the above studies are aware of the limitations of the exercise they have carried out. Neither has their approach escaped criticism. For example, Howell, Wolff and Ballantine (1997) argue that the assumption that producers from a number of countries could not coordinate their activities through cartel arrangements is disproved by historical experience. But independent of the appropriateness of any specific index included or not included in the market power test, it will be difficult to argue that an approach developed on the basis of sound economic analysis and regularly used in competition cases, is inappropriate for use for a similar purpose in AD cases.

The results of the empirical exercises cited above showed that the vast majority of the AD complaints included in the samples would not have got through the 'first tier' of competition policy-type tests. But this need not always be the case. As the record of competition policy cases in various WTO member countries shows, predation attempts can take place, be identified and blocked. In a business world characterised by asymmetry of resources and information, such a possibility cannot be discounted. Hence it would be a mistake on the part of the proponents of AD measures to oppose a proposal to confine AD actions to predation attempts, because of the fear that such a move would leave a country defenceless against anti-competitive attacks from abroad. Such a revision will of course make it impossible to camouflage selective '*de facto* safeguard' measures as AD actions.

The methods which could be used to appraise those complaints which might get through to the 'second tier' in a reformed AD regime could draw on the interesting proposals made by authors such as Baumol (1996), and which we have briefly reviewed on p. 88. They are starkly different from the 'fully allocated cost' tests which are currently being used in injury determination in a number of AD regimes. The use of appropriate cost-based tests in the second tier could be fruitfully combined with the 'rule of reason standard' proposed by Phlips (1995).

It is not the purpose of this chapter to delve into the institutional implications of the changes in the AD regulations which are suggested here. The interface between AD policy and competition policy is an important topic in its own right. The question of moving towards some sort of multilateral convergence of international competition standards is a matter of considerable discussion (see Jacquemin *et al.*, 1998; Lloyd, 1998). The confining of AD actions to cases of predatory pricing will make the handling of at least one aspect of the interface between competition policy and AD policy easier.

5 Concluding remarks

The AD mechanism has been deployed recently by a large number of WTO members. There is a real danger that AD practice will seriously erode the hard-won gains of multilateral trade liberalisation. The proliferation of AD actions by a number of countries carries with it the risk of its widespread use as a device for escalation and counter-escalation of selective, protectionist measures.

From an economic point of view, the first-best-solution would be to dismantle the current AD mechanism and try to bring about a convergence of competition policy practices in the trading countries. But not much progress has been achieved in this area. The next-best step would be to revise the WTO definition of dumping, confining the phenomenon to predatory pricing. Predatory price dumping is a case which leads to negative welfare effects and thus warrants some corrective action. The possibility of successful price predation taking place depends on a crucial set of assumptions, of which the market power of the predator and the credibility of the predatory threat are the most important. While confirmed cases of successful price predation are rare, they can indeed take place. Competition authorities in certain countries have developed and deployed useful methods for detecting predation attempts. The most appropriate among them is the so-called 'two-tier approach'.

In the first stage of any investigation of any complaint alleging predatory pricing behaviour, the extent of the market power of the supposed predator is assessed. Only those cases in which the existence of market power is confirmed will pass on to the second stage where appropriate price–cost comparisons and other relevant factors could be taken into account. Such an approach with the necessary adjustments for the international context can be effectively used in AD cases if the definition of harmful dumping is confined to the predatory kind.

Recent empirical studies show that if the above-mentioned type of tests were applied in the AD cases decided in some of the countries which are major users of AD measures, only a small proportion of the complaints would have reached the second 'tier'. This finding might stiffen the opposition of the proponents of the AD system to any revision of the WTO (and member state) definition of dumping. That would be a pity.

Bibliography

Anderson, S.P., N. Schmitt and J.-F. Thisse (1995) Who benefits from anti-dumping legislation?, *Journal of International Economics*, 38, pp. 321–37
Areeda, P. and D.F. Turner (1975) Predatory pricing and related practices under section 2 of the Sherman Act, *Harvard Law Review*, 38, pp. 697–733

Baker, J.B. (1989) Recent developments in economics that challenge Chicago School views, *Antitrust Law Journal*, pp. 645–55

Baumol, W.J. (1979) Quasi-permanence of price reductions: a policy for prevention of predatory pricing, *Yale Law Journal*, 89, pp. 1–26

—— (1996) Predation and the logic of the average variable cost test, *The Journal of Law and Economics*, 39, pp. 49–72

Belderbos, R.A. (1997a) Anti-dumping and tariff jumping: Japanese firms' FDI in the European Union and the United States, *Weltwirtschaftliches Archiv*, 133, pp. 419–57

—— (1997b) *Japanese Electronics Multinationals and Strategic Trade Policies*, Oxford: Clarendon Press

Blonigen, B.A. (1998) Foreign direct investment responses of firms involved in antidumping investigations, University of Oregon: Department of Economics, mimeo

Boltuck, R. and R.E. Litan (1991) *Down in the Dumps: Administration of the Unfair Trade Laws*, Washington, DC: Brookings Institution

Bork, R. (1978) The antitrust paradox, cited in Miller and Pautler (1985), pp. 495–502

Bourgeois, J.H.J. and P.A. Messerlin (1997) The European Community experience with antidumping policy, Washington, DC: Brookings Trade Policy Forum, mimeo

Carlton, D.W. and J.M. Perloff (1990) *Modern Industrial Organisation*, New York: HarperCollins

Commission of the European Communities (1997) Annual Report from the Commission to European Parliament on the Community's Anti-Dumping and Anti-Subsidy Activities, Brussels

Deardorff, A. (1990) Economic perspectives on antidumping law, in Jackson and Vermulst (1990), pp. 23–9

Djankov, S. and B. Hoekman (1998) Conditions of competition and multilateral surveillance, *The World Economy*, 21, pp. 1109–28

Dodgson, J.S., Y. Katsoulacos and C.R. Newton (1993) An application of the economic modelling approach to the investigation of predation, *Journal of Transport Economics and Policy*, 127, pp. 153–70

Easterbrook, F.H. (1981) Predatory strategies and counterstrategies, *University of Chicago Law Review*, 48, pp. 263–337

Finger, J.M. (1981) The inter-industry incidence of less than fair value cases in US import trade, *Quarterly Review of Economics and Business*, 21, pp. 259–77

—— (1993) *Antidumping: how it works and who gets hurt*, Ann Arbor: University of Michigan Press

Finger, J.M. and E. Murray (1993) Antidumping and countervailing duty enforcement in the United States, in Finger (1993), pp. 241–54

Gallaway, M.P., B.A. Blonigen and J.E. Flynn (1999) Welfare costs of the United States antidumping and countervailing duty laws, *Journal of International Economics*, 49, pp. 211–44

Haaland, J.I. and I. Wooton (1998) Antidumping jumping: reciprocal antidumping and industrial location, *Weltwirtschaftliches Archiv*, 134, pp. 340–62

Hansen, W.L. and T.J. Prusa (1996) Cumulation and ITC decision-making: the sum of the parts is greater than the whole, *Economic Inquiry*, 34, pp. 746–69

Hindley, B. (1991) The economics of dumping and antidumping action: is there a baby in the bathwater?, in Tharakan (1991), pp. 25–43

Howell, T.R., A.W. Wolff and D. Ballantine (1997) Does dumping matter? Commentary on Robert Willig's competition policy and antidumping: the economic effects of antidumping policy, Washington, DC: Brookings Trade Policy Forum, mimeo

Hyun Ja Shin (1994) The nature of US antidumping cases in the 1980s, Yale University, mimeo

Jackson, J.H. (1990) Dumping in international trade: its meaning and context, in Jackson and Vermulst (1990), pp. 1–22

Jackson J.H. and E.A. Vermulst (1990) *Antidumping Law and Practice: A Comparative Study*, New York: Harvester Wheatsheaf

Jacquemin, A., P.J. Lloyd, P.K.M. Tharakan and J. Waelbroeck (1998) Competition policy in an international setting: the way ahead, *The World Economy*, 21, pp. 1179–83

Joskow, P.L. and A.K. Klevorick (1979) A framework for analyzing predatory pricing policy, *The Yale Law Journal*, 89, pp. 213–71

Lindert, P.H. (1991) *International Economics*. 9th edn., Homewood, Il.: Richard D. Irwin

Lloyd, P.J. (1998) Multilateral rules for international competition law?, *The World Economy*, 21, pp. 1129–49

McGee, J. (1958) Predatory price cutting: the Standard Oil (NJ) Case, *Journal of Law and Economics*, 1, pp. 137–69

——— (1980) Predatory pricing revisited, *Journal of Law and Economics*, 23, pp. 238–330

Mennes, L.B.M. and J.A. Kol (eds.) (1988) *European Trade Policies and the Developing World*, London: Croom Helm

Messerlin, P.A. (1989) The EC Antidumping Regulations: a first economic appraisal 1980–1985, *Weltwirtschaftliches Archiv*, 125, pp. 563–87

Messerlin, P.A. and G. Reed (1995) Antidumping policies in the United States and the European Community, *The Economic Journal*, 105, pp. 1565–75

Milgrom, P. and J. Roberts (1982) Predation, reputation and entry deterence, *Journal of Economic Theory*, 27, pp. 280–312

Miller, J.C. III and P. Pautler (1985) Predation: the changing view in economics and the law, *Journal of Law and Economics*, 85, pp. 495–502

Miranda, J., R.A. Torres and M. Ruiz (1998) The international use of anti-dumping: 1987–1997, *Journal of World Trade*, 32(5), pp. 5–71

Niels, G. and A. ten Kate (1997) Trusting antitrust to dump antidumping: abolishing antidumping in free trade agreements without replacing it with competition law, *Journal of World Trade*, December, pp. 29–43

OECD (1989) *Predatory Pricing*, Paris: OECD

Phlips, L. (1985) *The Economics of Price Discrimination*, 2nd edn., Cambridge: Cambridge University Press

(1987) *Predatory Pricing*, Brussels: EC Commission

(1995) *Competition Policy: A Game-Theoretic Perspective*, Cambridge: Cambridge University Press

Phlips, L. and I.M. Moras (1993) The *AKZO* decision: a case of predatory pricing?, *Journal of Industrial Economics*, 41, pp. 315–21

Prusa, T. (1997) The trade effects of US antidumping actions, in R. Feenstra (ed.), *The Effects of US Trade Protection and Promotion Policies*, NBER: University of Chicago Press

Scherer, F.M. (1994) *Competition Policies for an Integrated World Economy*, Washington, DC: Brooking Institute

Selten, R. (1978) The chain store paradox, *Theory and Decision*, pp. 127–59

Stewart, T.P. (1991) Administration of the antidumping law: a different perspective, in Boltuck and Litan (1991), pp. 288–330

Telser, L.G. (1966) Cutthroat competition and the long purse, *Journal of Law and Economics*, 9, pp. 259–77

Tharakan, P.K.M. (1988) The sector–country incidence of anti-dumping and countervailing duty cases in the European Communities, in Mennes and Kol (1988), pp. 99–142

(1991) The political economy of anti-dumping undertakings in the European Communities, *European Economic Review*, 35, pp. 1341–59

(ed.) (1991) *Policy Implications of Antidumping Measures*, Amsterdam: North-Holland

(1999) Is anti-dumping here to stay?, *The World Economy*, 22, pp. 179–206

Tharakan, P.K.M., G. Greenaway and J. Tharakan (1998) Cumulation and injury determination of the European Community in antidumping cases, 134, *Weltwirtschaftliches Archiv*, pp. 320–39

Tharakan, P.K.M., E.A. Vermulst and J. Tharakan (1998) Interface between anti-dumping policy and competition policy: a case study, *The World Economy*, 134, pp. 1035–60

Tirole, J. (1988) *The Theory of Industrial Organization*, Cambridge, Mass.: MIT Press

USITC (1995) *The Economic Effects of Antidumping and Countervailing Duty Orders and Suspension Agreements*, Washington, DC: US International Trade Commission, Publication 2900

Viner, J. (1923) *Dumping: A Problem in International Trade*, Chicago: University of Chicago Press

Willig, R. (1997) Competition policy and antidumping: the economic effects of antidumping policy, Washington, DC: Brookings Trade Policy Forum, mimeo

WTO (1994) *WTO Anti-Dumping Agreement on Implementation of Article VI of the General Agreement on Tariffs and Trade 1994*, Geneva: WTO

5 Should pricing policies be regulated when firms may tacitly collude?

George Norman and Jacques-François Thisse

1 Introduction

Regulation of the conditions under which firms compete is common in the majority of Western industrialised countries. Such regulation is intended to prevent or control, for example, explicit or tacit collusion among firms, mergers and acquisitions, vertical restraints and firms' pricing policies – in particular, whether firms can employ discriminatory pricing. The common rationale for these regulatory policies is that they are needed to protect consumers from the abuse of monopoly power by firms that supply them with goods and services.

The purpose of this chapter is to suggest that care should be exercised by anti-trust authorities in their design of policies intended to promote competition in the market place. We do not deny the underlying '*raison d'être*' of competition policy but wish to suggest that a naive application of the idea that competition is always and everywhere desirable may have unforeseen and harmful effects. Our analysis can be summarised by the proposition that analysis of the effects of competition policy *should not take industry structure as given*. Policies that create too tough a competitive environment may result in perverse effects detrimental to consumer and social welfare because active anti-trust policy affects market structure through its impact on the medium- and long-run decisions of firms. The stronger are the structural effects of regulatory policy the more likely is it that blind adherence by the regulatory authorities to the benefits of competition will be misguided.

As a simple illustration, consider the case for cartel laws. The received wisdom has been that a high degree of coordination among firms benefits them through high profits but is detrimental to consumers through high prices, the losses of consumers generally outweighing the gains

We are grateful to Jim Friedman for comments on an earlier draft of this chapter.

of producers. This line of reasoning underpinned the tough anti-trust and merger policy that characterised regulation in the United States and Europe until the early 1980s. The desirability and acceptability of such tough policy has, however, been questioned on several grounds. Williamson (1968), for example, has argued that efficiency considerations may be grounds for defending coordination among firms if such coordination allows them to perform cost-saving activities, the benefits of which outweigh the price-increasing or quantity-reducing effects of coordination.[1] This kind of trade-off appears especially relevant in the setting considered in this chapter and more broadly defined as 'semi-collusion' by Phlips (1995, p. 151). Phlips describes this as a market structure in which 'decisions have to be made in a competitive way but with the understanding that product market collusion will follow or, alternatively, when collusive decisions are made with the understanding that they will be followed by competition on the product market'.

Selten (1984) develops an argument that is related to the ideas we develop in this chapter. He shows that if the market within which cartel laws are being enacted is characterised by free entry 'joint profit maximisation permits a greater number of competitors in a market than non-collusive behavior' (p. 183). As a consequence 'cartel laws are good for business in the sense of greater average joint profits' (p. 214).

Our focus in this chapter is on the regulation of firms' pricing policies, which was widely accepted up to the early 1980s to be in the public interest. Norman and Thisse (1996) provide several examples of such regulation: of the prices charged by United States and European airline industries, the application of resale price maintenance (RPM), the policies articulated by the United Kingdom Price Commission and the Federal Trade Commission (FTC) in the United States attacking discriminatory pricing. In a related context, the 1980s saw increasingly strict application by the United States and Europe of anti-dumping (AD) legislation ('dumping' can be viewed as price discrimination in the international market place). For example, from 1980 to 1987 the EC ruled against foreign firms in 249 cases affecting some 3 billion ECU of imports (Tharakan, 1991, table 1; see also chapter 4 in this volume).

This relatively tough regulatory regime has been considerably relaxed since 1987. The Robinson–Patman Act has not been applied in the United States, the Price Commission was abolished in the United Kingdom and more generally firms have been left freer to choose their pricing policies,

---

[1] German law allows 'rationalisation' and 'specialisation' cartels on the grounds that they lead to efficiency gains (see Kühn, 1993).

as a result of which (spatial) discriminatory pricing is a more likely outcome (Thisse and Vives, 1988).

Justification for the relaxation in policy can be found in modern developments in spatial pricing which argue that spatial price discrimination may be better for consumers than mill pricing: see, for example, Norman (1983), Thisse and Vives (1988). The way the argument runs is that discriminatory pricing is tougher for firms than mill pricing and so is pro- rather than anti-competitive:

denying a firm the right to meet the price of a competitor on a discriminatory basis provides the latter with some protection against price attacks. The effect is then to weaken competition, contrary to the belief of the proponents of naive application of legislation prohibiting price discrimination like the Robinson–Patman Act, or similar recommendations of the Price Commission in the United Kingdom. (Thisse and Vives, 1988)

It is of interest to note, for example, that discriminatory prices can be defended against action under the Robinson–Patman Act or international AD legislation if they are intended to 'meet the competition'.

The benefits claimed for discriminatory pricing have been called into question in analyses by Armstrong and Vickers (1993) and Norman and Thisse (1996). The common theme of these works is that current policy-based analysis is flawed because it takes no account of an important feedback loop between market conduct and market structure.[2] *If discriminatory pricing is, indeed, more competitive for incumbent firms it will act as an entry deterrent.* As a result, the essentially short-run benefits that the more competitive regime generates through lower prices may be more than offset by the longer-run effects it has on market structure: by reducing in the number of firms that wish to enter the market or the scale at which they enter.

Our specific contribution in this chapter is that we extend the Norman–Thisse analysis by relaxing an important assumption: that post-entry prices are one-shot Bertrand equilibrium prices. We consider, instead, the situation in which the incumbent firms recognise that the price game is a *repeated* game. Before turning to this analysis, we develop some further preliminary ideas in section 2. Our formal model is then presented in section 3 and the price equilibria for this model are identified in section 4.

---

[2] Armstrong and Vickers consider a situation in which a monopolist serves two markets, one of which is captive and the other subject to the threat of entry by a price taking entrant. They show that entry is more likely and the scale of entry is larger when price discrimination is banned. Norman and Thisse consider a free-entry Salop-style market and show that price discrimination may inhibit entry sufficiently as to be against the interests of consumers and society. See d'Aspremont and Motta (2000, chapter 6 in this volume) for a model in a related vein.

Section 5 presents a welfare comparison of the two pricing policies and our main conclusions are summarised in section 6.

2 Some preliminary analysis

Let us try to make the ideas presented above more concrete by examining how we might structure a general case capable of identifying the supposed benefits of tough regulatory policies. Assume that a market (as defined for policy purposes) contains N active firms, where N is to be determined endogenously through some entry and/or exit process. The payoff to each firm is a function of two sets of variables:

(i) A set R describing the regulatory regime within which the firms operate. R may be determined by government, for example describing the class of acceptable pricing policies or the toughness of anti-trust policy, or by (a subset of) the incumbent firms, for example, specifying 'orderly' pricing regimes such as basing-point pricing; consumer incentives; price-matching guarantees.

(ii) A set P of strategic variables chosen by the firms more or less non-cooperatively: prices, product specifications; locations; quantities.

A subgame perfect Nash equilibrium (SPE) in N and P is identified from some m-stage game. For a given regulatory regime R, this equilibrium specifies a payoff to each firm of the form:

$$\Pi_i^*(P^*(N^*), N^*:R) \quad \text{for } i = 1 \dots N^* \tag{5.1}$$

which will have associated welfare properties. Now consider alternative regulatory regimes, where we define a 'tougher' regime $\hat{R} > R$ as being a regime that is more competitive for the firms in, or contemplating entry to, the market. For example, assume that the regulatory authority tries to promote fierce competition in this market by abolishing facilitating practices, or outlawing the trade association to avoid contacts among the firms, or warning the firms that they are suspected of collusive behaviour.[3] For a given N it is to be expected that:

$$\Pi_i^*\left(P^*(N), N:\hat{R}\right) < \Pi_i^*(P^*(N), N:R) \quad \text{if } \hat{R} > R \tag{5.2}$$

with the reduction in profit (partially) transferred to consumers. Equation (5.2) would appear to justify governments' preference for tough rather than soft regulatory regimes.

[3] An interesting example occurred in the gas market in the United Kingdom, where British Gas was forced to yield market share to potential competitors.

However, (5.2) is essentially short-run, in that it takes market structure as given. It is also to be expected that increased toughness of the regulatory regime will reduce the number of active firms in the market in the medium- and long-run. When firms have to decide whether to renew plants or to update their products or to incur other fixed costs, it may be that the decreased future stream of expected profits will not cover these costs. The exit of some firms is to be expected, increasing profitability for the firms remaining in the market:[4]

$$\Pi_i^*(P^*(N_1), N_1 : R) < \Pi_i^*(P^*(N_2), N_2 : R) \quad \text{if } N_1 > N_2 \quad (5.3)$$

The overall effect of an increase in the toughness of the regulatory regime is a combination of (5.2) and (5.3) and might be expressed as follows. Let $\Delta R > 0$ be some measure of increased toughness of R. Then

$$\left.\frac{\Delta \Pi_i}{\Delta R}\right|_N = \frac{\Delta \Pi_i}{\Delta P}\frac{\Delta P}{\Delta R} < 0 \quad \text{and} \quad \left.\frac{\Delta \Pi_i}{\Delta N}\right|_R < 0$$

but

$$\frac{\Delta \Pi_i}{\Delta R} = \underbrace{\frac{\Delta \Pi_i}{\Delta P}\frac{\Delta P}{\Delta R}}_{(a) < 0} + \underbrace{\left[\frac{\Delta \Pi_i}{\Delta P}\frac{\Delta P}{\Delta N} + \frac{\Delta \Pi_i}{\Delta N}\right]\frac{\Delta N}{\Delta R}}_{(b) > 0} = ? \quad (5.4)$$

In other words, increased toughness of R has:

(a) a profit-reducing effect in the short run through its impact on P for a given N, and
(b) a profit-increasing effect in the longer run through induced exit and stronger entry deterrence.

For increased toughness to benefit consumers (a) must dominate (b). Otherwise increased market concentration will make consumers worse off – for example, through reduced product variety or a longer travel distance to shops and, more generally, through higher prices. Note the similarity between this analysis and Selten's (1984) argument that *collusion may lead to lower concentration and lower total profits in an industry*. A qualitatively similar conclusion would be reached if our measure of the desirability of changes in R were some weighted average of producer and consumer surplus.[5] In short, policy that establishes too tough a competitive

---

[4] A possible exception would be if there were extensive network externalities between firms.
[5] There are further considerations that we do not consider in this chapter. For example, price discrimination facilitates market segmentation by multiproduct firms, increasing prices and profits but reducing consumer surplus.

environment may have some unforeseen effects with the (apparently) paradoxical result of being detrimental to the community's welfare.

An important limitation of almost all current analysis is that the equilibrium of the post-entry subgame, on whatever strategic variables it is based, is assumed to be the outcome of a one-shot game. This, as we shall show, is an important assumption. If price, for example, is the strategic variable, discriminatory pricing is, indeed, more competitive than non-discriminatory (referred to hereafter as mill) pricing in spatial markets, or their non-spatial analogues, precisely because the prices that emerge are the result of a Bertrand-at-every point process. But if the price subgame is *repeated* it is not at all clear that the same conclusion will hold.

We know that a monopolist always prefers discriminatory pricing to mill pricing and it might be expected that the same will be true when the prices charged by firms correspond to a tacitly collusive outcome for an infinitely repeated price subgame.[6] Assume, for example, as we do in the remainder of our analysis, the familiar Hotelling/Salop spatial model in which consumer demand is perfectly inelastic for prices below some reservation price. With demand of this type it trivially follows from the Folk Theorem that a set of discriminatory prices arbitrarily close to the consumers' reservation price will be SPE prices for some discount factor sufficiently close to unity (see Friedman, chapter 3 in this volume). Consequently, these prices will be higher than the SPE mill prices almost everywhere, even if market structure is endogenously determined.

It would appear, in other words, that the 'endogenous market structure' argument is irrelevant to the choice of allowable pricing practices once we introduce the possibility that firms are aware that they are in competition over time and incorporate this into their pricing decisions. But this over-looks the importance of a crucial part of the argument: that the discount factor be 'sufficiently close to unity'. The question we need to investigate is *how close* the discount factor must be to unity for a particular set of discriminatory or mill prices to be sustainable as an SPE. This question arises from the nature of SPE prices. These are sustained through some credible punishment strategy which is designed to ensure that the short-term gains from deviating from the (tacitly) agreed prices are more than offset by the long-term losses that will be incurred once the punishment phase is implemented. Looking at this another way, the ability to raise prices above their Bertrand–Nash equilibrium levels is constrained by the potential gains a firm will make by deviating from these prices. Such gains are likely to vary significantly with different pricing policies and so will

---

[6] We can assume the price subgame to be infinitely repeated or to be repeated with some known, constant probability in each period t that the subgame will continue.

impose different limits on the SPE prices. This suggests that we might approach the problem from a somewhat different perspective by asking: *for a given discount factor*, what is the upper limit on the discriminatory and mill prices that firms can charge? We can then investigate the welfare properties of these prices.

Two other remarks are in order at this stage. First, the punishment strategy on which we focus in this chapter is what is sometimes referred to as a 'grim trigger strategy': any deviation from the tacitly agreed prices induces reversion to the one-shot Bertrand–Nash equilibrium prices forever. Other punishments are available to firms (Friedman, chapter 3 in this volume) but it is reasonable to suggest that the qualitative properties of our analysis would remain valid for a larger class of such alternative strategies.

Secondly, it will be shown below that the discount factor is an amalgam of the discount rate, which is largely outside the control of regulators (and firms), and firms' price flexibility in response to deviation by their rivals, which is potentially controllable by regulators. Under what circumstances (if any) might the authorities wish to impose controls on the speed with which firms can change their prices? Our analysis, in other words, introduces a further important element to regulatory control that has not been much discussed, primarily because the currently available analysis is static. The dynamic approach followed here brings with it a new dimension of competition in that the discount factor can be made endogenous to the market.

We show that, provided consumers' reservation prices impose no effective constraints on firms, the upper limits on the tacitly agreed prices are such that discriminatory prices are almost always and almost everywhere lower than mill prices. In other words, consumers gain and firms lose from discriminatory pricing. The ease with which firms can revise their location decisions (the degree of spatial contestability), which was central to the welfare properties of our 1996 analysis, now has a more limited role. Firms gain less and consumers lose less from mill pricing when the market is spatially non-contestable.

We also show, however, that explicit account must be taken of the consumer reservation price since this imposes a more severe constraint on mill prices than on discriminatory prices. If this constraint is strong enough and if pricing decisions are flexible enough, the welfare properties of the two pricing policies are reversed, with consumers losing and firms gaining from discriminatory pricing. The required degree of price flexibility for this to happen is lower in more concentrated market structures. This implies that *if market concentration is already high, deregulation of pricing policies is less likely to benefit consumers unless the regulatory authorities are willing to impose accompanying restrictions intended to reduce price flexibility.*

3 The model

We conduct our analysis in the context of the Hotelling/Salop location model, in which the economy is assumed to be a circle C over which consumers are uniformly distributed at unit density. The interpretation of this model as a model of horizontal product differentiation is now so familiar that we need not repeat it here.

We assume that each time period t is γ units long, where γ measures the speed of response of incumbent firms to any perceived price deviation, and that the continuous rate of time discount is ρ. Firms entering this market offer products that are identical in all characteristics but their locations. Production costs in any period t are assumed to be identical for all firms, given by:

$$C^t(Q^t) = f + cQ^t \tag{5.5}$$

where f can be thought of as the flow-equivalent present value of set-up costs – if aggregate set-up costs are F, then $f = F \big/ \sum_{t=0}^{\infty} \int_{t\gamma}^{(t+1)\gamma} e^{-\rho\tau} \, d\tau = F/\rho - c$ are marginal costs and Q^t is total output of the firm in period t. Production thus exhibits economies of scale, limiting the number of firms that will wish to enter the market. We assume that f is sufficiently small for us to be able to ignore integer problems and we normalise $c = 0$ without loss of generality.

The set $N = \{1, 2, \dots n, \dots\}$ denotes all potential entrants and the set $\aleph$ denotes the firms that actually choose to enter.[7] Each firm chooses a location $x_i \in C \cup \Phi$, where $x_i \in C$ if firm i chooses to enter the market and $x_i = \Phi$ otherwise. This entry stage establishes a *location configuration* denoted by the vector $x = (x_i)$ in which we assume that the set $\aleph$ corresponds to the first $\#(\aleph)$ elements of x. It will prove convenient below to refer to the time-dependent location configuration x^t where, unless otherwise stated, it is to be expected that $x^t = x$ for all $t = 1 \dots \infty$.

Firms are assumed to make their pricing decisions after they have made their entry/location decisions. In each post-entry period t, each firm $i \in \aleph$ establishes the price schedule $p_i^t(r|x^t)$ giving its delivered price to each consumer location $r \in C$. Transport costs are assumed to be linear in

---

[7] This implies that all firms make their entry decisions simultaneously. In the analysis that follows we shall concentrate upon entry processes that lead to the loosest packing of firms consistent with the relocation costs that firms might incur. As a result, we could equivalently think of the entry process as being sequential provided that the post-entry price game is played non-cooperatively until the entry process has been completed.

distance and quantity transported with transport rate s, so that with mill pricing the delivered price schedule for firm i in period t is:

$$p_i^t(r|x^t) = m_i^t + s\|x_i - r\| \qquad \forall i \in \aleph, \ r \in C \tag{5.6}$$

With discriminatory pricing we assume only that firms never price below marginal costs:

$$p_i^t(r|x^t) \geq s\|x_i - r\| \qquad \forall i \in \aleph, \ r \in C \tag{5.7}$$

and we normalise $s = 1$ without loss of generality. The firms' pricing decisions made in each period are denoted by the vector

$$p^t(x^t) = \{p_i^t(r|x^t)\}, \qquad i \in \aleph$$

and

$$P_i^t(x^t), \qquad i \in \aleph$$

denotes the set of feasible delivered price schedules for each entrant in period t. Let $s^t = (x^t, p^t(x^t))$ and $s = \{s^0, s^1, \ldots, s^t, \ldots\}$.

Consumers purchase from the firm offering the product at the lowest delivered price. If there is a price tie, we assume that consumers act in a socially optimal manner by purchasing from the nearest firm. Consumer demand is perfectly inelastic at prices below a reservation price v, with demand to firm $i \in \aleph$ from consumers at location r given by:

$$\begin{cases} q_i^t(s^t) = 1 & \text{if } p_i^t(r|x^t) \leq v \text{ and } p_i^t(r|x^t) = \min_j [p_j^t(r|x^t)] \\ \qquad = 0 & \text{otherwise} \end{cases} \tag{5.8}$$

The per-period rate of profit to firm $i \in \aleph$ is:

$$\pi_i^t(s^t) = \int_C \int_{t\gamma}^{(t+1)\gamma} [p_i^t(r|x^t) - \|x_i - r\|] q_i^t(s^t) e^{-\rho\tau} \, d\tau \, dr$$

$$- f \int_{t\gamma}^{(t+1)\gamma} e^{-\rho\tau} \, d\tau \tag{5.9}$$

$$= \frac{1-\delta}{\rho} \delta^t \left[\int_C [p_i^t(r|x^t) - \|x_i - r\|] q_i^t(s^t) \, dr - f \right]$$

where $\delta = e^{-\gamma\rho}$ is the *discount factor*, with $0 \leq \delta \leq 1$. The discounted present value of firm i is:

$$V_i(s) = \sum_{t=0}^{\infty} \pi_i^t(s^t) \tag{5.10}$$

Since the discount factor δ is determined by both γ and ρ it can be taken as a measure of price flexibility in the relevant market which, as we noted in section 2, is potentially controllable by the regulatory authorities. In other words, the discount factor can be made endogenous to the market by the regulator.

In analysing equilibrium in this market we distinguish between the initial entry stage and subsequent periods in which incumbent firms can take explicit account of the repeated nature of price competition between them. Since in these later periods 'profits will normally be shared on the basis of market areas ... we may expect the process by which market areas are determined to be a very aggressive one.' (MacLeod, Norman and Thisse, 1987, p. 192). Specifically, we assume that market areas are determined by a two-stage entry/price game in which equilibrium for the price subgame is Bertrand–Nash. This is defined in the usual way as the set of price functions $p_b^t(x^t)$ such that for all $i \in \aleph$:

$$\pi_i^t\left(x^t, p_b^t(x^t)\right) \geq \pi_i^t\left(x^t, p_i^t(x^t), p_{-ib}^t(x^t)\right) \quad \forall\, p_i^t(x^t) \in P_i^t(x^t)$$

$$(5.11)$$

Denote $s_b^i = \left(x^t, p_b^t(x^t)\right)$.

Equilibrium for the first-stage entry game is a location configuration x such that:

$$\pi_i^t\left(x, p_b^t(x)\right) \geq \pi_i^t\left((x_i, x_{-i}), p_b^t(x_i, x_{-i})\right) \quad \forall x_i \in C \cup \Phi \text{ and } i \in \aleph$$

$$(5.12)$$

We follow a well established tradition and confine our attention to location configurations in which incumbent firms are symmetrically located on C.

Once firms' market areas have been determined by this entry/price process the identities of the incumbent firms are known and it becomes possible for them to coordinate their pricing decisions to reflect the repeated nature of the price game in which they are now involved. We can relabel as $t = 0$ the beginning of the post-entry repeated-price game. Given the equilibrium $\left(x, p_b^t(x)\right)$ identified by (5.11) and (5.12), it is always possible to find a set of prices $\tilde{p} = \{\tilde{p}_i\}$ for $i \in N$ such that $\pi_i^t(x, \tilde{p}) \geq \pi_i^t\left(x, p_b^t(x)\right)$. MacLeod, Norman and Thisse (1987) show that the pricing strategy:

$$P_i^{t*} = \begin{cases} p_{ib}^t(x^t) & \text{if } \{x^t \neq x\} \text{ or} \\ \quad \{x^\tau = x \text{ and } p^\tau \neq \tilde{p} \text{ for some } 0 \leq \tau \leq t-1\} & (5.13) \\ \tilde{p}_i^t & \text{otherwise} \end{cases}$$

is an SPE pricing strategy provided that:

$$\pi_i^t(x, \tilde{p}) - \delta \pi_i^t\left(x, p_b^t(x)\right) \geq (1 - \delta) \max_{p_i} \pi_i(x, p_i, \tilde{p}_{-i})$$

$$(5.14)$$

Equation (5.14) ensures that deviation from the prices $\tilde{p}$ is not profit-able for any incumbent firm, while the initial entry process and the pricing strategy (5.13) guarantee that new entrants will not be attracted to the market. MacLeod, Norman and Thisse do not identify what the prices $\tilde{p}$ might be and it is to this question that we now turn.

4 Price equilibrium in the repeated-price game

In determining the prices $\tilde{p}$ we need to identify, first, the 'shape' of the firms' delivered price schedules and, secondly, their one-period profit maximising deviation from these prices. We simplify the analysis by assuming that at the entry stage each firm is committed to a particular *pricing policy*. In the non-discriminatory case, this implies that all firms are committed to mill pricing whether or not they abide by the agreed prices.[8] If the firms adopt discriminatory pricing, we assume that they are committed to a uniform delivered pricing policy.[9] It should be clear that the optimal one-period deviation from a tacitly agreed uniform delivered price is a uniform delivered price.

Assume for the moment that the market is of unit length[10] and that it contains n symmetrically located firms, that no further entry is possible and that the consumer reservation price is sufficiently high or the number of firms sufficiently great that firms are in the competitive regions of their demand curves (Salop, 1979). For the moment we can suppose the no-entry condition to be determined either exogenously by institutional constraints or endogenously as the result of the free-entry process we have detailed in section 3.

Mill pricing

The free-entry Bertrand–Nash equilibrium mill prices are:

$$m_i^b = 1/n, \qquad i = 1 \ldots n \tag{5.15}$$

---

[8] This implies that with mill pricing the consumers control collection of the goods. In the product-differentiation analogy, it implies that the deviating firm is committed at the entry stage to a specialised technology that cannot produce a range of differentiated products.

[9] This is not unreasonable given our assumption that demand is perfectly inelastic for all prices less than the reservation price ν. In the production-differentiation analogue, the uniform pricing assumption implies that all firms are committed to charging the same price for all the product variants they offer. It is interesting to note that the Ford Motor Company, for example, is increasingly employing this type of pricing policy over parts of the product spectrum that they feel to be reasonably distinct.

[10] This normalisation does not affect the analysis so long as the consumer reservation price is non-binding. We shall relax this assumption on p. 115 when we consider the effects of a binding reservation price.

After the entry stage has been completed we assume that the firms reach a tacit agreement on a set of mill prices $\tilde{m}_i^a = \tilde{m}/n$, $i = 1\ldots n$, with instantaneous flow profits to each firm inclusive of fixed costs of:

$$\pi_i^a = \tilde{m}/n^2 \qquad i = 1\ldots n \tag{5.16}$$

We wish to identify the highest mill prices $\tilde{m}_i^a(\delta)$ that can be an SPE for the discount factor δ. As we have noted, these prices must exactly balance the one-period rewards from cheating on the agreed prices against the long-term losses when such deviation is punished. The punishment phase is easily defined: we assume that firms revert to the one-shot Bertrand–Nash prices of (5.15) forever. If firm i decides to deviate from the tacitly agreed prices, more complex considerations arise. In particular, firm i must decide how many of its neighbouring firms it will undercut (stealing their entire markets).

It is convenient to use the following definition.

Definition: Let

$$h(\delta) = \frac{2\delta - 1 + \sqrt{3\delta^2 - 3\delta + 1}}{2(1 - \delta)} \tag{5D}$$

and define $j|[\delta]|$ to be the smallest integer j greater than $h(\delta)$. Note that $j|[\delta]|$ is increasing in δ.

We can show (see the mathematical appendix, p. 119) that if firm i deviates from the agreed prices it will do so in such a way that it undercuts exactly $j|[\delta]|$ neighbouring firms on each side. Firm i will not, however, set prices such that it undercuts $j|[\delta]|$ neighbours and takes part of the markets of the $(j|[\delta]| + 1)$th neighbours. We then have the following:

Proposition 1:[11] The highest mill price that can be an SPE for the repeated price game when the market contains n symmetrically located firms, no further entry is possible and the discount factor is δ is:

$$\tilde{m}_i^a(\delta) = \min\left[v - \frac{1}{2n}, \frac{\delta\left(1 + j|[\delta]| + 2j|[\delta]|^2\right) - j|[\delta]|(1 + 2j|[\delta]|)}{\delta(1 + 2j|[\delta]|) - 2j|[\delta]|} \cdot \frac{1}{n} \right] \tag{5.17}$$

where $j|[\delta]|$ is defined by (5D) and is such that $1 \leq j|[\delta]| \leq n/2$.

---

[11] Proofs of all propositions are given in the mathematical appendix (p. 119).

It is easy to show, as we would expect,[12] that $\partial \tilde{m}_i^a(\delta)/\partial \delta > 0$. The upper limit on the SPE mill price is an increasing function of the discount factor, or equivalently, of the degree of price flexibility.

Discriminatory pricing

We know[13] that provided no firm has monopoly power in any segment of its market area the Bertrand–Nash equilibrium discriminatory pricing schedule for each entrant is:

$$p_i^b(r|x) = \max\left(\|x_{i-r}\|, \min_j\|x_j - r\|\right), \qquad i = 1 \ldots n \qquad (5.18)$$

Now assume that after the entry stage has been completed the firms tacitly agree each to charge a uniform delivered price $\tilde{u}$. As with discriminatory pricing, we wish to identify the highest uniform delivered prices $\tilde{u}_i^a(\delta)$ that can be an SPE for the discount factor δ. Once again, these have to balance reward and punishment, where now (5.18) gives the prices that will apply forever in the event of cheating. With discriminatory pricing it is easy to identify the best-possible deviation for firm i: price should be reduced marginally below the tacitly agreed uniform delivered price $\tilde{u}_i^a(\delta)$, giving the cheating firm a market area of $\tilde{u}_i^a(\delta)/s = \tilde{u}_i^a(\delta)$ with our normalisation $s = 1$. We then have:

Proposition 2: The highest uniform delivered price that can be an SPE when the market contains n symmetrically located firms, no further entry is possible and the discount factor is $\delta > 0.5$ is:

$$\tilde{u}_i^a(\delta) = \min\left[v, \frac{1 + \sqrt{\delta(2\delta - 1)}}{2(1 - \delta)} \cdot \frac{1}{n}\right] \qquad (5.19)$$

As with the mill price, $\partial \tilde{u}_i^a(\delta)/\partial \delta > 0$. The upper limit on the uniform delivered price is an increasing function of the discount factor (or the degree of price flexibility).

5   The welfare effects of deregulating firms' pricing policies

The analysis of section 4 identifies upper limits on the prices that firms can charge, but we know from the Folk Theorem that any prices between these upper limits and the Bertrand–Nash prices can be sustained as

---

[12] This is most easily done numerically since, for any given n, the mill price is a function only of δ.

[13] See, for example, Gee (1976); Lederer and Hurter (1986).

equilibrium prices for the relevant discount factor δ. This makes welfare comparison of the alternative pricing policies impossible without the imposition of some further structure on the model. The approach we adopt is to assume that self-interest among the incumbent firms leads them to settle on the highest possible prices that can be charged consistent with there being no incentive to deviate. In other words, for the remainder of this chapter, we assume that (5.17) and (5.19) describe the actual prices that will be charged by the incumbent firms after the entry stage has been completed.

A simple result characterises the comparison of discriminatory and mill prices for the one-shot price subgame, as illustrated by figure 5.1. If there are n active firms with each pricing policy as in figure 5.1a no consumer loses from discriminatory pricing. By contrast, if there are n active firms with mill pricing but only $n/2$ with discriminatory pricing as in figure 5.1b no consumer gains from discriminatory pricing.

It turns out that a similar property holds for the SPE prices of (5.17) and (5.19).

Proposition 3:   Assume that the reservation price is not binding and that there are $\bar{n}$ active firms with mill pricing:

(i) $\tilde{u}_i^a(\delta)|_{n=\bar{n}} < \tilde{m}_i^a(\delta)|_{n=\bar{n}} \ \forall \ \bar{n} \geq 2$: If there are also $\bar{n}$ active firms with discriminatory pricing, all consumers gain from discriminatory pricing.

(ii) If no consumer is to gain from discriminatory pricing, there will have to be no more than $\bar{n}/2$ firms with discriminatory pricing.

These are actually stronger results than for the one-shot price subgame. It would appear that the advantage to consumers of discriminatory pricing relative to mill pricing is even greater with the repeated-price game. This might on first-sight seem surprising since, as figure 5.1a makes clear, the punishment phase with discriminatory pricing is much more severe than with mill pricing. The reason is to be found in the very different rewards that accrue to price undercutting with the two pricing policies. When firms employ mill pricing, a firm which wishes to cut price to one set of consumers must also offer reduced prices to all of its existing customers, dissipating at least some of the benefits of the reduced prices. A price-cutting firm suffers no such loss of revenue with discriminatory pricing since prices to its existing customers are maintained effectively unchanged, strengthening the temptation to cut prices. The need to offset the one-period gains to price cutting imposes a sufficiently strong constraint on the tacitly agreed discriminatory prices as to lead to proposition 3.

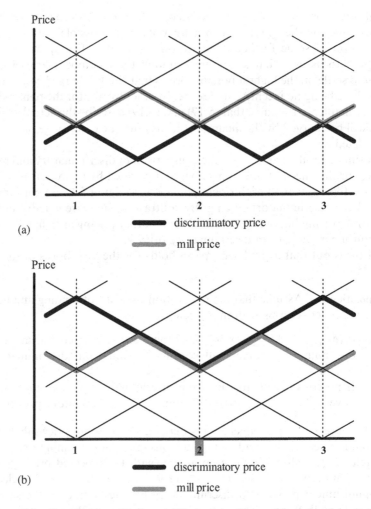

(a)

(b)

Figure 5.1   Comparison of price equilibria: (a) n firms with each pricing policy (b) n firms with mill pricing; $n/2$ firms with discriminatory pricing

In order to extend our comparisons of the two pricing policies we need to be more precise about the outcome of the entry stage detailed in section 3. A key property that affects entry, market structure, and so the effects of price deregulation, is the degree of spatial contestability. When incumbents can relocate their activities costlessly the industry is defined to be spatially contestable (SC). At the other extreme, if relocation costs are prohibitive, making location choice once-for-all, the industry is defined to be spatially non-contestable (SNC).

In a free-entry equilibrium with spatial contestability each entrant firm just breaks even. We take as the free-entry SNC equilibrium the loosest packing of firms consistent with there being no further entry. At this equilibrium the incumbents fully exploit the entry-deterring advantage of being committed to their locations. As a result, the free entry number of entrants is:[14]

$$
\begin{cases}
n_d^{SC} = (2f)^{-1/2}; & n_f^{SC} = (f)^{-1/2} \\[2mm]
n_d^{SNC} = (8f)^{-1/2}; & n_f^{SNC} = \dfrac{\sqrt{3/2}}{\sqrt{(2+\sqrt{3})f}}
\end{cases}
\qquad (5.20)
$$

Since $n_d^*/n_f^* > 1:2$ we cannot conclude that the entry-deterring effect of discriminatory pricing more than offsets its pro-competitive benefits for consumers. We must, therefore, turn to more aggregate comparisons. In doing so, it turns out that we must also distinguish between cases in which the reservation price is not binding and those in which it is.

Welfare comparisons: non-binding consumer reservation price

Throughout this subsection we shall assume that the consumer reservation price imposes no effective constraint on firms' prices. The complex nature of the price equilibria makes analytical results difficult to derive. However, given (5.17), (5.19) and (5.20), set-up costs appear as a common multiplier provided that the consumer reservation price is not binding. As a result, all comparisons are determined by the discount factor δ and numerical comparisons provide a complete description of the relative merits of the two pricing policies. Recall that $\delta = e^{-\gamma \rho}$, with the result that, for a given continuous rate of time discount, δ will be greater the faster the speed of response of incumbents (the lower is γ). Figure 5.2 and table 5.1 summarise the welfare effects of the two pricing policies. In table 5.1 we also repeat our results for the one-shot price subgame to facilitate comparison.

Consider, first, the impact of pricing policy on delivered prices (figure 5.2a). *If the market is SC every consumer is better off with discriminatory pricing for any discount factor greater than 0.5 and if the market is SNC every consumer is better off with discriminatory pricing provided the discount factor is greater than 0.601.* The benefits to consumers of the pro-competitive effects of discriminatory prices with a given market structure

---

[14] See Norman and Thisse (1996) for a detailed discussion of these results. The subscript d denotes discriminatory pricing and the subscript f denotes mill (or FOB) pricing.

extend to endogenous market structures when prices are determined by
(5.17) and (5.19). Discriminatory pricing increases market concentration
and so increases prices (which is why the difference between the mill price
and uniform delivered price is lower when the market is SNC). However,
this is more than offset by the need to make price undercutting unprofitable

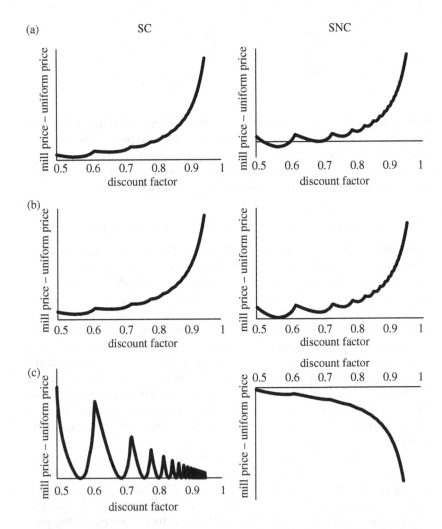

Figure 5.2 Welfare comparison of non-discriminatory versus discriminatory pricing. (a) Difference between mill price and uniform delivered price
(b) Difference in total revenue (c) Difference in individual firm profits
(d) Difference in aggregate profit

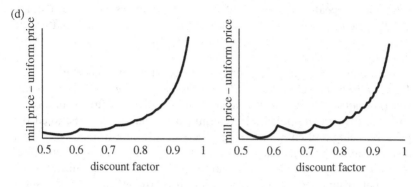

Figure 5.2 (*cont.*)

Table 5.1 *Welfare comparisons*

	Spatial contestability	Spatial non-contestability
Repeated-price game[a]		
Prices	$\tilde{m}_i^a(\delta) > \tilde{u}_i^a(\delta)$ if $\delta > 0.5$	$\tilde{m}_i^a(\delta) > \tilde{u}_i^a(\delta)$ if $\delta > 0.601$
Consumer surplus	$CS_f < CS_d$	$CS_f < CS_d$
Supernormal profit	$\pi_{if} > \pi_{id}$	$\pi_{if} < \pi_{id}$
	$\Pi_f > \Pi_d$	$\Pi_f > \Pi_d$
Total surplus	$TS_f < TS_d$	$TS_f > TS_d$
One-shot price game		
Consumer surplus	$CS_f < CS_d$	$CS_f > CS_d$
Supernormal profit	—	$\pi_{if} < \pi_{id}$
		$\Pi_f < \Pi_d$
Total surplus	$TS_f < TS_d$	$TS_f > TS_d$

Note: [a]The welfare comparisons relate to cases in which the consumer reservation price is non-binding.

which, as we have already indicated, imposes a stronger constraint on pricing when firms employ discriminatory pricing.

The impact of discriminatory pricing on aggregate consumer surplus is straightforward. If firms' total revenue is denoted $TR(n)$ and aggregate consumer surplus is denoted $CS(n)$ then it follows from our definition of individual consumer demand that $CS(n) = v - TR(n)$. From figure 5.2b *mill pricing generates higher total revenues and so lower aggregate consumer surplus than discriminatory pricing no matter the degree of spatial contestability*. This is in contrast to the one-shot price subgame, in which mill pricing benefits consumers if the market is SNC. When the price subgame is repeated, the ability of firms to raise prices when they employ a mill pricing policy is sufficiently strengthened that, no matter the degree of spatial contestability, consumers unambiguously benefit from discriminatory prices.

Now consider the impact of pricing policy on profitability (figure 5.2c). *If the market is SC (SNC) mill (discriminatory) pricing gives greater supernormal profits to the individual firm.*[15] Individual firm profitability with the two pricing policies is determined by the interplay between the price-reducing and entry-deterring effects of allowing firms to employ a discriminatory pricing policy. If the market is SC the price-reducing effect is dominant. By contrast, if the market is SNC (5.20) indicates that the entry-deterring effect of price deregulation is strengthened. This is sufficient, at the individual firm level, to offset the profit-reducing effects of fiercer price competition.

Such ambiguity does not characterise aggregate profits: figure 5.2d. *Aggregate profit is greater with mill pricing than discriminatory pricing no matter the degree of spatial contestability.* This is in sharp contrast to our analysis of spatial non-contestability with a one-shot price subgame (see table 5.1). The difference derives once again from our discussion of proposition 3 in which we saw that the competitive disadvantage of discriminatory pricing is strengthened when the price subgame is repeated.

The comparison of total surplus is just as in Norman and Thisse (1996). If total costs are $TC(n)$ then total surplus is $v - TC(n)$. Since the entry process we have assumed is independent of the nature of the post-entry price subgame, total costs are also independent of the nature of the post-entry price subgame. *If the market is SNC (SC) mill pricing will generate higher (lower) total surplus than discriminatory pricing.*

To summarise, when the price subgame is repeated *and the consumer reservation price is non-binding*, discriminatory prices benefit consumers almost always individually and always in the aggregate while mill prices benefit producers in the aggregate (and individually if the market is SC). Although the impact of discriminatory prices on aggregate surplus is determined by the degree of spatial contestability when consumer surplus and producer surplus are weighted equally, it is clear that there will be some additional weighting of consumer surplus above which regulators should unambiguously favour discriminatory prices.

---

[15] There is a slight exception to this. With spatially contestability the difference in profits between mill and discriminatory pricing is a series of quadratics, one for each value of j. Each such quadratic has a turning point at the discount factor $\delta(j) = 4j^2/(4j^2 + 4j - 1)$ at which individual profits are equal for the two types of firm.

It is important to note, however, that our results in this subsection are based upon the assumption that the consumer reservation price imposes no effective limit on firms' choice of prices as given by (5.17) and (5.19). We now examine the effect of relaxing this assumption.

Welfare comparisons: binding consumer reservation price

It will emerge below that if the consumer reservation price is binding, welfare comparisons of the two pricing policies are affected by market length. As a result, assume that the market is of length Λ. Given the entry process described in section 3, the free-entry number of entrants is now equal to:

$$
\begin{cases}
n_d^{SC} = (\Lambda/2f)^{1/2}; \quad n_f^{SC} = (\Lambda/f)^{1/2} \\[2mm]
n_d^{SNC} = (\Lambda/8f)^{1/2}; \quad n_f^{SNC} = \dfrac{\sqrt{3\Lambda/2}}{\sqrt{(2+\sqrt{3})f}}
\end{cases}
\tag{5.20a}
$$

We know that the highest mill price any firm will wish to charge is $v - \Lambda/2n$ and that the highest uniform delivered price that can be charged is v. An important implication of the previous subsection is also that, no matter the degree of spatial contestability, the discount factor $\hat{\delta}_f$ above which the consumer reservation price is binding is lower with mill pricing than with discriminatory pricing. We take advantage of these two properties in this subsection. Our discussion turns the analysis of the previous subsection on its head to an extent, by seeking to answer the following questions:

(i) Under what circumstances will *all* consumers be worse off with discriminatory pricing as compared to mill pricing and how is this affected by the degree of spatial contestability?

For this to be the case it must be that the uniform delivered price is exactly equal to the consumer reservation price v, since we know that the maximum delivered price with mill pricing is v and this applies to a zero measure of consumers. So what does the critical discount factor $\hat{\delta}_f$ have to be for a uniform delivered price $\tilde{u}_i^a(\hat{\delta}_f) = v$ to be sustainable as an SPE? We can then show how this critical discount factor is affected by market size, the consumer reservation price and the firms' set-up costs.

(ii) Under what circumstances will consumers *on average* be worse off with discriminatory pricing and how is this affected by the degree of spatial contestability?

For this to be the case the uniform delivered price must be greater than $v - \Lambda/4n$. So above what discount factor will a uniform delivered price of $v - \Lambda/4n$ be sustainable as an SPE? Again, we can investigate how this discount factor is affected by market size, the consumer reservation price and the firms' set-up costs.

(iii) Under what circumstances will firms either individually or on aggregate benefit from price deregulation and how is this affected by the degree of spatial contestability?

The approach we adopt is straightforward. Equation (5.19) identifies the maximum uniform delivered price that is sustainable as an SPE for a given discount factor. Inverting this equation, therefore, gives us the lowest discount factor for which a particular uniform delivered price is sustainable as an SPE. Assume that the uniform delivered price is $\kappa/n \leq v$ for some parameter $\kappa \geq 1$. From (5.19), the discount factor $\hat{\delta}_d(\kappa)$ for which the uniform delivered price $\tilde{u}_i^a(\hat{\delta}_d(\kappa))$ equals κ/n is:

$$\hat{\delta}_d(\kappa) = \frac{(2\kappa - 1)^2}{2(2\kappa^2 - 1)} \geq 0.5 \qquad \text{for } \kappa \geq 1 \qquad (5.21)$$

It follows immediately from (5.21) that $\partial\hat{\delta}_d(\kappa)/\partial\kappa \geq 0$. In other words, the critical discount factor $\hat{\delta}_d(\kappa)$ is increasing in κ.

Consider first the critical discount factor above which *all* consumers will be worse off with discriminatory pricing. We have already noted that for this to be the case $\tilde{u}_i^a(\hat{\delta}_d(\kappa_1)) = \kappa_1/n = v$, so that $\kappa_1 = v \cdot n$, and from (5.20a) we have:

$$\kappa_1^{SC} = \hat{v}\sqrt{\frac{\Lambda}{2}} > \kappa_1^{SNC} = \frac{\hat{v}}{2} \cdot \sqrt{\frac{\Lambda}{2}} \qquad (5.22)$$

where $\hat{v} = v/\sqrt{f}$. *When the consumer reservation price imposes an effective constraint on firms' mill prices, the critical discount factor above which all consumers are worse off with discriminatory pricing is lower when the market is SNC than when it is SC.*

For consumers *in the aggregate* to lose from discriminatory pricing, it must be the case that $\tilde{u}_i^a(\hat{\delta}_d(\kappa)) \geq \kappa_2/n = v - \Lambda/4n$, which gives a lower limit on κ of $\kappa_2 = v \cdot n - \Lambda/4$. Substituting from (5.20a) gives:

$$\kappa_2^{SC} = \hat{v}\sqrt{\frac{\Lambda}{2}} - \frac{\Lambda}{4} > \kappa_2^{SNC} = \frac{\hat{v}}{2} \cdot \sqrt{\frac{\Lambda}{2}} - \frac{\Lambda}{4} \qquad (5.23)$$

and we obtain the same qualitative conclusion.

Note further that $\partial \kappa_i^{\bullet} / \partial \hat{v} > 0$ and $\partial \kappa_i^{\bullet} / \partial \Lambda > 0$ $(i = 1, 2)$[16] imply-ing that *when mill prices are constrained by the reservation price, consumers individually and in the aggregate are more likely to lose from discriminatory pricing if the market is 'small', the reservation price is 'low' and/or firms' set-up costs are 'high'.*

For firms individually to benefit from discriminatory pricing the lower limit on κ is such that (see the mathematical appendix, p. 122):

$$\begin{cases} \kappa_3^{SC} = 0.5\hat{v}\sqrt{\Lambda} \\ \kappa_3^{SNC} = 0.079\hat{v}\sqrt{\Lambda} + 0.225 \end{cases} \Rightarrow \kappa_3^{SC} > \kappa_3^{SNC} \qquad (5.24)$$

When mill prices are constrained by the reservation price, the critical discount factor above which firms individually gain from discriminatory pricing is lower when the market is SNC than when it is SC. By the same argument as in n. 16, we have $\partial \kappa_3^{\bullet} / \partial \hat{v} > 0$ and $\partial \kappa_3^{\bullet} / \partial \Lambda > 0$, implying that when mill prices are constrained by the reservation price, firms individually are more likely to gain from discriminatory pricing if the market is 'small', the reservation price is 'low' and/or firms' set-up costs are 'high'.

Finally, we can show that for firms in the aggregate to gain from discriminatory pricing the lower limit on κ is:

$$\begin{cases} \kappa_4^{SC} = 0.707\hat{v}\sqrt{\Lambda} - 0.104\Lambda - 0.207 \\ \kappa_4^{SNC} = 0.354\hat{v}\sqrt{\Lambda} + 0.138\Lambda - 0.433 \end{cases} \Rightarrow \kappa_4^{SC} > \kappa_4^{SNC}$$

$$(5.25)$$

When mill prices are constrained by the reservation price, the critical discount factor above which firms will gain from discriminatory pricing is lower when the market is SNC than when it is SC. Once again, we have $\partial \kappa_4^{\bullet} / \partial \hat{v} > 0$ and $\partial \kappa_4^{\bullet} / \partial \Lambda > 0$, implying that *when mill prices are constrained by the reservation price, firms in the aggregate are more likely to gain from discriminatory pricing if the market is 'small', the reservation price is 'low' and/or firms' set-up costs are 'high'.*

These results take us back more nearly to those presented in Norman and Thisse (1996) for the one-shot price subgame. When mill prices are constrained by the consumer reservation price, there will be a degree of price flexibility above which consumers will lose and producers will ben-efit from discriminatory pricing. The degree of price flexibility necessary

---

[16] It must be the case that $v \geq \Lambda/n$ and we know from (5.20a) that $n = \sqrt{(\Lambda/\eta f)}$ where $\eta \geq 1$. It follows that $v/\sqrt{f} > \sqrt{\Lambda}$.

for this to be the case is lower if the market is SNC than if it is SC, reflecting the stronger entry-deterring nature of spatial non-contestability. We are also brought back to our question in the introduction of whether there is a potential role for the regulatory authorities in influencing the degree of price flexibility. Equations (5.17) and (5.19) indicate that, no matter the allowable pricing policy, prices can be expected to be higher the more flexible are firms' pricing decisions, since a high degree of price flexibility translates to a high discount factor. We have shown that when the consumer reservation price does not impose an effective constraint on firms, consumers always benefit from price deregulation. We now see that these benefits will be even greater if price flexibility can be reduced. When the consumer reservation price does impose an effective constraint, our analysis indicates that consumers will not gain from price deregulation, particularly in more concentrated markets, unless the degree of price flexibility is sufficiently low, where the definition of 'sufficient' can be implied from our formal analysis.

It would appear, therefore, that there are, indeed, consumer benefits to be had if price deregulation is accompanied by policies that reduce price flexibility, perhaps by the regulator imposing some type of minimum period within which prices cannot be changed. The intuition behind this is familiar from the Folk Theorem. Low price flexibility reduces the effectiveness of the punishment phase that sustains the tacitly collusive prices above the one-shot Bertrand–Nash level and so lowers the maximum sustainable prices.

6   Conclusions

In this chapter we have extended our earlier analysis of the relative merits of soft and tough price regimes to the situation in which post-entry price equilibria reflect the repeated nature of the post-entry price subgame. We derive welfare conclusions that contrast reasonably sharply with our one-shot analysis. If the constraint implicit in the consumer reservation price is non-binding then aggregate consumer surplus is greater and aggregate profits are lower with discriminatory pricing than with mill pricing no matter the degree of spatial contestability of the market. In addition, provided that price decisions are sufficiently flexible ($\delta > 0.601$) *every* consumer will benefit from price discrimination. The entry-deterring effect of discriminatory pricing is more than offset by its pro-competitive effect.

The reason for this contrast lies in the very different constraints the two pricing policies impose on firms' abilities to raise their prices above the Bertrand–Nash prices. Such constraints exist since any set of tacitly agreed prices must be sensitive to the temptation each firm has to cheat on these prices and so must be supported by some credible punishment strategy in the event that cheating occurs. The punishment strategy on which we have focused in this chapter is the grim trigger strategy in which, if deviation occurs, firms move to the one-shot Bertrand–Nash prices forever. Given the relatively aggressive entry process we have proposed, we know from our previous analysis that at these prices firms individually and in the aggregate earn at least as great profits with discriminatory pricing as with mill pricing. With a mill pricing policy any attempt by one firm to undercut its rivals requires that the firm also offers the lower prices to all of its existing customers. There is no such requirement with discriminatory pricing, as a result of which the gains from cheating are greater with discriminatory pricing than with mill pricing. This combination of weaker punishment of and greater gains to cheating with a discriminatory pricing policy leads to the consumer gains and producer losses we have noted.

If our analysis were to stop here it would appear that we could be much more sanguine about the benefits of deregulation of firms' pricing policies even if this were to affect market structure in the ways we have suggested. Our analysis has also shown, however, that the consumer reservation price has an important part to play in determining the welfare properties of alternative pricing policies. If the reservation price effectively constrains mill prices then there exists a degree of price flexibility above which our welfare conclusions are reversed, with firms gaining and consumers losing from discriminatory pricing. The degree of price flexibility above which this will apply is greater when the market is SNC; when market size is small; when the consumer reservation price is low; and when firms' set-up costs are high.

Each of these conditions implies that there are less likely to be benefits to consumers from price deregulation in markets already characterised by high levels of market concentration. They further imply a role for the regulatory authorities that has, so far as we are aware, not been considered in the literature, primarily because most of the pre-existing analysis is static rather than dynamic. We have shown that the discount factor has a crucial role to play in determining the benefits that consumers are likely to derive from price deregulation. Simply put, consumers are likely to gain more from price deregulation if the discount factor is low. The discount factor is itself determined by the (continuous) rate of time discount, which is generally outside the control of the regulatory authorities, and the speed with which firms can react to deviation from the tacit agreed prices, which is conceivably *within* the control of the authorities. Our analysis indicates that price deregulation is more likely to be successful if it is accompanied by policies that impose a period over which prices cannot be changed. Interestingly, this is especially likely to be the case in concentrated markets and these are the markets in which response speeds might be expected to be greatest.

6 Mathematical appendix

Proof of Proposition 1:

(a) Assume that firms have tacitly agreed on the mill price m/n, where $m > 1$. Assume further that a price-cutting firm charges a price $(m - j)/n$ that just undercuts $j > 1$ neighbouring firms. This gives a market radius to the price-cutting firm of $j/n + 1/2n$ and instantaneous gross profit of:

$$\pi^c = (m - j)(2j + 1)/n^2 \tag{5A.1}$$

Instantaneous gross profit with the agreed mill price m/n is:

$$\pi^a = m/n^2 \tag{5A.2}$$

The Bertrand–Nash equilibrium mill price is $1/n$ with instantaneous gross profit

$$\pi^b = 1/n^2 \tag{5A.3}$$

For such price-cutting to be unprofitable we require that:

$$\pi^a - \delta\pi^b \geq (1 - \delta)/\pi^c$$

Solving for m gives the upper bound on the tacitly agreed price:

$$\frac{\tilde{m}(\delta, j)}{n} = \frac{\delta(1 + j + 2j^2) - j(1 + 2j)}{\delta(1 + 2j) - 2j} \cdot \frac{1}{n} \tag{5A.4}$$

By a similar analysis, if the price-cutting firm just undercuts $j + 1$ neighbours the upper bound on the mill price is:

$$\frac{\tilde{m}(\delta, j + 1)}{n} = \frac{\delta(4 + 5j + 2j^2) - (j + 1)(3 + 2j)}{\delta(3 + 2j) - 2(j + 1)} \cdot \frac{1}{n} \tag{5A.5}$$

These upper bounds are equal when $\delta(j) = 4j(j + 1)/(1 + 8j + 4j^2)$. Thus the upper bound on the mill price is $\tilde{m}(\delta, j)/n$ for $\delta \in [\delta(j - 1), \delta(j))$ for the price-cutting firm to wish just to undercut exactly j neighbours to each side. Inverting $\delta(j)$ gives $h(\delta)$ in the text.

(b) We now check that the price-cutting firm would not prefer an interior solution in which it undercuts j neighbours to each side and takes only part of the market of the $(j + 1)$th neighbours.

If the tacitly agreed mill price is $\tilde{m}(\delta, j)/n$ and the price-cutting firm charges a price c/n it gets market radius $(1 + \tilde{m}(\delta, j) + j - c)/2n$

and earns instantaneous gross profit of $c(1 + \tilde{m}(\delta, j) + j - c)/n$ giving the optimal price:

$$\frac{c(\delta, j)}{n} = \frac{1 + \tilde{m}(\delta, j) + j}{2n} \tag{5A.6}$$

We need merely check that $(c(\delta, j) + j)/n \geq m(\delta, j)/n$. Substituting from (5A.5) and simplifying gives:

$$\Delta = c(\delta, j) + j - \tilde{m}(\delta, j) = \frac{j(4\delta(j + 1) - (4j + 1))}{2(\delta(2j + 1) - 2j)} \tag{5A.7}$$

Differentiating Δ with respect to δ gives:

$$\frac{\partial \Delta}{\partial \delta} = \frac{(1 - 2j)j}{2(\delta(2j + 1) - 2j)^2} < 0 \text{ for } j \geq 1 \tag{5A.8}$$

Thus we need only evaluate Δ at $\delta(j)$. This gives:

$$\Delta|_{\delta = \delta(j)} = \frac{2j - 1}{4} > 0 \tag{5A.9}$$

It follows that the corner solution (5A.5) is always the preferred method for a price-cutting firm. ∎

Proof of Proposition 2: Assume that firms have tacitly agreed on a uniform delivered price u, where $u \geq 1/n$. A price-cutting firm will just undercut this price, giving it a market radius of u/n and instantaneous gross profit:

$$\pi^c = 2 \int_{r=0}^{u/n} \left(\frac{u}{n} - r\right) dr = u^2/n^2 \tag{5A.10}$$

Instantaneous gross profit with the agreed uniform delivered price is:

$$\pi^a = 2 \int_{r=0}^{u/n} \left(\frac{u}{n} - r\right) dr = (4u - 1)/4n^2 \tag{5A.11}$$

The Bertrand–Nash equilibrium prices give instantaneous gross profits of:

$$\pi^b = 1/2n^2 \tag{5A.12}$$

For price-cutting to be unprofitable we require that:

$$\pi^a - \delta\pi^b \geq (1 - \delta)\pi^c$$

Solving for u/n gives the upper bound on the tacitly agreed uniform delivered price:

$$\frac{\tilde{u}(\delta)}{n} = \frac{1 + \sqrt{\delta(2\delta - 1)}}{2(1 - \delta)} \cdot \frac{1}{n} \tag{5A.13}$$

The upper limit on this price is, of course, the consumer reservation price v. ∎

Proof of Proposition 3:

(i) For a given n and provided that the reservation price is not binding, the difference between the tacitly agreed mill and uniform delivered prices is:

$$\Delta_1 = \frac{\delta\left(1 + j|[\delta]| + 2j|[\delta]|^2\right) - j|[\delta]|(1 + 2j|[\delta]|)}{\delta(1 + 2j|[\delta]|) - 2j|[\delta]|} \cdot \frac{1}{n}$$

$$- \frac{1 + \sqrt{\delta(2\delta - 1)}}{2(1 - \delta)} \cdot \frac{1}{n} \tag{5A.14}$$

For a given n this is a function solely of the discount factor δ and so can be examined numerically. This examination confirms that $\Delta_1 > 0$ as required.

(ii) For a given n and provided that the reservation price is not binding, the difference between the maximum delivered mill price with n firms and the uniform delivered price with $n/2$ firms is:

$$\Delta_2 = \frac{\delta\left(1 + j|[\delta]| + 2j|[\delta]|^2\right) - j|[\delta]|(1 + 2j|[\delta]|)}{\delta(1 + 2j|[\delta]|) - 2j|[\delta]|} \cdot \frac{1}{n}$$

$$+ \frac{1}{2n} - \frac{1 + \sqrt{\delta(2\delta - 1)}}{2(1 - \delta)} \cdot \frac{2}{n}. \tag{5A.15}$$

For a given n this is a function solely of the discount factor δ and so can be examined numerically. This confirms that $\Delta_2 \geq 0$ but that $\Delta_2 = 0$ for exactly one value of δ for each value of $j|[\delta]|$. It follows that for at least some consumers to prefer mill pricing there will have to be fewer than $n/2$ firms with uniform delivered pricing.

Proof of (5.24) and (5.25): If the mill price is constrained to $v - \Lambda/2n$ then individual firm and aggregate profit are respectively:

$$\begin{cases} \pi_f = \Lambda v/n_f - f - \Lambda^2/2n_f^2 \\ \Pi_f = \Lambda v - f \cdot n_f - \Lambda^2/2n_f \end{cases} \tag{5A.16}$$

where from (5.20a) we know that:

$$n_f = \sqrt{\Lambda/\alpha f} \tag{5A.17}$$

with $\alpha = 1$ or $3/(2(2+\sqrt{3}))$. Substituting in (5A.16) gives:

$$\begin{cases} \pi_f = \dfrac{f}{2}\left(2\hat{v}\sqrt{\alpha\Lambda} - \alpha\Lambda - 2\right) \\ \Pi_f = \dfrac{\sqrt{\Lambda f}}{2\sqrt{\alpha}}\left(2\hat{v}\sqrt{\alpha\Lambda} - \alpha\Lambda - 2\right) \end{cases} \qquad (5A.18)$$

Assume that the uniform delivered price is u/n_d. Then individual firm and aggregate profit with uniform delivered pricing are:

$$\begin{cases} \pi_d = \Lambda u/n_d^2 - f - \Lambda^2/4n_d^2 \\ \Pi_d = \Lambda u/n_d - f \cdot n_d - \Lambda^2/4n_d \end{cases} \qquad (5A.19)$$

and we know that:

$$n_d = \sqrt{\Lambda/\beta f} \qquad (5A.20)$$

where $\beta = 2$ or 8. Substituting in (5A.19) gives:

$$\begin{cases} \pi_d = \dfrac{f}{4}(4\beta u - \beta\Lambda - 4) \\ \Pi_d = \dfrac{\sqrt{\Lambda f}}{4\sqrt{\beta}}(4\beta u - \beta\Lambda - 4) \end{cases} \qquad (5A.21)$$

Solving $\pi_d \geq \pi_f$ and $\Pi_d \geq \Pi_f$ for u gives the critical values of κ above which $\pi_d \geq \pi_f$ and $\Pi_d \geq \Pi_f$. Substituting for α and β in these equations gives (5.24) and (5.25).   ■

Bibliography

Armstrong, M. and J. Vickers (1993) Price discrimination, competition and regulation, *Journal of Industrial Economics*, 41, pp. 335–59

d'Aspremont, C. and M. Motta (2000) Tougher price competition or lower concentration: a trade-off for anti-trust authorities? (chapter 6 in this volume)

Friedman, J.W. (1997) A guided tour of the Folk Theorem (chapter 3 in this volume)

Gee, J.M.A. (1976) A model of location and industrial efficiency with free entry, *Quarterly Journal of Economics*, 90, pp. 557–74

Kühn, K.U. (1993) Protecting the freedom to compete: an overview of German competition policy, mimeo

Lederer, P.J. and A.P. Hurter (1986) Competition of firms: discriminatory prices and locations, *Econometrica*, 54, pp. 623–40

MacLeod, W.B., G. Norman and J.-F. Thisse (1987) Competition, tacit collusion and free entry, *Economic Journal*, 385, pp. 189–98

(1988) Price discrimination and equilibrium in monopolistic competition, *International Journal of Industrial Organization*, 6, pp. 429–46

Norman, G. (1983) Spatial pricing with differentiated products, *Quarterly Journal of Economics*, 98, pp. 291–330

Norman, G. and J.-F. Thisse (1996) Product variety and welfare under tough and soft pricing regimes, *Economic Journal*, 106, pp. 76–91

Phlips, L. (1995) *Competition Policy: A Game-Theoretic Perspective*, Cambridge: Cambridge University Press

Salop, S.C. (1979) Monopolistic competition with outside goods, *Bell Journal of Economics*, 10, pp. 141–56

Selten, R. (1984) Are cartel laws bad for business?, in H. Hauptmann, W. Krelle and K.C. Mosler (eds.), *Operations Research and Economic Theory*, Berlin: Springer Verlag

Tharakan, P.K.M. (1991) The political economy of anti-dumping undertakings in the European Communities, *European Economic Review*, 35, pp. 1341–59

Thisse, J.-F. and X. Vives (1988) On the strategic choice of spatial price policy, *American Economic Review*, 78, pp. 122–37

Williamson O.E. (1968) Economies as an antitrust defense: the welfare trade-offs, *American Economic Review*, 58, pp. 18–36

6 Tougher price competition or lower concentration: a trade-off for anti-trust authorities?

Claude d'Aspremont and Massimo Motta

1 Introduction

Looking at the history of anti-trust laws, their first and possibly main objective seems to have been the forbidding of price collusion – that is, to prevent different sellers to agree in fixing the price of their product. For instance, the Sherman Act (1890) was, in its early period, generally interpreted as a law against cartels and moreover 'in the enforcement of the Sherman Act against cartels, emphasis has been placed upon establishing the fact of an agreement pertaining to price' (Posner, 1977, p. 213). The application of the Act to mergers came only later and was subject to controversy. Judges[1] did not immediately use the argument that, by consolidation into a single-firm, cartel members could evade the law. As a result, following the Sherman Act, there was a sharp increase in the number of mergers in United States industry at the end of the nineteenth century as documented, among others, by Bittlingmayer (1985). More recently a similar evolution was observed in the European Community legislation. For years it had been discussed whether articles 85 and 86 of the Rome Treaty (1957), could have been directly applied to mergers and acquisitions. It was only in 1989 that a new regulation[2] on such cases

Thanks are due to Luis Cabral, Isabel Grilo and Jean-Pierre Ponssard for helpful discussions. A first-version of this chapter was presented in the workshop on 'Competition and Regulation in Concentrated Industries', CORE (May 1993) and at the 'Jornadas de Economia Industrial', Madrid (September 1993). This chapter presents research results of the Belgian programme on inter-university poles of attraction initiated by the Belgian state, Prime Minister's Office, Science Policy Programming. The scientific responsibility is assumed by its authors.

[1] As mentioned by Posner (1977), in the *Northern Securities* case, the judge's position that the Sherman Act (1890) was inapplicable to mergers was rejected by a majority of the Supreme Court.
[2] Council of the European Communities, Council Regulation EES 89, 'On the Control of Concentration between Undertakings' (21 December 1989).

was adopted 'in the 1992 perspective and given the corresponding wave of mergers and takeovers'.[3]

In both cases, it is only after observing that forbidding price agreements leads to higher concentration in industries that the legislator tries to limit such adverse effect by restricting mergers and acquisitions. This adverse effect is even more dramatic if one takes into account the fact that after a merger there is a smaller number of firms in the industry, and this circumstance makes it more likely for collusion to arise.

One might then argue whether tough anti-trust law and anti-trust enforcement might provoke an undesirable increase in concentration. Such an increase in concentration may result from voluntary consolidation by firms to avoid the law, as already mentioned. It may also result from involuntary exits or bankruptcies, owing to excessive price competition.[4] An example is the Resale Prices Act (1964) in the United Kingdom which prohibited the practice of resale price maintenance (RPM) and contributed to the decline of a great number of independent food retailers.[5] Indeed such a danger has been sometimes officially recognised, as it was for some industries in the United States by the National Recovery Administration's Code of Fair Competition during the 1930s (until such arrangements were declared unconstitutional).

This is an argument dear to Louis Phlips, who has warned us about the possible adverse effect of tough competition and too low profitability for producers. In Phlips (1998, p. 24), he says, for instance, that 'there is probably general agreement that anti-trust authorities should do what is necessary to get prices down towards marginal cost. But how far should they go down? Until they are equal to marginal cost?'

The purpose of this chapter is to analyse whether tougher price competition might have an overall negative effect on welfare. In general, there exists the following trade-off. On the one hand, tougher price competition improves allocative efficiency for any given industrial structure. On the other hand, it might cause a reduction in the number of firms operating in the industry, which in turn has a negative effect on welfare. *A priori*, it is unclear whether the first effect always outweighs the second, so that tougher price competition would always be beneficial. In this chapter we show that under certain (admittedly strong) conditions, intermediate degrees of price competition might be optimal. Before misinterpreting our results, however, we should emphasise that pure collusion, where the joint profit maximising price is chosen by a group

---

[3] See Jacquemin (1990).
[4] See Sutton (1991) and in particular his study of the United States salt industry.
[5] See Everton (1993).

of firms, leaves too little room for competition, thus causing unambiguously total welfare losses. Under no circumstance do we find that collusion increases welfare with respect to any other benchmark of product market competition. The way in which we deal with the idea that softer price competition *might* avoid an increase in concentration and therefore *might* increase welfare is to compare welfare under Cournot (i.e. quantity) competition and under Bertrand (i.e. price) competition. That Cournot competition implies some form of price coordination, and therefore softer price competition, is clear from a theoretical point of view. For instance, in d'Aspremont, Dos Santos Ferreira and Gérard-Varet (1991a), it is shown that Cournot competition can be viewed as competition in prices and in quantities, where price competition is coordinated by a 'pricing scheme', establishing the market price, but under the influence of the prices announced by the individual firms. The problem is to recognise Cournot competition in practice. The main feature of Cournot competition is not that firms choose strategically their own quantities, but that they take the total quantities produced by the others in the industry as given, assuming that they are ready to adjust their prices to keep their market shares. Then, facing a residual demand, it does not really matter for a firm whether the price or the quantity is the main strategic variable (as in a pure monopoly). We have thus a sharing of the market which is implemented, and each firm respects the market shares of the others (taking for granted that if a firm's market share is threatened this firm will adjust its price). In this perspective it is interesting to quote, as an example, the use by an industry of what has been called 'facilitating practices'. These are contractual clauses or conventions, or norms of conduct, in an industry to implement coordination of prices. Examples are the 'meet-or-release clause' (whereby a firm should meet the price of a competitor or release its customer), the 'most-favoured customer clause' (whereby a firm cannot discriminate a customer with respect to other customers) and the 'advance-notice' of price changes. Combining these with the possibility of rebates, Holt and Scheffman (1987) showed that such practices turn out to be of the kind implied by Cournot competition in an industry. The possibility of rebates is crucial, because it explains why a firm can anticipate that its competitor will keep its own customers.[6]

We will contrast Cournot competition with Bertrand competition, where competition in prices is more severe. As the theory shows, this kind of competition leads in general to lower prices or creates more problems for the existence of an equilibrium. Our story is simple. Imposing

---

[6] Without the possibility of rebates, and in a symmetric oligopoly, one would get the pure collusion solution. See Salop (1986); Kalai and Satterthwaite (1986).

Bertrand competition in an industry, instead of allowing 'fair competition' in the Cournot sense, might be destructive in the sense of forcing some firms to exit and thereby increasing concentration. Indeed, this increase of concentration might be very damaging to consumers, thus having a detrimental effect on global welfare.[7] To give a first example, consider an homogeneous good industry composed of two firms facing the demand function $q = S(1 - p)$, where q and p denote, respectively, total quantity and the market price, and where S measures the 'size' of the market. Suppose the present situation in the industry to be of the Cournot type, with (short-run) profits at the Cournot equilibrium (each firm selling a quantity $\frac{S}{3}$ at a price equal to $\frac{1}{3}$) sufficient to cover some (not too high) fixed costs $K > 0$. Imagine now that regulation against price agreements forces the firms into Bertrand competition. Short-run profits are driven down to zero, so that only one firm can survive in the long run, and this single firm is only selling the quantity $\frac{S}{2}$ at the price $\frac{1}{2}$. Even more, computing the respective producers' surpluses ($\frac{2S}{9} - 2K$ in the Cournot case and $\frac{S}{4} - K$ in the monopoly case) and the consumers' surplus ($\frac{2S}{9}$ and $\frac{S}{8}$, respectively), total welfare is decreased. Of course, this example is extreme, since starting with two firms, we end up with a monopoly. Our purpose is to generalise this example to a larger oligopoly, where in addition product differentiation owing to differences in location also plays a role. This last feature is important because, with spatial differentiation, some sort of price coordination is unavoidable: each firm has to adopt a 'pricing policy' to take into account transportation costs (whether pure discrimination or FOB pricing or 'basing-point' pricing or anything else). Coordination cannot be avoided, and the problem becomes more a question of degree. How much coordination should be tolerated?

In section 2 we present our example. In section 3 we look for equilibrium in both the Cournot and Bertrand cases and, in section 4, we make welfare comparisons; section 5 concludes.

2 The model

We consider an industry with a maximum number of three firms which, in the Launhardt/Hotelling tradition,[8] are supposed to be located on the real-line. In the long run the number of firms will depend on market and cost

---

[7] The idea that less intense competition, in the form of cooperative agreements on R&D in the line of d'Aspremont and Jacquemin (1988), allows for a higher number of firms in the industry, having possible desirable effects on welfare, has been proposed by Motta (1992). The idea that collusion may lead to lower concentration and lower profits is treated in Selten (1984).

[8] See Hotelling (1929) or, less well known, Launhardt (1885).

conditions, but also on the type of pricing arrangement. For simplicity we assume that locations are fixed (owing, for example, to the locations of mineral resources) and limit ourselves to the two-firm and the three-firm cases, firms A and B being installed at point 0 and point 1, respectively, with (or without) an intermediate firm C at point $(1/2)$. Each firm is supposed to produce the same homogeneous good under the same cost conditions. Variable production costs are given by the function $-\frac{1}{2}q^2$ and fixed costs by $K > 0$. Hence if a firm j, sells a quantity q_j at a price p_j, its profit is:

$$\pi_j = p_j q_j - \frac{1}{2}q_j^2 - K$$

Later we will denote $\Pi_j = p_j q_j - \frac{1}{2}q_j^2$, the profit when fixed costs are sunk. Potential consumers are uniformly distributed on the real-line (or at least on an interval much larger than [0, 1] and containing it) and each buys one unit of the good if the price is less than a reservation price $S > 0$. The pricing policy used by each firm is *FOB mill pricing*, according to which a consumer buying from firm $j(j = A, B$ or C) pays j's mill price p_j plus a transportation cost of t per unit of distance. Of course, each consumer will choose to buy from the firm proposing the lowest price at delivery, if this is lower than his reservation price S.

For each vector of mill prices p, each firm, in its location, can serve two sides of the market, given by the potential customers on its right and the potential customers on its left. Likewise each firm i, on each side, can either enjoy a position of (local) monopoly, having its demand D_i^0 on this side depend only on its own price and on the reservation price S, i.e.:

$$D_i^0(p) = \frac{S - p_i}{t} \tag{6.1}$$

or it can share this side of the market with another firm j (the two market areas overlapping), and have its demand $D_i^j(p)$ depend on their distance, say Δ_{ij}, and on the difference between the two prices, i.e.:

$$D_i^j(p) = \frac{1}{2}\left(\Delta_{ij} + \frac{p_j - p_i}{t}\right) \tag{6.2}$$

Figure 6.1 illustrates these two possibilities. To compute $D_i^0(p)$ and $D_i^j(p)$ one has simply to solve in x the respective two equations:

$$p_i + tx = S$$
$$p_i + tx = p_j + t(\Delta_{ij} - x)$$

Note that $D_i^j(p)$ should be interpreted as a demand addressed to firm i if and only if $0 < D_i^j(p) < \Delta_{ij}$. At $D_i^j(p) = 0$ (or equivalently if

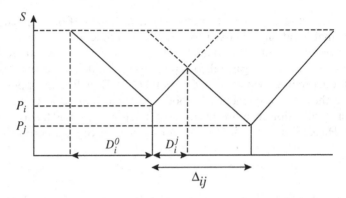

Figure 6.1   Market areas

$p_j + t\Delta_{ij} = p_i$) there is a discontinuity, since then all the remaining potential customers of firm i are indifferent whether to go to firm j. For $D_i^j(p) < 0$ firm j undercuts ($p_j + t\Delta_{ij} < p_i$) the price of firm i and all customers prefer to go to firm j. A similar reasoning applies to $D_i^j(p) \geq \Delta_{ij}$ (this is equivalent to $D_j^i(p) \leq 0$). We should also restrict our considerations to $D_i^0(p) \geq 0$.

Knowing how demand is shared between two adjacent firms we can now easily derive the complete demand schedule for both the two-firm and the three-firm cases. Indeed, for $i = A$, B and $j \neq i$, the total demand to firm i can be defined (with $p = (p_A, p_B)$ in the two-firm case and $p = (p_A, p_B, p_C)$ in the three-firm case) by the following three expressions. The first refers to the case where firm i has zero demand on both sides, the second refers to the case where it has a local monopoly on both sides and the third to the case of local monopoly on one side and overlapping of market areas on the other:

$$D_i(p) = 0 \quad \text{if } p_i > S \text{ or } p_i > p_j + t\Delta_{ij}, \text{ for some } j \neq i \qquad (6.3)$$

$$= 2D_i^0(p), \quad \text{if } D_i^j(p) > 0, p_i + tD_i^j(p) \geq S \text{ or } p_j > p_i + t\Delta_{ij}$$
$$\text{for all } j \neq i \qquad (6.4)$$

$$= D_i^0(p) + D_i^j(p), \quad \text{if } p_i + tD_i^j(p) < S \text{ and } 0 < D_i^j(p) < \Delta_{ij}$$
$$(6.5)$$

This definition of the demand function applies to both firms A and B ($i, j = A$ or B), in the two-firm case, or in the three-firm case whenever firm C price is too high: $p_C > p_j + t\Delta_{jC} (= p_j + \frac{t}{2})$, for $j = A$ or B. Otherwise, one should put $j = C$ in (6.3) and define in addition the demand schedule of firm

C. The following expressions (6.3'), (6.4') and (6.5') correspond to the cases (6.3), (6.4) and (6.5) already described. The only new case is given by (6.6), where we have overlapping market areas on both sides of the middle firm:

$$D_C(p) = 0, \quad \text{if } p_C > S \text{ or } p_C > p_j + t\Delta_{Cj}, \text{ for some } j \neq C \qquad (6.3')$$

$$= 2D_C^0(p), \quad \text{if } D_C^j(p) > 0, p_C + tD_C^j(p) \geq S \text{ or } p_j > p_C + t\Delta_{Cj}$$

$$\text{for all } j \neq C \qquad (6.4')$$

$$= D_C^A(p) + D_C^B(p), \quad \text{if } p_C + tD_C^i(p) < S \text{ and } 0 < D_C^i(p) < \Delta_{Ci},$$

$$\text{for } i = A, B \qquad (6.6)$$

$$= D_C^0(p) + D_C^j(p), \quad \text{otherwise for } j = A \text{ or } B \qquad (6.5')$$

Notice that in the above conditions $\Delta_{Ci} = \Delta_{jC} = \frac{1}{2}$ and $\Delta_{ij} = 1$ for $i, j = A, B$. Notice also that we have left undetermined here the demand functions at each point of discontinuity – namely, for each pair (i, j) at the point p where $D_i^j(p) = 0$ (or $D_j^i(p) = \Delta_{ij}$). This will be done, when required, along the way.

The knowledge of the demand schedules for each firm is not sufficient to specify the profit functions completely. We need to establish what type of competition is taking place among the firms. In that respect, beyond the hypothesis that all the firms agree to adopt the mill pricing policy, there might be additional coordination. Of course the highest degree of price coordination is pure collusion where the FOB–mill pricing scheme is chosen so as to maximise some joint profit (with one, two or three firms effectively producing) which may have to be shared among firms. However we shall limit ourselves to two 'non-collusive' pricing schemes, involving no sharing of profit, the first implying more coordination than the second, and leading to two different types of equilibrium.

The first is an equilibrium of the Cournot type.[9] As mentioned in the introduction, the main feature of Cournot competition is that, whenever a firm fixes its price (and its production), it takes as given the quantities to be sold by the other firms. This implies a need for the other firms to adjust their prices (using, for instance, various kinds of discounts or rebates) in order to keep their customers. In the pure homogeneous case, with a simple market price, it is possible and convenient to use the inverse total demand function.

---

[9] Or, more precisely, of the Cournot–Walras type in the sense of Gabszewicz and Vial (1972).

In the present case of product differentiation owing to different locations, there is no total demand function to invert, but a system of demand functions given by the definition above. Formally a 'Cournot equilibrium' is defined as a price vector p^c and a quantity vector q^c such that, for each firm i, the profit $\pi_i^c = p_i^c q_i^c - \frac{1}{2}(q_i^c)^2 - K$ is the maximum attainable under the constraints: $p \geq 0$, $0 \leq q_i \leq D_i(p)$, and $D_j(p) = q_j^c$, for all $j \neq i$. Two remarks are in order. On the one hand, for a firm, to undercut the mill price of another firm is not effective: to keep its market share this other firm would indeed immediately adjust its own mill price. This means we can exclude the cases where firm i obtains the whole market[10] of firm j through undercutting: $p_j > p_i + t\Delta_{ij}$. On the other hand, when two adjacent firms are in a situation of local monopolies with respect to each other (their market areas being disjoint), each can change its own price (locally) without affecting the market share of the other. So the cases where inverting of the demand system could still be considered are when the market areas overlap: a firm should lower its price to sell more, but the other firm would adjust its own price to keep its market share unchanged.

The second type of equilibrium we shall use introduces less coordination: it is of the Bertrand/Hotelling type. Any firm takes as given the prices announced by the other firms. Hence any firm may consider the possibility of undercutting the price of some other firm in order to capture its whole market. Such behaviour increases the likelihood of a price war and makes the existence of an equilibrium more problematic.[11] Formally a 'Bertrand equilibrium' is defined as a price vector p^b and a quantity vector q^b such that, for any firm i, the profit $\pi_i^b = p_i^b q_i^b - \frac{1}{2}(q_i^b)^2 - K$ is the maximum attainable under the constraints: $p_i \geq 0$ and $0 \leq q_i \leq D_i(p_i, p_{-i}^b)$, where p_{-i} denotes the $(n-1)$ vector $(p_j)_{j \neq i}$.

In section 3 we shall determine, for our example, values of the parameters S and t for which a Cournot equilibrium exists, when there are three firms, and a Bertrand equilibrium exists, when there are two or three firms already installed and fixed costs are considered as sunk. However, considering the preliminary stage where firms decide to enter or not in the industry, there will be values of the fixed cost K such that all three firms would enter under Cournot competition, but only the two extreme firms (A and B) under Bertrand competition.[12]

---

[10] As observed by Eaton and Lipsey (1989), 'the undercutting temptation is removed when competition is in quantities'.

[11] See d'Aspremont, Gabszewicz and Thisse (1979).

[12] Since the conditions binding the parameters will be restated in section 4, devoted to the welfare implications of such a situation, the computations in the following can be skipped without lost of continuity.

3 Equilibrium computations

Three-firm Cournot equilibrium

Although there are different regimes of equilibria, it is enough for our purpose to study Cournot equilibrium with the three market areas overlapping (strictly): $p_i < p_i + tD_i^j(p) < S$, for $i = A, B$ and $j = C$, as well as for $i = C$ and $j = A, B$ (see (6.5) and (6.6) above). Also, without loss of generality, we will adopt the normalisation $t = 1$. The demand system becomes (using (6.1), (6.2), (6.5) and (6.6)):

$$q_i = (S - p_i) + \left(\frac{1}{4} + \frac{p_C - p_i}{2} \right) = S + \frac{1}{4} + \frac{1}{2}p_C - \frac{3}{2}p_i \quad i = A, B$$

$$q_C = \left(\frac{1}{4} + \frac{p_A - p_C}{2} \right) + \left(\frac{1}{4} + \frac{p_B - p_C}{2} \right)$$

$$= \frac{1}{2} + \frac{1}{2}(p_A + p_B) - p_C \tag{6.7}$$

Inverting this system we get:

$$p_i = S + \frac{1}{2} - \frac{5}{6}q_i - \frac{1}{6}q_j - \frac{1}{2}q_C \quad i,j = A, B; \ i \neq j$$

$$p_C = S + 1 - \frac{1}{2}(q_i + q_j + 3q_C) \quad i,j = A, B; \ i \neq j \tag{6.8}$$

Computing the gross profit functions $\Pi_i = p_i q_i - \frac{1}{2}q_i^2$, for $i = A, B$ and C, and solving the system of first-order conditions, we get the following solution:

$$q_A^c = q_B^c = \frac{3(3 + 7S)}{65}; \qquad q_C^c = \frac{14 + 11S}{65}$$

$$p_A^c = p_B^c = \frac{11(3 + 7S)}{130}; \qquad p_C^c = \frac{14 + 11S}{26} \tag{6.9}$$

$$\Pi_A^c = \Pi_B^c = \frac{12(3 + 7S)^2}{4225}; \qquad \Pi_C^c = \frac{2(14 + 11S)^2}{4225}$$

Of course we need that profits, net of fixed costs, π_i^c, be positive: for $i = A, B, C$:

$$\min_i \{\Pi_i^c\} > K > 0 \tag{6.10}$$

For this to be a solution we have first to check that strict overlapping is respected: $p_i^c < p_i^c + \frac{1}{4} + \frac{1}{2}(p_j^c - p_i^c) < S$ for $i = A, B$ and $j = C$, and for $i = C$ and $j = A, B$. It may be verified that these conditions hold if:

$$S > \frac{21}{26} \tag{6.11}$$

In addition, for the candidate solution to be a Cournot equilibrium, we have to exclude the possibility for any firm i to gain more by selecting a higher production level, while all prices adjust so that $p_i = p_j - \Delta_{ij}$ for some $j \neq i$, and the quantities of the other firms are maintained at the same level ($q_j = q_j^c$ for all $j \neq i$). Take the case of firm C and $p_C = p_j - \frac{1}{2}$ for $j = A, B$. The demand function it faces is given by (whenever positive):

$$q_C = 2(S - p_C) - q_A^c - q_B^c$$

or

$$p_C = S - \frac{1}{2}(q_A^c + q_B^c) - \frac{1}{2}q_C$$

Maximising its profit $\Pi_C = p_C q_C - \frac{1}{2}q_C^2$ one gets the optimal deviation (q_C', p_C') and the optimal profit accordingly:

$$\Pi_C' = \frac{(44S - 9)^2}{16900}$$

Comparing Π_C' with Π_C^c we get a no-deviation sufficient condition:

$$S < 3.771 \tag{6.12}$$

Consider now the case of an extreme firm (say, firm A) deviating and let it choose $p_A = p_C - \frac{1}{2}$, thus absorbing C's market area, while maintaining an overlapping with B's market area. Then $q_A = S + \frac{1}{2} + \frac{1}{2}p_B - \frac{3}{2}p_A - q_C^c$, where p_B is such that: $S + \frac{1}{2} + \frac{1}{2}p_A - \frac{3}{2}p_B = q_B^c$. These two equations lead to $p_A = S + \frac{1}{2} - \frac{3}{4}q_A - \frac{3}{4}q_C^c - \frac{1}{4}q_B^c$. The quantity q_A' that maximises the deviating profit $\Pi_A = p_A q_A - \frac{1}{2}q_A^2$ is given by: $q_A' = (79 + 206S/650)$. The corresponding profit is $\Pi_A' = (79 + 206S)^2/338,000$ which is never greater than Π_A^c.

It is also easy to exclude that A would be tempted to absorb both B's and C's market areas. Indeed it is enough to compute the pure monopoly quantity $q^m = \frac{S}{2}$, which is the solution to the problem $\max_x[P(x)x - \frac{1}{2}x^2]$ with $x \geq 0$ and $P(x) \equiv S - \frac{1}{2}x$ denoting the inverse demand function, and to impose that the quantity that A can sell under the Cournot hypothesis – namely ($q^m - q_B^c - q_C^c$) is negative. This is the very weak condition:

$$S \leq 46 \tag{6.13}$$

Up to now we have only considered deviations leading to lower prices. We should also analyse deviations where firm i produces less, but sells at a higher price, so that its market area does not overlap any longer with the market area of a competitor. The Cournot hypothesis implies that the other firms also raise their prices in order to keep selling the same quantities. However the vector of adjusted prices should be such that for the deviating firm i, $D_i^j(p) > 0$ and $p_i + D_i^j(p) \geq S$ for all $j \neq i$ (see (6.4) and (6.4')). When i is firm C, such a deviation implies that all three firms are local monopolies, with firms A and B selling their Cournot equilibrium quantities. Then it is easy to compute the maximal quantity firm C can sell in such a deviation. This is $\bar{q}_c = 1 - 2(S - \bar{p})$, where $\bar{p}$ is the price such that $2(S - \bar{p}) = q_A^c = q_B^c$. But such a deviation is excluded as soon as this maximal quantity $\bar{q}_c$ is smaller than $q^m = \frac{S}{2}$, the quantity C would choose to sell as a pure monopoly (indeed, it would then mean that the deviation price has been pushed too far up). This leads to the condition

$$S > \frac{112}{107} \tag{6.14}$$

Suppose now that the firm considering such a deviation (leading to a price high enough to ensure a local monopoly) is an extreme firm, say firm A. Applying the Cournot hypothesis again, the maximal quantity firm A can hope to sell is limited to $\bar{q}_A \equiv 2\left(\frac{1}{2} - \frac{1}{2}q_C^c\right) = (1 - q_C^c)$, since A avoids overlapping the market area of C in the zone between their respective locations. Applying the same argument as above, such a deviation is excluded if $\bar{q}_A < q_m$, that is

$$S > \frac{100}{87} \tag{6.15}$$

Two-firm Bertrand equilibrium

The two-firm Bertrand equilibrium is simpler to compute than the three-firm Cournot equilibrium.[13] There are only three possible regimes: one where S is large enough so that both firms reach the pure monopoly profit, a second regime where they are closer (with adjacent market areas) and have local monopoly profits (i.e. with $q_i = (S - p_i)$, $i = A, B$), and a third regime where their market areas strictly overlap. For brevity's sake, we shall limit our computations to this last regime.

Demand is given by:

$$q_i = (S - p_i) + \left(\frac{1}{2} + \frac{p_j - p_i}{2}\right) \qquad i, j = A, B; \ i \neq j$$

and we can directly maximise the gross profit, $\Pi_i = p_i q_i - \frac{1}{2}q_i^2$, in the price p_i (for $i = A, B$). The solution we get is:

$$p_A^b = p_B^b = \frac{5 + 10S}{16}$$

$$q_A^b = q_B^b = \frac{3(1 + 2S)}{16}$$

$$\Pi_A^b = \Pi_B^b = \frac{21(1 + 2S)^2}{512}$$

---

[13] For a complete description of all the equilibria, see d'Aspremont, Dos Santos Ferreira and Gérard-Varet (1991b).

Again we need a condition on fixed costs:

$$\Pi_i^b \geq K > 0 \tag{6.16}$$

and a condition to ensure strict overlapping:

$$p_i^b < p_i^b + \tfrac{1}{2} + \tfrac{1}{2}(p_j^b - p_i^b) < S, \quad i \neq j$$

Since $p_j^b - p_i^b = 0$, this simply amounts to:

$$S > \frac{13}{6} \tag{6.17}$$

To get an equilibrium in prices we should also exclude any deviation. To exclude a deviation by firm i, choosing a higher price and getting a situation of two local monopolies, it is enough to verify that the maximal quantity i can sell, i.e. $1 - (S - p_B^b)$, is smaller than the pure monopoly quantity $q^m = \tfrac{S}{2}$. We get the condition

$$S > \frac{3}{2} \tag{6.18}$$

To prohibit deviations by a lower price, it should be taken into account that, in contrast to the Cournot approach, a firm i has the possibility to eliminate a competitor j by undercutting its price – that is, by choosing a price $p_i = p_j - 1 - \varepsilon$, for some $\varepsilon > 0$. Choosing ε small enough this leads to a deviation maximal profit

$$\Pi_i' \simeq [S - (p_j^b - 1)](p_j^b - 1) - \frac{1}{2}[S - (p_j^b - 1)]^2$$

$$= \frac{12S^2 - 44S - 121}{64}$$

which should be less than Π_i^b, or

$$S < 38 \tag{6.19}$$

But this constraint, as well as (6.18), is not binding, so that a Bertrand equilibrium of the overlapping type exists in the two-firm case if and only if (6.16) and (6.17) hold.

Three-firm Bertrand equilibrium

Finally we consider the three-firm case again and suppose that Bertrand competition is imposed. We shall show that under this kind of competition, the three-firm market structure can be excluded for some values of the fixed costs, deterring entry by the middle firm. First to determine the conditions under which an equilibrium with overlapping market areas exists, we consider each profit function $\Pi_i = p_i q_i - \tfrac{1}{2}q_i^2$ where q_i is the demand of firm i as given by (6.7). Taking first-order conditions we get a system of equations in prices:

$$\frac{5}{2}S + \frac{5}{8} - \frac{21}{4}p_i + p_C = 0 \qquad i = A, B$$

$$1 + p_A + p_B - 3p_C = 0 \qquad i,j = A, B; \, i \neq j$$

The solution of this system is:

$$\hat{p}_A = \hat{p}_B = \frac{5(5 + 12S)}{106}; \qquad \hat{p}_C = \frac{2(13 + 10S)}{53}$$

$$\hat{q}_A = \hat{q}_B = \frac{3(5 + 12S)}{106}; \qquad \hat{q}_C = \frac{(13 + 10S)}{53}$$

$$\hat{\Pi}_A = \hat{\Pi}_B = \frac{21(5 + 12S)^2}{22472}; \qquad \hat{\Pi}_C = \frac{3(13 + 10S)^2}{5618}$$

Note that $\hat{\Pi}_A = \hat{\Pi}_B > \hat{\Pi}_C$ for

$$S > 1.087 \tag{6.20}$$

So it is valid to take $\hat{\Pi}_C \geq K$ as the condition determining entry of the middle firm and, thus, the three-firm market structure under Bertrand competition.

Again restricting ourselves to a strict overlapping regime we have to check that a consumer indifferent between buying from firm A (say) or not buying, and located at the point $(S - \hat{p}_A)$, is on the right of the consumer indifferent between buying from firm A and firm C, who is located at the point $\left[\frac{1}{4} + \frac{1}{2}(\hat{p}_C - \hat{p}_A)\right]$. This gives the condition

$$S > \frac{65}{56} \tag{6.21}$$

Then to exclude the undercutting by firm C of the equilibrium prices of firms A and B, involving a deviation price p'_C slightly less than $\left(\hat{p}_A - \frac{1}{2}\right) = \left(\hat{p}_B - \frac{1}{2}\right)$ and a quantity of at most $q'_C = 2(S - p'_C) = 2S + 1 - 2\hat{p}_A$, one has to ensure that the corresponding deviation profit $\hat{\Pi}'_C = p'_C \, q'_C - \frac{1}{2}(q'_C)^2$ is less than the equilibrium profit Π^b_C, i.e.:

$$S < 9.26 \tag{6.22}$$

Now it is easy to verify that it is never profitable for an extreme firm (say, firm A) to undercut firm C but not firm B by choosing a price p'_A satisfying $\hat{p}_B - 1 < p'_A < \hat{p}_C - \frac{1}{2}$ (which is possible for $S < 4$). Similarly it is not profitable for firm A to undercut both firms B and C by choosing $p'_A < \hat{p}_B - 1$. Finally we have to exclude deviations involving price increases. If firm C chooses a price high enough to get a situation of total monopolies, the maximal quantity it can sell is given by $[1 - (S - \hat{p}_A) - (S - \hat{p}_B)]$, which is less than the pure monopoly quantity q^m whenever

$$S > \frac{156}{145} \tag{6.23}$$

So, we have established a set of conditions which are sufficient to ensure the existence of both a Bertrand equilibrium and a Cournot equilibrium in the three-firm case and of a Bertrand equilibrium in the two-firm case. We return now to the conditions on fixed costs, which are crucial to determine the number of firms in the market, and to collective welfare considerations.

4 Welfare comparisons

The computations above allow us to construct an example having the following features. If Cournot competition prevails, a three-firm market structure will emerge since a three-firm Cournot equilibrium exists that ensures a positive equilibrium profit π_i^c to every firm (this is condition (6.10)). If Bertrand competition prevails, we can find values of the fixed cost K (still satisfying condition (6.10)) such that a three-firm Bertrand equilibrium would lead to a negative equilibrium profit for the middle firm – i.e. $\hat{\Pi}_C < K$. In other words the middle firm would not enter the industry under such a condition and, instead, a two-firm Bertrand equilibrium would be established (whenever $\Pi_i^b > K$ for $i = A$ and B). Since there are obviously values of K ensuring

$$\min\{\Pi_A^b, \Pi_C^c\} > K > \hat{\Pi}_C$$

(at least for $S > 1$ and under the normalisation of the transportation cost parameter $t = 1$), our example is simply obtained if we fix the reservation parameter S in the interval:

$$2.1 < S < 3 \tag{6.24}$$

This condition implies a three-firm market structure under Cournot competition and a two-firm market structure under Bertrand competition. We thus have a trade-off: more competition (the Bertrand case) implies more concentration.

We shall now go further and evaluate the welfare implications of such a situation. We shall see that, for some values of the fixed cost K, not only the consumers' surplus but even the total surplus (net of fixed costs) is larger at the three-firm Cournot equilibrium (where the fixed cost is counted three times) than at the two-firm Bertrand equilibrium (where the fixed cost is counted twice).

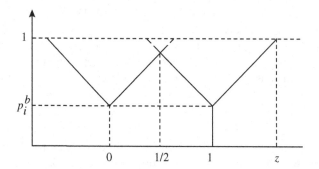

Figure 6.2 Two-firm Bertrand case

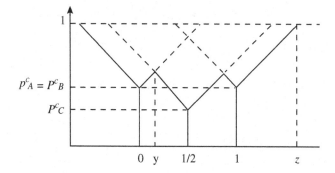

Figure 6.3 Three-firm Cournot case

To determine these, one may first compute the consumers' surplus in the two cases. First consider the Bertrand two-firm case (see figure 6.2). The consumer surplus is computed using the following formula:

$$CS^b = 2 \int_0^{1/2} \left[S - p_i^b - x \right] dx + 2 \int_1^z \left[S - p_i^b - (x - 1) \right] dx$$

with $p_i^b = p_A^b = p_B^b$ and $z = (11 + 6S)/16$, we get: $CS^b = \frac{1}{256}(36S^2 + 36S - 119)$. Then consider the consumer surplus in the three-firm Cournot case (see figure 6.3).

$$CS^c = 2 \int_0^y \left[S - p_A^c - x \right] dx + 2 \int_y^{1/2} \left[S - p_C^c - \left(\frac{1}{2} - x \right) \right] dx$$
$$+ 2 \int_1^z \left[S - p_B^c - (x - 1) \right] dx$$

with $y = (51 - 11S)/130$ and $z = (97 + 53S)/130$, we get $CS^c = (3051S^2 + 4008S - 7034)/16900$. Comparing the two consumers' surpluses, it is easy to check that $CS^c > CS^b$ in the relevant interval given by (6.23). Hence Bertrand competition is directly damaging for the consumers. This is essentially due to the fact that in the three-firm Cournot case all prices are lower than the Bertrand price:

$$p_C^c < p_A^c = p_B^c < p_A^b = p_B^b$$

However, to complete our example, we should compare total surplus in the two cases. This means that we should add to the consumer surplus, in each case, the total profits (gross of fixed costs), that is:

$$TS^b = CS^b + \Pi_A^b + \Pi_B^b = \frac{1}{128}(60S^2 + 60S - 49)$$

$$TS^c = CS^c + \Pi_A^c + \Pi_B^c + \Pi_C^c = \frac{1}{1,300} + (671S^2 + 808S - 354)$$

and verify the following condition, for some values of K,

$$TS^c - TS^b > K > \hat{\Pi}_C \tag{6.25}$$

A sufficient condition on S for that is:

$$S < 3.3$$

Therefore the final conditions to determine our example are: $t = 1$ and $2.1 < S < 3$.

5   Conclusions

The example we have constructed shows that it may be better, in some oligopolistic situations, to allow for more coordination in prices since it amounts to allowing for lower concentration. However 'more coordination in prices' should not be assimilated to pure collusion[14] but to something like Cournot competition which is known to introduce more coordination than Bertrand competition. Our example used a spatial model of the Hotelling type with linear transportation cost and finite reservation price for the consumers. We have also introduced fixed costs and quadratic variable costs of production, and these have played a crucial role in our construction. To simplify the computations, the key condition for the example

---

[14] It may be verified that the total surplus at the pure collusive solution, where the three firms maximise joint profits, is equal to $\left[\frac{1}{400}(191S^2 + 224S - 116) - 3K\right]$, which is lower than the total surplus at the three-firm Cournot equilibrium.

was put on the consumer's reservation price, normalising the unit transportation cost. However it should be interpreted as a condition on the ratio of these two parameters, meaning that the result holds when the transportation cost, although still lower than the reservation price, is relatively large. A final word of warning about the interpretation of the results is needed. Our chapter shows that some intermediate degree of price coordination might in some (very specific) circumstances be preferable than a tougher degree of price competition. In this sense, the chapter confirms the intuition of some authors who have indicated the possible danger of too harsh competition.

However, the practical use of our chapter depends very much on the possibility of identifying exactly the real-world practices which would correspond to Cournot competition. In the introduction we mentioned the literature on 'facilitating practices'. But there are other directions to be further investigated, such as the one indicated by the work of Kreps and Scheinkman (1983) on quantity pre-commitment through capacity choice. Moreover, the conditions that we have derived, in order to defend a policy allowing coordination in prices of the Cournot type, are very strong, and the informational requirements on the anti-trust authorities too demanding. It would be worthwhile to see whether such conditions could be relaxed, or if other types of coordination in prices could lead to similar results, before making any precise recommendation.

Bibliography

d'Aspremont C., R. Dos Santos Ferreira and L.A. Gérard-Varet (1991a) Pricing schemes and cournotian equilibria, *American Economic Review*, 81(3), pp. 666–73

(1991b) Concurrence en prix et équilibres cournotiens, *Revue Economique*, 42(6), pp. 967–96

d'Aspremont, C., J.J. Gabszewicz and J.-F. Thisse (1979) On Hotelling's stability in competition, *Econometrica*, 47, pp. 1145–50

d'Aspremont, C. and A. Jacquemin (1988) Cooperative and noncooperative R & D in duopoly with spillovers, *American Economic Review*, 78, pp. 1133–1137

(1990) Erratum, *American Economic Review*, 80, pp. 641–2

Bittlingmayer, G. (1985) Did anti-trust policy cause the great merger wave?, *Journal of Law and Economics*, 28, pp. 77–118

Eaton, B.E. and R.G. Lipsey (1989) Product differentiation, in R. Schmalensee and R.D. Willig (eds.), *Handbook of Industrial Organization*, I, Amsterdam: North-Holland, pp. 723–68

Everton, A.R. (1993) Discrimination and predation in the United Kingdom: small grocers and small bus companies – a decade of domestic competition policy, *European Competition Law Review*, 17–14

Gabszewicz, J.J. and J.P. Vial (1972) Oligopoly à la Cournot in a general equilibrium analysis, *Journal of Economic Theory*, 4, pp. 381–400

Holt, C.A. and D.T. Scheffman (1987), Facilitating practices: the effects of advance notice and best-price policies, *Rand Journal of Economics*, 18(2), pp. 187–97

Hotelling, H. (1929) Stability in competition, *Economic Journal*, 39, pp. 41–57

Jacquemin, A. (1990) Horizontal concentration and European merger policy, *European Economic Review*, 34, pp. 539–50

Kalai, E. and M.A. Satterthwaite (1986) The kinked demand curve, facilitating practice's and oligopolistic coordination, *MEDS Discussion Paper*, 677, Northwestern University

Kreps, D. and J. Scheinkman (1983) Quantity pre-commitment and Bertrand competition yield Cournot outcomes, *Bell Journal of Economics*, 14, pp. 326–37

Launhardt, W. (1885) *Mathematische Begründung der Volkswirtschaftslehre*, Leipzig

Motta, M. (1992) Cooperative R & D and vertical product differentiation, *International Journal of Industrial Organisation*, 10

Phlips, L. (1998) Introduction, in L. Phlips (ed.), *Applied Industrial Economics*, Cambridge: Cambridge University Press

Posner, R.S. (1977) *Economic Analysis of Law*, Boston: Little Brown & Co.

Salop, S.C. (1986) Prices that (credibly) facilitate oligopoly coordination, in G.F. Mathewson and J.E. Stightz (eds.), *New Developments in the Analysis of Market Structure*, Cambridge, Mass.: MIT and London: Macmillan, pp. 265–90

Selten, R. (1984) Are cartel laws bad for business?, in H. Hauptmann, W. Krelle and K.C. Mosler (eds.), *Operations Research and Economic Theory*, Berlin: Springer Verlag

Sutton, J. (1991) *Sunk Costs and Market Structure*, Cambridge, Mass.: MIT Press

7 The strategic effects of supply guarantees: the raincheck game

Jonathan H. Hamilton

1 Introduction

Why might a firm sell its product at prices less than marginal cost? If each firm posts its price in advance of learning its demand, the quantity demanded could exceed the maximum quantity a firm wishes to supply when competitors charge higher than expected prices or demand is strong. Such a firm then faces a choice of whether to ration its customers or to serve all demand. There are many reasons why a firm might forgo the strategy of short-run profit maximisation and serve all demand. Among them are encouraging shopping by consumers who buy both advertised and unadvertised goods, maintaining a positive reputation with consumers, and inducing risk-averse consumers with significant shopping costs to seek out low prices by removing the risk of finding the store stocked out.

Some firms effectively commit to serve all demand by offering 'rainchecks'. Many supermarket chains in the United States issue coupons to consumers to buy items advertised at special prices when the supermarket runs out of its supply. The consumer can then return after the store restocks and obtain the product at the special price. Trade deals with manufacturers often enable stores to offer special low prices, so offering to sell the good after the sale period at the low price is an offer to sell at a price below marginal cost. While maintaining goodwill is an obvious explanation, there are at least two others. First, the Federal Trade Commission (FTC) regulates advertising. To prevent the use of 'bait-and-switch' tactics,

I thank Duke University, UNC–Chapel Hill, and the Institut d'Anàlisi Econòmica (Barcelona) for their hospitality during the early part of this research. I thank DGICYT (Spanish Ministry of Education and Science) and the University of Florida College of Business Administration for financial support. I thank Gary Biglaiser, Ramon Caminal, James Friedman, Dan Kovenock, Carmen Matutes, Hervé Moulin, Jozsef Sakovics, Xavier Vives and Megan Werner for helpful comments, and John Rollins and Rajiv Sharma for research assistance. Any remaining errors are my sole responsibility.

stores must be able to demonstrate that they have sufficient inventory to meet anticipated demand for advertised products. Stores which offer rainchecks do not need to prove that they have sufficient inventory.

The second explanation lies in the strategic effects of offering rainchecks. When a store offers rainchecks as a general policy, both the store and its competitors take account of this in choosing equilibrium prices. In this chapter, the only reason for firms to offer rainchecks is to influence the subsequent pricing game.

Selling strategies in oligopoly have been an important focus of the game-theoretic revolution in industrial organisation. Beyond developing a fuller understanding of traditional Bertrand and Cournot models, researchers have explored a great variety of firm behaviour. Non-price competition, such as advertising policies and product attribute choices, has received much attention. Research on sophisticated selling strategies includes most-favoured customer clauses (Cooper, 1986) and other techniques (Salop, 1986). An important insight from this research is that, relative to perfect competitors or monopolists, oligopolists have additional strategic incentives to use these sophisticated practices. Rainchecks share this property.

Another strain of oligopoly research starts from Grossman's (1981) model of competition in supply functions. Rather than setting price or quantity as in Bertrand or Cournot games, firms choose how much to supply at each possible price. Klemperer and Meyer (1989) have extended this approach to allow for uncertain market demand. Dixon (1992) develops a simpler type of strategy where each firm chooses both a price and the maximum quantity it will supply. Supply function equilibria are certainly appealing as a way for firms to protect themselves against some of the uncertainties they face, but it seems problematic that all oligopolists can avail themselves of this flexibility. Retail firms' price advertisements commit the firm to the advertised price. It seems implausible that a firm could advertise a conditional commitment to charge prices which depend on the state of demand, given that consumers are unlikely to be able to form reliable estimates of the state of demand or to verify the firm's claim. Especially when consumers' search and shopping decisions depend on expected prices, forcing consumers to calculate expected price would seem to leave a firm vulnerable to unconditional price commitments from competitors, even at higher expected prices.

Instead of taking the supply function approach, I analyse a simpler model which corresponds to a static analogue of an explicit form of retail competition. Firms announce prices and also whether or not those prices will pertain in all states of demand. The only flexibility the firm has is whether it will supply the good to all customers even if its marginal cost exceeds the price it has already set. A dynamic interpretation of this commitment is giving rainchecks – a firm commits to deliver one unit of the good at the advertised price to consumers even when it has run out of stock. Thus, each firm announces a price and whether that price is a conditional or an unconditional commitment. My approach thus contrasts with Dixon (1990). In his model, firms simply face an explicit cost from turning away customers. In my model, if a firm chooses to offer rainchecks, the cost of turning away customers becomes infinite.

Thepot (1995) analyses Bertrand competition with increasing costs. His interest is in avoiding the need to consider mixed strategy equilibria. His model considers 'production-to-order' rules versus 'production-to-expectation' rules for firms, but does not let firms choose which rule to follow. Thus, he does not endogenise the analogue of the raincheck decision.

In this chapter, I eliminate all other influences from consideration to focus on the one which has been neglected to date. How does offering rainchecks affect the incentives for price competition among rivals? If offering rainchecks deters vigorous competition by oligopolists, then that in itself may explain the use of rainchecks by firms. Studying this choice of price policies also extends the literature on price formation. Most of the models referred to above study only one type of competition.[1] Here, I endogenise the choice of the type of price competition – with or without rainchecks – which occurs.

I analyse two models of price competition with rainchecks. In the first, duopolists with identical cost functions produce homogeneous products. Absent rainchecks, the price equilibrium is in mixed strategies. Furthermore, the higher-priced firm faces a positive demand in some states of the world. This model with the addition of rainchecks has a rather startling outcome – multiple pure strategy price equilibria. There is a large interval of prices such that both firms charging the same price is a Nash equilibrium.

In the second model of differentiated products, with no rainchecks, pure strategy equilibria always exist. To allow a role for rainchecks, I introduce exogenous uncertainty about consumer demand. Even though each firm can predict the prices which all firms will charge, no firm can predict what its final demand will be in equilibrium. A firm prefers to turn customers away in states of the world where demand for its product is strong. By offering rainchecks, a firm removes this option. No matter how many customers wish to purchase the good, the firm supplies all of them. With increasing marginal costs, this commitment has an obvious direct cost to

---

[1] An exception is Singh and Vives (1986), who embed price-setting and quantity-setting in a two-stage game for firms producing differentiated products.

Klemperer and Meyer (1986) also compare price-setting and quantity-setting in a model of demand uncertainty.

the firm when marginal cost exceeds price, but it also shifts the equilibrium prices in a way that favours the firm offering rainchecks. For moderate values of the demand uncertainty parameter, offering rainchecks is the equilibrium of the first stage of the game. Hence, we do not need to resort to legal restrictions or demand-enhancement arguments to uncover motivations for committing to guarantee supply.

In section 2, I present the homogeneous products model and some basic results. Section 3 presents the model with differentiated products and analytical results. Section 4 presents simulation results to describe when firms choose to offer rainchecks. Section 5 contains some conclusions and discusses the welfare effects of rainchecks.

2   The homogeneous products case

Economists have long recognised that Bertrand equilibria with homogeneous products depend crucially on the properties of cost functions. With constant average and marginal production costs, the unique equilibrium price equals marginal cost. With increasing returns to scale, the only equilibria are in mixed strategies. Similarly, with decreasing returns to scale, the only equilibria are in mixed strategies. Tirole (1988) demonstrates this for one particular rationing rule and shows that it holds as well for a broad class of rationing rules.

Crucial to Tirole's analysis is the incorporation of an additional (implicit) assumption – that each firm can choose to supply less than the quantity demanded at its announced price. With this assumption, Bertrand competition is no longer a direct analogue to traditional Cournot competition. In the Cournot game, each firm chooses what quantity to produce. Firms make no further decisions and market clearing determines the equilibrium price. Under price-setting, allowing each firm to choose how much to supply after learning about its demand (which depends on all prices set by the competing firms) effectively expands the strategic framework for firms.

With increasing marginal costs, each firm's supply decision is actually quite simple – sell the lesser of the quantity demanded and the quantity such that marginal cost equals its price (the quantity on its competitive supply curve at that price). No other supply decisions constitute a subgame perfect equilibrium (SPE) in the two-stage game where firms first choose prices and then decide on what quantities to supply.[2] With constant or increasing returns to scale, this second stage is irrelevant, since each firm is always willing to supply the entire market at any price at which the firm had been

---

[2] Thus, Dixon's (1992) results do not seem particularly robust.

willing to supply anything at all. Thus, without increasing costs, firms never ration consumers.

With increasing marginal costs, the firm offering the lower price often prefers to ration consumers. Hence, the firm charging the higher price may still find itself facing a positive demand. Consequently, the higher-price firm need not be willing to match the lower-price firm, preventing the competitive market price from being an equilibrium (Tirole, 1988).

If each firm is constrained to serve all demand at its announced price, the higher-price firm never faces a positive demand, providing a strong incentive to match the lower price. However, the fact that the low-price firm must serve the entire market discourages each firm from cutting its price to capture additional sales. As a consequence, there are multiple equilibria. There is an interval of prices such that each firm charging equal prices is an equilibrium.

To see this, assume there are two identical firms, each with the cost function $C(q_i)$, where q_i is the quantity firm i produces and sells, with $C'(q_i) > 0$ and $C''(q_i) > 0$. The market demand curve is $D(p)$, which I assume to be continuous and downward-sloping for all prices with positive demand.

If both firms offer rainchecks, the demand function facing each firm is:

$$D_i^R(p_i, p_j) = \begin{cases} 0 & \text{if } p_i > p_j \\ D(p_i)/2 & \text{if } p_i = p_j \\ D(p_i) & \text{if } p_i < p_j \end{cases}$$

The profit function is:

$$\Pi_i^R(p_i, p_j) = p_i D_i^R(p_i, p_j) - C(D_i^R(p_i, p_j))$$

The first result is that the 'competitive equilibrium' where each firm supplies the quantity such that marginal cost equals price and the market clears is always a Nash equilibrium with rainchecks.

Proposition 1:   Assume that firms have identical cost functions with C'' $(q_i) > 0$ for all q_i. Let $S_i(p_i)$ denote the quantity such that marginal cost equals price (the competitive supply). A Nash equilibrium of the game with the demand functions $D_i^R(\cdot)$ is (p_c, p_c) where p_c solves $D(p^c) = S_i(p^c) + S_j(p^c)$.

Proof: For any price set by firm j, firm i will never strictly prefer to charge a price greater than p_j if $\Pi_i^R(p_j, p_j) \geq 0$ since $\Pi_i^R(p_i, p_j) = 0$ for all $p_i > p_j$. Given that firm j is charging p_c, firm i cannot gain from charging a price $p_i < p_c$, since it must then serve the entire market. For $p_i = p_c$,

$D_i^R(p_c, p_c) = S_i(p_c)$, and for all $p_i < p_c$, $D_i^R(p_i, p_c) > S_i(p_i)$. Thus, p_c is the best-reply to p_c since a lower price would decrease revenue and increase production cost.   ■

We thus have a model of price competition that gives us the competitive equilibrium as a Nash equilibrium with only two firms with increasing costs. However, this pricing game has considerably more equilibria. Any pair of equal prices in a large interval will be a Nash equilibrium. The competitive price is strictly interior to this interval of equilibrium prices.

Proposition 2: Any price pair $(\tilde{p}, \tilde{p})$ is a Nash equilibrium for the game with demand functions $D_i^R(p_i, p_j)$ if the following conditions hold:

$$\Pi_i^R(\tilde{p}, \tilde{p}) \geq 0 \tag{7.1}$$

and

$$\Pi_i^R(\tilde{p}, \tilde{p}) \geq \tilde{p}D(\tilde{p}) - C(D(\tilde{p})) \tag{7.2}$$

Proof: Condition (7.1) guarantees that firm i will not strictly prefer to charge a price higher than p_j, which would result in zero demand and zero profits. Condition (7.2) compares profits from matching price to profits from undercutting firm j's price. As long as firm i prefers to share the market rather than capture all the market demand, $\tilde{p}$ will be an equilibrium price.   ■

The lower bound on the equilibrium price is that price at which both firms share demand equally and earn zero profits. The upper bound is the price at which sharing demand equally yields a profit identical to that from an ε-undercut of the rival's price. The upper bound is also less than or equal to the monopoly price from its construction. It is somewhat startling that the change in the rule on whether firms can or cannot turn away customers causes a switch from multiple pure strategy equilibria to no pure strategy equilibrium.

Without rainchecks, Shapley (1957) first showed that the equilibrium incorporates mixed strategies. Dixon (1984) and Dasgupta and Maskin (1986) have proved the existence of the mixed strategy equilibrium. However, construction of the equilibrium price distributions for a downward-sloping demand function and convex cost function is a difficult task. To endogenise the decision to offer rainchecks, one must solve for equilibrium mixed strategies and make an equilibrium selection from the set of equilibria under rainchecks. Rather than attack that complex task, I turn to a model with differentiated products.

3 Differentiated products with demand uncertainty

With differentiated products, the Bertrand model no longer yields such stark results. Two firms are not enough competition to reach the perfectly competitive outcome. With a linear demand structure and sufficient differentiation between the firms' outputs, the price equilibria when neither firm issues rainchecks are unique and in pure strategies. Since there are no surprises about the rival's price choice and thus no surprises about one's demand, there is no apparent need for rainchecks. To introduce the possibility of firms desiring to ration consumers in the simplest way, I assume that the demand functions are subject to random shocks. Firms observe these shocks only after choosing prices. Thus, this model reasonably describes price competition where the advertising or marketing process enforces a time lag between sellers' choice of prices and consumers' learning of these choices.

Let demand for firm i's product be:

$$D_i(p; \varepsilon) = a - bp_i + cp_j + \varepsilon_i, \qquad i = 1, 2, \quad i \neq j$$

where ε_i is a random variable, p is the vector (p_i, p_j) of both firms' prices, and a, b and c are all positive constants. Obviously, with differentiated products, $b > c$. The random draws for the two firms' demand functions are independent and identically distributed. I further assume that ε_i is uniformly distributed on the interval $[-A, +A]$. The firms have identical cost functions:

$$c(q_i) = q_i^2 \qquad i = 1, 2$$

I first solve for the price equilibria in three different subgames: when both firms offer rainchecks, when neither firm offers rainchecks, and when only one offers rainchecks.

The simplest subgame is when both firms offer rainchecks. Quantities sold always equal quantities demanded. Firm i's profit function is:

$$
\begin{aligned}
\pi_i^{RR}(p; \varepsilon) &= p_i D_i(p_i, p_j) - C_i(D_i(p_i, p_j)) \\
&= p_i[a - bp_i + cp_j + \varepsilon_i] - [a - bp_i + cp_j + \varepsilon_i]^2
\end{aligned}
$$

where the RR superscript indicates that both firms offer rainchecks. As long as demand is always positive, since ε_i is drawn from a distribution that is symmetric about zero, expected profit equals:

$$\Pi_i^{RR}(p_i, p_j) = p_i[a - bp_i + cp_j] - [a - bp_i + cp_j]^2 - \sigma_\varepsilon^2$$

where σ_ε^2 is the variance of ε_i.[3] Note that with this demand and cost parametrisation, each firm's pricing decision exhibits action certainty equivalence in this subgame.[4]

Given that all realisations of demand for firm i's product are non-negative, the best replies solve:

$$\frac{\partial \Pi_i^{RR}}{\partial p_i} = a - bp_i + cp_j - bp_i + 2b(a - bp_i + cp_j) = 0$$

Therefore,

$$p_i(p_j) = \frac{(a + cp_i)(1 + 2b)}{2b(1 + b)} \qquad i = 1, 2, \quad i \neq j$$

Differentiating profit with respect to own price again, I find:

$$\frac{\partial^2 \Pi_i^{RR}}{\partial p_i^2} = -2b - 2b^2 < 0$$

so profits for both firms are strictly concave. The best replies for both firms have slopes less than one. Given these properties, there exists a unique pure strategy price equilibrium in the RR subgame at the intersection of these best replies. These equilibrium prices are:

$$p_1^{RR} = p_2^{RR} = \frac{a(1 + 2b)}{2b + 2b^2 - c - 2bc}$$

Expected sales equal:

$$Eq_1^{RR} = Eq_2^{RR} = \frac{ab}{2b + 2b^2 - c - 2bc}$$

and equilibrium profits equal:

$$\Pi_1^{RR}(p_1^{RR}, p_2^{RR}) = \Pi_2^{RR}(p_1^{RR}, p_2^{RR}) = \frac{a^2 b(1 + b)}{[2b + 2b^2 - c - 2bc]^2} - \sigma_\varepsilon^2$$

Given that $b > c$, the equilibrium price increases as a and c increase, decreases as b increases, and remains constant as σ_ε^2 changes.

The raincheck offer becomes relevant only if ε_i ever takes on values large enough that $D_i(p_i^{RR}, p_j^{RR}) > p_i/2$, which is the quantity that a price taker with the same cost function would supply. Thus, the raincheck offer is

---

[3] Throughout the remainder of the chapter $\pi_i(p; \varepsilon)$ denotes profits given the demand state and $\pi_i(p)$ denotes expected profits (taking expectation over ε_i and ε_j).

[4] See Newbery and Stiglitz (1981) for a discussion of action certainty equivalence.

binding in some states of the world as long as:

$$A > p_i/2 + bp_i - cp_j - a$$

Hence, in the simulation analysis I consider only parameter values in this range. There is also an upper bound on the disturbance term ε_i to prevent violations of the assumption that $D_i(\cdot)$ is never negative in any state of the world. Given the equilibrium prices, this is easily checked.

Next, consider the subgame where firm 1 offers rainchecks, but firm 2 does not. I label this the 'NR subgame'. (The RN subgame where firm 1 offers rainchecks and firm 2 does not is completely symmetric to this NR subgame.) Both firms' profit functions differ from those in the RR subgame. Firm 1's profit takes two different functional forms depending on whether or not it rations consumers. While firm 2 never rations consumers, its demand depends on whether or not firm 1 rations. When firm 1 rations consumers, firm 2 faces some spillover demand. Some consumers who prefer to buy the good from firm 1, but are unable to do so, buy the good from firm 2. Friedman (1988) discusses alternative models of rationing and spillover demand with differentiated products, including analogues of both proportional (as in Davidson and Deneckere, 1986) and parallel rationing (as in Kreps and Scheinkman, 1983). I use Friedman's version of parallel rationing as the simplest alternative – the lower-priced firm first serves the consumers with the greatest willingness to pay.[5]

Firm 1 does not offer rainchecks, and its profit function equals:

$$\pi_1^{NR}(p;\varepsilon) = \begin{cases} p_1 D_1(p;\varepsilon) - [D_1(p;\varepsilon)]^2 & \text{if } D_1(p;\varepsilon) \leq p_1/2 \\ p_1^2/4 & \text{if } D_1(p;\varepsilon) > p_1/2 \end{cases}$$

Define firm 2's spillover demand as:

$$s_2(p;\varepsilon) \equiv \max\{(c/b)[a - (b-c)p_2 + \varepsilon_1 - p_1/2, 0]\}.$$

Firm 2's profits take two different functional forms depending on the value of ε_1. Thus:

$$\pi_2^{NR}(p;\varepsilon) = \begin{cases} p_2 D_2(p;\varepsilon) - [D_2(p;\varepsilon)]^2 & \text{if } \varepsilon_1 \leq p_1/2 + (b-c)p_2 - a \\ p_2[D_2(p;\varepsilon) + s_2(p;\varepsilon)] \\ \quad -[D_2(p;\varepsilon) + s_2(p;\varepsilon)]^2 & \text{if } \varepsilon_1 > p_1/2 + (b-c)p_2 - a \end{cases}$$

---

[5] In the case of homogeneous goods, there is another interpretation of parallel rationing. If the model is one of identical consumers with downward-sloping demand curves, then the lower-price firm sells each customer the same quantity of the good. Note that Tirole (1988) calls this system 'efficient rationing'.

The Nash equilibrium in prices for the NR subgame does not have an analytic solution. In addition, establishing existence of a pure strategy equilibrium in this subgame is more complicated. First, firm 1's profit function is not concave. I can write Π_1 (expected profits) as the sum of two terms – a concave term which is profits when firm 1 does not ration its customers and a convex term which is profits when it rations its customers – weighted by the probability of rationing. Since this probability depends on price, Π_1 cannot be guaranteed to be concave. However, I can still show that there exists a pure strategy price equilibrium in this subgame with asymmetric raincheck policies.

Proposition 3: In the NR subgame, there always exists a pure strategy Nash equilibrium in prices.

Proof: First, it can be shown that $\partial^2 \Pi_1 / \partial p_1 \partial p_2$ is always positive. Thus, $p_1^{NR}(p_2)$ is monotone increasing (see Novshek, 1985, or Vives, 1990). Firm 2, which continues to give rainchecks, has a concave profit function and therefore a continuous best-reply function. It is also monotone increasing. Hence, I can apply Vives' (1991) result that monotone increasing best-reply functions have a pure strategy equilibrium on a compact strategy set by imposing an arbitrary upper bound on price above each firm's monopoly price level. Uniqueness cannot be guaranteed without further information, but the numerical analysis never turned up instabilities of the type that non-uniqueness might lead to.   ∎

The NN subgame where neither firm offers rainchecks is more complicated because of the spillover demands. There are six regions for the functional form of demand: neither firm faces excess demand; both firms do; one firm does and the other does not, even with the spillover demand (two regions); and one firm faces excess demand, while the second only does so after including the spillover demand (again, two regions). Let $q_i = D_i(p; \varepsilon)$ be firm i's own demand *ex post* and s_i be its spillover demand *ex post*. Denote the six regions as:

$$
\begin{array}{llll}
\text{I} & q_1 \leq p_1/2 & \text{and} & q_2 \leq p_2/2 \\
\text{II} & q_1 > p_1/2 & \text{and} & q_2 > p_2/2 \\
\text{III} & q_1 > p_1/2 & \text{and} & q_2 + s_2 \leq p_2/2 \\
\text{IV} & q_1 > p_1/2 & \text{and} & q_2 + s_2 > p_2/2 > q_2 \\
\text{V} & q_1 + s_1 \leq p_1/2 & \text{and} & q_2 > p_2/2 \\
\text{VI} & q_1 + s_1 > p_1/2 > q_1 & \text{and} & q_2 > p_2/2
\end{array}
$$

Figure 7.1 displays the six regions in $(\varepsilon_1, \varepsilon_2)$ space. In region I, firm 1's profit is:

$$\pi_1(p; \varepsilon) = p_1 q_1 - q_1^2$$

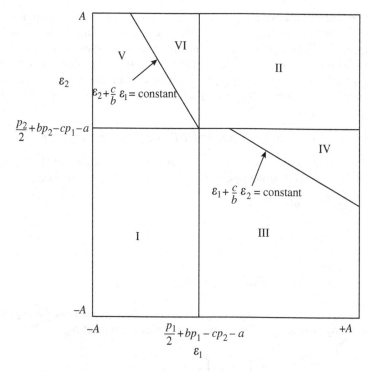

Figure 7.1   The six regions for the profit functions (assuming $p_1 < p_2$)
Note: I, No rationing; II, Both ration without spillover demand; III, 1 rations, 2 doesn't;
IV, Both ration with 2's spillover demand; V, 2 rations, 1 doesn't; VI, Both ration with 1's
spillover demand.

and in regions II, III, IV and VI, it is:

$$\pi_1(p;\varepsilon) = p_1^2/4$$

and in region V, it is:

$$\pi_1(p;\varepsilon) = p_1(q_1 + s_1) - (q_1 + s_1)^2$$

The profit functions for firm 2 can be similarly derived. As with the *NR* subgame, the equilibrium for the *NN* subgame cannot be found analytically. Furthermore, the *NN* subgame does not necessarily have an equilibrium in pure strategies. This fact should not be a surprise since we know that the homogeneous products version of the subgame never has an equilibrium in pure strategies. However, in the simulation analysis, I perform a numerical search to confirm that the numerical solution is indeed a Nash equilibrium.

Even without analytic solutions in some subgames, some comparisons of the two firms' best-reply functions between these subgames are possible. These results illustrate some of the incentives to offer rainchecks. The first comparison is how the best reply of the firm whose rival offers rainchecks shifts when it drops rainchecks. Perhaps not surprisingly, since the firm does not have to serve all demand when demand is high, it is willing to charge a lower price.

Lemma 4:   Comparing the NR and RR subgames, $p_1^{NR}(p_2) < p_1^{RR}(p_2)$.

Proof: For $\varepsilon_1 \le p_1(1+2b)/2 - cp_2 - a$, $\pi_1(p;\varepsilon)$ and $\partial\pi_1(p;\varepsilon)/\partial p_1$ are identical across the subgames. For $\varepsilon_1 > p_1(1+2b)/2 - cp_2 - a$:

$$\frac{\partial \pi_1^{NR}}{\partial p_1} = \frac{p_1}{2}$$

and

$$\frac{\partial \pi_1^{RR}}{\partial p_1} = (1+2b)(a - bp_1 + cp_2 + \varepsilon_1) - bp_1$$

Let $\varepsilon_1 = p_1(1+2b)/2 - cp_2 - a + \delta$, where $\delta > 0$ everywhere in this region. Substituting this into the above expression and subtracting:

$$\int_{-A}^{A} \left[\frac{\partial \pi_1^{RR}}{\partial p_1} - \frac{\partial \pi_1^{NR}}{\partial p_1} \right] d\varepsilon_1 = \int_{0}^{\Delta} \delta\, d\delta > 0$$

where 0 and $\Delta = A - \{p_1(1+2b)/2 - cp_2 - a\}$ are the lower and upper bounds for δ.

Since the derivative with respect to own price for the RR subgame is larger than the derivative for the NR subgame, $p_1^{NR}(p_2) < p_1^{RR}(p_2)$, since the derivative is decreasing in own price in the neighbourhood of the equilibrium (from concavity).   ∎

Similarly, the best-reply function of a firm whose rival does not offer rainchecks shifts up when it adopts rainchecks.

Lemma 5:   Comparing the NN and NR subgames, $p_1^{RN}(p_2) > p_1^{NN}(p_2)$.

Proof: Since the presence of spillover demand affects only the probabilities that a firm rations its customers, the analysis of lemma 4 applies here as well.   ∎

Other comparisons across different subgames are ambiguous. Consider 1's best-reply functions in the NN and NR subgames. In expected terms, the demand curve facing firm 1 shifts out and becomes flatter (more elastic) if firm 2 drops rainchecks. While this is sufficient to show that firm 1's expected sales are greater (holding p_1 constant) when firm 2 does not offer rainchecks, the effect on firm 1's best-reply function cannot be established. Without this comparison, qualitative comparisons of the equilibrium prices in the four subgames are impossible to derive. Since expected costs change across the subgames, price comparisons are inefficient to solve the raincheck games. I now turn to numerical simulations of the solution to the full game.

4   Simulation results with differentiated products

Given the specific functional forms of demand and costs of the differentiated products model, there are four parameters: a, b, c and A. The cost function $c_i(q_i) = q_i^2$ has no independent parameters and, in effect, plays the role of a normalisation. For a range of different values of a, the demand intercept, and then searching exhaustively over feasible values for b and c, the demand slope parameters and A, the demand variability parameter, I compute equilibrium prices and profits in all subgames. For the NN and NR subgames, computer routines with an iterative equation solver find solutions to the first-order conditions.[6] After finding the equilibrium in the NN subgame, I perform a grid search to verify that the solution to the first-order conditions are the true best replies. Parameter values for which the NN equilibrium prices fail the grid search are not included in the results. This problem arises only for values of c quite close to b, so that the degree of product differentiation is small. (Copies of FORTRAN programs are available from the author on request.)

All three types of pricing subgames are part of subgame perfect Nash equilibria for different parameter values. Table 7.1 reports some results for unilateral changes in a single parameter, holding the other parameters constant. It is an equilibrium of the full game to offer rainchecks over a large fraction of parameter space – they are not a phenomenon that occurs only in knife-edge cases.

In all simulations, as demand uncertainty increases, the equilibrium of the first-stage game changes from both firms offering rainchecks to multiple equilibria (one firm offers and the other does not offer rainchecks, and vice versa) to neither firm offering rainchecks. Since the direct cost of offering rainchecks increases with the degree of demand uncertainty, this should not be too surprising. The multiple equilibrium region can be quite small, so it does not always turn up in a coarse grid search.

---

[6] The computer routines use a version of Brent's (1973) method by Moré and Cosnard (1980).

Table 7.1 *Equilibrium types: comparative statics with respect to demand uncertainty*

$a = 50.0$

$b = 1.0$ $c = 0.4$	
$A = [9.0, 13.14]$	Both offer rainchecks
$[13.15, 13.16]$	Multiple equilibria (only one firm offers rainchecks)
$[13.16, 17.50]$	Neither firm offers rainchecks
$b = 1.0$ $c = 0.6$	
$A = [11.50, 17.50]$	Both offer rainchecks
18.00	Multiple equilibria (only one firm offers rainchecks)
$[18.50, 22.0]$	Neither firm offers rainchecks
$b = 2.0$ $c = 1.4$	
$A = [5.50, 8.50]$	Both offer rainchecks
9.0	Multiple equilibria (only one firm offers rainchecks)
$[9.50, 18.0]$	Neither firm offers rainchecks
$b = 2.0$ $c = 1.6$	
$A = [6.50, 11.0]$	Both offer rainchecks
11.5	Multiple equilibria (only one firm offers rainchecks)
$[12.0, 22.0]$	Neither firm offers rainchecks
$b = 3.0$ $c = 2.6$	
$A = [5.0, 8.50]$	Both offer rainchecks
$[9.00, 10.00]$	Multiple equilibria (only one firm offers rainchecks)
$[10.50, 21.50]$	Neither firm offers rainchecks
$b = 4.0$ $c = 3.4$	
$A = [5.00, 5.50]$	Both offer rainchecks
$[6.00, 6.50]$	Multiple equilibria (only one firm offers rainchecks)
$[7.0, 17.0]$	Neither firm offers rainchecks
$b = 4.0$ $c = 3.6$	
$A = [5.0, 8.0]$	Both offer rainchecks
$[8.50, 9.50]$	Multiple equilibria (only one firm offers rainchecks)
$[10.0, 21.0]$	Neither firm offers rainchecks

What is more surprising is that not offering rainchecks arises as the equilibrium of the first-stage game under circumstances where the firms would do better if both offered rainchecks. In other words, not offering rainchecks can sometimes be a 'Prisoners' Dilemma' outcome of the first-stage game. Table 7.2 reports firm 1's price and profits in all four subgames as the degree of demand uncertainty changes.

One can also investigate other comparative statics through simulations. Holding constant all but one parameter, one varies the last parameter. As b (the slope of demand with respect to own price) increases, the equilibrium of the first-stage game shifts from both firms giving rainchecks to neither firm doing so. As c (the slope of demand with respect to the other firm's price) increases, the equilibrium shifts in the opposite way – low values of c have equilibria without rainchecks, while high values of c have equilibria with rainchecks.

5   Concluding remarks

Firms may offer supply guarantees to their customers for a variety of reasons. This chapter analyses yet another one – the effect that supply guarantees have on oligopoly price competition. With homogeneous products and increasing marginal costs of production, without supply guarantees the only Nash equilibria utilise mixed strategies. With supply guarantees, there is a great range of Nash equilibria, with both firms charging equal prices.

It is considerably easier to consider the decision of whether or not to offer supply guarantees in a model with differentiated products. The main finding is that offering supply guarantees changes the ensuing price competition game in such a way that a firm may benefit enough to cover the *ex post* costs of meeting its supply commitments. Equilibria in the game where firms first choose whether or not to offer these guarantees can be of three types, depending on parameter values. In the different types of equilibria, both firms, neither firm, or a single firm choose to offer supply guarantees. As one might expect, for low levels of demand uncertainty, the cost of offering these guarantees is smaller and that is when firms choose to offer the guarantees.

I do not compute social welfare in the different subgames. For a complete understanding of whether supply guarantees enhance or reduce welfare, the effect of the guarantees on consumers matters. The demand rationing scheme specifies only the effect on consumer demand from being unable to purchase a good from one's preferred supplier. It requires even more structure to establish the effects of supply guarantees on the utilities of individual consumers. What this chapter demonstrates is

Table 7.2   *Profits and prices in the four subgames*
$(a = 50.0, b = 1.0, c = 0.40)$

$A = 13.14$			Firm 2	
			No rainchecks	Rainchecks
		No rainchecks	580.13 (52.99)	580.02 (53.21)
	Firm 1	Rainchecks	580.15 (53.41)	580.02* (53.57)

$A = 13.15$			Firm 2	
			No rainchecks	Rainchecks
		No rainchecks	580.005 (52.99)	580.012* (53.21)
	Firm 1	Rainchecks	580.006* (53.41)	580.011 (53.57)

$A = 13.17$			Firm 2	
			No rainchecks	Rainchecks
		No rainchecks	579.88* (52.98)	579.95 (53.21)
	Firm 1	Rainchecks	579.88 (53.41)	579.94 (53.57)

$A = 13.24$			Firm 2	
			No rainchecks	Rainchecks
		No rainchecks	579.31* (52.97)	579.38 (53.19)
	Firm 1	Rainchecks	579.26 (53.41)	579.32 (53.57)

$A = 13.30$			Firm 2	
			No rainchecks	Rainchecks
		No rainchecks	578.83* (52.96)	578.89 (53.19)
	Firm 1	Rainchecks	578.87 (53.41)	578.79 (53.57)

Note: *denotes the equilibrium outcome. Only firm 1's profits are listed in each cell. Firm 2's profits equal firm 1's in the *NN* and *RR* subgames. Firm 2's profits in the *NR* subgame equal firm 1's in the *RN* subgame. Firm 1's price is given in parentheses beside the profit figures.

that policy makers should anticipate that requiring supply guarantees may have adverse effects on price competition that limit the benefits that consumers could obtain from supply guarantees. Since some firms offer such guarantees unilaterally, this news should not shock policy makers too much.

This simple model demonstrates another example of an important message that game-theory has contributed to our understanding of oligopoly. Pricing and practices that monopolists and perfectly competitive firms never use (or never use except to enhance efficiency) may be used for strategic reasons in oligopoly. Strategic factors may similarly change our view of whether a pricing practice is beneficial or harmful to consumers. That oligopolists behave differently from both monopolists and perfectly competitive firms need not be evidence of collusive behaviour on their part. One needs to examine closely the effects of a particular pricing practice on prices, profits and consumers for good public policy evaluation.

Louis Phlips' (1983) study of basing-point pricing systems in the steel industry in Western Europe before and after the founding of the EEC was an early example of research with this message. Louis and his colleagues have taught us much about how to analyse carefully the economics of business practices as they actually occur.

Bibliography

Brent, R.P. (1973) Some efficient algorithms for solving systems of nonlinear equations, *SIAM Journal of Numerical Analysis*, 10, pp. 327–44

Cooper, T. (1986) Most-favored-customer pricing and tacit collusion, *Rand Journal of Economics*, 17, pp. 377–88

Dasgupta, P. and E. Maskin (1986) The existence of equilibrium in discontinuous economic games, II: Applications, *Review of Economic Studies*, 53, pp. 27–41

Davidson, C. and R. Deneckere (1986) Long-run competition in capacity, short-run competition in price, and the Cournot model, *Rand Journal of Economics*, 17, pp. 404–15

Dixon, H. (1984) The existence of mixed strategy equilibria in a price-setting oligopoly with convex costs, *Economics Letters*, 16, pp. 205–12

(1990) Bertrand–Edgeworth equilibria when firms avoid turning customers away, *Journal of Industrial Economics*, 39, pp. 131–46

(1992) The competitive outcome as the equilibrium in an Edgeworthian price–quantity model, *Economic Journal*, 102, pp. 301–9

Friedman, J. (1988) On the strategic importance of prices versus quantities, *Rand Journal of Economics*, 19, pp. 607–22

Grossman, S. (1981) Nash equilibrium and the industrial organization of markets with large fixed costs, *Econometrica*, 49, pp. 1149–72

Klemperer, P. and M. Meyer (1986) Price competition vs. quantity competition: the role of uncertainty, *Rand Journal of Economics*, 17, pp. 618–38

(1989) Supply function equilibria in oligopoly under uncertainty, *Econometrica*, 57, pp. 1243–77

Kreps, D. and J. Scheinkman (1983) Quantity precommitment and Bertrand competition yield Cournot outcomes, *Rand Journal of Economics*, 14, pp. 326–37

Moré, J. and M. Cosnard, BRENTM, A FORTRAN subroutine for the numerical solution of systems of nonlinear equations, *ACM Transactions on Mathematical Software*, 6, pp. 240–51

Newbery, D. and J. Stiglitz (1981) *The Theory of Commodity Price Stabilization*, Oxford: Clarendon Press

Novshek, W. (1985) On the existence of Cournot equilibrium, *Review of Economic Studies*, 52, pp. 85–98

Phlips, L. (1983) *The Economics of Price Discrimination*, Cambridge: Cambridge University Press

Salop, S. (1986) Practices that (credibly) facilitate oligopoly coordination, in G.F. Mathewson and J. Stiglitz (eds.), *New Developments in the Analysis of Market Structure*, Cambridge, Mass.: MIT Press and London. Macmillan

Singh, N. and X. Vives (1986) Price and quantity competition in a differentiated duopoly, *Rand Journal of Economics*, 17, pp. 546–54

Shapley, L. (1957) A duopoly model with price competition (abstract), *Econometrica*, 25, pp. 354–5

Thepot, B. (1995) Bertrand duopoly with decreasing returns to scale, *Journal of Mathematical Economics*, 24, pp. 689–718

Tirole, J. (1988) *The Theory of Industrial Organization*, Cambridge, Mass.: MIT Press

Vives, X. (1990) Nash equilibrium in oligopoly games with monotone best responses, *Journal of Mathematical Economics*, 19, pp. 305–21

8 Product market competition policy and technological performance

Stephen Martin

Too much of anything...isn't necessarily a good thing. (*The Trouble with Tribbles*)

1 Introduction

One of the persistent strands in Louis Phlips' contributions to industrial economics is that competition policy can and should be informed by economic analysis (for example, Phlips, 1993, 1995, 1996). In this chapter I make an effort in that direction.

There is a large literature that examines the impact of R&D cooperation on technological performance.[1] In Martin (1996), I show that R&D cooperation makes it more likely that tacit collusion will be an equilibrium strategy. Here I investigate the impact of product market competition policy on technological performance.

In a market system, firms invest in new technology and new product development because of the profit they expect to earn after discovery and development. More precisely, a firm's incentive to invest in R&D depends on the difference between the profit it earns before innovation and the profit it expects to earn after innovation.[2]

Competition or anti-trust policy exposes firms to the possibility of fines and injunctions if they engage in prohibited conduct.[3] But the

I am grateful to seminar participants at the January 1998 meetings of the Industrial Organisation Society, BETA, Université Louis Pasteur, Universidad Complutense de Madrid and to Paul Geroski for useful comments. Responsibility for errors is my own.
[1] For contributions and references to this literature, see Jorde and Teece (1997); Martin (1997); Meißner and Markl (1997); and Suzumura and Goto (1997).

[2] See the literature that follows from Arrow (1962), in particular Gilbert and Newbery (1982, 1984); Reinganum (1983).

[3] In some circumstances, individuals responsible for decisions to infringe competition rules open themselves to the possibility of criminal penalties, including imprisonment. Such penalties do occur, but they are exceptional, and are not modelled here.

proscriptions of competition law will not be binding constraints unless the probability that violations will be detected is sufficiently high and the penalties that follow conviction are sufficiently great. In practice, neither of these conditions is likely to be met, with the result that the effect of competition policy will be to deter and ameliorate the condemned behaviour, not to completely prevent it.

Competition policy thus typically prohibits naked collusion, which nonetheless occurs. Colluding firms may think that with a certain probability, their actions will not come to light; or if their actions do come to light, that with a certain probability authorities will not meet the standards of proof laid down by the courts; or that in contrary states of the world, any fines eventually imposed are likely to be small relative to collusive profits.

Profit maximising firms will alter their behaviour to take expected anti-trust penalties into account. Colluding firms, for example, may raise price above the non-cooperative equilibrium level of a one-shot game,[4] but deliberately hold price below the joint profit maximizing level, to reduce the probability of attracting the attention of enforcement agencies.[5]

This argument suggests a model of anti-trust enforcement-limiting behaviour on the part of firms, and implies that product market competition policy will reduce profitability both before and after innovation. This means that product market competition policy will affect firms' incentives to invest in innovation.

In the model of competition policy that is developed here, stricter competition policy reduces expected payoffs before and after innovation, but reduces pre-innovation payoffs relatively more than post-innovation payoffs, and therefore increases the equilibrium level of R&D activity. Tough product market competition policy stimulates innovation.

There is, however, an inverted-U relationship between competition policy and expected welfare. Making competition policy tougher always promotes innovation; it increases welfare up to a certain point, beyond which decreasing returns set in and welfare begins to decline.

The model also yields insights into the effect of R&D spillovers on expected welfare, on R&D efforts and on the expected time to discovery of a cost-saving innovation.

---

[4] Or 'a non-cooperative equilibrium level of a one-shot game', if there are multiple equilibria.

[5] In both *Trenton Potteries* and the electrical equipment conspiracies of the 1950s, the enforcement authorities' attention was brought to the offending conduct, in the first instance, by customers whose suspicions were aroused by prices that they regarded as excessive.

2   Monopoly equilibrium with competition policy

The market

Write the equation of the inverse demand curve as

$$p = p(q) + \varepsilon \qquad (8.1)$$

I assume that expected demand $p(q)$ is downward-sloping and otherwise well behaved.

The error term ε has continuous and differentiable density function[6] $f(\varepsilon)$, with mean 0 and variance σ^2.

The density function is defined over the range

$$\underline{\varepsilon} \leq \varepsilon \leq \bar{\varepsilon} \qquad (8.2)$$

where

$$\underline{\varepsilon} < 0 < \bar{\varepsilon} \leq \infty \qquad (8.3)$$

There is always some range of prices over which demand is positive:

$$p(0) + \underline{\varepsilon} > 0 \qquad (8.4)$$

Modelling competition policy

Competition authorities have limited resources and imperfect information. Imperfect information manifests itself in two ways that are central for the administration of competition policy.

First, imperfect information affects the competition authority's decisions about the allocation of enforcement resources. The competition authority does not directly observe firm conduct. It observes the market outcome – here, the realised price. The realised price is influenced but not completely determined by the firm's actions.[7]

To model the competition authority's decision making process, I suppose that it sets an industry-specific threshold price g. If the realised price rises above g, the competition authority investigates the industry. Investigation means that the competition authority devotes some resources to acquiring additional information about the industry, after which it either decides to prosecute firms in the industry for violating the law, or lets the matter drop.[8]

---

[6] For an elaboration of the model with linear inverse demand and a uniform distribution of ε, see Martin (1998).

[7] In this sense the competition authority and the firm stand in a principal–agent relationship, with the competition authority as principal.

[8] Souam (2000) outlines a model in which such a policy is optimal. In this chapter, g is treated as a parameter under the control of the competition authority. In Martin (2000) I examine the competition authority's problem of setting threshold prices when it monitors several industries subject to an overall budget constraint.

It is realistic to suppose that competition authorities have imperfect information about firm conduct, that they monitor industry conditions and that then they decide whether or not to examine a particular industry in detail based on what they observe. The specification that the competition authority considers a single variable when it makes its investigation decision is used for simplicity – in practice, a vector of variables would be observed.

The other way in which imperfect information affects the working of competition policy regards the decision to prosecute and the outcome of such a prosecution, if it should occur.[9] A high realised price may reflect a large value of ε or it may reflect the exercise of monopoly power. If the competition authority investigates an industry, it might conclude that the high observed price is not due to the exercise of market power. Alternatively, it might decide that the high observed price is due to the legal exercise of market power. Competition policy typically does not prohibit the exercise of market power as such; what it prohibits is strategic behaviour aimed at acquiring or maintaining a position of market power[10] that is thought to infringe the rules of acceptable business behaviour in some way. Collusive outcomes reached through genuinely non-cooperative behaviour typically do not violate competition policy. In such cases, a high realised price would trigger an investigation but not result in any liability for the firm.

But this is not the only uncertain element of the enforcement process. The competition authority may institute a legal proceeding against the incumbent, but it may not prevail. The competition authority may fail because it is found not to have respected the legal rights of the firm. It may fail because it is not able to meet the standards of proof laid down by the letter or interpretation of the law. It may fail because competition law conflicts with some other branch of the law and courts resolve the conflict against the application of competition law.[11]

From the point of view of firms, all these factors make it uncertain whether an anti-trust fine would be levied, if a high realised price should trigger an investigation. To capture all of this uncertainty about the result of an investigation, I suppose there is a parameter γ, which is common

[9] Besanko and Spulber (1989) present a model of competition policy with imperfect information that has much in common with models of limit pricing: the competition authority knows that production cost is high or low, but it does not know which. This approach does not allow for uncertainty about the functioning of the legal system.

[10] Under the terminology 'monopolisation', 'conspiracy to monopolise', 'abuse of a dominant position', or 'collusion'.

[11] For example, it might have been held that United States anti-trust law applied to OPEC collusion in the 1970s. In the event, the decision was that foreign policy considerations ruled this out (see Grossack, 1986).

knowledge – that is, the probability of investigation, legal challenge – and conviction if price rises above the investigation threshold price g. If the firm is found to have offended the provisions of competition law, it pays a fine F. The expected fine in the event that an investigation is undertaken – if price rises above g – is γF.[12]

Competition policy and static monopoly payoffs

Given the threshold price g and the distribution of ε, a monopolist's expected payoff when unit cost is c is

$$\pi(q; c, g) = [p(q) - c]q - \gamma F \int\limits_{g-p(q)} f(\varepsilon) \, d\varepsilon \qquad (8.5)$$

The first term on the right-hand side is profit from the sale of q units of output. The second is the expected value of anti-trust fines. The lower limit of the integral, $g - p(q)$, is the critical value of the random element of demand, given output and the implied expected price chosen by the firm. If the realised value of ε exceeds $g - p(q)$, the observed price exceeds the investigation threshold price and investigation takes place.

In the second term on the right-hand side,

$$\tau(g) = \Pr[p(q) + \varepsilon \geq g] = \Pr[\varepsilon \geq g - p(q)] = \int\limits_{g-p(q)} f(\varepsilon) \, d\varepsilon$$

$$(8.6)$$

is the probability that the competition authority undertakes an investigation. It depends on the investigation threshold price g and on output q. A low investigation threshold price means a strict competition policy, a high investigation threshold price represents a lenient competition policy.

A tougher competition policy (lower g) increases the probability of investigation, all else being equal:

$$\frac{\partial \tau}{\partial g} = -f[g - p(q)] < 0 \qquad (8.7)$$

---

[12] It would be possible to endogenise γF, by making it a function of the levels of resources devoted to prosecution and to defence, or of some index of the severity of the offence. But both γ and F are likely to depend in part on the received standards of the legal system, in ways that the legislature and the competition authority can influence but not completely control. In United States anti-trust law, the elaboration of the concept of 'anti-trust injury' is an example. (For evolutionary views of the development of the common law, see Priest, 1977; Rubin, 1977.)

I will assume that there are decreasing returns to lowering the investigation threshold, in the sense that

$$\frac{\partial^2 \tau}{\partial g^2} = -f'[g - p(q)] > 0 \tag{8.8}$$

There are positive but decreasing returns to deterring the exercise of monopoly power.

The first-order condition to maximise $\pi(c)$ is[13]

$$\frac{\partial \pi}{\partial q} = p(q) - c + q\,\frac{dp}{dq} - \gamma F f[g - p(q)]\,\frac{dp}{dq} \equiv 0 \tag{8.9}$$

It follows that the profit maximising firm selects an output that makes marginal revenue less than marginal production cost,

$$p(q) + q\,\frac{dp}{dq} = c + \gamma F f[g - p(q)]\,\frac{dp}{dq} < c \tag{8.10}$$

The firm expands output above the unconstrained monopoly level to reduce the probability of an anti-trust investigation.

Now turn to the question of comparative statics with respect to the threshold price. Differentiating the first-order condition with respect to g gives

$$\frac{dq}{dg} = -\frac{\partial^2 \pi / \partial g \partial q}{\partial^2 \pi / \partial q^2} \tag{8.11}$$

Differentiating (8.9) with respect to g and noting that (8.8) implies $f' < 0$ gives

$$\frac{\partial^2 \pi}{\partial g \partial q} = -\gamma F f' p' < 0 \tag{8.12}$$

Hence

$$\frac{dq}{dg} < 0 \tag{8.13}$$

---

[13] The second-order sufficient condition for profit maximisation is

$$\frac{\partial^2 \pi}{\partial q^2} = 2\frac{dp}{dq} - \gamma F f'\left(\frac{dp}{dq}\right)^2 + (q - \gamma F f)\frac{d^2 p}{dq^2} < 0$$

This is satisfied for linear demand, and is henceforth assumed.

lowering the investigation threshold g induces greater equilibrium output.[14]

Totally differentiating (8.5) with respect to g, the comparative static impact of a change in g on the firm's equilibrium payoff is

$$\frac{d\pi}{dg} = \frac{\partial\pi}{\partial q}\frac{dq}{dg} + \frac{\partial\pi}{\partial g} = \gamma Ff[g - p(q)] > 0 \qquad (8.14)$$

(making use of the envelope theorem). Tougher competition policy (a lower investigation threshold g) lowers equilibrium profit.

Example:

Monopoly Consider a market with linear inverse demand curve

$$p = 110 - Q + \varepsilon \qquad (8.15)$$

Let marginal cost be constant, 10 per unit, and suppose there are no fixed costs. If the industry were perfectly competitive, long-run equilibrium price would be 10.

Let the density of the random part of demand be exponential,[15]

$$f(\varepsilon) = \frac{1}{10}\exp-\left(\frac{\varepsilon + 10}{10}\right) \qquad (8.16)$$

This has range $(-10, \infty)$ (see figure 8.1). ε has mean 0 and variance $\sigma^2 = 100$. For this density function, it is more likely that ε will fall in a range of modestly negative values than in a higher range of identical length.

Table 8.1 reports the main characteristics of monopoly equilibrium without competition policy and for threshold prices ranging from 70 to 10. Without competition policy, monopoly profit is 2,500 per time period. The figures reported in table 8.1 are calculated for $\gamma F = 1,000$. This is 40 per cent of the no-competition policy payoff.

Here and in what follows, I measure expected net social welfare as the sum of expected economic profit and expected consumers' surplus,[16] on the ground that from a normative point of view this is what an impartial competition authority would maximise.[17]

---

[14] One can also show that an increase in γF increases equilibrium output.

[15] A truncated normal distribution would yield similar results, except that such a case would always have equilibrium $g - p > 0$. In this sense, the exponential specification implies a weak competition policy.

[16] When the discussion moves to innovation, this is measured in terms of expected present discounted values.

[17] The expected value of fines is a transfer from firms to the competition authority, and thus not lost to society; enforcement costs must be set against such transfers. Proper consideration of net enforcement cost requires a model of the behaviour of a competition authority that allocates scarce enforcement resources across several industries, and is the subject of ongoing research.

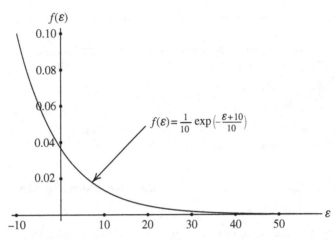

Figure 8.1   Exponential density function

Table 8.1   *Static monopoly market performance, alternative investigation thresholds* $p = 110 - Q$, $c = 10$, $\gamma = 1/2$, $F = 2000$, $\sigma = 10$

g	q_m	p_m	τ	π_m	CS	$\pi_m + CS$
No cp	50.00	60.00	na	2,500.0	1,250.0	3,750.0
70	54.37	55.63	0.087	2,393.5	1,478.1	3,871.6
65	56.08	53.92	0.122	2,341.6	1,572.3	3,913.9
60	58.15	51.85	0.163	2,270.7	1,690.5	3,961.2
55	60.56	49.45	0.211	2,177.5	1,833.5	4,011.0
50	63.27	46.73	0.265	2,058.6	2,001.4	4,060.0
45	66.24	43.76	0.392	1,911.3	2,194.1	4,105.4
40	69.45	40.56	0.389	1,733.0	2,411.3	4,144.3
35	72.84	37.16	0.457	1,521.8	2,652.6	4,174.4
30	76.39	33.61	0.528	1,275.7	2,917.7	4,193.4
25	80.08	29.92	0.602	993.5	3,206.5	4,200.0
20	83.89	26.11	0.678	673.7	3,518.7	4,192.4
15	87.80	22.20	0.756	315.4	3,854.2	4,169.6
10	91.79	18.21	0.836	−82.5	4,213.0	4,130.5

$g = 70$ is a relatively high threshold price, one standard deviation above the no-competition policy monopoly price. It results in a relatively small probability of investigation – 8.7 per cent – but also an 8.7 per cent expansion in output and a 3.2 per cent increase in net social welfare, compared with the no-competition policy case.

As the threshold price falls, output and consumers' surplus rise and economic profit falls. For high and intermediate values of $g(g \geq 45)$, the expected price is below the threshold price. For lower values of g, the expected price is above the threshold price.

Despite the increase in output, the equilibrium probability of investigation rises as g falls. When g falls, the comparative static response of the monopolist is to expand output, but the monopolist does not expand output so much that the direct effect of a lower threshold price on the probability of investigation is neutralised or reversed.

Even for low threshold prices, when the equilibrium expected price is above g, the probability of investigation is less than one: there is always some chance that a large negative ε will push the realised price below the investigation threshold.

There is an inverted-U relationship between g and net social welfare: beyond a certain point ($g \approx 25$ for this example), further increases in the severity of competition policy reduce net social welfare. For threshold prices at low levels, the reductions in expected profit (after allowing for expected fines) that follow from further reductions in g more than offset further gains in consumers' surplus. This is a consequence of the assumption that there are decreasing returns to lowering the investigation threshold.

Oligopoly Qualitatively similar results obtain for non-cooperative oligopoly. Table 8.2 gives numerical results for the market of the monopoly example when there are two quantity-setting firms and each firm non-cooperatively maximises its own expected payoff,

$$\pi_i(q_1, q_2; c, g) = [p(q_1 + q_2) - c]q_i - \frac{1}{2} \gamma F \int\limits_{g-p} f(\varepsilon)\, d\varepsilon \qquad (8.17)$$

The final term on the right-hand side implies that if there is a successful prosecution, each firm expects to pay one-half of the resulting fine.[18] This specification is appropriate for joint offences against competition policy, such as tacit collusion or joint strategic entry deterrence. It would not be appropriate for single-firm violations of competition policy, such as (for example) abuse of a dominant position.

As in table (8.1), output, the probability of investigation, and consumers' surplus all rise as competition policy becomes stricter – as g falls.

[18] Anticipating situations in which firms have different unit costs and therefore different equilibrium market shares, one might wish to investigate a model in which a firm expects to pay a fraction of the expected fine equal to its market share. Such a specification would complicate first-order conditions, compared with (8.17); it would not change equilibrium total output, and is not examined here.

Table 8.2 *Static duopoly market performance, alternative investigation thresholds*
$p = 110 - Q$, $c = 10$, $\gamma = 1/2$, $F = 2000$, $\sigma = 10$

g	q_N	p_N	τ	π_N	CS	$2\pi_N + CS$
No cp	33.33	43.33	na	1,111.1	2,222.2	4,444.4
70	33.73	42.55	0.024	1,085.9	2,275.0	4,446.8
65	33.95	42.09	0.037	1,071.0	2,305.7	4,447.8
60	34.29	41.42	0.057	1,048.7	2,351.6	4,449.0
55	34.77	40.47	0.086	1,016.2	2,417.5	4,449.9
50	35.41	39.18	0.125	970.9	2,507.9	4,449.7
45	36.24	37.53	0.174	910.5	2,626.9	4,446.9
40	37.25	35.51	0.235	832.8	2,774.5	4,439.9
35	38.43	33.15	0.306	736.6	2,953.3	4,426.5
30	39.76	30.47	0.386	621.2	3,162.2	4,404.7
25	41.23	27.53	0.474	486.0	3,400.3	4,372.3
20	42.82	24.36	0.569	330.5	3,666.8	4,327.7
15	44.50	21.00	0.670	154.3	3,960.1	4,269.5
10	46.27	17.46	0.776	−42.7	4,281.5	4,196.1

Economic profit falls as g falls. Once again, there is an inverted-U relation between g and net social welfare. A moderately strict competition policy improves net social welfare.

The size of the impact of competition policy on market performance is less for duopoly than for monopoly (without competition policy, expected net social welfare is 4,444.4; maximum expected net social welfare with competition policy is approximately 4,449.9, for $g \approx 55$). This is a consequence of the improvement in market performance when there are two firms rather than one.

3 Competition policy and innovation

Monopoly

Racing for cost-saving innovation
I will use a standard racing model of cost-saving innovation.[19] Initially the monopolist produces with unit cost c_1. By setting up a research project, it can develop a more efficient technology, reducing unit cost to c_2 per unit. If it does set up such a research project, the time at which

---

[19] Because the basic model is well known, I give it an abbreviated treatment. For further discussion, see Reinganum (1989) or the appendix to Martin (1997).

the new technology comes on line is a random variable. The random discovery time I has a Poisson distribution,

$$\Pr(I \leq t) = 1 - e^{-ht} \tag{8.18}$$

where h is the level or intensity of the R&D project.

The expected time of discovery is the inverse of the R&D intensity,

$$E(I) = \frac{1}{h} \tag{8.19}$$

A greater level of R&D activity therefore brings forward the expected time of discovery.

A greater level of R&D activity is also more costly: the R&D cost function is $z(h)$, with positive and increasing marginal cost of R&D effort:

$$z'(h) > 0 \qquad z''(h) > 0 \tag{8.20}$$

The expected present discounted value of the monopolist is

$$
\begin{aligned}
V_m &= \int_{t=0}^{\infty} e^{-(r+h)t} \left[\pi_m(c_1, g) - z(h) + \frac{h\pi_m(c_2, g)}{r} \right] dt \\
&= \frac{\pi_m(c_1, g) - z(h) + (h\pi_m(c_2, g)/r)}{r + h}
\end{aligned}
\tag{8.21}
$$

where

$$
\begin{aligned}
\pi_m(c_1, g) &= \text{instantaneous pre-innovation payoff} \\
\pi_m(c_2, g) &= \text{instantaneous post-innovation payoff}
\end{aligned}
\tag{8.22}
$$

and $c_2 < c_1$ implies that the payoff is greater after innovation:

$$\pi_m(c_2, g) > \pi_m(c_1, g) \tag{8.23}$$

The first-order condition to maximise V_m is[20]

$$\frac{\partial V_m}{\partial h} = \frac{(r+h)[(\pi_m(c_2, g)/r) - z'(h)] - [\pi_m(c_1, g) - z(h) + (h\pi_m(c_2, g)/r)]}{(r+h)^2} \tag{8.24}$$

$$= \frac{\pi_m(c_2, g) - \pi_m(c_1, g) + z(h) - (r+h)z'(h)}{(r+h)^2} = 0 \tag{8.25}$$

---

[20] The assumption that $z'' > 0$ is sufficient to ensure that the first-order condition identifies a maximum.

Comparative statics with respect to g
Differentiate the numerator of (8.25) with respect to g and rearrange terms to obtain

$$\frac{dh}{dg} = \frac{1}{(r+h)z''(h)} \frac{\partial[\pi_m(c_2,g) - \pi_m(c_1,g)]}{\partial g} \tag{8.26}$$

In view of (8.20), the comparative static derivative has the same sign as the derivative of the profit increment,

$$\frac{\partial[\pi_m(c_2,g) - \pi_m(c_1,g)]}{\partial g} = -\int_{\alpha=c_2}^{\alpha=c_1} \frac{\partial^2\pi_m(\alpha,g)}{\partial\alpha\partial g}\,d\alpha \tag{8.27}$$

A sufficient condition for $dh/dg < 0$ is that

$$\frac{\partial^2\pi_m(c,g)}{\partial c\partial g} > 0 \tag{8.28}$$

To interpret this condition, write

$$\frac{\partial^2\pi_m(c,g)}{\partial c\partial g} = \frac{\partial}{\partial c}\left(\frac{d\pi_m}{dg}\right) \tag{8.29}$$

and recall from (8.14) that $d\pi_m/dg > 0$.

If condition (8.28) holds, then innovation, which reduces unit cost, reduces the impact of a reduction in g on the firm's profit.[21] In other words, if (8.28) holds, one incentive for the firm to innovate is to shield itself from the threat of anti-trust fines.

Using (8.14) to evaluate (8.27),

$$\frac{\partial[\pi_m(c_2,g) - \pi_m(c_1,g)]}{\partial g} = \gamma F\{f[g - p_m(c_2)] - f[g - p_m(c_1)]\} \tag{8.30}$$

Equation (8.30) is negative, as shown in figure 8.2. The lower cost that follows successful innovation implies a lower monopoly price, leading to

$$0 < p_m(c_2) < p_m(c_1) \tag{8.31}$$

---

[21] The analogy with strategic substitutability is clear. Note that (1) Bulow, Geanakoplos and Klemperer (1985) normalise variables so that greater values indicate more aggressive play, while here lower values of g indicate more aggressive monitoring by the competition authority and lower values of c imply greater output; and (2) c is not a choice variable of the firm.

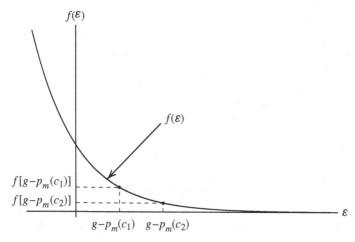

Figure 8.2   Equilibrium $g - p(c_i)$

$$g - p_m(c_2) > g - p_m(c_1) \tag{8.32}$$

$$0 < f[g - p_m(c_2)] < f[g - p_m(c_1)] \tag{8.33}$$

Consequently

$$\frac{dh}{dg} < 0 \tag{8.34}$$

This gives the first result of the model:

Theorem 1:   *Stricter product market competition policy increases monopoly equilibrium R&D intensity.*

A tougher competition policy compresses the incumbent's pre- and post-innovation payoffs. But it compresses the incumbent's pre-innovation payoff more than the incumbent's post-innovation payoff, resulting in greater R&D effort and (in view of (8.19)), a shorter expected time to discovery.

One assumption behind this result is that the investigation threshold is held fixed after innovation. A competition authority implementing a dynamic policy would lower investigation thresholds as lower-cost technologies are put into place. Such a policy would reduce but not eliminate the relatively greater impact of competition policy on pre-innovation profit that lies behind theorem 1.

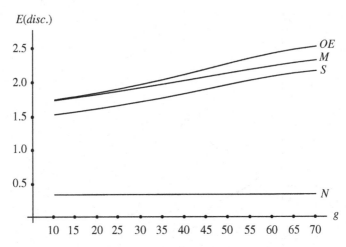

Figure 8.3   Expected time to discovery, monopoly and alternative duopoly cooperation regimes, $s = 1/3$

Note: $n = 2$, $a = 110$, $c_1 = 10$, $c_2 = 5$, $\sigma = 10$, $u = 10$, $v = 1,000$, $\lambda = 1$. N indicates non-cooperative R&D, OE indicates an operating entity joint venture, S indicates a secretariat R&D joint venture.

Figure 8.3 illustrates theorem 1 for the linear demand example underlying table 8.1 and the demand uncertainty density shown in figure 8.1. The innovation is moderate: unit cost after production is 5 rather than 10; the interest rate is 10 per cent. The R&D cost function is quadratic,

$$z(h) = uh + vh^2 \tag{8.35}$$

for $u = 10$, $v = 1,000$.

The curve labelled 'M' shows the investigation threshold–expected time to discovery relationship. Expected time to discovery is 2.4 time periods without competition policy, 2.3 if $g = 70$, and falls steadily to 1.7 for $g = 10$.

The negative relationship between g and expected discovery time translates into an inverted-U relationship between g and expected present-discounted net social welfare, as shown in figure 8.4.

Net social welfare is 40,158 without competition policy, 41,402 for $g = 70$. Net social welfare rises to 45,428 for $g = 20$, then falls to 45,113 for $g = 10$.[22]

---

[22] If $g = 10$, the firm's instantaneous payoff is negative when marginal cost is 10, positive when marginal cost is 5, and the firm's expected present-discounted value is 2,596.8. This compares with an expected present-discounted value of 26,723 without competition policy.

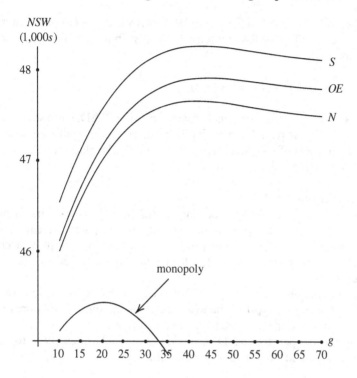

Figure 8.4   Net social welfare, alternative R&D regimes, $s = 1/3$
Note: $n = 2$, $a = 110$, $c_1 = 10$, $c_2 = 5$, $\sigma = 10$, $u = 10$, $v = 1,000$, $\lambda = 1$.

Duopoly

I wish to compare monopoly and duopoly market performance, allowing for R&D spillovers and for the possibility of alternative R&D cooperation arrangements.

Spillovers
Each firm picks its own R&D intensity h_i, interpreted as above. Spillovers influence the firm's *effective* R&D intensity, μ_i,

$$\mu_i = h_i + sh_j \tag{8.36}$$

for $i, j = 1, 2$ and $i \neq j$. The spillover parameter s lies between zero and one. Zero indicates the absence of spillovers, one indicates that a firm's R&D activity benefits its rival as much as itself.

The probability that a firm completes its R&D project at or before time t depends on effective R&D intensity; the distribution of random discovery time is then

$$\Pr(I_i \leq t) = 1 - \exp(-\mu_i t) \tag{8.37}$$

Spillovers reduce a firm's incentive to spend on R&D, since some of the research effort it pays for benefits its rival. However, spillovers increase the effectiveness of such R&D spending as does take place, since a portion of each firm's spending increases the likelihood of discovery of all firms.

Non-cooperative R&D
If the two firms carry out independent R&D projects, the first firm to develop the cost-saving process receives an effective patent. In calculating the winning firm's post-innovation payoff, I assume that it licenses use of the new technology to the losing firm for a fee $c_1 - c_2$ per unit of output.[23]

Let π_W denote the static payoff of the firm that wins the innovation race, π_L the static payoff of the loser. $\pi_N(c_i)$ is the static non-cooperative Cournot duopoly payoff if both firms operate with unit cost c_i.[24]

For non-cooperative R&D, firm i picks its R&D intensity h_i to maximise its expected present-discounted value,

$$
\begin{aligned}
V_i^N &= \frac{\pi_N(c_1) - z(h_i) + ((\mu_i \pi_W + \mu_j \pi_L)/r)}{r + \mu_1 + \mu_2} \\
&= \frac{\pi_N(c_1) - z(h_i) + ((\pi_W + s\pi_L)h_i + (s\pi_W + \pi_L)h_j)/r}{r + (1+s)(h_1 + h_2)}
\end{aligned} \tag{8.38}
$$

(for $j \neq i$).

Operating entity joint venture
If the two firms form an operating entity joint venture,[25] they carry out one R&D project and evenly share the cost. The R&D intensity h of the

---

[23] I use this specification for its simplicity, not for its realism. It is possible to generalise the model to allow for imperfect post-innovation appropriability (see Martin, 1999). While there is good reason to think that patents do not ensure absolute appropriability, there is also evidence that in many sectors there are other appropriability devices that are effective (Levin *et al.*, 1987).

[24] For notational simplicity, the functional dependence of payoffs on g is not explicitly noted.

[25] Vonortas (1994) attributes the terminology 'operating entity joint venture' and 'secretariat joint venture' to Ouchi (1989).

project is chosen to maximise expected firm value,

$$V_i^{OE} = \frac{\pi_N(c_1) - (z(h)/2) + h(\pi_N(c_2)/r)}{r + h} \qquad (8.39)$$

This assumes that there is non-cooperative product market rivalry before and after innovation.

Secretariat joint venture
With a secretariat joint venture, each firm carries out its own R&D project. Results are shared; when discovery takes place, both firms have access to the new technology. The value of a single firm is

$$V_i^S = \frac{\pi_N(c_1) - z(h_i) + (\mu_1 + \mu_2)(\pi_N(c_2)/r)}{r + \mu_1 + \mu_2}$$

$$= \frac{\pi_N(c_1) - z(h_i) + (1 + s)(h_1 + h_2)(\pi_N(c_2)/r)}{r + (1 + s)(h_1 + h_2)} \qquad (8.40)$$

(for $i = 1, 2$).

Results
Theorem 2, which is proved in the appendix (p. 182), outlines the competition policy–R&D intensity relationship for the alternative R&D regimes.

Theorem 2: *(a) For non-cooperative R&D,*

$$\frac{dh_N}{dg} = -\frac{1}{D_1} \left\{ \frac{1}{1 + s} \left[\frac{d(\pi_W - \pi_N)}{dg} - s \frac{d(\pi_N - \pi_L)}{dg} \right] \right.$$

$$\left. + (1 - s) \frac{h}{r} \frac{d(\pi_W - \pi_L)}{dg} \right\} \qquad (8.41)$$

for

$$D_1 = (1 - s) \frac{\pi_W - \pi_L}{r} - z'(h) - \left(\frac{r}{1 + s} + 2h \right) z''(h) < 0 \qquad (8.42)$$

and

$$dh_N/dg < 0$$

for linear demand

(b) for an operating entity joint venture,

$$\frac{dh_{OE}}{dg} = \frac{2}{(r + h_{OE})z''(h_{OE})} \frac{d[\pi_N(c_2) - \pi_N(c_1)]}{dg} \tag{8.43}$$

(c) for a secretariat joint venture,

$$\frac{dh_S}{dg} = \frac{1}{z'(h_S) + (r/(1 + s) + 2h_S)z''(h_S)} \frac{d[\pi_N(c_2) - \pi_N(c_1)]}{dg} \tag{8.44}$$

Part (a) shows that for linear demand, stricter competition policy increases non-cooperative equilibrium R&D intensity. For parts (b) and (c), a condition analogous to (8.28) is sufficient for stricter competition policy to increase equilibrium R&D intensity. As in the monopoly case, if cost reduction reduces the marginal impact of competition policy on payoffs, then stricter competition policy increases R&D intensity.

Figure 8.3 illustrates the investigation threshold–expected discovery relationship for linear demand and exponential distribution of ε. The spillover rate is $1/3$, which is relevant for non-cooperative (N) and secretariat (S) R&D.[26] Under all three oligopoly regimes, stricter competition policy shortens the expected time to discovery. Non-cooperative R&D, with multiple research paths and high R&D levels, induced by the lure of high payoffs from first success and the threat of low payoffs otherwise, brings by far the shortest expected discovery time. Expected discovery time with non-cooperative R&D falls as the threshold price g falls, but the magnitude of the impact is slight. With either type of cooperative R&D, R&D levels are much lower, and expected time to discovery is much longer than with non-cooperative R&D (and comparable to expected discovery time under monopoly).

The alternative cooperation regimes rank quite differently in terms of expected net social welfare (figure 8.4). Of the three cooperation regimes, secretariat R&D yields the greatest welfare, independent R&D the least. Secretariat R&D dominates operating entity R&D because two research projects translate into two independent possibilities of bringing the innovation on line. Secretariat and operating entity R&D both dominate non-cooperative R&D because they imply that both firms have access to the new technology after discovery.

---

[26] The spillover rate does not affect the outcome for an operating entity joint venture, since with this form of R&D cooperation there is just one research project.

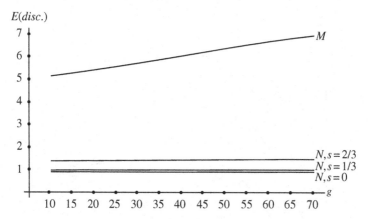

Figure 8.5   Expected time to discovery, alternative spillover levels
Note: $n = 2$, $a = 110$, $c_1 = 10$, $c_2 = 5$, $\sigma = 10$, $u = 10$, $v = 1,000$, $\lambda = 1$.

All three duopoly cooperation regimes yield greater expected net social welfare than monopoly. For the most part, this reflects better static market performance under duopoly; expected discovery times under monopoly and cooperative R&D are comparable.

For non-cooperative R&D, increases in spillovers increase the expected time to discovery (figure 8.5), although the magnitude of the effect is slight. Increases in spillovers also increase expected net social welfare (figure 8.6). Greater spillover levels reduce the single firm's incentive to spend on R&D, since they make it more likely that firm's R&D will lead the other firm to discovery first. But this also means that such R&D as does take place is more effective, increasing welfare.

Whether secretariat R&D or operating entity R&D yields a shorter expected time to discovery depends on the level of spillovers (figure 8.7). For low spillover levels, expected discovery time is less with an operating entity R&D. As spillover levels increase, expected discovery time for secretariat R&D goes down, and beyond a critical level falls below that of operating entity R&D. With secretariat R&D, greater spillovers improve technological performance. This contrasts with non-cooperative R&D (figure 8.5). The difference between the two regimes is that with a secretariat joint venture, all firms have equal access to the new technology after innovation.

Secretariat R&D consistently yields greater expected net social welfare than operating entity R&D (figure 8.8). The welfare level with secretariat R&D rises with the level of spillovers, as for non-cooperative R&D.

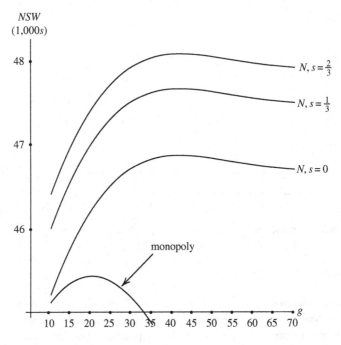

Figure 8.6 Net social welfare, non-cooperative R&D regimes, alternative spillover levels

Note: $n = 2$, $a = 110$, $c_1 = 10$, $c_2 = 5$, $\sigma = 10$, $u = 10$, $v = 1,000$, $\lambda = 1$; N indicates non-cooperative R&D, OE indicates an operating entity joint venture, S indicates a secretariat R&D joint venture.

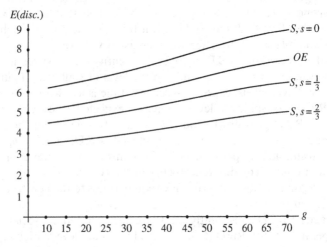

Figure 8.7 Expected time to discovery, cooperative R&D regimes, alternative spillover levels

Note: $n = 2$, $a = 110$, $c_1 = 10$, $c_2 = 5$, $\sigma = 10$, $u = 10$, $v = 1,000$, $\lambda = 1$.

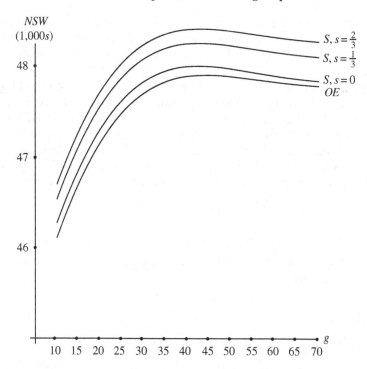

Figure 8.8   Net social welfare, cooperative R&D regimes, alternative spillover levels

Note: $n = 2$, $a = 110$, $c_1 = 10$, $c_2 = 5$, $\sigma = 10$, $u = 10$, $v = 1,000$, $\lambda = 1$; N indicates non-cooperative R&D, OE indicates an operating entity joint venture, S indicates a secretariat R&D joint venture.

4   Conclusion

Competition policy reduces expected firm profits by exposing firms to the possibility of fines if they engage in privately profitable but socially disapproved-of behaviour. If enforcement agencies make decisions by monitoring market performance, profit maximising firms expand output, simultaneously reducing the probability of investigation and improving static market performance. They also increase R&D efforts, reducing the expected time to development of lower-cost production methods (which will also lower the probability of anti-trust prosecution).

There is an inverted-U relationship between competition policy and the combined welfare of producers and consumers. A moderately strict competition policy improves their welfare; very strict competition policy worsens it.

Spillovers lower the expected time to discovery for secretariat R&D and increase it for non-cooperative R&D. Spillovers improve net social welfare under both regimes. In the examples considered here, the shortest time to discovery occurs for non-cooperative R&D and zero spillovers. The greatest expected social welfare occurs for secretariat R&D and high-spillover levels. If society wishes to promote technological progress as a goal in and of itself, the recipe suggested by the model developed here is independent R&D with an effective appropriability mechanism.[27] If society wishes to promote expected net social welfare, the recipe is secretariat R&D with spillovers and moderately tough competition policy, which brings multiple R&D paths, diffusion of results and improved static market performance.

5   Appendix: proof of theorem 2

Parts (b) and (c) are immediate from differentiation of the respective first-order conditions.

dh/dg

Firm 1's expected present-discounted value is

$$V_1 = \frac{\pi_N - z(h_1) + 1/r[((\pi_W + s\pi_L))h_1 + (s\pi_W + \pi_L)h_2]}{r + (1+s)(h_1 + h_2)} \qquad (8\text{A}.1)$$

The first-order condition to maximise V_1 is

$$
\begin{aligned}
[r + (1+s)(h_1 + h_2)]^2 \, \frac{\partial V_1}{\partial h_1} \\
= \pi_W - \pi_N - s(\pi_N - \pi_L) + (1 - s^2)\frac{\pi_W - \pi_L}{r} \\
+ (1+s)z(h_1) - [r + (1+s)(h_1 + h_2)]z'(h_1) = 0
\end{aligned}
\qquad (8\text{A}.2)
$$

The second partial derivative, evaluated along the first-order condition, is

$$\frac{\partial^2 V_1}{\partial h_1^2} = -\frac{z''(h_1)}{r + (1+s)(h_1 + h_2)} \qquad (8\text{A}.3)$$

The assumption that $z''(h_1) > 0$ is sufficient to ensure that the first-order condition identifies a maximum.

---

[27] Broadly defined, long-lived patents, for example (although it is not clear that there is in fact much government can do to enhance effective appropriability).

Differentiate the first-order condition with respect to h_1 to obtain an expression for the slope of firm 1's R&D reaction function,

$$\frac{\partial h_1}{\partial h_2} = \frac{1}{z''(h_1)} \frac{(1-s)((\pi_W - \pi_L)/r) - z'(h_1)}{r/(1+s) + h_1 + h_2} \tag{8A.4}$$

Stability requires that this be less than one in absolute value in the neighbourhood of equilibrium. Setting $h_1 = h_2 = h$, this implies

$$D_1 = (1-s)\frac{\pi_W - \pi_L}{r} - z'(h) - \left(\frac{r}{1+s} + 2h\right)z''(h) < 0 \tag{8A.5}$$

This will henceforth be assumed.[28]

Now set $h_1 = h_2 = h$ in (8A.2) to obtain the equation that determines non-cooperative equilibrium R&D intensity:

$$\frac{\pi_W - \pi_N - s(\pi_N - \pi_N)}{1+s} + (1-s)\frac{\pi_W - \pi_L}{r}h + z(h)$$

$$- \left(\frac{r}{1+s} + 2h\right)z''(h) = 0 \tag{8A.6}$$

Differentiate (8A.6) with respect to g to obtain

$$\frac{dh}{dg} = -\frac{1}{D_1}\left\{\frac{1}{1+s}\left[\frac{d(\pi_W - \pi_N)}{dg} - s\frac{d(\pi_N - \pi_L)}{dg}\right]\right.$$

$$\left. + (1-s)\frac{h}{r}\frac{d(\pi_W - \pi_L)}{dg}\right\} \tag{8A.7}$$

In view of (8A.5), dh/dg and the term in braces on the right-hand side in (8A.7) have the same sign. Sufficient conditions for $dh/dg \leq 0$ are

$$\frac{d(\pi_W - \pi_N)}{dg} \leq 0 \tag{8A.8}$$

$$\frac{d(\pi_N - \pi_L)}{dg} \geq 0 \tag{8A.9}$$

$$\frac{d(\pi_W - \pi_L)}{dg} \leq 0 \tag{8A.10}$$

---

[28] Stability conditions were satisfied for the simulations reported in the text.

Comparative statics, post-innovation market

First evaluate (8A.10). I assume that demand is linear. Payoffs are

$$\pi_W = [p(Q) - c_2]q_W + (c_1 - c_2)q_L - \frac{1}{2}\gamma F \int\limits_{g-p(Q)} f(\varepsilon)\,d\varepsilon \quad (8A.11)$$

$$\pi_L = [p(Q) - c_2]q_L - \frac{1}{2}\gamma F \int\limits_{g-p(Q)} f(\varepsilon)\,d\varepsilon \quad (8A.12)$$

where

$$Q = q_W + q_L \quad (8A.13)$$

is non-cooperative equilibrium output in the post-innovation market.

The first-order conditions for profit maximisation are

$$\frac{\partial \pi_W}{\partial q_W} = p(Q) - c_2 + q_W p' - \frac{1}{2}\gamma Ffp' = 0 \quad (8A.14)$$

$$\frac{\partial \pi_L}{\partial q_L} = p(Q) - c_1 + q_L p' - \frac{1}{2}\gamma Ffp' = 0 \quad (8A.15)$$

Note that (8A.14) and (8A.15) imply

$$q_W - \frac{1}{2}\gamma Ff = -\frac{p - c_2}{p'} > 0 \quad (8A.16)$$

and

$$q_L - \frac{1}{2}\gamma Ff = -\frac{p - c_1}{p'} > 0 \quad (8A.17)$$

respectively.

Differentiate π_W and π_L with respect to g to obtain:

$$\frac{d\pi_W}{dg} = \frac{\partial \pi_W}{\partial q_W}\frac{dq_W}{dg} + \frac{\partial \pi_W}{\partial q_L}\frac{dq_L}{dg} + \frac{\partial \pi_W}{\partial g} \quad (8A.18)$$

$$\frac{d\pi_L}{dg} = \frac{\partial \pi_L}{\partial q_W}\frac{dq_W}{dg} + \frac{\partial \pi_L}{\partial q_L}\frac{dq_L}{dg} + \frac{\partial \pi_L}{\partial g} \quad (8A.19)$$

(8A.14) makes the first term on the right-hand side in (8A.18) equal to zero; (8A.15) makes the second term on the right-hand side in (8A.19) equal to zero; this is the envelope theorem. By inspection, (8A.11) and (8A.12) imply

$$\frac{\partial \pi_W}{\partial g} = \frac{\partial \pi_L}{\partial g} \quad (8A.20)$$

Hence

$$\frac{d(\pi_W - \pi_L)}{dg} = \frac{\partial \pi_W}{\partial q_L} \frac{dq_L}{dg} - \frac{\partial \pi_L}{\partial q_W} \frac{dq_W}{dg} \qquad (8A.21)$$

Differentiate (8A.11) with respect to q_L:

$$\begin{aligned}\frac{\partial \pi_W}{\partial q_L} &= p'q_W + c_1 - c_2 - \frac{1}{2}\gamma Ffp' \\ &= p'\left(q_W - \frac{1}{2}\gamma Ff\right) + c_1 - c_2 \\ &= p'\left(-\frac{p - c_2}{p'}\right) + c_1 - c_2 \\ &= -(p - c_1)\end{aligned} \qquad (8A.22)$$

(using (8A.16)).

Differentiate (8A.12) with respect to q_W:

$$\frac{\partial \pi_L}{\partial q_W} = p'q_L - \frac{1}{2}\gamma Ffp' = -(p - c_1) \qquad (8A.23)$$

(using (8A.17)).

Substitute (8A.22) and (8A.23) into (8A.21) to obtain

$$\frac{d(\pi_W - \pi_L)}{dg} = (p - c_1)\left(\frac{dq_W}{dg} - \frac{dq_L}{dg}\right) \qquad (8A.24)$$

Now subtract (8A.15) from (8A.14) and rearrange terms to obtain

$$q_W - q_L = -\frac{c_1 - c_2}{p'} > 0 \qquad (8A.25)$$

This implies

$$\frac{d(q_W - q_L)}{dg} = 0 \qquad (8A.26)$$

Hence

$$\frac{d(\pi_W - \pi_L)}{dg} = 0 \qquad (8A.27)$$

and (8A.10) is satisfied.

Comparative statics, pre-innovation market

Now turn to consideration of (8A.8) and (8A.9).

If both firms operate with unit cost c_1, firm 1's payoff is

$$\pi_1 = [p(q_1 + q_2) - c_1]q_1 - \frac{1}{2}\gamma F \int_{g - p(q_1 + q_2)} f(\varepsilon)\,d\varepsilon \qquad (8A.28)$$

Equilibrium per-firm output q_N satisfies the condensed first-order condition

$$p(2q_N) - c_1 + p'\left(q_N - \frac{1}{2}\gamma Ff\right) = 0 \qquad (8A.29)$$

This implies

$$q_N - \frac{1}{2}\gamma Ff = -\frac{p(2q_N) - c_1}{p'} > 0 \qquad (8A.30)$$

Differentiating (8A.29) with respect to q_N gives the comparative static derivative

$$\frac{dq_N}{dg} = \frac{1}{2}\frac{\gamma Ff'}{3 + p'\gamma Ff'} = \frac{1}{2}\frac{1}{p' + (3/\gamma Ff')} < 0 \qquad (8A.31)$$

The indicated sign depends on $f'(g - p) < 0$, which is henceforth assumed.

Firm 1's equilibrium payoff is

$$\pi_N = [p(2q_N) - c_1]q_N - \frac{1}{2}\gamma F \int_{g - p(2q_N)} f(\varepsilon)\,d\varepsilon \qquad (8A.32)$$

Differentiate (8A.32) with respect to g:

$$\frac{d\pi_N}{dg} = \frac{d\pi_N}{dq_N}\frac{dq_N}{dg} + \frac{\partial \pi_N}{\partial g} \qquad (8A.33)$$

To evaluate $d\pi_N/dq_N$, differentiate (8A.32) with respect to q_N:

$$\frac{d\pi_N}{dq_N} = p - c_1 + 2q_N p' - \gamma Ffp'$$
$$= \left(q_N - \frac{1}{2}\gamma F\right)p' = -[p(2q_N) - c_1] \qquad (8A.34)$$

Subtract (8A.33) from (8A.18):

$$\frac{d(\pi_W - \pi_N)}{dg} = \frac{\partial \pi_W}{\partial q_L}\frac{dq_L}{dg} - \frac{d\pi_N}{dq_N}\frac{dq_N}{dg} + \frac{\partial(\pi_W - \pi_N)}{\partial g} \qquad (8A.35)$$

First consider the final term:

$$\frac{\partial \pi_W}{\partial g} = \frac{1}{2}\gamma Ff[g - p(Q)]$$ (8A.36)

$$\frac{\partial \pi_N}{\partial g} = \frac{1}{2}\gamma Ff[g - p(2q_N)]$$ (8A.37)

Since

$$Q > 2q_N$$ (8A.38)

$$p(Q) < p(2q_N)$$ (8A.39)

$$g - p(Q) > g - p(2q_N)$$ (8A.40)

$$f[g - p(Q)] < f[g - p(2q_N)]$$ (8A.41)

and finally

$$0 < \frac{\partial \pi_W}{\partial g} < \frac{\partial \pi_N}{\partial g}$$ (8A.42)

or

$$\frac{\partial(\pi_W - \pi_N)}{\partial g} < 0$$ (8A.43)

the final term on the right-hand side in (8A.35) is negative.
Now turn to

$$\frac{\partial \pi_W}{\partial q_L}\frac{dq_L}{dg} - \frac{d\pi_N}{dq_N}\frac{dq_N}{dg}$$

$$= -[p(Q) - c_1]\frac{dq_L}{dg} + [p(2q_N) - c_1]\frac{dq_N}{dg}$$

$$= \frac{p(2q_N) - c_1}{(3/f'[g - p(2q_N)]) + \gamma Fp'} - \frac{p(Q) - c_1}{(3/f'[g - p(Q)]) + \gamma Fp'}$$

(8A.44)

Assume that $f' < 0, f'' > 0$ over the range of ε that is relevant for the pre- and post-innovation equilibria. This is a regularity condition on the distribution of the random part of demand.
Then

$$f'[g - p(2q_N)] < f'[g - p(Q)] < 0$$ (8A.45)

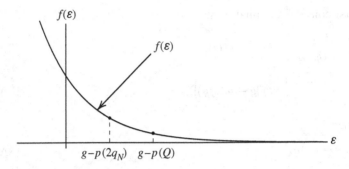

Figure 8A.1   Equilibrium $g - p(2q_N)$, $g - p(Q)$

(see figure 8A.1);

$$\gamma F f'[g - p(2q_N)] < \gamma F f'[g - p(Q)] < 0 \qquad (8A.46)$$

$$\frac{3}{\gamma F f'[g - p(Q)]} < \frac{3}{\gamma F f'[g - p(2q_N)]} < 0 \qquad (8A.47)$$

$$p' + \frac{3}{\gamma F f'[g - p(Q)]} < p' + \frac{3}{\gamma F f'[g - p(2q_N)]} < 0 \qquad (8A.48)$$

$$\frac{1}{p' + (3/\gamma F f'[g - p(2q_N)])} < \frac{1}{p' + (3/\gamma F f'[g - p(Q)])} < 0 \qquad (8A.49)$$

Combining (8A.48) and (8A.49) gives

$$\frac{p(2q_N) - c_1}{p' + (3/\gamma F f'[g - p(2q_N)])} < \frac{p(Q) - c_1}{p' + (3/\gamma F f'[g - p(Q)])} < 0 \qquad (8A.50)$$

Hence

$$\frac{\partial \pi_W}{\partial q_L} \frac{dq_L}{dg} - \frac{d\pi_N}{dq_N} \frac{dq_N}{dg} < 0 \qquad (8A.51)$$

Combined with (8A.43), this establishes that (8A.8) is satisfied.
Essentially the same arguments, with appropriate sign changes, show that (8A.9) is satisfied. This establishes part (a) of theorem 2.

Bibliography

Arrow, K.J. (1962) Economic welfare and the allocation of resources for Invention, in K.J. Arrow, *The Rate and Direction of Inventive Activity: Economic and Social Factors*, NBER, Princeton: Princeton University Press, pp. 609–25

Baron, D.P. and R.B. Myerson (1982) Regulating a monopolist with unknown costs, *Econometrica*, 50, pp. 911–30

Besanko, D. and D. Spulber (1989) Anti-trust enforcement under asymmetric information, *Economic Journal*, 99, pp. 408–25

Bulow, J.I., J.D. Geanakoplos and P.D. Klemperer (1985) Multimarket oligopoly: strategic substitutes and complements, *Journal of Political Economy* 93(3), pp. 488–511

Gilbert, R.J. and D.M.G. Newbery (1982) Preemptive patenting and the persistence of monopoly, *American Economic Review*, 72(3), pp. 514–26

(1984) Uncertain innovation and the persistence of monopoly: comment, *American Economic Review*, 74(1), pp. 238–42

Grossack, I.M. (1986) OPEC and the anti-trust laws, *Journal of Economic Issues*, 20(3), pp. 725–41

Jorde, T.M. and D.J. Teece (1997) Harmonizing competition policy in regimes of rapid technological change, in L. Waverman, W.S. Comanor and A. Goto (eds.) *Competition Policy in the Global Economy*, London and New York: Routledge

Levin, R.C., A.K. Klevorick, R.R. Nelson and S.G. Winter (1987) Appropriating the returns from industrial research and development, *Brookings Papers on Economic Activity Microeconomics*, pp. 783–820

Martin, S. (1996) R&D joint ventures and tacit product market collusion, *European Journal of Political Economy*, 11(4), pp. 733–41

(1997) Public policies towards cooperation in research and development, in L. Waverman, W.S. Comanor and A. Goto (eds.), *Competition Policy in the Global Economy*, London and New York: Routledge

(1998) Competition policy: publicity vs. prohibition and punishment, in S. Martin (ed.), *European Competition Policies*, Amsterdam: Elsevier–North Holland

(1999) Spillovers, appropriability, and R&D, February, paper presented to the January 2000 meeting of the American Economic Association, Boston

(2000) Resource allocation by a competition authority, in E. Hope (ed.), *Foundations of Competition Policy Analysis*, London: Routledge

Meißner, W. and R. Markl (1997) International R&D cooperations, in L. Waverman, W.S. Comanor and A. Goto (eds.), *Competition Policy in the Global Economy*, London and New York: Routledge

Ouchi, W.G. (1989) The new joint R&D, *Proceedings of the IEEE*, 77(9), pp. 1318–26

Phlips, L. (1993) The *AZKO* decision: a case of predatory pricing?, *Journal of Industrial Economics*, 41(3), pp. 315–21

(1995) *Competition Policy: A Game-Theoretic Perspective*, Cambridge: Cambridge University Press

(1996) On the detection of collusion and predation, *European Economic Review*, 40(3–5), pp. 495–510

Priest, G. (1977) The common law process and the selection of efficient rules, *Journal of Legal Studies*, 6(1), pp. 65–82

Reinganum, J.F. (1983) Uncertain innovation and the persistence of monopoly, *American Economic Review*, 73(4), pp. 741–8

(1989) The timing of innovation: research, development, and diffusion, chapter 14 in R. Schmalensee and R.D. Willig (eds.), *Handbook of Industrial Organization*, 1 Amsterdam: North-Holland, pp. 849–908

Rubin, Paul H. (1977) Why is the common law efficient?, *Journal of Legal Studies*, 6(1), pp. 51–63

Souam, S. (2000) Optimal antitrust policy under different regimes of fines, *International Journal of Industrial Organization*, forthcoming

Suzumura, K. and A. Goto (1997) Collaborative R&D and competition policy, in L. Waverman, W.S. Comanor and A. Goto (eds.), *Competition Policy in the Global Economy*, London and New York: Routledge

Vonortas, N.S. (1994) Inter-firm cooperation with imperfectly appropriable research, *International Journal of Industrial Organization*, 12(3), pp. 413–35

9 On some issues in the theory of competition in regulated markets

Gianni De Fraja

1 Introduction

Writing in 1962, Louis Phlips observed that 'la réalisation d'un marché concurrentiel en Europe peut être facilitée par *une intégration des marchés européens*', which is 'un moyen d'aboutir à des comportements plus concurrentiels',[1] and stressed that a positive intervention may be needed in order to stimulate the forces of competition: 'il ne suffit pas cependant de l'intégrer négativement, de se borner à la suppression des barrières artificielles aux échanges: il faut aussi l'integrer de façon positive, en améliorant son functionnement.'[2]

While Phlips was concerned with the lowering of barriers between national markets which the Common Market was intended to demolish, the concern nowadays is with the barriers to enter certain industries, which have traditionally been monopolised: in the 1980s and 1990s, it became increasingly obvious that the simple opening up of a market to any firm which wished to enter it was not sufficient to guarantee the establishment of competitive conditions in markets for goods such as the supply of electricity, telecommunications service, water and gas. Government and competition authorities realised that they needed to maintain a degree of scrutiny over these industries, and often undertook positive actions in order to enhance the competitive pressure. The complexity of these industries throws up a host of problems which, while of considerable interest to the

A preliminary version of this chapter was presented at the 20th Conference of *l'Industria*, Piacenza, Italy, (27–28 September 1996). I would like to thank Paola Valbonesi for comments. I acknowledge the financial support of the ESRC research Programme on Contracts and Competition, Phase II, grant L114251031.
[1] 'The creation of competitive markets in Europe can be brought forward by the *integration of the European markets*, because it determines a more competitive behaviour' (Phlips, 1962, p. 75, emphasis in the original).
[2] 'However, it is not sufficient to integrate negatively, eliminating artificial barriers to trade: it is also essential to integrate actively, improving the working of the market' (Phlips, 1962, p. 75).

economic theorist, also highlight the inadequacy of a stylised view of the world according to which there are only two types of industries. On the one hand are industries which are either competitive, and hence do not need regulation or intervention or oligopolies, for which traditional anti-trust intervention is necessary, and on the other are industries where no competition is possible, and therefore price and/or rate of return regulation (or even nationalisation) is necessary. It is now accepted that political developments (privatisation, the abolition of statutory monopolies, etc.) and technological advances (which have lowered economies of scale), are increasingly allowing the introduction of some form of competitive pressure on erstwhile natural monopolies, at least for part of their activities. Conversely, incumbent firms have the incentive and, often, the means, to hinder this competitive pressure, and governments and competition authorities may need to intervene to prevent socially costly activities of this type.

Theoretical developments have shown how competition and regulation can affect the performance of an industry, and how their interaction can result in varying structures, depending on the rules designed to operate the regulatory mechanisms. In this chapter I look at some of the problems that come up in the analysis of the interplay between regulation and competition; the main point which will emerge is the variety of situations that can occur, and the consequent need of a case-by-case approach to the modelling of this interplay. This contrasts with the simple situation where there is a single regulated monopolist, and corresponds to the complex variety of models developed by the theory of industrial organisation for the analysis of oligopoly situation *vis-à-vis* the relatively straightforward modelling of monopoly and of perfect competition. The richness of the set of situations that emerges is also reflected in the more complex possibilities that industrial policy makers need to consider. In many situations, a case-by-case approach might be called for, whereas in the traditional set up, the application of a certain set of rules might have sufficed. To put it schematically: one firm or many firms: straightforward; few firms: complex.

Early models of regulation studied took the existing regulatory mechanisms as given without inquiring as to their *raison d'être*; by contrast, the 'new theory of regulation' (the origin of which can be ascribed to the papers of Baron and Myerson, 1982, and Laffont and Tirole, 1986, both inspired by Loeb and Magat, 1979) takes the constraints as given and studies the *optimal* regulation within those constraints (Laffont, 1994). The most powerful of such constraints has been identified in the different knowledge possessed by the two parties in a contractual relationship. A typical stylised example of this may depict a situation where a regulated firm may be in a position to claim higher costs or more difficult technical problems than actually exist, and demand higher prices than strictly necessary to cover its costs and reward the capital adequately. As long as the regulator is unable to verify such claims (in the jargon, as long as there is asymmetry of information), the firm will obtain a higher reward than the market rate of profit. One of the most interesting points that can be inferred from the results of the optimal regulation literature is that the contracts offered in practice by procurement agencies have features which tally somehow with the prescriptions of the models (see below, and the discussion in Laffont and Tirole, 1993, pp. 72 ff.). This approach has the added advantage of unifying regulation and procurement theory, as highlighted by Laffont and Tirole in the title of their book: in the benchmark case for both situations a welfare maximising principal offers a contract to a profit maximising firm, and in both situations the latter has an informational advantage over the principal.

This chapter focuses on the effects of competition in regulation and procurement. After briefly sketching, in section 2, the basic Laffont–Tirole model, I describe in section 3 a number of applications of this model to more complex situations where more than one firm is potentially operating in the market. The chapter ends in section 4 with an analysis of competition in procurement. I show how potential competition can alleviate the inefficiency caused by the possibility of opportunistic behaviour identified by the literature on incomplete contracts. While the various models illustrated are deliberately not closely linked to each other, they develop a common theme: the presence of competition, potential or actual, often alters policy conclusions reached in the presence of a single firm, and therefore theoretical analyses developed for the single-firm case need in general to be extended to the case of more than one firm before policy conclusions are drawn and implemented.

2   Competition in regulated markets

The basic one-firm model

In an influential article, Laffont and Tirole (1986) built a model of regulation which sheds important light on the theoretical problems of regulation and their possible solutions. In the model, a welfare maximising regulator sets the price for the (single-product) firm she supervises. The firm operates in a technologically advanced environment where cost reductions are possible, for example through investment in R&D. The regulator can observe the realised cost of production, but cannot distinguish between low cost due to 'luck' (easier than expected technological conditions) and low cost due to 'effort' (high R&D). The regulator would like to reward the latter without transferring costly social resources to a firm which just happens to be lucky. Formally, if we denote with β the exogenous level of cost, with e the firm's cost-reducing effort, with p the regulated firm's price and with λ the distortionary and administrative cost of public funding, the model can be described as follows (a fuller discussion can be found in Laffont and Tirole, 1993, chapters 1, 2):

$q(p)$ is the regulated firm's demand: $q'(p) < 0$, with elasticity $\eta(p)$

$\psi(e)$ is the utility cost of the regulated firm's cost-reducing effort (R&D, managerial effort, etc.): it satisfies $\psi'(e), \psi''(e) > 0$ and $\psi'''(e) \geq 0$ (the last is a technical assumption which ensures an interior solution)

$(\beta - e)q$ is the regulated firm's production cost

$F(\beta)$ is the distribution function of the exogenous parameter β, $\beta \in \left[\underline{\beta}, \bar{\beta}\right]$, $f(\beta) = F'(\beta)$, $F(\underline{\beta}) = 0$, $F(\bar{\beta}) = 1$

$$\text{and } \frac{d}{d\beta}\left(\frac{F(\beta)}{f(\beta)}\right) \geq 0.$$

The realised value of β is the regulated firm's private information: the regulator only knows the distribution function

t is the monetary transfer from the regulator to the firm

$S(q)$ is the consumer's surplus

$\pi(p, e, t) = t + (p - \beta + e)q(p) - \psi(e)$ is the regulated firm's profit

$W(p, e, t) = S(q(p)) - (1 + \lambda)t + \pi(p, e, t)$ is the regulator's payoff function.

The regulator maximises her payoff function, by choosing a relationship between p and t, and allowing the firm to select any combination of p and t satisfying this relationship. Laffont and Tirole (1986) compare the solution of this problem in conditions of both symmetric and asymmetric information, and obtain a number of results which can be summarised as follows:

- The regulated firm's price is given by Ramsey pricing both in symmetric and asymmetric information:

$$\frac{p - \beta + e}{p} = \frac{1}{\eta(p)} \frac{\lambda}{1 + \lambda}$$

This is defined as the dichotomy property; when it holds prices and incentives can be separated: asymmetry of information affects only the provision of incentives, not the pricing rule. A necessary condition for this to happen is the observability of cost: when cost is not observable, as in Baron and Myerson (1982), then price distortions must be introduced.

- Effort is lower in the presence of asymmetric information, except when $\beta = \underline{\beta}$:

  Symmetric information: $q(p) = \psi'(e)$

  Asymmetric information: $q(p(\beta)) = \psi'(e(\beta))$

  $$- \frac{\lambda}{1 + \lambda} \frac{F(\beta)}{f(\beta)} \psi''(e(\beta))$$

This of course implies that, for every value of $\beta \in (\underline{\beta}, \bar{\beta}]$, price is also higher with asymmetric information; this is caused by the fact that cost is higher: the rule of price determination is unaffected by the asymmetry of information.

- 'Lucky' firms, (firms with low β) extract rent from the regulator; this is appropriately defined 'informational rent', because it is absent with symmetric information:

  Symmetric information : $U = \pi(p, e, t) = 0$

  Asymmetric information : $U(\beta) = \pi(p(\beta), e(\beta), t(\beta))$

  $$= \int_{\beta}^{\bar{\beta}} \psi'(e(\tilde{\beta})) \, d\tilde{\beta}$$

They also show that some of the theoretical features of contracts are also observed in actual relationship between regulators and regulated firms, and between procurement agencies and their contractors. As their book (Laffont and Tirole, 1993) testifies, this model can be extended in numerous directions and used to shed considerable light on the interaction between parties in more complex, and realistic, relationships, such as multiproduct firms, situations where quality matters and dynamic situations, where the regulator and the regulated firm interact over a period of time. A substantial part of the book is devoted to situations where more than one potential supplier is potentially capable of satisfying the regulator's needs. I concentrate on these specific cases in the remainder of this section, illustrating the rich variety of situations that emerge and the developments that have occurred since the publication of Laffont and Tirole (1993).

Multiple suppliers

While there undoubtedly do exist situations where only one firm can economically supply a certain market, it is now generally accepted that, in the vast majority of cases, competition, whether actual or potential, has a role to play. This can be the case when a domestic market is opened up to foreign suppliers, as is happening at a very fast pace in the European telecommunication markets; another related instance is the power industry in the United Kingdom, where most households have the opportunity to buy gas from electricity suppliers and electricity from gas suppliers. In these cases the regulator faces a two-fold problem: on the one hand, she needs to choose the actual supplier (or, indeed, suppliers) among several potential ones; on the other, she needs to find ways of allowing competitive forces to play their role and reduce, if possible, the two sources of cost identified above, the actual production cost $(\beta - e)$ and the regulated firm's informational rent.

This is still an area where the theoretical developments are rapidly evolving, and one can therefore expect further insights into the topic. Nevertheless, it is possible to propose a rough classification of the various problems considered. In particular, we can distinguish between:

- *Symmetric competition* – whereby all firms are treated symmetrically; and within it:
  - auction-type situations
  - market-type situations.
- *Asymmetric competition*, whereby some of the firms are in a different position; this can happen:
  - either because one firm has some advantage or disadvantage (typically in regulated industries it produces a necessary input in conditions of natural monopoly, as it owns the network connecting each household to the service)
  - or because, for reasons which may not have an economic rationale, only some of the firms are subject to regulation (thus, for example, the opening of the national European markets such as electricity and telephony, might result in a situation where the French regulator imposes price constraints on the French companies, but not on the German, British or Spanish companies willing to supply French consumers).

Roughly speaking we may label 'market-type' the situations where the regulator takes separate decisions on the number of entrants and their prices (e.g. Auriol and Laffont, 1992; Biglaiser and Ma, 1995; McGuire and Riordan, 1995). The optimal number of firms will be determined as a trade-off between costs and benefits. The cost of an increase in the number of firms is the duplication of fixed costs (which parallels the negative effect of entry in oligopoly markets). To counter this cost, there are two types of benefits: first if the selected contractors offer different goods, there is the beneficial effect of an *increase in variety* (as in McGuire and Riordan, 1995; this trade-off between variety and fixed cost forms the basis of Spence, 1976, and Dixit and Stiglitz, 1977, analysis of monopolistic competition). The second type of benefit, less paramount in theoretical models of industrial organisation, is the *information effect*. In the first place if, as it seems likely, cost conditions are correlated between firms, then the regulator can reduce their profits (which are socially costly), by making one firm's payment dependent on the others' actions (see Caillaud, 1990, for a model highlighting this effect); secondly, as Auriol and Laffont (1992) point out, increasing the number of potential suppliers also increases the sample and hence the probability of finding a low-cost supplier. These considerations suggest that the simultaneous presence of firms should occur more often where economies of scale are weak and where the benefits of variety and of information are high.

Bidding for contracts or franchises

Whilst auctions have long been used in procurement, it has been suggested that one way to introduce competition in markets that are known to be natural monopolies would be to auction off the right to be such a monopolist to the highest supplier (Demsetz, 1968). An early example that received considerable attention was the auctioning of the franchise for cable TV in parts of the United States (Posner, 1972; Williamson, 1976). More recently, the FCC auctioned off the spectrum for mobile telephone communication, in what was dubbed – for once, probably truthfully – the greatest auction in history (*New York Times*, March 16, 1995, p.1A.17; see McAfee and McMillan, 1996, for a description and theoretical considerations).

In 1993, the UK Independent Television Commission (ITC) auctioned off the right to broadcast terrestrial television in the frequencies used by the third channel in 16 different geographical regions in the United Kingdom. This auction has received relatively little attention, despite the fact that it displayed some interesting features, in particular with reference to quality. In an ordinary auction the seller of the auctioned object wants to maximise the revenues from its sale. This was the case in the FCC spectrum auction, and in the early United States cable TV auctions mentioned above: bidders could be ruled out on the grounds that they did not offer adequate guarantees about the financial viability of their plans, but if this guarantee was met, then the highest bidder won the franchise; on the other hand, the ITV auction in the United Kingdom had explicit concerns for quality. Firms had to present a broadcasting plan, describing in some detail the programmes they intended to show. In half of the 16 regions the franchise was not awarded to the highest bidder, on the ground that their quality level was lower than that of lower-bidding firms. Concern for quality is of course paramount in military procurement, and it is therefore not surprising that the theoretical literature has concentrated mostly on the auctions used in practice by the United States Department of Defense. In general terms, the latter has the two-fold problem of choosing the right supplier (or suppliers) on the one hand and, on the other, of providing the selected supplier with the right incentive for cost reduction.

The analysis of this situation is in Laffont and Tirole (1987). They use their benchmark model, sketched on pp. 193–5 above, and extend it by assuming that rather than just one firm, there are n of them, identical in all respects except the realised value of their efficiency parameter, $\beta \in [\underline{\beta}, \bar{\beta}]$. The regulator (or, more likely in this case, the procurement agency), asks each firm, i, to report its own $\beta_i, i = 1, \ldots, n$, and commits itself to a mechanism for selecting the winner and to offering a contract for the sale of one unit of output to the winner, based on all the reports, $\beta = (\beta_1, \ldots, \beta_n)$. The regulator must award the contract to a single firm (an assumption that can be relaxed), but may use a stochastic mechanism: it can (commit to) award the contract to firm i with probability x_i, with $x_i = x_i(\beta)$. The regulator's payoff function is therefore the expectation of:

$$
S \sum_{i=1}^{n} x_i - (1 + \lambda) \sum_{i=1}^{n} t_i - (1 + \lambda) \sum_{i=1}^{n} x_i(\beta_i - e_i)
$$
$$
+ \sum_{i=1}^{n} (t_i - x_i \psi(e_i))
$$

where S, t_i, e_i and ψ are defined as on p. 194. Laffont and Tirole show that the solution to the regulator's problem satisfies the following properties:

- The contract is awarded to the firm with the lowest β_i.
- The winning firm is required to exercise the same level of effort as it would exercise if it were the only supplier: organising an auction does not increase the firms' investment.
- The transfer received by the winning firm is, however, reduced by competition, and consequently so is its informational rent. Specifically, if firms are re-labelled so that firm 1 is the one with the lowest β and firm

2 that with the second lowest β (i.e. if $\beta_1 \leq \beta_2 \leq \beta_j, j = 3, \ldots, n$), then $U_1(\beta) = \int_\beta^{\beta_2} \psi'(e^*(\tilde{\beta})) d\tilde{\beta}$ – that is, the transfer (and the informational rent) received by the winning firm is the same which it would receive in a single-firm regulatory relationship where, however, the distribution is truncated at $\beta = \beta_2$ – that is, where the regulator knows that the firm's β is at most β_2.

Note the close analogy with the mechanism of a standard English auction for the sale of, say, a painting. This is equivalent to a mechanism by which all participants report their maximum willingness to pay, the painting is awarded to the person reporting the highest willingness to pay, who is, however, required to pay a price equal only to the second-highest willingness to pay reported by the bidders.

The results obtained by Laffont and Tirole, in a plausible model, contain (at least) two important lessons. First, competition for contracts reduces, but does not eliminate, informational rents, except in the limit as the number of firms goes to infinity. This has an exact parallel in the standard industrial organisation result that oligopoly reduces the monopoly rent (and consequent deadweight loss) but eliminates it in only the limit, as the number of firms becomes large. Secondly, perhaps less intuitively, while competition does reduce costs, it reduces only the first of the two sources of costs we have identified above – namely, the regulated firm's profit – and leaves unaltered the level of effort and the production costs: as we have just seen, the winner of the competition has the same level of production cost that it would have had if it had been the sole supplier to begin with.

In a paper inspired by the United Kingdom television auction, Cabizza and De Fraja (1998) study the case where firms do not exert a cost-reducing effort, but can alter, at a cost, the quality of their supply. Some of the results obtained mirror the Laffont–Tirole ones: the franchise is awarded to the most efficient firm, the quality level offered by each firm, $q(\beta)$, is not affected by the extent of competition,[3] while the price paid for the franchise

---

[3] Quality is given by the condition

$$\frac{S'(q)}{(1+\lambda)} = C_q(q, \beta) \qquad\qquad \text{with symmetric information}$$

$$\frac{S'(q)}{(1+\lambda)} = C_q(q, \beta) + \frac{\lambda}{1+\lambda} \frac{F(\beta)}{f(\beta)} C_{\beta q}(q, \beta) \quad \text{with asymmetric information}$$

Here q is quality and S denotes the consumer's utility from quality. Thus, as one might expect from the analysis on p. 195, quality is reduced by asymmetry of information, except for the lowest-β firm, and in a way which depends on the distribution function of β and on the shadow cost of public funding, λ, is. Note that the formulae do not contain n: quality does not depend on the number of bidders.

is. With regard to the relationship between the franchise fee paid and the quality of programmes broadcast by the winning television station, they found that, when there is no auction, the franchise fee is a decreasing function of the quality supplied: low-cost firms broadcast higher-quality programmes but pay a lower fee for the franchise; this is the opposite of what happens in conditions of symmetric information. However, this is reversed as the number of competitors goes up: in this case it may happen that low-cost firms not only offer better programmes, but also bid a higher price for the right to do so. These conclusions allow them to interpret the rejection of the higher bid in the ITV auction as a consequence of the limited number of bidders.

I have so far assumed that there is only one winner in the auction. While it must clearly be the case that only one mobile telephone company is allowed to use a certain frequency in a given area, it is entirely plausible that the supply of, say, uniforms to the Navy, be split between two or more producers. The United States Department of Defense makes considerable use of auctions with multiple winners, known as 'split award auctions'. While it does not use the optimal mechanism (which, even in very simple set ups, is in general fiendishly complex), it does require the submission of quite elaborate bids, asking each participating contractor to bid a price for the supply of the entire requirement and a price for the supply of $1/n$th of the requirement, where n is the number of participants and is known in advance to bidders.[4] There is still considerable controversy in practice with regard to the merit of the split award auction (see Anton and Yao, 1992). The forces at work are conceptually simple. On the one hand, splitting the award reduces the informational rent of the winners; on the other hand awarding the contract to a single bidder makes the most of economies of scale in production. Therefore, not surprisingly, Anton and Yao (1992) show that, with diseconomies of scale, when the firms have similar costs a split award is preferable; only if one of them has a substantial cost advantage should it be awarded the whole contract. In a related paper, Anton (1995) studies the case of economies of scale, and obtains similar results, with the additional conclusion that the split award auction does not happen as often as it should from an efficiency viewpoint. In both these papers, while whether the award is split or whole is determined endogenously *after* the bids are submitted, the way in which the award is split is exogenously given. This reflects current practice by the United States Department of Defense, but is in general not optimal.

---

[4] See Simmons (1996) for a comparison between the performance of the various mechanisms used and the optimal one.

Regulation and entry

Within the group of models which consider situations where the firms are treated asymmetrically I concentrate here on those where competition is potential, rather than actual (as, for example, in Laffont and Tirole, 1993, chapter 5.2; Biglaiser and Ma, 1995): the issue here is that regulation and entry deterrence interact, in the sense that the policies designed by the regulator for the regulated firm inevitably affect the profitability of entry. To understand how this should be the case, it is sufficient to consider the standard limit-pricing model: this model is normally described as theoretically unsound because it displays 'time-inconsistency': if the incumbent firm could commit not to change its price after entry, then it would indeed be profitable for it to lower its price so as to make entry unprofitable. But entry-deterrence via limit pricing does not work precisely because the potential entrant knows that the pre-entry price can be easily changed in the event of entry. The incumbent would like to commit to maintain its price in the event of entry, but it has no way of doing so. However, if this price is set once for all by the regulator, then the entrant knows that it will in fact remain at that level, and this may provide the incumbent with the degree of commitment which is necessary to deter entry. This sketchy example is unrealistic: it implicitly assumes no ability to commit for an incumbent monopolist in an unregulated firm, and unlimited commitment ability to commit on the regulator's part. In reality, it is likely that the regulator's ability to commit is determined by the design of the institutional mechanism for regulation: a typical example is the length of the interval between regulatory reviews: this is typically fixed by the government, and cannot normally be modified by the regulator.

De Fraja (1997) investigates the role of the regulator's commitment on prices and on the incentives for cost reduction and obtains some surprising results. For example, he shows that price cuts and marginal cost reductions, which are unambiguously welcome in the standard monopoly regulation can, in the presence of potential competitors in the industry, clash with the regulator's objective function, and consequently prove undesirable. This occurs because of the adverse effect of the regulated firm's price and cost reduction on any potential competitors and the likelihood of their entry into the industry. The way in which the regulator's conflicting goals of fostering competition and inducing price decreases and technology improvements interact with each other is determined by the design of the institutional framework for regulation. For example, with regard to the interval between regulatory reviews, if this gap is short, then prices are lower and the cost-reducing effort higher than they would be with a longer interval. Again, this is exactly the opposite of what happens when there is only one firm in the industry, where a longer gap gives a monopoly more time to reap profits from a cost-reducing investment.

Monopoly ownership of inputs: the access problem

The problem of access pricing can be described in the following simplified terms: a utility supplies a necessary input under conditions of national monopoly: the standard example is the network of pipes or cables connecting each individual consumer to the national grid. This network is owned and maintained by a water or gas (in the case of pipes) or electricity or telephone (in the case of cables) company, who also supplies the final product. In order to supply the final customers, any alternative supplier would have to use the network owned by their competitor. In some cases it is possible to split the firm up so that the owner of this input is not a competitor in the final market (this was the case with the divestiture of AT&T in the United States, and in the British power and rail industries). In other cases, for technological reasons (or political choices) this cannot be done. The question arises in this case: how should the price to be paid for access to the network be set? Is there a risk that the monopolistic owner of the network might set so high a price for access that competition is barred? Can this lead to inefficient allocation of production, in the sense that the firm who can supply the service at the least cost is prevented from supplying it by the excessively high price set for access? Conversely, wouldn't the possibility of not being able to supply the final customers and extract profit from them weaken the network's owner from efficiently maintaining the network – e.g. by investing in state-of-the-art technology? The crux of the economic problem that arises in the situation described is that, since the intermediate output is produced in a condition of natural monopoly, marginal cost is above average cost, and the standard marginal cost pricing rule would leave the network owner unable to cover the fixed costs of running the network.

This situation has recently received considerable attention in the telephony industry, where extremely fast technological developments have put scores of suppliers in the position of requiring access to the monopoly-owned network. It is indeed this industry that has recently brought the access problem to the attention of the courts, when anti-trust litigation between *Clear Communications* and the privatised New Zealand Telecom company was decided by the (British) Queen's Privy Council, who approved the use of the so-called Efficient Component Pricing Principle, or Baumol–Willig Rule (Baumol and Sidak, 1994).[5] According to this rule,

---

[5] This rule was first conceived in the context of rail services, by which a train operator would have to lease the track it owns to a competitor (Baumol, 1983).

the price paid by the competitor to use the monopoly-owned input should be set at a level that repays the latter for *all* the costs incurred in making the network available to the former, including the lost profit caused by the inability to sell itself the units of the output sold by the competitors. In economic terms, this is simply the opportunity cost of allowing the competitor to use the network. The importance of this rule is that, if the price for the final output of the owner of the network is set efficiently by the regulator (i.e. if it equals the latter's marginal cost) then:

(i) the rule gives the socially correct incentives for adequate investment in the network
(ii) the rule selects, as the final suppliers, the firm whose cost of running the long-distance line is lower and
(iii) the rule does not require the regulator to set the terms at which the network owner charges the firms requiring access to the network.

Subsequent research has extended the original work by defining the rule for more complex technological situations (Armstrong, Doyle and Vickers, 1996; Armstrong, 1998) and by studying the case where the condition that the final output price is set efficiently cannot hold – for example, because of some informational advantage of the first contractor. An important source of informational rent is the ability to shift (accounting) costs from one source of (economic) costs to another. De Fraja (1999a) shows that, when the regulator observes only the network owner's total cost and is unable to determine whether it derives from the running of the network or the long-distance line, then the Baumol–Willig rule is not (constrained) optimal. In this case, the competitor should be favoured: the access price should be set below the marginal cost of providing access, so that the competitor supplies the market even if it has higher production costs in the long distance than the owner of the network. Moreover (see also Anton and Yao, 1987) the regulator cannot leave the determination of the access price to negotiation. Laffont and Tirole (1993, chapter 5) consider the case in which the regulator can separate the source of the network owner's costs (namely whether they generate from the network or the long-distance transfer), and show that, in a set up similar to that considered on pp. 193–5, asymmetry of information increases the cost of running the network, and hence will require less supply by the competitor. In practice, the optimal policy towards firms requiring access to a monopoly network is given by the relative strength of these two forces pulling in opposite direction.

Incentive issues within the firm

The introduction of competition in regulated markets may interact in unexpected ways with the internal organisation of regulated firms.

204   **Gianni De Fraja**

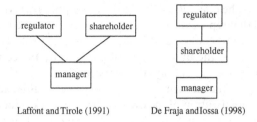

Laffont and Tirole (1991)   De Fraja and Iossa (1998)

Figure 9.1   The structure of the industry in two- and three-agent models

Surprisingly, given its importance, this is a relatively unexplored area. The reason is probably owing to the difficulty of constructing manageable models. We sketch briefly two such models here. Their common aim is the comparison between two stylised institutional designs. Laffont and Tirole (1991) compare the optimal mechanism in publicly owned firms and in privately owned regulated firms; De Fraja and Iossa (1998) compare two simple regulatory schemes. These two papers also have in common the interaction of three parties with contrasting objectives, a utility maximising manager (whose utility depends on monetary reward and on leisure), a profit maximising shareholder and a welfare maximising regulator. The difference between the models is in the structure of the firms: this could be defined 'in parallel' in Laffont and Tirole (1991), and 'in sequence' in De Fraja and Iossa (1998) (see figure 9.1).

In their model, Laffont and Tirole assume that both the shareholder and the regulator offer the manager a contract, according to which she is rewarded in a fashion similar to that considered on p. 194 – namely, with a cash payment dependent on the realised value of cost. It is therefore a case of common agency (Bernheim and Whinston, 1986; Stole 1990), with the added feature that the manager can also undertake an additional investment, which is non-contractible and which would yield a greater benefit if used by outsiders (expropriated). The main result of the Bernheim and Whinston paper is that effort is lower in the regulated private firm than in a publicly owned firm: this creates a conflict between incentive schemes, and is conceptually analogous and technically quite 'similar to the classic double marginalisation on two complementary goods sold by non-cooperative monopolists' (Laffont and Tirole, 1993, p. 637). This is the cost of private ownership. On the other hand, the cost of public ownership is that the manager will not undertake the investment, because she knows that it will be redeployed better to serve the owner's social goals: a private owner is not interested in social goals, so the manager of a private firm will not worry about this possibility.

This 'in parallel' structure of the model may be not fully convincing, even when reinterpreted as the regulator offering a payment to the shareholders and the shareholder simultaneously offering a payment to the manager. The reason is that it seems plausible to assume that internal mechanisms can be changed more quickly than external ones. This is reflected in a hierarchical structure, where the shareholders take the constraints imposed by the regulator as given when choosing the incentive contract offered to their managers. De Fraja and Iossa (1998) show that, in the presence of competition from a group of entrepreneurial firms, the regulatory mechanism affects the incentive structure of the firm. In particular they assume that the regulator imposes a rule on the firm, and that the shareholders, taking this rule as given, impose a mechanism scheme on their managers. Analogously to p. 000, this mechanism maximises the shareholders' profit, given the information constraints (the managers know the cost function, the shareholders do not). De Fraja and Iossa (1998) compare two simple regulatory mechanisms: the *price cap*, used in the regulation of the UK privatised utilities, by which the regulator chooses the maximum level of price which can be charged by the regulated firm, and the *output floor*, where the regulator sets a minimum level of output that the regulated firm must supply. The paper shows that the two mechanisms are equivalent when the regulated firm is a monopoly; however, in the presence of the competitive fringe, the two rules differ. This is because the demand function of the regulated firm is affected by the fringe. At the optimum, the utility of a manager whose cost parameter is β, is

$$u(\beta) = \int\limits_{\beta}^{\bar{\beta}} \psi'\left(e^{j}(\tilde{\beta})\right)\left(1 - \frac{\partial R^{j}(j,\tilde{\beta})}{\partial \beta}\right) d\tilde{\beta}$$

where j takes value and p with a price cap and q with an output floor, and $R^{j}(j,\beta)$ is the revenue function of the regulated firm. The important point of this model is that the regulated firm's revenue depends on the cost parameter, β: this is so because in the presence of a competitive fringe, with the plausible assumption that the cost realisations are correlated between firms, a low cost for the regulated firm implies a low cost for the firms in the fringe. When there is no competitive fringe, $R^{j}(j,\beta)$ does not vary with β, the second term in the integral is one, and the two regimes are equivalent. With a competitive fringe, however, $R^{p}(p,\beta)$ and $R^{q}(q,\beta)$ are different functions; this implies that the managerial utility, for given β, is different depending on the regime chosen by the regulator. The paper shows that, for high values of β, in all conditions, and for all values of β, in plausible conditions, an output floor has better incentive properties than a price cap – that is, the shareholders can demand a higher level of cost reduction from their managers for a given reward.[6]

3   Hold-up, renegotiation and multiple suppliers

A simple model of sequential suppliers

I end the chapter by considering a more specific case of the effects of competition in procurement situations. I consider a stylised relationship between two parties engaged in a long-term relationship (such as a Ministry of Defence and its high-tech suppliers). The model builds on Hart and Moore's (1988) seminal work which shows the inefficiency effects of incomplete contracts. In their model, a buyer and a seller enter a contractual relationship for the exchange of a complex product. Benefits to the buyer depend on his investment; conversely, the cost to the seller depends on his own investment. Both parties' investment must be undertaken before a payoff-relevant variable is realised. The parties write a long-term contract before the realisation of the random variable is known. This contract is incomplete because, even if it were possible to conceive all the possible circumstances that might arise, it would be impossible or immensely costly to write them down in sufficiently unambiguous manner so that a court could determine which clause to apply.[7] Note that the parties have symmetric information: they can both observe the realisation of the state of the world: it is the court who cannot tell which state of the world has occurred. After the investment has been made, and the state of the world has become known, the parties can renegotiate the original contract, specifying a new price and a new quantity. Hart and Moore showed that even when there are no direct external effects of the investment (i.e. even when one party's investment affects only his own benefit or cost), the possibility of renegotiation creates an indirect externality, and the level of investment is below the socially optimal level. Subsequent research (Chung, 1991; Aghion, Dewatripont and Rey, 1994) has shown that, so long as direct externalities are at most one-sided, the parties can use the original contract to constrain themselves to follow certain specific renegotiation procedures (which amount to

[6] As a consequence, since the price is determined by the worst possible conditions, it follows that price is lower with an output cap; the regulator is able to induce the shareholder to make the most of the presence of a competitive fringe when she selects an output level rather than a price cap.

[7] This is where the requirement that the product be complex is important: in the example of the high-tech contractor of the Ministry of Defence, a complete contract would need to specify, among others things, what to do in each of a very large number of possible outcomes of the performance of early prototypes.

attributing all the *ex post* bargaining power to one of the two parties) which lead to the choice of the first-best investment level. If, however, the direct externalities are two-sided, then the attribution of all the bargaining power to one party is not sufficient to eliminate inefficiencies (De Fraja, 1999b, proposition 1).

I consider below an extension of the Hart and Moore (in Chung's notation) model where:

- there are two-sided direct externalities
- the *ex ante* parties can agree to allocate all the *ex post* bargaining power to the seller and
- the buyer can find another seller at the renegotiation stage, but not vice versa.

While generally applicable to several contractual relationships, the three assumptions above are particularly apt in the presence of government contracting: direct externalities, while probably pervasive, seem especially relevant in situations such as those involving government purchases such as defence or space exploration equipment, regulation in complex environments such as telecommunications, or long-term contracts where quality is important, observable, but hard to describe *ex ante*, in unambiguous terms, such as in health services and education. The ability to allocate the bargaining power to one party depends on penalties for delays, and forms typically part of public procurement contracts. The crucial assumption is the third: it introduces a powerful asymmetry between the parties – the procurement agency can find another supplier, the contractor cannot find another buyer. This reflects the situation typical in defence: contractors are often forbidden from dealing with foreign governments in certain areas, whereas a government can normally find a new contractor if the terms offered by the original contractor are no longer acceptable.

The result: the presence of multiple suppliers reduces inefficiency

I now proceed to establish the main result of this section. It shows that the presence of potential competition reduces the inefficiency in investment determined by the incompleteness of contracts. However, in view of the presence of relation-specific investment, it cannot eliminate it completely, even when the imperfection of competition, proxied by the time delay necessary to find a new partner, tends to zero. The situation described informally on p. 206 can be formally seen as an infinite sequence of identical five-stage games, separated by a time interval of

$\tau > 0$ from one another. The typical ith subgame can be described as follows:

Stage 1:   the buyer and the seller write a contract specifying q_i, t_i, a quantity to be traded and a payment in exchange, and attributing the *ex post* bargaining power to the seller.

Stage 2:   simultaneously and independently, the buyer chooses β_i and the seller chooses σ_i, their investment levels; these investments have a cost of $h_b(\beta)$ and $h_s(\sigma)$, respectively, they are observed by the parties, but not by the courts in the event of a dispute.

Stage 3:   nature chooses $\omega_i \in \Omega$; this is also observed by the parties but not by the court.

Stage 4:   the seller proposes q_i^r and t_i^r, the new values of the quantity and payment.

Stage 5:   the buyer chooses among the following:
    (a)   accept the seller's proposal q_i^r and t_i^r
    (b)   go to court and enforce the original contract (q_i, t_i, stipulated in stage 1); or
    (c)   abandon the relationship with buyer i.

If the buyer chooses, (a) or (b) in stage 5, the game ends; if the buyer chooses (c), the game proceeds to subgame $i + 1$; and so on. The payoffs to the parties are $v(q, \omega, \beta, \sigma) - t - h_b(\beta)$ to the buyer and $t - c(q, \omega, \beta, \sigma) - h_s(\sigma)$ to the seller. The buyer's payoff is discounted by a factor δ.

Consider stage 4. Assume that, for every ω, β, σ there exists q such that $v(q, \omega, \beta, \sigma) - c(q, \omega, \beta, \sigma) > 0$, then the total surplus is positive, and the seller will clearly prefer to continue the relationship with the buyer, and will therefore offer a contract q_i^r, t_i^r, which he knows the buyer will accept. This is the case if:

$$v(q^r, .) - t^r \geq v(q, .) - t \tag{A}$$

$$v(q^r, .) - t^r \geq \delta^\tau \mathscr{B}(q_{i+1}, t_{i+1}) \tag{B}$$

where '.' stands for 'ω, β, σ', the subscript i is omitted to lighten the notation and $\mathscr{B}(q_{i+1}, t_{i+1})$ is the value, to the buyer, of the subgame starting with subgame $i + 1$, given that the players are expected to choose q_{i+1}, t_{i+1} optimally for the stage 1 contract of the $(i + 1)$th subgame. Constraint (A) (resp. (B)) says that the buyer is better off accepting the new offer than going to court to enforce the original contract (resp., than switching to a new partner).

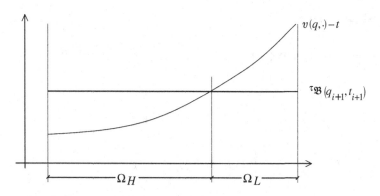

Figure 9.2   The functions $v(q,\cdot) - t$ and $\delta^\tau \mathcal{B}(q_{i+1}, t_{i+1})$

The seller will therefore choose q_i^r, t_i^r, as follows:

$$q^r, t^r = \arg\max_{q,t}\{t - c(q,.) - h_s(\sigma)\} \qquad \text{(s.t.: (A) and (B))}$$

It is straightforward to check that the solution satisfies $q^r = q^*(\omega, \beta, \sigma)$, where $q^*(\omega, \beta, \sigma)$ is the socially optimal choice of quantity, which satisfies

$$q^*(\omega, \beta, \sigma) = \arg\max_q\{v(q, \omega, \beta, \sigma) - c(q, \omega, \beta, \sigma)\}$$

and

$$t^r = v(q^*(\cdot), \cdot) - \max\{v(q,.) - t, \delta^\tau \mathcal{B}(q_{i+1}, t_{i+1})\}$$

Next, let $\Omega_H = \{\omega \in \Omega | \delta^\tau \mathcal{B}(q_{i+1}, t_{i+1}) > v(q, \cdot) - t\}$, and $\Omega_L = \Omega \backslash \Omega_H$. That is, Ω_H (resp. Ω_L) is the set of states of the world where constraint (B) (resp (A)) binds and, thus, $t^r = v(q^*(\cdot), \cdot) - \delta^\tau \mathcal{B}(q_{i+1}, t_{i+1})$ if $\omega \in \Omega_H$, $t^r = v(q^*(\cdot), \cdot) - v(q, \cdot) + t$ if $\omega \in \Omega_L$ (see figure 9.2).

At stage 2, β and σ are chosen simultaneously by the parties; let $\tilde{\beta}$ and $\tilde{\sigma}$ be the equilibrium choices; they satisfy:

$$\tilde{\beta} = \arg\max_\beta\left\{\int_{\omega \in \Omega} [v(q^*(\omega, \beta, \tilde{\sigma})) - t^r(q, t, \omega, \beta, \tilde{\sigma})]\, dF(\omega) - h_b(\beta)\right\}$$

$$\tilde{\sigma} = \arg\max_\sigma\left\{\int_{\omega \in \Omega} [t^r(q, t, \omega, \tilde{\beta}, \sigma) - c(q^*(\omega, \tilde{\beta}, \sigma))]\, dF(\omega) - h_s(\sigma)\right\}$$

substituting gives:

$$\tilde{\beta} = \arg\max_{\beta} \left\{ \int_{\omega \in \Omega_L} [v(q^*(\omega, \beta, \tilde{\sigma})) - t^r(q, t, \omega, \beta, \tilde{\sigma})] \, dF(\omega) \right.$$

$$\left. + \delta^\tau \mathscr{B} \mu(\Omega_H) - h_b(\beta) \right\}$$

$$\tilde{\sigma} = \arg\max_{\sigma} \left\{ \int_{\omega \in \Omega} [v(q^*(\omega, \tilde{\beta}, \sigma), \omega, \tilde{\beta}, \sigma) \right.$$

$$- c(q^*(\omega, \tilde{\beta}, \sigma), \omega, \tilde{\beta}, \sigma)] \, dF(\omega) - \int_{\omega \in \Omega_L} [v(q, \omega, \tilde{\beta}, \sigma)$$

$$\left. - t^r(q, t, \omega, \tilde{\beta}, \sigma)] \, dF(\omega) - \delta^\tau \mathscr{B} \mu(\Omega_H) - h_s(\sigma) \right\}$$

where $\mu(\cdot)$ is a measure in Ω. The first-order conditions are:

$$\int_{\omega \in \Omega_L} [v_\beta(q^*(\omega, \tilde{\beta}, \tilde{\sigma}))] \, dF(\omega) - h'_b(\tilde{\beta}) = 0$$

$$\int_{\omega \in \Omega} [v_\sigma(q^*(\omega, \tilde{\beta}, \tilde{\sigma}), \omega, \tilde{\beta}, \tilde{\sigma}) - c_\sigma(q^*(\omega, \tilde{\beta}, \tilde{\sigma}), \omega, \tilde{\beta}, \tilde{\sigma})] \, dF(\omega) \qquad \text{(C)}$$

$$- \int_{\omega \in \Omega_L} v_\sigma(q, \omega, \tilde{\beta}, \tilde{\sigma}) \, dF(\omega) - h'_s(\tilde{\sigma}) = 0$$

Note that changes in the sets Ω_H and Ω_L cancel each other out, because at the boundary between the two sets $v(q, \cdot) - t = \delta^\tau \mathscr{B}(q_{i+1}, t_{i+1})$. The second of the two conditions contains the main insight of the section. At the first-best choice of investment, σ satisfies:

$$\int_{\omega \in \Omega} [v_\sigma(q^*(\omega, \beta, \sigma), \omega, \beta, \sigma)$$

$$- c_\sigma(q^*(\omega, \beta, \sigma), \omega, \beta, \sigma)] \, dF(\omega) - h'_s(\sigma) = 0$$

Thus if v_σ is identically zero, and if β is at its first-best level, then the first-order conditions, (C), determine the same level of the seller's investment as the first best; moreover, as Chung (1991) shows, it is possible, under mild conditions, to choose t and q, the initial contractual terms, to ensure any choice of buyer's investment that is required. If, however, v_σ is positive (that is, if there are direct externalities), then the choice of σ will not satisfy the

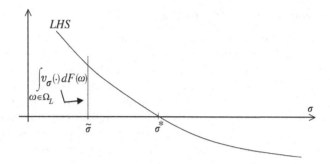

Figure 9.3   The function

$$LHS = \int\limits_{\omega \in \Omega} \left[v_\sigma \big(q^* (\omega, \tilde{\beta}, \sigma), \omega, \tilde{\beta}, \sigma \big) - c_\sigma \big(q^* (\omega, \tilde{\beta}, \sigma), \omega, \tilde{\beta}, \sigma \big) \right] dF(\omega) - h'_s(\sigma)$$

conditions for first-best optimality. To see this, rewrite the second line of (C) as:

$$\int\limits_{\omega \in \Omega} \left[v_\sigma \big(q^* (\omega, \tilde{\beta}, \tilde{\sigma}), \omega, \tilde{\beta}, \tilde{\sigma} \big) - c_\sigma \big(q^* (\omega, \tilde{\beta}, \tilde{\sigma}), \omega, \tilde{\beta}, \tilde{\sigma} \big) \right] dF(\omega) - h'_s(\tilde{\sigma})$$

$$= \int\limits_{\omega \in \Omega_L} v_\sigma \big(q, \omega, \tilde{\beta}, \tilde{\sigma} \big) \, dF(\omega) > 0$$

Figure 9.3 illustrates the situation; the standard assumptions of the model (Chung, 1991, assumption p. 1035; De Fraja 1999b, assumption 2) ensure that the left-hand side of the expression above is a decreasing function of σ. When $\tau = +\infty$, then $\delta^\tau \mathscr{B}(q_{i+1}, t_{i+1}) = 0$ and $\Omega_L = \Omega$; thus we are in the one-seller situation (De Fraja 1999b, (A1)). However, as τ decreases, the line $\delta^\tau \mathscr{B}(q_{i+1}, t_{i+1})$ in figure 9.2 moves up, constraint (B) becomes binding for sufficiently unlucky realisations of ω and the set Ω_L shrinks. This reduces the height of the function at $\tilde{\sigma}$, and therefore the distance between $\tilde{\sigma}$ and the first-best choice of σ, σ^* in figure 9.3.

Note, however, that even when $\tau = 0$, the measure of Ω_L remains strictly positive; therefore, even if there is no time interval between offers, the inefficient choice of investment remains a feature of the model. The reason is simply the fact that investment has to be sunk, and therefore there is a very real cost in leaving the first partner, in addition to the delay in obtaining the product.

4   Discussion and concluding remarks

The model sketched above contains some lessons on the role of competition in regulated and procurement markets: potential competition – that is, the threat made by the procurement agency or the regulator to cease the relationship started with the existing supplier – has the effect of binding the future behaviour of the parties, and improves the payoff of the party who has the ability to call on a new partner. This is well known; however what results from the above analysis, and is probably surprising, is that the presence of competing suppliers enhances the *ex ante* payoff of both parties, the seller as well as the buyer. To see this, suppose that, at stage 1, the buyer and the seller split 50/50 any expected surplus from their relationship (this can be achieved by varying the choice of t, with no effect on any of the other variables). In this case, the increase in efficiency brought about by the presence of competition increases the total surplus, and hence the benefit of both parties.

The contract is always completed with the first seller; thus competition remains potential, the threat of the regulator destroying her own invest-ment in order to improve the contractual terms is never carried out. The mechanism by which the threat operates is such that it simply increases the participation constraint: in the event of a bad realisation of the state of the world, the regulator could, as it were, have another go with a different partner; this suggests that it is quite straightforward to expand the model in order to allow for the possibility of 'divorce': some realisations of ω could be so bad that the expected gain from a new draw is high enough to offset the loss of the investment.

Bibliography

Aghion, P., M. Dewatripont and P. Rey (1994) Renegotiation design with unverifiable information, *Econometrica*, 62, pp. 257–82
Anton, J.J. (1995) Equilibrium bids and scale economies in split-award auctions, Duke University, mimeo
Anton, J.J. and D.A. Yao (1987) Second sourcing and the experience curve: price competition in defense procurement, *Rand Journal of Economics*, 18, pp. 57–76
    (1992) Coordination in split award auctions, *Quarterly Journal of Economics*, 107, pp. 681–707
Armstrong, M. (1998) Network interconnection in telecommunications, *Economic Journal*, 108, pp. 545–64
Armstrong, M., C. Doyle and J. Vickers (1996) The access pricing problem – a synthesis, *Journal of Industrial Economics*, 44, pp. 131–50

Auriol, E. and J.-J. Laffont (1992) Regulation by duopoly, *Journal of Economics and Management Strategy*, 1, pp. 507–34

Baron, D.P. and R. Myerson (1982) Regulating a monopolist with unknown cost, *Econometrica*, 50, pp. 911–30

Baumol, W.J. (1983) Some subtle pricing issues in railroad regulation, *International Journal of Transport Economics*, 10, pp. 341–55

Baumol, W.J. and J.G. Sidak (1994) The pricing of inputs sold to competitors, *Yale Journal of Regulation*, 11, pp. 171–202

Bernheim, D. and M. Whinston (1986) Common agency, *Econometrica*, 54, pp. 923–42

Biglaiser, G. and C.A. Ma (1995) Regulating a dominant firm: unknown demand and industry structure, *Rand Journal of Economics*, 26, pp. 1–19

Cabizza, M.M. and G. De Fraja (1998) Quality considerations in auctions for television franchises, *Information Economics and Policy*, special issue on Media and Multimedia Economics, 10, pp. 9–22

Cabral, L.M. and M.H. Riordan (1989) Incentives for cost reduction under price cap regulation, *Journal of Regulatory Economics*, 1, pp. 93–102

Caillaud, B. (1990) Regulation, competition, and asymmetric information, *Journal of Economic Theory*, 52, pp. 87–110

Chung, T. (1991) Incomplete contracts, specific investments, and risk sharing, *Review of Economic Studies*, 58, pp. 1031–42

De Fraja, G. (1997) Entry, prices, and investment in regulated industries, *Journal of Regulatory Economics*, 11, pp. 257–70

(1999a) Regulation and access pricing with asymmetric information, *European Economic Review*, 43, pp. 109–34

(1999b) After you sir. Sequential investment as a solution to the hold-up problem, *Games and Economic Behavior*, 26, pp. 22–39

De Fraja, G. and E. Iossa (1998) Price caps and output floors: a comparison of simple regulatory rules, *Economic Journal*, 108, pp. 1404–21

Demsetz, H. (1968) Why regulate utilities?, *Journal of Law and Economics*, 11, pp. 55–66

Dixit, A.K. and J.E. Stiglitz (1977) Monopolistic competition and optimum product diversity, *American Economic Review*, 67, pp. 297–308

Hart, O.D. and J. Moore (1988) Incomplete contracts and renegotiation, *Econometrica*, 56, pp. 755–85

Laffont, J.-J. (1994) The new economics of regulation ten years after, 1992 Econometric Society Presidential Address, *Econometrica*, 1994, 62, pp. 507–37

Laffont, J.-J. and J. Tirole (1986) Using cost observation to regulate firms, *Journal of Political Economy*, 94, pp. 614–41

(1987) Repeated auctions of incentive contracts, investment and bidding parity, *Rand Journal of Economics*, 19, pp. 516–37

(1991) Privatization and incentives, *Journal of Law, Economics and Organization*, 6, pp. 1–32

(1993) *A Theory of Incentives in Procurement and Regulation*, Cambridge, Mass.: MIT Press

Loeb, M. and W. Magat (1979) A decentralised method of utility regulation, *Journal of Law and Economics*, 22, pp. 399–404

McAfee, R.P. and J. McMillan (1996) Analyzing the airwaves auction, *Journal of Economic Perspectives*, 10, pp. 159–75

McGuire, T.G. and M. Riordan (1995) Incomplete information and optimal market structure: public purchases from private providers, *Journal of Public Economics*, 56, pp. 125–41

Phlips, L. (1962) *De l'integration des marches*, Louvain: Editions E. Nauwelaerts

Posner, R. (1972) The appropriate scope for regulation in the cable television industry, *Bell Journal of Economics*, 3, pp. 98–129

Simmons, P. (1995) Procurement auctions with multiple sourcing, University of York, Economics Department, *Discussion Paper*, 95/11

Spence, M.A. (1976) Product selection, fixed costs, and monopolistic competition, *Review of Economic Studies*, 43, pp. 217–35

Stole, L. (1990) Mechanism design under common agency, MIT, mimeo

Williamson, O.E. (1976) Franchise bidding for natural monopolies: in general and with respect to CATV, *Bell Journal of Economics*, 7, pp. 73–104

10 Modelling the entry and exit process in dynamic competition: an introduction to repeated-commitment models

Jean-Pierre Ponssard

1 Introduction

This chapter provides an introduction to game-theoretic models of dynamic competition based on repeated commitments (Gromb, Ponssard and Sevy, 1997). The following stylised facts about entry motivate this approach (Geroski, 1995):

(i) entry is mostly associated with innovative processes, higher productivity and a context in which the current industry structure and technology are out of line with exogenous changes
(ii) entrant firms suffer a high-rate of failure and an eventual success can hardly be assessed before a period of 5–10 years
(iii) entry of innovative firms, whenever successful, leads to the exit of inefficient incumbents.

A number of econometric studies support these facts. Detailed industry analyses illustrate further how the selective reactions to entry may depend on the relative position of the competing firms (Scherer, 1992). These industry analyses focus on the entry of foreign rivals into home markets in a context of increased international competition. More generally, firms enjoying natural markets due to transportation or switching costs may face a similar context when these costs drop due to some external changes.

Under such circumstances, the reactions of incumbent firms appear to be selective: some firms prefer to progressively give up their market share, milking their current business, while others react aggressively through large R&D investments so as to catch back their rivals. According to Scherer, RCA adopted a milking strategy in television sets while Gillette strongly reacted in wet-shaving apparatus. The cement industry (see chapter 1 in this volume), an industry traditionally with large transportation cost and then selectively affected by a massive decrease in the cost of sea freight, also provides a good example illustrating both types of reactions (Dumez and Jeunemaître, 2000).

The repeated-commitment approach is particularly well suited to formalise the stylised facts reported by Geroski and to investigate the rationale behind the selective reactions detailed by case studies.

The repeated-commitment approach features an incumbent and an entrant which repeatedly compete for a natural monopoly situation. The incumbent firm has to balance between low short-term profit (and high entry cost) versus high short-term profit (and low entry cost). The relative efficiency of competing firms determines their respective best strategy – that is, the one which maximises their respective long-term profit. This approach combines some features of previous models of dynamic competition such as Eaton and Lipsey (1980), Maskin and Tirole (1988) and Ponssard (1991). It offers the unique advantage of explicitly considering the case of asymmetric firms while these previous approaches did not.

This approach is also consistent with Phlips' requirement about genuine competitive behaviour in dynamic games (Phlips, 1995, ch. 2). Ordinarily, dynamic games exhibit many Nash equilibria, some of which clearly feature tacit cooperation. These equilibria should be excluded, at least from a reference standpoint. Phlips' requirement consists in selecting only equilibria which cannot be sustained through threats, thus excluding tit-for-tat behaviour. The approach adopted in Gromb, Ponssard and Sevy (1997) allows only for short-term commitments. Under a finite horizon, there is a unique perfect equilibrium.

Altogether this approach appears as a nice and simple framework to address the economic issues pointed out in the empirical literature. As an illustration of the relevance of these models, this chapter will also detail a specific application designed to emphasise the specific trade-off between competitive advantage and mobility barriers. The strategic value of incumbency, as defined in Gilbert (1989), will be derived for various strategic configurations. The specific application is constructed along two key parameters. Competitive advantage is modelled as a lower-cost position resulting in higher efficiency; mobility barriers are introduced through the duration of the short-term commitment – i.e. through a discount factor. Then the impact of these two parameters on the strategic value of incumbency and on the entry/exit trajectories is exhaustively analysed.

It turns out that the higher the mobility barrier the longer the exit time in the model. This presumably can leave room for an inefficient incumbent to catch back on competitiveness. For very high mobility barriers the exit time may even be infinite, in which case entry of an efficient firm would be blockaded.

A more subtle outcome of the model refers to the impact of a decrease of mobility barriers on the strategic value of incumbency for an efficient firm: this value may increase. This is owing to the fact that this efficient firm is protecting itself against an inefficient one which would be the most affected by this decrease in mobility barriers, were it be the incumbent. To put it differently, the increase in competition does not lead to a lower short-term profit for the efficient incumbent because the more competitive market would be worth less for its less efficient rival. Depending on their relative efficiency, firms do have different expectations with respect to an increase in competition, even with a 100 per cent market share.

These theoretical results are well in line with the empirical literature mentioned earlier. They could be applied to assess the value of protection in international trade, a subject extensively discussed in Scherer (1992). Indeed, this is a context in which inefficiency of the home industry is often assumed to be temporary; a protection is then limited to the transitory period needed for the home industry to catch back in competitiveness. Our dynamic model could be used to explicitly investigate the social welfare of the various trade policies.

This chapter is organised as follows. Section 2 briefly recalls previous results on dynamic competition in the case of symmetric firms. These results can be used as a benchmark when asymmetry is considered and highlights the novelty of the repeated-commitment approach. This approach and the associated new results are summarised in section 3. Section 4 contains the detailed discussion of the application under study. The final sections discusses other economic applications and related results.

2   Previous results

In order to fix ideas, the economic situation is supposed to correspond to the following stylised representation. It is assumed that the market can support only one firm with durable positive profit (natural monopoly). Then the incumbent policy, denoted x, simultaneously determines both the incumbent ongoing streams of profit – say, $v(x)$ per unit of time – and the entry barrier – i.e. the cost the entrant would have to pay to displace the incumbent, given its policy x. Denote by $C(x)$ this entry cost. For notational convenience take the precise duration which would be required to displace the incumbent as the unit of (discrete) time. This is called the *commitment period*, the incumbent advantage due to its mobility barrier is assumed to be totally exhausted after that period.

With symmetric firms, the functions C and v are independent across the industry. Then one gets the key recursive equation of dynamic competition (Wilson, 1992):

$$C(x) = \delta v(x)/(1 - \delta) \qquad (10.1)$$

Equation (10.1) states that, at equilibrium, the entry cost generated by the incumbent policy is exactly the total rent of the incumbent, discounted back from the time the displacement would occur (the discount factor δ is such that $0 \leq \delta \leq 1$). This equation was first derived through a focal-point argument: suppose both the entrant and the incumbent analyse the situation through the same angle, a successful entrant will be an incumbent in the future and so will reason at that stage exactly as the current incumbent perceives its position now. The equation directly results from this argument. However, it is because firms are symmetric in their characteristics that this argument can work.

Observe that this solution is striking in two respects. First, in dynamic games one would ordinarily expect to obtain many solutions. Here the proposed solution is unique. Second, one may also expect that collusion could easily be obtained through some form of non-cooperative behaviour. No collusion is apparent here. Consequently the proposed solution is a good normative model of dynamic competition.

This economic relevance is indeed even more apparent when one considers the limiting case of shorter and shorter commitment periods (i.e. δ converging to 1). From (10.1) one gets that, as long as the entry cost is bounded (which is a natural assumption) the ongoing profit stream must converge to zero. This is known as the *rent dissipation property*: whenever the duration of commitments is small so that successful entry can occur extremely fast, the incumbent instantaneous rent is forced to zero. This form of competition corresponds to what should be expected in that limiting case.

All these well behaved properties make it worthwhile to formalise the focal-point argument. Two directions have been proposed in relationship with this question: Markov equilibria (Maskin and Tirole, 1988) and forward induction (Ponssard, 1991). Broadly speaking, Markov equilibria are such that 'bygones are bygones', and only the future matters. In a way, this approach restricts the possibility of collusion through retaliation strategies.

In a quite different fashion forward induction also is a way to limit retaliation: it allows a player to signal some unambiguous continuation equilibrium path, favourable to him, independently of the fact that there may exist other paths which could be used as credible threats by the other player. Thus in forward induction equilibria, as opposed to Markov equilibria, both the past and the future are important.

In spite of their conceptual differences, these two approaches lead to (10.1). However direct generalisations to asymmetric situations appear problematic both ways. In these extensions the least efficient firm may indefinitely remain the incumbent and may even enjoy a higher rent than the one the most efficient firm would get if it were the incumbent (Ponssard, 1990; Lahmandi-Ayed, Ponssard and Sevy, 1995). This is clearly not satisfactory from an economic perspective since one would expect that dynamic competition would eventually lead to the selection of the most efficient firm.

At this point, the repeated-commitment approach is the only one that provides a more satisfactory framework to discuss dynamic competition with symmetric and asymmetric firms.

3   The repeated-commitment approach: the main result

The precise way competition is modelled in this approach is now introduced. The economic situation features two firms competing for a natural monopoly. One firm is strong (S) and the other one is weak (W).

The game consists in the repetition of a stage game. At the beginning of each stage, one firm is the incumbent (I) and the other one is the potential entrant (E).

Each stage is played as follows.

Step 1:   Firm I decides to compete at that stage or not. If not, positions I and E are immediately reversed, and two reversals of positions end the current stage and the overall game with zero payoffs. If firm I decides to compete, it selects some x, a real number, and the game goes to step 2.

Step 2:   Firm E decides to enter or not at that stage. If it does not enter, then firm I gets $v_I(x)$, with $v_I(x)$ increasing in x, firm E gets zero and the game proceeds to the next stage with unchanged positions. If firm E decides to enter, it incurs a cost $C_E(x)$, with $C_E(x)$ decreasing in x, firm I gets $-d$ (with $d > 0$) and the positions are reversed for the next stage.

This stage game is repeated n times, given that one has in mind a very large n, possibly going to infinity. The initial incumbent may be either S or W. The two corresponding games will be denoted $G_n(S)$ and $G_n(W)$, respectively. It is further assumed that the two firms maximise their total discounted profits using the same discount factor δ.

The asymmetry between firms is introduced as follows.

Assumption 1   (asymmetry):   *Let Δ be a positive real number, the payoff functions of the two firms are such that*:

$$v_W = v_S - \Delta$$

$$C_W = C_S + \Delta$$

Incumbency is worth less and entry is more costly for the weak firm.

Assumption 2 states that deterring entry costs less in profit reduction than the increase in entry cost inflicted to the competitor. It plays a key role in the selection property.

Assumption 2   (increasing returns in the entry barrier): *For S and W, v +C is a decreasing function.*

This completely specifies the model. Any such game, $G_n(S)$ or $G_n(W)$, because of its perfect information structure, can be solved using backward induction.

An economic context which fits almost perfectly this formulation is one in which x is the age of an equipment, the duration of which is H. To remain on the market, this equipment has to be renewed repeatedly. Through selecting $x < H$ the incumbent reduces its profit but it generates an entry barrier. Indeed an entrant would be in a duopolistic situation for at least the residual life-time of the equipment of the incumbent (it is assumed that an equipment, once in place, can be operated at no cost). During that time, duopolistic profits will be lower in comparison with the monopolistic profit expected when a firm is alone. The entry cost $C(x)$ is precisely the difference between this monopolistic profit and the duopolistic one over that period. The smaller x, the higher the entry cost $C(x)$ but the smaller the profit per equipment $v(x)$. This model, when firms are symmetric, is due to Eaton and Lipsey (1980). The precise solution of this game with asymmetric firms can be found in Louvert and Steinmetz (1997). There the asymmetry refers to firms with different fixed costs for renewing the capital investment.

We can now state the main result of the repeated commitment approach.

Proposition 1   (selection property): For all $\Delta > 0$ there exists a δ close enough to 1 and an integer n^* such that at the unique perfect equilibrium of any $G_n(W)$, $n > n^*$, firm W is never an incumbent after n^* stages.

4   An economic application

This approach is now applied to a specific situation in which the two parameters Δ and δ have the following interpretation. Δ can be seen as the competitive advantage of firm S over firm W. δ can be related to the mobility barriers: the less discounting the shorter the commitment period and thus the closer the situation to one of perfect contestability (Baumol, Panzar and Willig, 1992). In order to obtain an analytical solution a simplifying assumption will be made relative to the payoff functions.

Assumption 3: $v_S(x) = x$; $C_S(x) = 1 - x$.

A complete derivation of the model can be made for all values of the two parameters Δ and δ. Observe that we have $C + v = cst$ so that proposition 1 does apply for δ close to 1, but nothing can be said for other values of δ.

In this simplified framework, the analysis will be carried out with the following questions in mind:

- Is it necessary for the commitment period to be short (δ close to 1) to obtain selection?
- When selection occurs, what process does it take?
- Do more efficient firms enter earlier with higher expected rents?
- When selection does not occur, does higher efficiency lead to higher rent?
- More generally, what underlying theory results from this approach in terms of strategic incumbency value?

Further notation

In this example it is convenient to think of x as a price commitment. The following additional notation is introduced.

- Denote by x_S^L the value of x such that $v_S(x) = 0$, x_S^L can be seen as average cost pricing, in our example $x_S^L = 0$
- For the weak firm $x_W^L = \Delta$ since $\Delta > 0$ the average cost of the weak firm is higher than the one of the strong firm
- Denote by x_S^L the value of x such that $C_W(x) = 0$; in order to make entry costly for its rival, the strong firm should commit to a price smaller than x_S^L, with $x_S^L = 1 + \Delta$
- The similar threshold for the weak firm to prevent an immediately profitable entry is $x_W^L = 1$, thus it is more constrained than the strong firm.

We now detail how the games $G_n(S)$ and $G_n(W)$ can be solved through backward induction. It will be convenient to use the index N for the total number of stages and n for intermediate games such that $1 \leq n \leq N$; furthermore, stages will be labelled, backwards.

Solving G_1

Consider first $G_1(S)$ and $G_1(W)$. Two cases appear:

- For $0 \leq \Delta \leq 1$ any of the two firms can remain in place through an optimal commitment that prevents entry. Denote by $\bar{x}_S^1$ and $\bar{x}_W^1$, respectively, these two commitments. Clearly:

$$\bar{x}_S^1 = x_S^L = 1 + \Delta$$

$$\bar{x}_W^1 = x_W^L = 1 \leq \bar{x}_S^1$$

Denote by V_S^1 and V_W^1, in G_S^1 and G_W^1, respectively, the associated payoff for the leader :

$$V_S^1 = v_S(\bar{x}_S^1) = \bar{x}_S^1 = 1 + \Delta$$

$$V_W^1 = v_W(\bar{x}_W^1) = \bar{x}_W^1 - \Delta = 1 - \Delta \leq V_S^1$$

- For $\Delta > 1$ the leadership advantage of firm W in $G^1(W)$ disappears. Its equilibrium strategy is not to compete in step 1, then firm S commits to $\bar{x}_S^1 = x_S^L = 1 + \Delta$.

This preliminary discussion helps to understand the solution of longer games. Focus on the case $\Delta < 1$ and increase the number of stages n. The following recursive argument applies: if the strong firm would get a higher payoff in being a leader in a game of $n - 1$ stages than the weak firm would – that is, $V_S^{n-1} > V_W^{n-1}$ – the entry-deterring commitment of the weak firm to secure its future rent is more constrained than that of the strong firm – that is, $\bar{x}_S^n > \bar{x}_W^n$. Consequently the stage payoffs associated with the initial entry-deterring commitments would be higher for the strong firm than for the weak firm – that is, $v_S(\bar{x}_S^n) > v_W(\bar{x}_W^n)$ – which makes the argument apply in a game of n stages, and thus recursively.

Thus, for long enough games it may certainly happen that deterring entry becomes costly for the weak firm – i.e. its associated stage payoff would be negative $(v_W(x_W^n) < 0)$. Eventually it may have to give up its initial leading advantage (V_W^n would be negative). When this is true, there is a clear similarity between a large cost advantage in a short game (such as in the case $\Delta > 1$ and $n = 1$) and a small cost advantage in a long game: in both cases, selection would occur. This whole argument is now detailed with due attention to the role of the discount factor.

Solving G_N

Assume $0 \leq \Delta \leq 1$. For short enough games the sequence of optimal commitments in $G_n(S)$ and $G_n(W)$, $\bar{x}_S^n$ and $\bar{x}_W^n$, respectively, are obtained through the following dynamic program:

$$C_W(\bar{x}_S^n) = \delta v_W(\bar{x}_W^{n-1}) + \delta^2 v_W(\bar{x}_W^{n-2}) \cdots + \delta^{n-1} v_W(\bar{x}_W^1)$$

$$C_S(\bar{x}_W^n) = \delta v_S(\bar{x}_S^{n-1}) + \delta^2 v_S(\bar{x}_S^{n-2}) \cdots + \delta^{n-1} v_S(\bar{x}_S^1)$$

or equivalently

$$C_W(\bar{x}_S^n) = \delta(C_W(\bar{x}_S^{n-1}) + v_W(\bar{x}_W^{n-1}))$$

$$C_S(\bar{x}_W^n) = \delta(C_S(\bar{x}_W^{n-1}) + v_S(\bar{x}_S^{n-1}))$$

In the case of our example, one gets:

$$1 + \Delta - \bar{x}_S^n = \delta(1 - \bar{x}_S^{n-1} + \bar{x}_W^{n-1})$$

$$1 - \bar{x}_W^n = \delta(1 - \bar{x}_W^{n-1} + \bar{x}_S^{n-1})$$

so that, through adding and subtracting both equations, one respectively obtains:

$$\bar{x}_S^n + \bar{x}_W^n = 2(1 - \delta) + \Delta$$

$$(\bar{x}_S^n - \bar{x}_W^n) - 2\delta(\bar{x}_S^{n-1} - \bar{x}_W^{n-1}) = \Delta$$

This last equation gives, plugging in initial values for the two sequences:

$$(\bar{x}_S^n - \bar{x}_W^n) = \Delta(1 - (2\delta)^n)/(1 - 2\delta)$$

So that finally, we obtain the two sequences for $n \geq 2$:

$$\bar{x}_S^n = 1 - \delta + (\Delta/2)(1 + (1 - (2\delta)^n)/(1 - 2\delta))$$

$$\bar{x}_W^n = 1 - \delta + (\Delta/2)(1 - (1 - (2\delta)^n)/(1 - 2\delta))$$

Assume for the time being that Δ is strictly positive. For $n \geq 2$, the first sequence is increasing in n while the second one is decreasing. This means that the optimal entry-preventing policy of firm S becomes less and less tight as the game becomes longer while the one of firm W becomes tighter and tighter. The discussion can now proceed in two steps.

Consider first the case in which the sequences do not converge, i.e. $\delta \geq 1/2$. It is clear that firm W will be better off for a long enough game to decide not to compete rather than preventing entry. Consider now the case in which the sequences do converge. This can make sense for firm W only if it converges to a policy which leaves it some ongoing profit – i.e. which is higher than its average cost. This will be so if:

$$1 - \delta + (\Delta/2)(1 - 1/(1 - 2\delta)) \geq \Delta$$

that is

$$1 - 2\delta \geq \Delta$$

If this inequality is not satisfied, firm W is better off deciding not to compete.

One can use the expression that gives $(\bar{x}_S^n - \bar{x}_W^n)$ to compute the minimal number of stages n^* it would take to make it unprofitable to the weak firm for deterring entry in a long game (when it exists). This n^* is the smallest integer, if any, such that $V_W^{n^*} = (C_W(\bar{x}_S^{n^*+1}))/\delta < 0$. That is:

$$C_W(\bar{x}_S^{n^*+1}) = \delta[1 - (\bar{x}_S^{n^*} - \bar{x}_W^{n^*})] < 0$$

or

$$\Delta > (1 - 2\delta)/(1 - (2\delta)^{n^*})$$

This discussion leads to the following result.

Proposition 2:   The selection property depends both on the relative cost advantage Δ and on the mobility barrier δ. More precisely:

- for $1/2 \leq \delta \leq 1$, n^* exists independently of Δ, as long as $\Delta > 0$
- for $\delta < 1/2$, n^* exists as long as $\Delta > 1 - 2\delta$
- for $\delta < 1/2$, and $\Delta < 1 - 2\delta$, there is no selection.

Figure 10.1 summarises proposition 2.

Consider now the case $\Delta = 0$, then selection is not at stake. The two sequences are identical and stationary from rank 2 (this stationarity comes from assumption 3 and is not a general property).

We now turn to a discussion of the equilibrium strategies when $\Delta > 0$. When n^* exists, a game consisting of precisely n^* stages is similar to a one-stage game in which $\Delta > 1$. The weak firm cannot exploit its leading advantage and its equilibrium strategy is not to compete at the initial stage. This makes the two games $G_{n^*}(W)$ and $G_{n^*}(S)$ payoff-equivalent. Consequently, a game consisting of $n^* + k$ stages, with $0 < k < n^*$, is now strategically equivalent to a game consisting of precisely k stages, since it differs only in a translation of payoffs. This construction can be repeated again and again for solving a game of any duration $N = qn^* + k$ as an initial k-stage game followed by q games of exactly n^* stages.

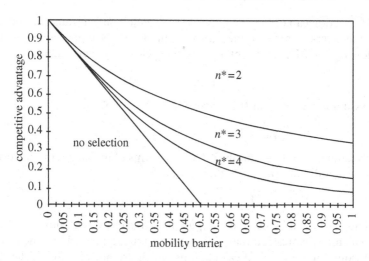

Figure 10.1   The selection property (n^* as a function of Δ and δ)

The reader will observe that backward induction is used at two levels. First to obtain the solution in short games and second to obtain the solution in long games, given that a discontinuity appears for a duration of n^* (the weak firm has to quit immediately). This makes the overall solution counterintuitive, at least at first sight.

This construction gives the exit process of the weak firm. Its strategy can be interpreted as a 'milking policy' through which it exploits its incumbent position, making it clear that it will move out within some given time. This approach does provide a precise calculation for the exit time but this calculation depends on the exact duration of the game to obtain the position of the initial stage within a cycle of n^*. This is not completely satisfactory. As for the strategy of the strong firm, once it is the incumbent, it uses a periodic policy which aims at preventing a temporary return of the weak firm. At any time, the position within the cycle depends on the total length of the game. This time-dependence of the equilibrium illustrates a surprising feature of competitive behaviour under a known horizon. The firms use their common knowledge of this horizon to coordinate on the entry date without ever engaging in a price war. It would be nice to get rid of this coordination so as to approach what is intuitively meant by 'genuine competition' under a long horizon.

We now turn to a discussion of the rent associated with the equilibrium strategies. We want to characterise the average rent per stage over a game G_n with n going to infinity. Two cases should be considered, depending on whether selection may or may not occur.

If selection can occur, the weak firm will enjoy only a transient rent. As for the average rent of the strong firm it can be approached in the following way. Its total rent $V_S^{n^*}$ over a cycle is, by construction

$$V_S^{n^*} = C_S(\bar{x}_W^{n^*+1})/\delta = 1 - \bar{x}_W^{n^*} + \bar{x}_S^{n^*}$$

Assuming equality in the expression that gives n^* one gets

$$\bar{x}_S^{n^*} - \bar{x}_W^{n^*} = 1$$

so that the total rent is simply 2. Now, in terms of average rent on a cycle of n^* when discounting at δ, this amounts to:

$$2(1 - \delta)/(1 - \delta^{n^*})$$

This result can be used to compute firm S average rent along the lines on which the expression that gives n^* is an equality; elsewhere one has to go through more detailed calculations which are not reproduced here.

If selection cannot occur, the corresponding calculations are much simpler. In that case one can use the limit values of the sequences $(\bar{x}_S^n)$ and $(\bar{x}_W^n)$. Denote these limits by x_S^∞ and x_W^∞. We have:

$$x_S^\infty + x_W^\infty = 2(1 - \delta) + \Delta$$

$$x_S^\infty - x_W^\infty = \Delta/(1 - 2\delta)$$

so that

$$x_S^\infty = (1 - \delta)[1 + \Delta/(1 - 2\delta)]$$

$$x_W^\infty = (1 - \delta)[1 - \delta\Delta/(1 - 2\delta)(1 - \delta)]$$

In this case, the average rent for the strong firm is simply x_S^∞, while for the weak firm it is $x_S^\infty - \Delta$. Observe that these rents are, respectively, equal to $1 + \Delta$ and 0 on the selection frontier ($\Delta = 1 - 2\delta$). Note that the rent of the strong firm is also $1 + \Delta$ at $\delta = 0$.

Let us now check that the rent of the strong firm also converges to $1 + \Delta$ when the frontier $\Delta = 1 - 2\delta$ is reached from the selection zone. Then n^* goes to infinity so that $2(1 - \delta)/(1 - \delta^{n^*})$ goes to $2(1 - \delta)$ (recall that in that case $\delta < 1/2$), which is precisely $1 + \Delta$. The continuity of the rent is, however, lost when one goes from the selection zone n^* to the $(n - 1)^*$ one.

These calculations are summarised in propositions 3 and 4.

Proposition 3 (strategic value of incumbency and competitive advantage): When selection occurs, a competitive advantage results in a permanent rent which increases with this advantage while a competitive disadvantage results in a transient rent. When selection does not occur, the incumbency rent of the strong firm is higher than the incumbency rent of the weak firm.

Proposition 4 (strategic value of incumbency and mobility barrier): When selection occurs, the incumbency rent of the strong firm decreases as the mobility barriers are decreased. When selection does not occur, incumbency rate of the strong firm is U-shaped while the incumbency rent of the weak firm decreases as the mobility barriers are decreased.

To get a complete picture, one should also compare the repeated-commitment approach with the standard approach in case of symmetric firms. When $\Delta = 0$ the firms' optimal strategies are stationary from rank 2 and satisfy the key recursive equation of entry games, that is:

$$C(x) = \delta v(x)/(1 - \delta)$$

Consequently the incumbency rent is now simply $1 - \delta$.

Proposition 5 (consistency): When firms have no competitive advantages the repeated-commitment approach gives the same limiting result as the standard approach of entry games.

In spite of this consistency result, there is an important difference between the pure symmetric case and a situation in which there is a slight asymmetry. There is a discontinuity in the incumbency rents which occurs at $\delta = 1/2$. If $\Delta = 0$ the symmetric rent is precisely $1/2$. When $\Delta \to 0$, the rent of the strong firm goes to 1 while the rent of the weak firm goes to zero. This discontinuity impacts all values of $\delta > 1/2$. This is illustrated in figure 10.2.

The rent-dissipation result which occurs nicely for $\Delta = 0$ is of course no longer valid for $\Delta > 0$. Furthermore, and this is more interesting, increasing the discount factor to one no longer results in a clear rent reduction for firm S. The reason is the following. A higher discount rate facilitates entry, this is good for the entrant and this puts pressure on the incumbent. But it also puts so much pressure on a weak firm that it can make a strong firm better off. To understand this result one has to keep in mind that the incumbent rent is determined by the height of the competitor's entry barrier. One may interpret this phenomenon by saying that the reduction of mobility barriers when competitors are uneven may generate stronger inequalities. This result may have interesting social welfare implications.

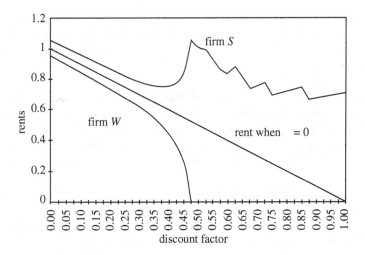

Figure 10.2   The strategic values of incumbency ($\Delta = 0.05$)

Altogether, these three propositions provide new and interesting insights for the strategic value of incumbency.

5   Related results

This section reviews some other applications of the repeated-commitment approach as well as some more technical issues. This gives some background materials to highlight the results obtained in the context of our specific example.

Economic applications

The general framework can be applied to other economic situations than the one considered here. Ponssard and Sevy (1995) develop an extension with price competition in the presence of switching costs. It is assumed that the weak firm catches back from its inefficiency after a known delay, typical of the industry (owing to imitation, technology transfer, loopholes in patent laws ...). Under these assumptions, a weak incumbent either fights to keep its position until it catches back or decides to 'milk its business', securing high short-run profits through a determined exit strategy. Some of the industry studies discussed by Scherer (1992) illustrate both situations. It is shown in that model that with short delays and low switching costs, potential entrants lack the incentive to invest for innovation and cost-reducing activities. Consequently, from an anti-trust point of view, switching costs are a substitute to an inefficient property right system.

Consider the Eaton and Lipsey model once again. There the mobility barrier refers to some sunk cost that has to be renewed from time to time. This sunk cost could, for instance, be associated with capital equipment or to advertising. This basic model can be extended to study the case of differentiated markets. For such markets Norman and Thisse (1996) consider the case of contestable markets versus non-contestable ones. In the first case investments can be instantaneously relocated at no cost, whereas in the second case investments are for ever. The proposed dynamic approach allows for intermediary situations with respect to these two extremal ones. In such a context, firms have three strategic variables – namely price, timing of capital renewal and location. An important result is that incumbent firms are better off through higher prices, earlier capital renewal and larger market shares (Steinmetz, 1998). Thus, in that case, potential competition leads to a high-level of capital waste. This point had already been mentioned, (see Maskin and Tirole, 1988 and Dasgupta and Stiglitz, 1988); however, these authors did not allow for a strategy which explicitly balances price increases with capital renewal.

Ponssard (1991) uses this spatial framework to discuss anti-trust policies in the cement industry. He argues that for such industries asset competition is more important than price competition, in particular because of the efficiency gains that may be obtained through asset restructuring in mature markets. Accordingly firms should be encouraged to acquire inefficient plants from competitors and close them rather than engage into a ruinous price competition. The restructuring process of the cement industry in Europe illustrates this idea quite well.

Technical issues

To obtain a completely satisfactory approach to dynamic competition, the current repeated-commitment approach should be extended to cover the following issues:

(i) *The selection property*
   The selection result depends on two features. First it depends on the precise game-form which is used: alternate move with endogenous leadership. The defence for this game-form is that it coincides with the Eaton and Lipsey original model of dynamic competition for strategic renewal of assets (Eaton and Lipsey, 1980). This game-form is also quite simple. More general game-forms such as repeated simultaneous play (Ponssard, 1991) would require us to get involved in elaborate Nash refinements.

Second, this adopted game-form itself is not enough to obtain selection. A sufficient condition refers on the existence of increasing returns in the construction of the entry barriers: (i.e. $v + C$ decreasing in x). This means that when the incumbent reduces its instantaneous profit by 1, it inflicts an entry cost to its rival of more than 1. A counter example, detailed in Louvert and Steinmetz (1997), proves that this condition is not necessary. It uses the Eaton and Lipsey model with no discounting and with a positive duopoly profit. Selection is obtained as long as the underlying situation is indeed a natural monopoly. On the other hand, with the quantity-competition model, the condition on $v + C$ does not hold and selection is not obtained (Lahmandi-Ayed, 1995). It would be interesting to provide a more complete picture of the forms of competition that favor selection.

(ii) *From one incumbent to an endogenous number of incumbents depending on the technology and on the market size*
The idea would be to develop the dynamic counterpart of static imperfect competition models; Lahmandi-Ayed (1995) provides a first step in that direction using quantity competition with linear demand and U-shaped cost functions. Under some assumptions she proves that repeated commitments lead to rent dissipation.

(iii) *Incomplete information*
A natural extension of the model would be to allow for incomplete information – say on the relative cost positions of the competing firms.

(iv) *From a finite to an infinite horizon*
It is not appealing to obtain results in long games which depend on the precise length of these games. In particular the periodicity of the optimal strategies introduces a combinatorial feature which is difficult to justify economically. The elimination of these difficulties appears quite complicated: simple Markov strategies, as already mentioned, are inadequate to bypass them. Still it may be possible to use more sophisticated Markov strategies.

In spite of these limitations, the present formalisation seems to provide an economically meaningful approach to dynamic competition.

Bibliography

Baumol, W.J., J.-C. Panzar and R.D. Willig (1992) *Contestable Markets and the Theory of Industry Structure*, New York: Harcourt Brace Jovanovich

Dasgupta, P. and J. Stiglitz (1988) Potential competition, actual competition and economic welfare, *European Economic Review*, 32

Dumez, H. and A. Jeunemaître (2000) *Understanding and Regulating the Market at A Time of Globalization: The Case of the Cement Industry*, London: Macmillan

Eaton, B. and R. Lipsey (1980) Exit barriers are entry barriers: the durability of capital as a barrier to entry, *Bell Journal of Economics*, 10, pp. 721–9

Geroski, P.A. (1995) What do we know about entry?, *International Journal of Industrial Organization*, 13, pp. 421–40

Gilbert, R. (1989) Mobility barriers and the value of incumbency in R. Schmalensee and R. Willig (eds.), *Handbook of Industrial Organization*, 1, Amsterdam: North-Holland, pp. 475–535

Gromb, D, J.-P. Ponssard and D. Sevy (1997) Selection in dynamic entry games, *Games and Economic Behavior*, 21, pp. 62–84

Lahmandi-Ayed, R. (1995) Natural oligopolies: efficiency through repeated commitments, PhD dissertation, ch. 3, Paris: Ecole Polytechnique

Lahmandi-Ayed, R., J.-P. Ponssard and D. Sevy (1995) Efficiency of quantity competition: a remark on Markovian equilibria, *Economics Letters*, 50, pp. 213–21

Louvert, E. and S. Steinmetz (1997) Entry deterrence through anticipated renewal: rent and selection issues, Laboratoire d'Econométrie, Ecole Polytechnique

Maskin, E. and J. Tirole (1988) A theory of dynamic oligopoly, part I: overview and quantity competition with large fixed costs, *Econometrica*, 56(3), pp. 549–69

Norman, G. and J.-F. Thisse (1996) Product variety and welfare under tough and soft pricing regimes, *The Economic Journal*, 106, pp. 76–91

Phlips, L. (1995) *Competition Policy: A Game-Theoretic Perspective*, London, Cambridge: Cambridge University Press

Ponssard, J.-P. (1990) Concurrence imparfaite et rendements croissants: une approche en termes de fair-play, *Annales d'Economie et de Statistique*, 15(16), pp. 152–72

(1991) Forward induction and sunk costs give average cost pricing, *Games and Economic Behavior*, 3, pp. 221–36

(1995) Concurrence stratégique et règlementation de la concurrence dans un oligopole naturel: l'exemple de l'industrie cimentière, *Revue d'Economie Industrielle*, numéro exceptionnel sur les développements récents en économic industrielle, pp. 385–401

Ponssard, J.-P. and D. Sevy (1995) Less short-term competition for more innovation, *Annales des Telecomunications*, 50, pp. 276–85

Scherer, F.M. (1992) *International High-Technology Competition*, Cambridge, Mass.: Harvard University Press

Steinmetz, S. (1998) Spatial preemption with finite lived equipments, *International Journal of Industrial Organization*, 16, pp. 253–70

Wilson, R. (1992) Strategic models of entry deterrence, in R.J. Aumann and S. Hart (eds.), in *Handbook of Game Theory*, 1, Amsterdam: Elsevier Science

11 Coordination failures in the Cournot approach to deregulated bank competition

André de Palma and Robert J. Gary-Bobo

1 Introduction

Many traditional analyses of the banking sector rely on the notion of perfect competition among banks (with the notable exception of some classic contributions such as Klein, 1971, and Monti, 1972). But if, for various reasons, the sector is concentrated, and if the market power of banks comes into play, the interaction of oligopolistic strategies with the principles of prudential regulation by the central banker should be reconsidered, with the help of some well defined game-theoretic model. This, we think, would essentially be the philosophy of Louis Phlips. In his 1995 address at the meeting of the European Economic Association (see Phlips, 1996), Louis explicitly advocated a more systematic use of game-theoretic reasoning within the field of competition policy (see also Phlips, 1983). In the banking sector, prudential regulation and competition policy are in many respects intertwined, and the present chapter can be viewed as an attempt to integrate contemporary industrial organisation methods with the theory of financial intermediation.

The way to this approach has been paved by a number of forerunners, who also based their approach on imperfectly competitive models of banking. Among other contributions, Yanelle (1988, 1995) studied Bertrand price competition among intermediaries on the input and output markets simultaneously; Gehrig (1996) shows how the theory of natural oligopoly in vertical differentiation models can be applied to financial intermediation; models of horizontal product differentiation have been used by various authors to discuss problems of regulation: see, for instance, Repullo (1990);

The authors thank B. Bensaid, T. Gehrig, R. Repullo, P. Rey, J.-C. Rochet and J. Tirole for helpful suggestions and comments. The present chapter is a revised version of a paper presented at a CEPR Workshop on Financial Intermediation held in Madrid (January 1995). This research was undertaken while both authors were consultants at the Bank of France, Centre de Recherche.

Rochet (1992b); Schmidt-Mohr and Villas-Boas (1993); Matutes and Padilla (1994); Matutes and Vives (1994); Chiappori, Perez-Castrillo and Verdier (1995) and Rochet and Tirole (1996) – and probably some others that we do not know – did in some sense anticipate our approach, introducing bankruptcy costs in a 'portfolio model', which is, in fact, a model of quantity competition, in which bankers choose asset portfolios, but he did not push the analysis of expected bankruptcy costs as far as we do it here.[1]

To be more precise, the purpose of this chapter is to construct and analyse a microeconomic model of competition among banks. The focus of the model is quantity (or Cournot) competition on the loan market. Our analysis is based on the existence of market imperfections: banks are endowed with market power on the loan market on the one hand, and loans cannot be costlessly resold on capital markets on the other: there are liquidation costs. It is shown that these market imperfections, combined with the agents' probabilistic beliefs on the future state of nature can generate non-concavities of the banks' objective functions. These non-concavities in turn lead to the possibility of, (i), multiple equilibria which can be ranked with respect to their associated level of credit supply and (ii), discontinuities of the aggregate equilibrium credit supply with respect to parameters such as banks' equity or the profitability of borrowing firms' investment projects.

The proposed model has the following features. There are banks, depositors and firms. Banks use standard demand deposits to finance risky loans demanded by limited liability firms. The profitability of borrowing firms is subject to some random shock. This shock is 'macro-economic' in nature and cannot be diversified away by banks: it affects all banks simultaneously. The probability of going bankrupt can vary from one bank to another, depending on their chosen loans to equity ratio. There is no deposit insurance and depositors are assumed well informed and perfectly rational: more precisely, they perceive each bank's riskiness correctly. It follows that a bank must adjust its deposit interest rate so as to exactly compensate for the risk borne by depositors. At some point in time, a signal is sent to all agents and reveals the true state of nature. Depositors must then decide either to withdraw their deposits, or to wait. Banks are therefore subject to the possibility of information-based, Nash equilibrium runs.

The analysis rests upon the existence of market imperfections. The market for loans is assumed imperfect, giving rise to a Cournot banking

---

[1] Other aspects of imperfect competition among financial intermediaries have been studied by Dermine, Neven and Thisse (1991); Gehrig and Jackson (1994); Yosha (1994); Bester (1995).

oligopoly. Each bank takes the impact of its loan supply on the lending rate into account. The financial markets on which loans can be resold are also imperfect: more precisely, early liquidation of bank loans is costly. But other possible sources of market imperfection (or incompleteness) are absent: the market for deposits is competitive, with rational depositors, and informational asymmetries do not play a role in the model. In particular, bankers have no privileged information about the quality of their assets.

These assumptions deserve some comments. The presence of market power on the loan market can first be substantiated with the idea that bank loans constitute a special category of assets. First, there are borrowers for whom non-bank sources of credit do not represent a perfect substitute for bank loans.[2] On the other hand, the reader can imagine that we consider a market on which a limited number of financial intermediaries, called banks, are endowed with some special knowledge about a pool of risky projects; these bankers then act as delegated monitors on behalf of depositors.[3] Thus, bankers deal with some moral hazard variable, but this is kept implicit. There is no explicit, built-in justification for bankers' market power in this chapter, we simply take it for granted, noticing that the assumption has some empirical relevance, since banking industries are highly concentrated in many countries, and particularly in European countries such as Belgium or France.

The presence of costly asset liquidation, we think, is not controversial. It captures the difficulties faced by a bank when it comes close to insolvency.[4] Liquidation costs summarise the impact of various forms of market incom- pleteness and transaction costs. The assumption of competitive deposit markets is also natural, since deposits have various close substitutes, and are supplied by a large number of firms and financial institutions.

The results obtained can be summarised as follows. The rather complicated story told above is shown to have a 'reduced form', the structure of which closely parallels that of a standard Cournot oligopoly. The bank's best-response function is then studied and it is shown that there exist two general types of market equilibrium: the *safe* and the *risky equilibria*. In safe equilibrium, banks bear no bankruptcy risk and supply a small amount of loans at high interest rates. In contrast, in risky equilibrium, banks supply a large amount of loans but bear a positive bankruptcy risk: bad signals can trigger a run. We show that a small change in basic model parameters such

---

[2] On this theme, see for instance Bernanke and Blinder (1988); Bernanke and Lown (1991).

[3] See the classic contribution of Diamond (1984).

[4] See Lucas and McDonald (1992); Donaldson (1993).

as bank equity and the average profitability of investments can induce a brisk, discontinuous transition from risky to safe equilibrium. For some parameter values, a safe and a risky equilibrium simultaneously exist. Any sunspot or extrinsic shock could then drive the market from risky to safe equilibrium. A consequence of such a change is a drastic reduction of aggregate lending. These phenomena happen when bank's profit functions are not single-peaked (not quasi-concave), a property which in turn stems from the agents' probabilistic beliefs about the uncertain return on investments. More precisely, profit functions typically exhibit two local maxima when the prior probability distribution of returns is bimodal. A bimodal probability density can be viewed as a mixture of two single-peaked densities, reflecting the agents' hesitations between two theories relative to the future course of events. We thus interpret bimodality of probabilistic beliefs as a description of a state of crisis.

The proposed model can be interpreted as a theory of deregulated (or free) banking competition. In the model, deposits are not insured, there are no capital requirements, and no deposit rate ceilings. An essential element in the debate on banking deregulation (and on the possibility of free banking) is the ability of depositors to correctly perceive the risk borne by banks.[5] Our assumptions of symmetrical information, combined with complete rationality and high information-processing abilities of depositors are clearly in favour of deregulation. Now, if complete markets, perfect competition and zero transactions costs were added to the set up, banks would be nothing but a 'financial veil', bank runs would not matter and there would be no ground for state intervention. If on the contrary, as we do here, there are market imperfections, as described above, then our analysis leads to the conclusion that a deregulated banking system is potentially highly unstable.

Finally, if we consider the relationships with the more recent literature, clearly the goal of our study is not to provide theoretical explanations for the mere existence and structure of financial intermediation, nor do we try to derive a theory of demand deposits as optimal contractual arrangements. These fundamental questions have been studied in numerous contributions.[6] The existence of institutions such as banks and demand deposits is taken as given in our analysis. This is also why our analysis is developed in an entirely risk-neutral economy. Risk-neutrality simplifies the analysis

---

[5] On the possibility of free competition and the theory of bank regulation, among many other contributions, see Kareken and Wallace (1978); Fama (1980); Smith (1984); Rochet (1992a); Dewatripont and Tirole (1993); Goodhart (1993); Hellwig (1994).

[6] See, among many other contributions, Diamond and Dybvig (1983); Boyd and Prescott (1986); Postlewaite and Vives (1987); Jacklin and Bhattacharya (1988); Calomiris and Kahn (1991); Bolton and Freixas (1994); Repullo and Suarez (1994); von Thadden (1995).

greatly from the technical point of view, and it is possible to show – although it might seem surprising – that nothing essential in our analysis depends on the restriction to risk-neutral agents. Our contribution focuses on the process of bank competition itself, showing how endogenous forces of competition can explain the behaviour of aggregate lending.

Section 2 describes the model – and, more precisely, the structure and timing of the game played by banks and depositors. The loan demand schedule is derived in section 3. Section 4 is then devoted to depositors' behaviour, and to the solution of the 'withdrawal subgames'. On the basis of the results obtained, the bank's optimal portfolio and loan supply is derived. Market equilibrium is then defined in section 5. This section also presents general properties of oligopoly equilibria. A class of examples, exhibiting non-concave profits, is then studied in section 6, showing how probabilistic beliefs and liquidation costs interfere to produce discontinuous equilibrium supply and multiple equilibria. Finally, section 7 gathers some concluding remarks.

2 The model

Basic assumptions

We construct a partial equilibrium, game-theoretic model of the bank loan and bank deposit markets in which three categories of agents explicitly intervene: banks, depositors and firms. All agents are risk-neutral and live one period. There are n banks, competing both on the credit and deposit markets, and indexed by $k = 1, \ldots, n$. Bank k's balance sheet is characterised by four variables: the bank's equity e_k, the mass of demand deposits d_k, the bank's reserve y_k and the amount of loans x_k. These variables are related by the balance sheet constraint

$$e_k + d_k = y_k + x_k$$

There exists a continuum of depositors. Banks supply deposits of size 1. We then assume that each depositor, either deposits 1 Franc in a bank, or purchases a one-period government bond yielding $(1 + \rho)$, where ρ denotes the riskless interest rate. Each bank k chooses the amount d_k of deposits it wishes to collect. The maximal deposit mass is assumed large enough so that banks can always collect their desired amount of deposits. We assume that the deposit market is competitive: each depositor is ready to deposit 1 Franc at bank k, provided that bank k's deposit interest rate, denoted i_k, guarantees an expected return at least equal to $(1 + \rho)$. Deposit interest rates i_k will then be greater than ρ only insofar as the banks' bankruptcy probabilities are not zero. The level of equity e_k of each bank is exogenously given. The bank invests $e_k + d_k$ in risky loans x_k, or reserves y_k. Reserves consist of one-period government bonds yielding $(1 + \rho)$.

Finally, there is a continuum of firms, each willing to invest in a single-period risky project and needing to borrow 1 Franc from banks. All firms are simultaneously subject to the same non-insurable, random 'macroeconomic' shock, which affects their profitability. For each value of the lending rate, denoted r, the firms whose expected rate of return on capital is greater than or equal to $(1 + \rho)$ apply for a loan. We assume here that each bank's share of the credit market is a perfect sample of the set of firms (or projects). Banks do not observe the quality of firms' investment projects and, to keep the model simple, they do not engage in screening. The macroeconomic shock affects all firms simultaneously and therefore, cannot be diversified away in bank portfolios.

Let x denote the total sum of loans granted, i.e. $x = \sum_{k=1}^{k=n} x_k$. The average rate of return on loans is a random variable denoted s, common to all banks, since its assumed source of randomness is 'macroeconomic'. Variable s is non-negative and has a probability distribution $G(s; x)$. It is crucial to note that G is parameterised by total credit supply x. This is because the average return on loans s depends on the amount of loans granted. Intuitively, the average quality of indebted firms decreases when the total amount of loans increases. This property is established in section 3. The expected value of the average return on loans is defined as

$$\bar{S}(x) = \int s \, dG(s; x) \tag{11.1}$$

The *ex ante* expected present value of bank k's loans x_k is then

$$\frac{x_k \bar{S}(x)}{1 + \rho}$$

In section 3, we derive the function $\bar{S}(x)$ from basic data and analyse its properties.

Timing of the game

There are three periods, $T = 0$, ε and 1. At $T = 0$, the state of the world is unknown. $T = \varepsilon < 1$ must be understood as some date, close to 0, at which the state of the world is revealed. $T = 1$ is the 'end of the economy'.

At time $T = 0$, each bank k chooses a quantity of loans x_k. Quantity competition on the loan market determines the lending rate r. Banks then compete to attract depositors and choose an amount of deposits d_k. Depositors decide either to deposit in a given bank k or to invest in government bonds. Perfect competition on the deposit market determines bank k's deposit rate i_k. In other words, bank k's deposit rate i_k must be adjusted so as to meet the depositor's participation constraint. Reserves are then automatically given by the balance sheet condition: $y_k = e_k + d_k - x_k$. At this stage, agents do not know the state of nature – i.e. they do not know the future realisation of the average yield on loans s.

At time $T = \varepsilon$, the state of nature is realised and determines the average yield s, which is revealed to all traders, bank managers and depositors. We thus assume that there are no informational asymmetries between agents.

Once s is revealed, depositors can non-cooperatively decide to withdraw their deposits or not. Massive withdrawal of all depositors of a given bank will be interpreted as a bank run. The interest i_k is not paid to depositors in case of (early) withdrawal at $T = \varepsilon$. Depositors invest the proceeds of their withdrawal in government bonds yielding $(1 + \rho)$ at $T = 1$, and each bank goes bankrupt at $T = \varepsilon$ if it cannot meet its obligations.

At time $T = 1$, bank loans and remaining depositors are reimbursed, and the bank is liquidated. Each bank can therefore go bankrupt, either at $T = \varepsilon$ if there is a run, or at $T = 1$, if the liquidation value of its assets is lower than the sum of its liabilities. In case of bankruptcy, depositors receive a proportionate share of the bank's liquidation value.

Liquidation costs

At $T = \varepsilon$, immediately after revelation of the state of nature, if the amount of withdrawals is too high, bank k's reserve will be insufficient and it will be forced to sell a fraction (or all) of its assets. To capture the illiquid character of bank assets, we introduce a liquidation cost, such that assets are sold at $T = \varepsilon$ with a discount. Let c, with $0 \leq c \leq 1$, describe the percentage of asset value that can be obtained on financial markets in case of early liquidation: x_k's liquidation value at $T = \varepsilon$ is

$$\frac{cx_k s}{(1 + \rho)}$$

The unit liquidation cost $(1 - c)$ is exogenously given. It can be interpreted as summarising all the costs incurred in case of early liquidation – that is, all transaction or securitisation costs, as well as discounts owing to short-term borrowing, when the bank is close to insolvency. Finally, c can also be viewed as summarising the impact of the lender of last resort's attitude towards 'problem banks': c will be close to 1 if the central banker is always ready to rescue the bank in case of a run, by means of short-term lending.[7] To sum up, there are various reasons why early liquidation is costly, and

---

[7] To illustrate this idea, assume that δ is the central bank's discount rate and that the central banker offers the most favourable conditions. Then, c can be rewritten as $c = (1 + \rho)/(1 + \delta)$, and $\delta \geq \rho$ implies $c \leq 1$.

our assumption provides a simple but tractable way to capture the existence of costs whose precise description would otherwise be very complex.

3   A model of the demand for loans

This section is devoted to the derivation of the probability distribution of s, based on a model of firm behaviour.

Let θ denote a firm type or project quality: θ is a real number and belongs to the interval $[\theta_0, \theta_1]$. Let $H(\theta)$ denote its cumulative distribution function. The mass of firms is normalised to 1.

Each firm has a small amount of capital $f > 0$ and wishes to invest in a project requiring $(1 + f)$. Investment projects are risky and their rate of return depends on the random state of nature, denoted ω, with cumulative probability distribution $J(\omega)$. Again, ω is a real number belonging to an interval denoted $\Omega = [\omega_0, \omega_1]$.

Each firm θ decides either to invest $1 + f$ at $T = 0$ in its project, or simply to invest f in government bonds yielding the riskless return $(1 + \rho)f$ at $T = 1$. All firms have limited liability, and are liquidated at $T = 1$. The return, at $T = 1$, of an investment made at $T = 0$ by firm θ is defined as $(1 + a(\theta, \omega))$, where $a(\theta, \omega)$ is a random variable satisfying $1 + a(\theta, \omega) \geq 0$. For convenience, we assume the following:

Assumption A1: $H(\theta)$ and $J(\omega)$ are differentiable and strictly increasing: $H'(\theta) \equiv h(\theta) > 0$ and $J'(\omega) \equiv j(\omega) > 0$.

Assumption A2: $a(\theta, \omega)$ is defined on $R \times \Omega$, continuously differentiable and strictly increasing with respect to both θ and ω, $\lim_{\theta \to -\infty} a(\theta, \omega) = -1$ and $\lim_{\theta \to +\infty} a(\theta, \omega) = +\infty$, for all ω in Ω.

Firms borrow 1 Franc and reimburse $(1 + r)$ at $T = 1$ if they are not bankrupt. In case of bankruptcy, the bank receives the liquidation value of the firm – i.e. $1 + a(\theta, \omega)$. It follows that the expected profit of firm θ at interest rate r is

$$\pi(\theta, r) = \int_\Omega \max\{0, a(\theta, \omega) - r\}dJ(\omega) \tag{11.2}$$

The firms which apply for a bank loan at interest rate r have types θ such that

$$\pi(\theta, r) \geq (1 + \rho)f \tag{11.3}$$

Under assumption A2, there exists a unique type, denoted $\hat{\theta}$ such that $\pi(\hat{\theta}, r) = (1 + \rho)f$. Note that $\hat{\theta}$ is a function of r and ρ. To simplify notation, this function is simply denoted $\hat{\theta}(r)$. It is easy to check (by an application of the Implicit Function Theorem) that $\hat{\theta}(r)$ is strictly increasing with respect to r, and this in turn implies that the lending rate r varies between bounds $r^{\min}$ and $r^{\max}$ when $\hat{\theta}(r)$ varies between θ_0 and θ_1.

Since each firm type $\theta \geq \hat{\theta}(r)$ demands a 1 Franc loan, the total demand for loans x can be computed as

$$x = A(r) = \int_{\hat{\theta}(r)}^{\theta_1} dH(\theta) \tag{11.4}$$

Under assumption A1, $A(r)$ is strictly decreasing. In addition, $A(r^{\min}) = 1$ and $A(r^{\max}) = 0$. The demand for loans can thus be expressed in inverse form, as a function $r : [0, 1] \rightarrow [r^{\min}, r^{\max}]$, where $r(x) \equiv A^{-1}(x)$. It is reasonable to assume:

Assumption A3: $r^{\min} < \rho < r^{\max}$.

The banks' average rate of return per loan (or per firm) is a random variable, parameterised by r, and defined as

$$\sigma(\omega, r) = \frac{1}{A(r)} \int_{\hat{\theta}(r)}^{\theta_1} \min\{1 + r, 1 + a(\theta, \omega)\} \, dH(\theta) \tag{11.5}$$

where the integral of (11.5) is the total (aggregate) revenue of the banks. For all $x \in (0, 1]$, the inverse demand for loans $r(x)$ can be used to define the average rate of return per loan as a function of x. That is, by definition,

$$\tilde{S}(\omega, x) \equiv \sigma(\omega, r(x)) \tag{11.6}$$

Define then $G(s; x)$ as the distribution of $\tilde{S}$ – i.e. $G(s; x) = \text{prob}(\{\omega | \tilde{S}(\omega, x) \leq s\})$. The expected average return on loans $\bar{S}(x)$ can then be expressed as

$$\bar{S}(x) = \int_{\Omega} \tilde{S}(\omega, x) \, dJ(\omega) = \int s \, dG(s; x)$$

The following result can be obtained with the help of standard calculus.

Proposition 1: Under assumptions A1 and A2, $\bar{S}(x)$ is continuous and non-increasing for all x in $[0, 1]$.

For future reference, it will be useful to study the properties of $G(s; x)$. Recalling (11.4)–(11.6), it is easy to see that the random variable $\tilde{S}$ is bounded above by $(1 + r(x))$. The minimal realisation of $\tilde{S}$ for given x is denoted $S^{\min}(x)$ and satisfies $S^{\min}(x) \equiv \sigma(\omega_0, r(x)) \geq 0$. Again, standard techniques permit one to establish the following result.[8]

Proposition 2:   Under assumptions A1 and A2, for all x in $[0, 1]$,

  (i) the support of $G(s; x)$ is $[S^{\min}(x), 1 + r(x)]$
  (ii) $G(s; x)$ is continuous for all $s < 1 + r(x)$
  (iii) $G(s; x)$ has an atom at $s = 1 + r(x)$
  (iv) $S^{\min}(x)$ is non-increasing with respect to x.

Proposition 2 (iii) shows that in the best states of nature, all active firms will be able to reimburse their loans, implying that the average return on loans $\tilde{S}$ reaches its maximal value $(1 + r(x))$ with positive probability.

4   Behaviour of depositors and the bank's expected profit

Withdrawal subgames

Consider a particular bank k which has chosen the variables (x_k, d_k, i_k). Assume that depositors have accepted k's deposit contract: the depositors' participation constraint implies $i_k \geq \rho$ for all k. At time $T = \varepsilon$, the value of s is revealed, and all depositors simultaneously and non-cooperatively decide whether or not to withdraw their deposits. Our next step is to solve this withdrawal subgame for its Nash equilibria (in pure strategies). Since all depositors are identical, we consider symmetric equilibria only.

   Remark that the (*ex post*) value of bank k at $T = 1$ can be expressed as $v_k = (1 + \rho)y_k + x_k s$, which is the sum of the values of reserves and loans. Using the balance sheet constraint and eliminating y_k yields the equivalent expression

$$v_k = (1 + \rho)(e_k - x_k) + x_k s + (1 + \rho)d_k \qquad (11.7)$$

The (*ex post*) value of bank k's debt is $(1 + i_k)d_k$ when the bank is solvent.
   At $T = \varepsilon$, and depending on the realised value of s, three different cases can occur.

Case 1 – The bank is solvent and there is no run: If s falls in the set $C_k^1 = \{s \mid v_k \geq (1 + i_k)d_k\}$, bank k is solvent at $T = 1$. Then, if all depositors wait until $T = 1$, they obtain $(1 + i_k)$, whereas a deviator who withdraws at $T = \varepsilon$ would receive $(1 + \rho) \leq (1 + i_k)$. It follows that it is a Nash equilibrium for all depositors not to withdraw prematurely.

---

[8] See the appendix in de Palma and Gary-Bobo (1994) for detailed proofs of propositions 1 and 2.

Case 2 – The bank is insolvent but depositors nevertheless wait until liquidation at $T = 1$: If s falls in the set $C_k^2 = \{s \mid (1 + \rho)d_k \leq v_k < (1 + i_k)d_k\}$, bank k is insolvent at $T = 1$. However, the payoff of a depositor who waits when all other depositors wait is the proportionate share of value v_k/d_k, which is greater than $(1 + \rho)$ if s belongs to C_k^2. Since the payoff of a deviator withdrawing early at $T = \varepsilon$ is $(1 + \rho)$, it follows that for all depositors waiting is a Nash equilibrium.

Case 3 – The bank is insolvent and there is a run at $T = \varepsilon$: If s falls in the set $C_k^3 = \{s \mid v_k < (1 + \rho)d_k\}$, bank k necessarily goes bankrupt. Early liquidation of the bank's assets yields $y_k + 1/(1 + \rho)cx_k s$ at $T = \varepsilon$. Since $c < 1$, it follows that the time $T = 1$ value of early liquidation is less than the $T = 1$ value of its debt. Formally,

$$(1 + \rho)y_k + cx_k s \leq v_k < (1 + \rho)d_k \leq (1 + i_k)d_k$$

The payoff to a depositor, when all depositors run at $T = \varepsilon$, is therefore $((1 + \rho)y_k + cx_k s)/d_k \geq 0$. A deviator who waits until $T = 1$ gets payoff 0, since the bank has already been liquidated and there is nothing left, showing that the bank run is a Nash equilibrium.

Bank k depositors' expected utility

Define the probability of case j as $P_k^j = \text{prob}(C_k^j)$, with $j = 1, 2, 3$. Clearly, since the three cases partition the set of possible values of s, $P_k^1 + P_k^2 + P_k^3 \equiv 1$. Further define

$$\bar{S}_k^j = \int_{C_k^j} s \, dG(s; x)$$

Then, for the same reasons,

$$\bar{S}_k^1 + \bar{S}_k^2 + \bar{S}_k^3 \equiv \bar{S}(x)$$

Finally, let U_k denote the expected utility of a typical bank k depositor.

Using these definitions, bank k depositors' expected utility can be computed as

$$U_k = \left(P_k^1(1 + i_k)\right) + \frac{1}{d_k}\left(P_k^2(1 + \rho)y_k + x_k\bar{S}_k^2\right) + \frac{1}{d_k}\left(P_k^3(1 + \rho)y_k + cx_k\bar{S}_k^3\right)$$

where the three terms between brackets of the right-hand side correspond to cases 1, 2 and 3 above. This expression can be easily rewritten as

$$[U_k - (1 + \rho)]d_k = P_k^1(i_k - \rho)d_k + (1 - P_k^1)(1 + \rho)(e_k - x_k)$$
$$+ x_k\bar{S}_k^2 + cx_k\bar{S}_k^3 \tag{11.8}$$

A rational and well informed depositor will then accept bank k's deposit contract only if bank k's portfolio variables (x_k, d_k, i_k) satisfy the *participation constraint*:

$$U_k d_k \geq (1 + \rho)d_k$$

Bank k's expected profit function

Let Π_k denote bank k's expected profit function:

$$\Pi_k = \int_{C_k^1} ((1 + \rho)y_k + sx_k - (1 + i_k)d_k)\, dG(s; x)$$

$$= P_k^1((1 + \rho)(e_k - x_k) + (\rho - i_k)d_k) + x_k \bar{S}_k^1 \tag{11.9}$$

Remark that bank k's expected profit Π_k and its depositors' expected utility U_k are functions of the variables (x, x_k, d_k, i_k). Bank k chooses its portfolio (x_k, d_k) so as to maximise Π_k while being forced to adjust i_k in order to ensure depositor participation. Formally, this is as if bank k chose (x_k, d_k, i_k) so as to solve the following program:

Program (I):

$$\max_{(x_k, d_k, i_k)} \Pi_k(x, x_k, d_k, i_k)$$

$$\text{s.t.} \quad e_k + d_k - x_k \geq 0, \quad d_k \geq 0, \quad 1 \geq x_k \geq 0, \quad i_k \geq \rho$$

$$U_k(x, x_k, d_k, i_k)d_k \geq (1 + \rho)d_k$$

It is intuitive that the depositors' participation constraint in program **(I)** should be binding at any optimal solution (for a rigorous proof, see the appendix, section A.1). A glance at (11.9) shows that Π_k is decreasing with respect to i_k, given that C_k^1 shrinks (or that P_k^1 decreases) when i_k increases. Define next the function $\Psi_k = \Pi_k + [U_k - (1 + \rho)]d_k$, which can be interpreted as the surplus of bank k and its depositors. Simple computations show that this function reduces to[9]

$$\Psi_k(x, x_k) = (1 + \rho)(e_k - x_k) + x_k \bar{S}(x) - (1 - c)x_k \bar{S}_k^3 \tag{11.10}$$

Remark that $\bar{S}_k^3$ depends neither on d_k nor on i_k, so that Ψ_k depends on (x, x_k) only. Therefore, U_k must be increasing with respect to i_k. Substitution of the participation constraint, written as an equality, in the bank's expected profit (11.9) yields $\Pi_k = \Psi_k$. It follows that Ψ_k can be viewed as bank k's objective function.

---

[9] Expression (11.10) is the sum of: (i) $(1 + \rho)(e_k - x_k)$, the net return on riskless reserves (which is by definition equal to $(1 + \rho)(y_k - d_k)$), (ii) $x_k \bar{S}(x)$, the total expected return on loans (including liquidation costs) and (iii) $-(1 - c)x_k \bar{S}_k^3$, minus expected liquidation costs, incurred when a bank run occurs.

Proposition 3 (proved in the appendix, section A.1) shows that bank k's profit maximisation program **(I)** reduces to unconstrained maximisation of Ψ_k with respect to x_k. To simplify notation, define $x_{-k} = \sum_{j \neq k} x_j$, for all k.

Proposition 3:   Under assumptions A1–A3,

(i) There exists an optimal solution of program **(I)**. It satisfies $P_k^1 > 0$.
(ii) (x_k^*, d_k^*, i_k^*) is an optimal solution of program **(I)** if and only if the three following conditions hold:

(a) x_k^* maximises $\Psi_k(x_k + x_{-k}, x_k)$ subject to $x_k \geq 0$
(b) d_k^* is any non-negative number satisfying $e_k + d_k^* - x_k^* \geq 0$
(c) i_k^* solves $[U_k(x_k^* + x_{-k}, x_k^*, d_k^*, i_k^*) - (1 + \rho)]d_k^* = 0$.

Proposition 3 shows that bank k's optimisation problem can be simplified and decomposed into a three-step procedure. The amount of loans x_k^* is first simply chosen so as to maximise the surplus $\Psi_k(x, x_k)$. The amount of deposits d_k^* can then be freely selected, provided that reserves are non-negative. Finally, the deposit interest rate i_k^* is set at a level such that the depositors' participation constraint is binding.

If the bank chooses a large amount of deposits, the value of its reserve will also be large and as a consequence, the bank will be safer. Thus, a small value of i_k^* will be sufficient to attract depositors. Proposition 3 implicitly shows the existence of a locus of pairs (d_k^*, i_k^*) such that $U_k = 1 + \rho$.

In the model, x_k^* is entirely determined by the characteristics of the demand for loans, and the magnitude of bank k's capital e_k. Once x_k^* is determined, d_k^* and i_k^* are simply adjusted so as to finance the difference $x_k^* - e_k$ and to compensate depositors for the risk borne.

Safe strategies, risky strategies

Proposition 4 (proved in the appendix, section A.2) shows that bank k has two types of strategies, corresponding to (i) and (ii), and hereafter called the *safe* and *risky* strategies.

Proposition 4:   Let (x_k, d_k, i_k) be such that $U_k = 1 + \rho$ and $\Pi_k > 0$. Then,

(i) $(i_k - \rho)d_k = 0$ if and only if $P_k^1 = 1$
(ii) $(i_k - \rho)d_k > 0$ if and only if $P_k^3 > 0$.

Assume that (x_k, d_k, i_k) is such that $P_k^1 = 1$. Such a strategy is called 'safe', since the probability of bankruptcy is zero – that is, $P_k^2 = P_k^3 = 0$. This is equivalent to saying that $(1 + \rho)(e_k - x_k) + x_k s \geq 0$ for all possible realisations of s – or, more conveniently, that $S^{\min}(x_k + x_{-k})x_k \geq (1 + \rho)(x_k - e_k)$, since $S^{\min}$ is by definition the smallest possible realisation of s. Since depositors bear no risk, the participation constraint boils down to $i_k = \rho$, and expected liquidation costs are zero, so that the bank's profit function can simply be written as $(1 + \rho)(e_k - x_k) + x_k \bar{S}(x)$.

By contrast, a 'risky' strategy is characterised by a positive probability of a bank run – that is, $P_k^3 < 0$ or, equivalently: $S^{\min}(x)x_k < (1 + \rho) \times (x_k - e_k)$. This naturally implies $x_k > e_k$ and $d_k > 0$, and to compensate rational and well informed depositors for bankruptcy risks, necessarily, $i_k > \rho$. In this case, the bank's profit function is given by (11.10) and expected liquidation costs $(1 - c)x_k \bar{S}_k^3$ are strictly positive.

The frontier separating the set of risky and safe strategies is defined as

$$S^{\min}(x_k + x_{-k})x_k = (1 + \rho)(x_k - e_k) \tag{11.11}$$

Since $S^{\min}(x)$ is a decreasing function of x, a solution of (11.11) in $[0, 1 - x_{-k}]$ is unique if it exists. Two cases can occur. Either there is no solution of (11.11) with respect to x_k in $[0, 1 - x_{-k}]$; the bank's supply of loans is then necessarily safe. This happens when bank capital e_k is large enough. Or, there exists a solution denoted $\bar{A}_k(x_{-k}, e_k)$, when e_k is sufficiently small. This solution[10] must be greater than e_k. Bank k's strategy x_k is then safe (resp. risky) if and only if $x_k \leq \bar{A}_k(x_{-k}, e_k)$ (resp. $x_k > \bar{A}_k(x_{-k}, e_k)$).

5 The banking oligopoly model

Definition of equilibrium

Proposition 3 shows that the problem of each bank k basically amounts to maximisation of Ψ_k with respect to x_k. A market equilibrium can simply be viewed as the non-cooperative equilibrium of a strategic-form game in which the banks' strategies are the quantities of loans x_k. This is clearly similar to a model of Cournot competition.

Definition of market equilibrium:[11]   A market equilibrium is an n-tuple $(x_1^*, \ldots, x_n^*) \geq 0$ such that for all $k = 1, \ldots, n$,

$$\Psi_k(x^*, x_k^*) \geq \Psi_k(x_{-k}^* + x_k, x_k)$$

for all x_k such that $0 \leq x_k \leq 1 - \sum_{j \neq k} x_j^*$.

---

[10] Bank k's profit function Ψ_k is not necessarily differentiable at $x_k = \bar{A}_k(x_{-k}, e_k)$. In other words, Ψ_k has a downward kink at $\bar{A}_k(x_{-k}, e_k)$. This stems from the presence of liquidation costs, the expected value of which is zero if $x_k \leq \bar{A}_k(x_{-k}, e_k)$ (since $C_k^3 = \emptyset$) and becomes strictly positive as soon as the bank selects a risky strategy.

[11] The structure of the game is analogous to that of a Cournot oligopoly. In expression (11.10), $\bar{S}(x)$ plays the role of an inverse demand function. The bank's revenue is $x_k \bar{S}(x)$, while its total cost is $x_k[(1 + \rho) + (1 - c)\bar{S}_k^3]$. The difference of total revenue and total cost is the bank's expected profit, net of the opportunity cost of capital $(1 + \rho)e_k$. When bank k plays a non-cooperative equilibrium strategy x_k^*, it chooses in fact an array of portfolio variables in a consistent way. More precisely, to each equilibrium quantity x_k^* is associated (i) a pair (d_k^*, i_k^*) such that depositors are ready to deposit the required amount d_k^* at interest i_k^* and (ii) a positive amount of reserves $y_k^* = e_k + d_k^* - x_k^*$ which determines bank k's level of risk for depositors.

The existence of market equilibria can be proved under standard profit quasi-concavity assumptions, but lack of quasi-concavity can stem from a non-convex expected liquidation cost. In the next subsection, we consider profit functions which are not quasi-concave. However, it is shown that equilibria can still be constructed.

Types of strategies

The frontier separating the set of risky and safe strategies, denoted $x_k = \bar{A}_k(x_{-k}, e_k)$ and defined as the solution of (11.11), is a strictly increasing function of e_k. In addition, the frontier $\bar{A}_k$ decreases when the other banks' loan supply x_{-k} increases.

Figure 11.1 represents the profit function Ψ_k of a bank (as defined by (11.10)) and its best replies in a non-concave case. The three drawings can be generated by the same example while varying e_k. Let Ψ_k^1 denote the profit of bank k without liquidation costs– i.e. $\Psi_k^1 = (1 + \rho)(e_k - x_k) + x_k \bar{S}(x)$. One has $\Psi_k^1 \geq \Psi_k$ and the two functions coincide over the set of safe strategies – that is, for all $x_k \leq \bar{A}_k$. In Figure 11.1a, the bank's best reply is denoted x_*^c and belongs to the risky interval. This stems from the fact that e_k, and thus $\bar{A}_k$, are relatively small. Such a strategy is called a *risky best response*. In figure 11.1b, corresponding to intermediate values of e_k, the bank's best reply is safe; it is denoted $\bar{x}_*$ and located at the frontier between the safe and risky intervals. This frontier corresponds to the kink of Ψ_k at $\bar{A}_k$. Such a strategy is called a *safe best response*. Finally, figure 11.1c corresponds to large values of e_k. The bank's best response, denoted x_*^1, is merely the maximum of Ψ_k^1. Such a strategy is called a *supersafe best response*.[12]

A paradoxical feature is that bank k's loan supply will be reduced suddenly when x_{-k} decreases, since this induces an increase of $\bar{A}_k$, and triggers a switch from the situation depicted by figure 11.1a to that depicted by figure 11.1b. In other words, bank k's best-response function will be discontinuous with an upward jump. Section 6 is devoted to the study of such non-convex cases.

Symmetric candidate equilibria

Assume now to simplify the discussion that $e_k = e$ for all k. The model possesses symmetric as well as asymmetric equilibria, and multiple

---

[12] If e_k is small or x_{-k} is large (figure 11.1a), bank k's safe strategies necessarily entail a relatively small amount of loan supply x_k. Risky strategies are then more profitable. If bank k selected a risky strategy x_k only slightly greater than $\bar{A}_k$ (see figure 11.1), the probability of a bank run, and thus expected liquidation costs, would increase very quickly without being compensated by a sufficient increase of revenue. This is why if a risky strategy x_*^c is chosen, it must be much larger than $\bar{A}_k$.

(a)

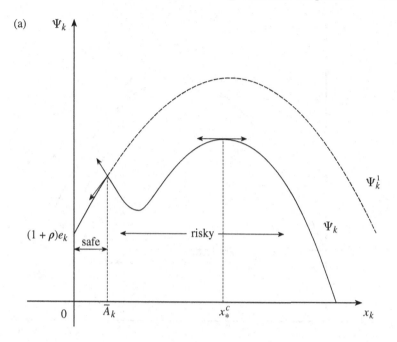

(b)

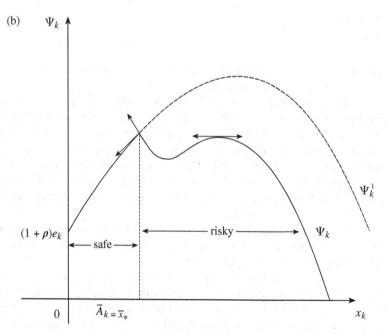

Figure 11.1 Best response: risky, safe and supersafe. (a) Risky best response
(b) Safe best response (c) Supersafe best response

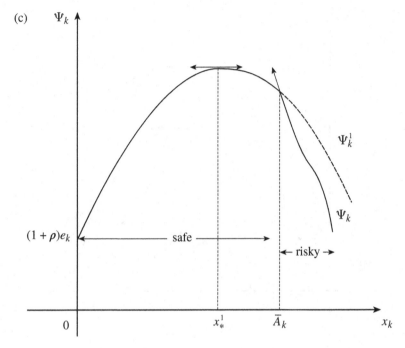

Figure 11.1   *(cont.)*

equilibria cannot be excluded (see section 6). We focus here on three types of symmetric equilibria with distinct features.

Equilibria such that all firms choose the same risky strategy x_*^c will hereafter be called *risky equilibria* (see figure 11.1a). These equilibrium points are characterised by $x_*^c > \bar{A}_k$ and $(\partial\Psi_k/\partial x_k)(nx_*^c, x_*^c) = 0$ for all k.

Equilibria such that all firms choose the same safe strategy are called *safe equilibria*, and are characterised by the fact that the choice of a strategy at the frontier of the safe and risky intervals is a best response to itself (see figure 11.1b). Such equilibrium strategies, denoted $\bar{x}_*$, necessarily satisfy $\bar{x}_* = \bar{A}_k[(n-1)\bar{x}_*, e]$ for all k.

Finally, *supersafe equilibria* are such that all firms choose the same supersafe strategy denoted x_*^1 (see figure 11.1c). This strategy is characterised by $(\partial\Psi_k^1/\partial x_k)(nx_*^1, x_*^1) = 0$ for all k.

The comparative statics of risky equilibria are very complex. However, under reasonable assumptions, one typically finds that $\partial x_*^c/\partial c > 0$, meaning that a reduction of the liquidation cost parameter $(1 - c)$ will lead to an increase of total bank loan supply. Similarly, $\partial x_*^c/\partial e \geq 0$. Intuitively, an increase of equity reduces the riskiness of banks, the probability of a run and thus expected liquidation costs. The analysis shows that $\partial x_*^c/\partial\rho \leq 0$ under 'normal conditions' – that is, in particular, if c is sufficiently close to 1. But the sign of this partial derivative could be positive, since an increase in ρ induces a favourable selection effect. More precisely, the average quality of loan applicants improves when ρ rises.

This is owing to the fact that $\hat{\theta}$ is an increasing function of ρ, implying that $\partial S^{\min}/\partial\rho \geq 0$. This latter property explains why an increase in ρ will tend to reduce expected liquidation costs. Interestingly, if this indirect effect is strong enough, an increase in ρ will counterintuitively increase the supply of loans.

The comparative statics of safe equilibria are much simpler. Clearly, liquidation costs do not affect safe equilibria locally (see (11.11)). A simple application of the Implicit Function Theorem to (11.11), evaluated at $x_k = \bar{x}_*$ and $x_{-k} = (n-1)\bar{x}_*$, proves that $\partial\bar{x}_*/\partial e > 0$. Intuitively, an increase in capital e shifts the frontier of safe strategies to the right, thus allowing the bank to expand credit without becoming risky. The sign of $\partial\bar{x}_*/\partial\rho$ is equal to the sign of $(e - \bar{x}_* + \bar{x}_*(\partial S^{\min}/\partial\rho))$. Since $(e - \bar{x}_*)$ is necessarily negative in safe equilibria, this partial derivative will have a counterintuitive sign if the favourable selection effect $\partial S^{\min}/\partial\rho$ is sufficiently strong.

Finally, supersafe equilibria $x_k = x_*^{1}$ exhibit the following properties: $\partial x_*^{1}/\partial c = 0$, $\partial x_*^{1}/\partial e = 0$, and $\partial x_*^{1}/\partial\rho < 0$. These properties are direct consequences of the expression of Ψ_k^{1}, which does not depend on c, of the fact that e is given and of the fact that $(1 + \rho)$ plays the role of a marginal cost for the supersafe bank.

6   Coordination Failures

Speculative markets and bimodal distributions of signal s

The shape of the signal's probability distribution G depends on the basic distribution J, and thus on the nature of the market on which firms operate. Investment profitability $a(\theta, \omega)$ is subject to macroeconomic shocks ω. The speculative and risky character of many markets, and thus of the corresponding investments and bank loans, is reflected in the agents' prior distributions of random shocks. It is common to assume that in the minds of many agents, a positive probability is attached to the possibility that currently observed high profitability is the result of a speculative bubble. If this is the case, agents believe that investment profitability can dramatically fall when bad signals are observed. A simple way to capture investment riskiness is then to assume that economic agents' beliefs, as represented by the probability distribution on states of nature $J(\omega)$, put weight on the possibility of a serious breakdown.

The speculative character of underlying investments can therefore be captured by the assumption that the probability density $j(\omega)$ is bimodal, and concentrated around both a high value, corresponding to continuation of favourable market conditions, and a low value, representing bubble collapse. Such a bimodal distribution can be viewed as a mixture of two single-peaked densities. In the framework of the static banking competition model studied here, a state of crisis can be simulated just by replacing a standard single-peaked prior density by some bimodal mixture, or by putting more weight around some bad state of nature, to represent increasing fears of market crash. Banks' profit functions will then typically be non-concave, as in figure 11.1.

A class of examples with discontinuous profit and reaction functions

We consider now a class of examples which can be viewed as a limiting case, obtained when the distribution $j(\omega)$ is bimodal and converges towards a discrete distribution over two states of nature. At the limit, the bank's profit function is no longer continuous. It exhibits a downward jump at the frontier separating the sets of risky and safe strategies. Although assumption A1 is then violated, this particular class is more easily tractable than a continuous probability example, and provides a qualitative view of oligopoly equilibrium behaviour for all its non-concave and continuous neighbours.[13]

We modify the basic assumptions of section 3 as follows.

Assumption A1': $H(\theta)$ is the uniform distribution over $[\theta_0, \theta_1]$. Distribution J is discrete with $J(\{\omega_0\}) = q$, $J(\{\omega_1\}) = 1 - q$, $0 < q < 1$, and $\Omega = \{\omega_0, \omega_1\}$.

We further specify the mapping $a(\theta, \omega)$ as follows:

Assumption A2': $a(\theta, \omega_0) \equiv \kappa + \theta - 1$ and $a(\theta, \omega_1) \equiv \theta$, where κ is a parameter satisfying: $-\theta_0 \leq \kappa < 1 - (\theta_1 - \theta_0) - f(1 + \rho)(1 - q)^{-1}$.

Under assumptions A1', A2' and A3, the random signal $\tilde{S}$ takes two different values – that is, $\tilde{S}(\omega_0, x) = S^{\min}(x) = \alpha_0 - \beta_0 x$ with probability q, and $\tilde{S}(\omega_1, x) = 1 + r(x) = \alpha_1 - \beta_1 x$ with probability $(1 - q)$, where α_0, α_1, β_0 and β_1 are positive numbers (see the appendix, section A.3 for a proof and precise definitions). These parameters are themselves functions of the

---

[13] Since models obtained under markedly bimodal distributions $J(\omega)$ are non-concave (see figure 11.1), it will become intuitively clear below that the best-response functions of such models and those of the limiting two-state approximations exhibit the same properties – in particular, the same type of discontinuities. In the limiting case, the structure of Nash equilibria in pure strategies is therefore closely analogous to that of approximating continuous models.

basic data $\rho, f, \theta_1, \theta_0, q$ and κ. It follows that the mean value of $\tilde{S}$ can be written:

$$\bar{S}(x) = qS^{\min}(x) + (1 - q)(1 + r(x)) = \alpha_q - \beta_q x \qquad (11.12)$$

where to simplify notation, $\alpha_q \equiv q\alpha_0 + (1 - q)\alpha_1$ and $\beta_q \equiv q\beta_0 + (1 - q)\beta_1$.

The derivation of bank k's profit function in section 4 applies to this limiting case with minor modifications which stem from the fact that, owing to the discreteness of $\tilde{S}$'s distribution, expected liquidation costs now discontinuously jump down as soon as x_k enters the set of risky strategies.

The bank's profit function Π_k is still given by (11.9) and the depositor's individual rationality constraint is still given by $U_k \geq 1 + \rho$ where U_k is defined by (11.8). The difference is now simply that P_k^l, the probability of being solvent, can take only a finite number of values – i.e. $P_k^l \in \{0, 1 - q, 1\}$. The following proposition (proved in the appendix, section A.4) restates proposition 3 in the discontinuous case considered here.

Proposition 5: Under assumptions A1′, A2′ and A3, proposition 3 remains true.

The particular expression of bank k's profit function Ψ_k is now derived. Safe strategies are characterised by $P_k^l = 1$ and $(U_k - (1 + \rho))d_k = (i_k - \rho)d_k = 0$ as usual. The frontier of the set of safe strategies is still given by (11.11) which is now quadratic with respect to x_k, and possesses a unique non-negative root whose expression[14] is

$$\bar{A}_k(x_{-k}, e_k) = \frac{1}{2\beta_0} \left([\alpha_0 - \beta_0 x_{-k} - (1 + \rho)] \right.$$
$$\left. + \sqrt{[\alpha_0 - \beta_0 x_{-k} - (1 + \rho)]^2 + 4e_k\beta_0(1 + \rho)} \right)$$

A strategy of k is safe (resp. risky) if and only if $x_k \leq \bar{A}_k(x_{-k}, e_k)$ (resp. $x_k > \bar{A}_k(x_{-k}, e_k)$). Recall that the set of risky strategies is open. The set of safe strategies shrinks when x_{-k} increases.

In the case studied here, as soon as x_k becomes risky, the probability P_k^3 jumps from 0 to q, inducing a sudden, discontinuous increase of expected liquidation costs which jump from 0 to $(1 - c)x_k\bar{S}_k^3 = (1 - c)x_kqS^{\min}(x)$. If x_k is safe, using (11.10) and (11.12), the expression of bank k's profit function is therefore

$$\Psi_k^l(x, x_k) = (1 + \rho)(e_k - x_k) + x_k(\alpha_q - \beta_q x) \qquad (11.13)$$

---

[14] It can be checked that $\bar{A}_k$ is positive if $e_k > 0$, equal to zero if $e_k = 0$, strictly increasing and strictly concave as a function of e_k, strictly decreasing and strictly convex, with a slope greater than $-1/2$, as a function of $x_{-k} \geq 0$.

If x_k is risky, using (11.10) and the expression of $S^{\min}(x)$, bank k's profit can be written $\Psi_k^c(x, x_k) = \Psi_k^1(x, x_k) - (1 - c)qx_k(\alpha_0 - \beta_0 x)$, showing that $\Psi_k^1(x, x_k) \geq \Psi_k^c(x, x_k)$. Let $\alpha_q^c \equiv qc\alpha_0 + (1 - q)\alpha_1$ and $\beta_q^c \equiv qc\beta_0 + (1 - q)\beta_1$. Then, $\Psi_k^c(x, x_k)$ can be conveniently rewritten as:

$$\Psi_k^c(x, x_k) = (1 + \rho)(e_k - x_k) + x_k(\alpha_q^c - \beta_q^c x) \tag{11.14}$$

A glance at (11.13) and (11.14) then shows that Ψ_k^1 and Ψ_k^c are quadratic and concave with respect to x_k (recall that $x = x_k + x_{-k}$).

The unique maximiser of Ψ_k^c over the set $x_k \geq 0$ is

$$Q_k^c(x_{-k}) = \frac{\max\{0, \alpha_q^c - \beta_q^c x_{-k} - (1 + \rho)\}}{2\beta_q^c} \tag{11.15}$$

and the unique maximiser of Ψ_k^1 over the set $x_k \geq 0$ is

$$Q_k^1(x_{-k}) = \frac{\max\{0, \alpha_q - \beta_q x_{-k} - (1 + \rho)\}}{2\beta_q} \tag{11.16}$$

Figure 11.2 shows that the choice of a risky versus a safe strategy depends on the relative heights of Ψ_k^1, evaluated at $\bar{A}_k$, and of Ψ_k^c, evaluated at its maximum Q_k^c. Bank k will be just indifferent between the safe strategy $\bar{A}_k$ and the optimal risky strategy Q_k^c if and only if $\bar{A}_k = B_k^c$, where B_k^c is the smallest root of the following quadratic equation in B: $\Psi_k^c(x_{-k} + Q_k^c, Q_k^c) = \Psi_k^1(x_{-k} + B, B)$, the solution of which is given by

$$B_k^c(x_{-k}) = Q_k^1(x_{-k}) - \sqrt{\left(Q_k^1(x_{-k})\right)^2 - \frac{\beta_q^c}{\beta_q}\left(Q_k^c(x_{-k})\right)^2}$$

Note that B_k^c does not depend on e_k. It is almost obvious that $0 \leq B_k^c < Q_k^1$, since $\Psi_k^1 > \Psi_k^c$ on the relevant domain. It is also true that[15] $B_k^c \leq Q_k^c$.

With the above-defined tools, bank k's best-response function, denoted $Q_k(x_{-k})$ can now be derived. A glance at figure 11.2 will help to understand the following proposition, the proof of which is fairly obvious.

Proposition 6:   Under assumptions A1′, A2′ and A3, bank k's best-response correspondence $Q_k(x_{-k})$ is equal to:

   (i) $Q_k^c(x_{-k})$ if $\bar{A}_k(x_{-k}, e_k) < B_k^c(x_{-k})$
   (ii) $\{Q_k^c(x_{-k}), \bar{A}_k(x_{-k}, e_k)\}$ if $\bar{A}_k(x_{-k}, e_k) = B_k^c(x_{-k})$
   (iii) $\bar{A}_k(x_{-k}, e_k)$ if $B_k^c(x_{-k}) < \bar{A}_k(x_{-k}, e_k) \leq Q_k^1(x_{-k})$
   (iv) $Q_k^1(x_{-k})$ if $Q_k^1(x_{-k}) \leq \bar{A}_k(x_{-k}, e_k)$

---

[15] It can be checked that (i) $Q_k^c = 0$ implies $B_k^c = 0$; (ii) B_k^c is strictly decreasing and convex with respect to all $x_{-k} \geq 0$ such that $Q_k^c > 0$; (iii) $Q_k^c = 0$ implies $\partial B_k^c / \partial x_{-k} = 0$; and (iv) $\partial B_k^c / \partial x_{-k} > -\frac{1}{2}$.

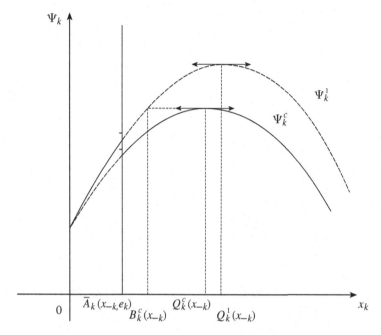

Figure 11.2   Expected profit in the discontinuous case

Analysis of duopoly equilibria: symmetric equilibria

The structure of symmetric equilibria can be analysed with the help of proposition 6. We assume that all banks are identical – that is, $e_k = e$ for all $k = 1, \ldots, n$. Since the frontier of safe strategies $\bar{A}_k$ increases with equity e, it will become clear below that risky equilibria occur for low values of e, safe equilibria occur for intermediate values of e and supersafe equilibria correspond to high values of e.

Figure 11.3a depicts a risky equilibrium in the duopoly case ($n = 2$). The bank's best-response function is represented as the discontinuous bold line which jumps down from Q_k^c to $\bar{A}_k$ at the intersection of $\bar{A}_k$ and B_k^c. The curve $\bar{A}_k$ lies everywhere below B_k^c when both curves lie above the diagonal: this is owing to the fact that e is relatively small. On this type of figure, any intersection of the best-response function and the diagonal is a symmetric duopoly equilibrium. A risky equilibrium appears in figure 11.3a at the intersection of Q_k^c and the diagonal. Formally, a risky equilibrium strategy, denoted x_*^c, is the unique solution of the following equation:

$$x_*^c = Q_k^c[(n-1)x_*^c] \tag{11.17}$$

(a)

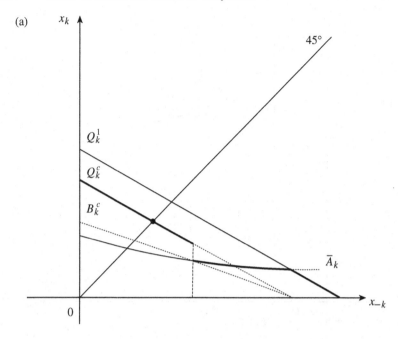

(b)

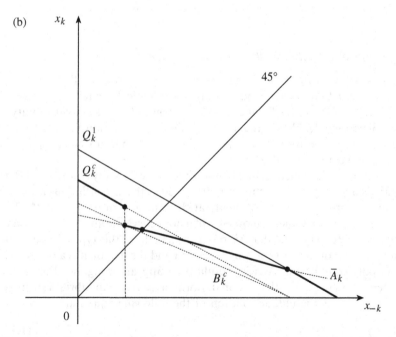

Figure 11.3   Equilibrium: risky, safe and supersafe (a) Risky equilibrium (b) Safe equilibrium (c) Supersafe equilibrium

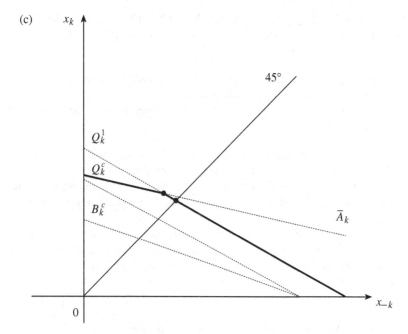

Figure 11.3 (*cont.*)

Figure 11.3b represents a case in which a safe equilibrium prevails. The curve $\bar{A}_k$ lies above B_k^c when both curves are below the diagonal: the value of e must be greater here than in Figure 11.3a. The bold line representing the bank's best response crosses the diagonal at a point such that the best response is equal to $\bar{A}_k$ (is safe). Formally, a safe equilibrium, denoted $\bar{x}_*$, is determined as the unique solution of the equation

$$\bar{x}_* = \bar{A}_k[(n-1)\bar{x}_*, e] \tag{11.18}$$

Finally, figure 11.3c depicts a supersafe equilibrium. The value of e is larger than in figure 11.3b and it follows that the curve $\bar{A}_k$ crosses Q_k^1 above the diagonal. The bank's best response is equal to Q_k^1 when it crosses the diagonal. Formally, a supersafe equilibrium, denoted x_*^1, is the unique solution of

$$x_*^1 = Q_k^1[(n-1)x_*^1] \tag{11.19}$$

The following proposition (proved in the appendix, section A.5) summarises our knowledge about symmetric equilibria.

Proposition 7:   Under assumptions A1′, A2′ and A3, and if $3\alpha_0 > \alpha_1$, there exist three threshold values e_1, e_2, e_3, satisfying $0 < e_1 < e_2$ and $0 < e_3 < e_2$, such that:

  (i) If $0 \le e \le e_1$, there exists a symmetric risky equilibrium
 (ii) If $e_3 \le e \le e_2$, there exists a symmetric safe equilibrium
(iii) If $e \ge e_2$, there exists a unique symmetric and supersafe equilibrium.

The thresholds e_1, e_2 and e_3 are functions of the basic parameters ρ, c, q, α_i and β_i, $i = 0, 1$. Note that the assumption $3\alpha_0 > \alpha_1$ is sufficient to guarantee $x_*^c < x_*^1$, which corresponds to the only reasonable configuration of the model, and is all that is really needed in the proof of proposition 7.

Depending on the value of basic parameters, it is possible to have either $e_3 < e_1$ or the opposite. Yet, a straightforward consequence of proposition 7 is that if $e_3 \le e_1$, there exists a symmetric equilibrium for all values of e.

Analysis of duopoly equilibria: asymmetric equilibria

If basic parameters are such that $e_1 < e < e_3$, none of our three candidates, the symmetric risky, safe and supersafe equilibria does exist, but asymmetric equilibria can then appear.

Figure 11.4 shows a duopoly example in which there are no symmetric equilibria, but two asymmetric equilibria exist. In each of the two equilibria, one of the firms chooses a safe strategy, while its competitor chooses a risky strategy. Such equilibria are characterised by the fact that a safe strategy is a best response to a risky strategy, and conversely. This possibility shows that heterogeneous riskiness of banks in a given market can be understood as an equilibrium phenomenon, even if banks are described by the same structural parameter values. We skip here the formal details of the description of such equilibria. It is, however, interesting to note that in the duopoly case, the average loan supply of banks is smaller in asymmetric equilibrium than in symmetric risky equilibrium, but larger than in symmetric safe equilibrium. This property is illustrated by figure 11.4, where average loan supply can be measured on the diagonal in the middle of the segment joining the two equilibria. Asymmetric equilibria generally exist for values of e belonging to an interval $[e_4, e_5]$ which includes $[e_1, e_3]$.

We now turn to a more uncommon phenomenon, which is the possibility of multiple symmetric equilibria.

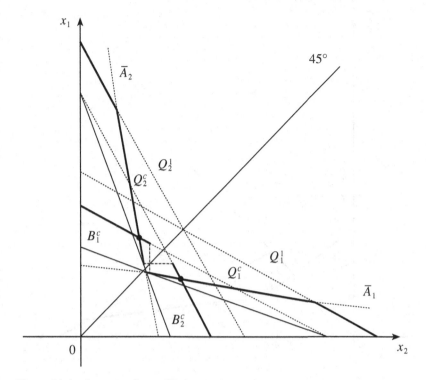

Figure 11.4   Asymmetric equilibria

Analysis of duopoly equilibria: multiple equilibria

Until now figures 11.3 and 11.4 illustrate the case in which $e_1 < e_3$. This can be seen on these figures since an increase of e shifts the curve $\bar{A}_k$ upwards. When e increases, starting from zero, $\bar{A}_k$ first cuts B_k^c just below the intersection of Q_k^c with the diagonal: this corresponds to e_1. When e continues to increase, $\bar{A}_k$ then crosses B_k^c just at the point at which B_k^c itself crosses the diagonal: this determines e_3. It follows that figures 11.3 and 11.4 are obtained under the assumption $e_1 < e_3$. Examples[16] in which $e_3 < e_1$ are necessarily such that $\bar{A}_k$ intersects B_k^c at least twice for intermediate values of e.

A consequence of proposition 7 is that a risky and a safe equilibrium simultaneously exist for all $e \in [e_3, e_1]$. Figure 11.5 represents an example

[16] It is possible to find numerical values of the model's parameters which correspond to all the examples discussed in section 6.

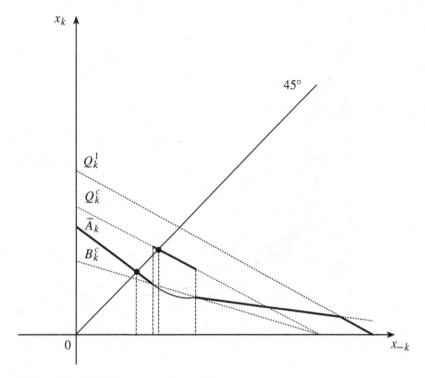

Figure 11.5   Multiple symmetric equilibria

with $e_3 < e_1$ and two symmetric equilibria. The fundamental property of this example is that equilibria can be ranked with respect to their total supply of loans. In other words, if the market is coordinated by the safe equilibrium, the supply of loans is markedly smaller than in risky equilibrium. A classical way of interpreting this result is to say that an exogenous shock, or the mere occurrence of a sunspot could induce a shift from risky to safe equilibrium. The corresponding reduction of loan supply can then be viewed as an endogenous 'credit crunch' phenomenon.

Equilibrium correspondence and discontinuous jumps of equilibrium credit

The results obtained above permit one to determine an aspect of the model's equilibrium correspondence. All other parameters being held fixed, an average equilibrium loan supply can be associated to each value of e.

Figure 11.6a represents the relation between average loan supply and equity e in the case $e_1 < e_3$. For relatively small values of e, the only equilibrium is risky. At the threshold $e = e_1$, the equilibrium supply jumps down and the structure of the banking industry changes to form an asymmetric equilibrium. As soon as $e \geq e_3$, loan supply again jumps down to a symmetric safe equilibrium. Then, the equilibrium supply increases with e and reaches a ceiling at $e = e_2$, at which the equilibrium becomes supersafe.

To sum up, the correspondence of figure 11.6a shows that market equilibrium necessarily exhibits discontinuities, with downward jumps of loan quantities (corresponding to upward jumps of the interest rate). This shows that the bank loan market behaviour is unstable with respect to underlying parameters.

The downward jump possibilities are even more striking on figure 11.6b, which represents the same equilibrium correspondence in the case $e_3 < e_1$. On this figure, symmetric safe and risky equilibria coexist

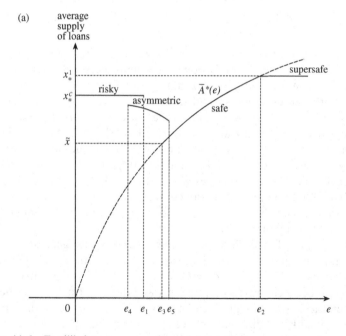

Figure 11.6   Equilibrium correspondence (a) Equilibrium correspondence when $e_1 < e_3$ (b) Multiple symmetric equilibria: equilibrium correspondence when $e_3 \leq e_1$

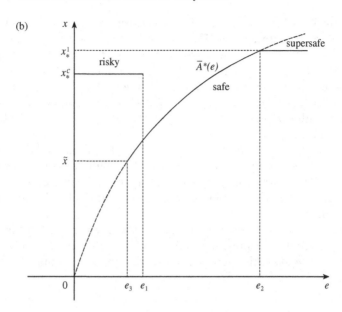

Figure 11.6   (*cont.*)

when $e \in [e_3, e_1]$. A 'crunch' (or a 'boom') might therefore happen for all values of e in this interval, and a downward jump necessarily occurs as soon as $e > e_1$ if the prevailing equilibrium is risky for $e \leq e_1$.

On both figures, the risky and supersafe supply of loans are constant with respect to e. The reason for this is that the expression of x_*^c and x_*^1 does not depend on e. (A glance at (11.15) and (11.16) shows that the maxima of Ψ_k^c and Ψ_k^1 are both independent of e.) In contrast, the safe equilibrium supply increases with e. To understand this property intuitively, recall that the set of safe strategies enlarges when e grows. In any safe equilibrium, each bank's loan supply is constrained by $\bar{A}_k$, the frontier of safe strategies. It follows that each bank increases its loan supply when this frontier shifts to the right (see figure 11.2).

The origin of the downward jump, and more generally of all discontinuities in equilibrium loan supply, can be intuitively understood at the bank level. When $\bar{A}_k = B_k^c$ (see figure 11.2), the bank is just indifferent between the risky strategy Q_k^c and the safe strategy $\bar{A}_k$. The gap between these two strategies can be explained as follows. At this critical point, the bank is indifferent between a relatively small amount of loans inducing a zero bankruptcy probability, and a risky, but large, amount of loans. When it operates in the risky interval, the bank must expand credit sufficiently to compensate for expected liquidation costs. This explains the paradoxical fact that an increase of e can trigger a downward jump.

At the market level, we find a similar behaviour of equilibrium loan supply. To understand why equilibrium credit falls from risky to asymmetric equilibria in figure 11.6a, consider the standard picture in figure 11.3a or 11.3b. This corresponds to a case in which $e_1 < e_3$. Remark first that the bank's best response is downward-sloping. It follows that bank loans are strategic substitutes (see Bulow, Geanakoplos and Klemperer, 1985). Consider a simple duopoly and assume that for some reason, bank 2 reduces its loan supply and reverts to a safe strategy. Such a reversion can be owing to an exogenous shock, or simply to irrational panic behaviour on the part of bank 2's managers. Bank 1's best response will then be to increase its loan supply and possibly to enter the risky interval if its previous choice was safe. This explains how an asymmetric equilibrium can emerge, starting from a symmetric risky or safe equilibrium.

The symmetric credit contraction phenomenon depicted in figure 11.6b can be explained with the help of figure 11.5, characterised by the coexistence of risky and safe equilibria. Consider again the duopoly case to simplify reasoning and assume that banks are in symmetric risky equilibrium. Remark that the banks' best-response function is no longer globally decreasing. More precisely, the loan supply variables are now local strategic complements. Then, if bank 2 reverts to a safe strategy for any exogenous reason, bank 1's best-response will also be to reduce its loan supply and choose a safe strategy. A symmetric safe equilibrium will soon emerge, linked with a drastic reduction of aggregate lending.

We have explored the behaviour of equilibrium credit when equity e varies. Similar results could be derived while varying other parameters such as ρ, c, or α_1. The level of the demand for loans is parameterised by α_1. In the above reasoning, the major role is in fact played by the ratio e/α_1 – i.e. the size of the bank relative to that of the market. A downward jump can naturally also be triggered by a slight decrease of α_1.

7 Concluding Remarks

First, it has been shown that the model can exhibit multiple equilibria, ranked according to total equilibrium lending. There exist safe equilibria, in which banks bear no bankruptcy risk, and risky equilibria, in which banks supply more loans, but face the risk of bankruptcy with positive probability. When both types of equilibria coexist, a perturbation, either extrinsic or intrinsic, can trigger a shift from risky to safe equilibrium. If this is the case, the equilibrium supply of loans decreases drastically. This feature of the model is more likely to arise when the prior probability densities describing the investments' future profitability reflect hesitation between two (or more) theories – in other words, during periods of transition between optimism and pessimism.

Second, it has been shown that the model's equilibrium correspondence can be discontinuous – i.e. a small change of underlying parameters, such as banks' capital/asset ratios, can induce a transition from risky to safe equilibria, corresponding to a discrete downward jump of equilibrium lending and a correlative upward jump of interest rates.

If the model is interpreted as representing a deregulated market, our results then predict that the behaviour of banks is potentially unstable. If liquidation costs can be manipulated by the central banker, an appropriate choice of the 'emergency lending' policy could completely correct this instability problem: just set $c = 1$. Unfortunately, this can be done only if the central bank is committed to rescue insolvent banks without limits at the smallest possible rate. It is intuitively clear that such a policy at least partially conflicts with any attempt to limit the banker's moral hazard and to promote the safety of depositors by the provision of appropriate incentives.

Our main results essentially depend on the presence of two types of market imperfection. First, banks are endowed with market power on the asset side, thus creating scope for strategic behaviour. Second, banks incur liquidation costs, since they cannot sell or securitise assets at their true fundamental values when close to insolvency.

Finally, these results have been produced in the framework of a simple but non-trivial partial equilibrium model which integrates the traditional portfolio choice problem of the bank with fully rational behaviour of depositors, leading to the possibility of information-based, Nash equilibrium runs. We have then been able to show that some cyclical patterns of banking activity could be explained as a response of the banking sector to outside shocks, which can be extrinsic (psychological) as well as intrinsic (macroeconomic), and that the forces driving this response are individual economic rationality and competition.

Appendix

A.1   Proof of proposition 3

Note that $\Psi_k(x_{-k} + x_k, x_k)$ is a function of x_k defined on the set $[0, 1 - x_{-k}]$. Assume that $x_{-k} \leq 1$. Ψ_k is continuous if G's atom at $1 + r(x)$ remains out of C_k^3 – that is, Ψ_k is continuous on the compact set $\{x_k | (1 + r(x))x_k \geq (1 + \rho)(x_k - e_k)\} \cap [0, 1 - x_{-k}]$. It follows that there exists a maximum of Ψ_k on this set, denoted x_k^*. We now show that x_k^* either belongs to the interior of the above set or is equal to zero. Assume first that $\bar{S}(x_k^* + x_{-k}) < (1 + \rho)$. Then, a glance at (11.10) shows that $\Psi_k < (1 + \rho)e_k$. But $\Psi_k(x_{-k}, 0) = e_k(1 + \rho) > 0$, a contradiction. Now, since $(1 + \rho) \leq \bar{S}(x_k^* + x_{-k}) \leq 1 + r(x_k^* + x_{-k})$, it easily follows that $(1 + r(x_k^* + x_{-k})) \times x_k^* > (1 + \rho)(x_k^* - e_k)$. Second, if $x_k^* + x_{-k} = 1$, then, since under assumption $A3$, $\rho > r(1)$, one finds $\bar{S}(1) \leq 1 + r(1) < 1 + \rho$, which in turn implies $\Psi_k(1, x_k^*) < (1 + \rho)e_k = \Psi_k(x_{-k}, 0)$, a contradiction.

Choose any value $d_k^* > 0$ such that $e_k + d_k^* - x_k^* \geq 0$. We now prove that there exists i_k^* such that $U_k(x_k^* + x_{-k}, x_k^*, d_k^*, i_k^*) = 1 + \rho$ and such that (x_k^*, d_k^*, i_k^*) satisfies

$$(i_k^* - \rho)d_k^* + (1 + \rho)(x_k^* - e_k) \leq (1 + r(x_k^* + x_{-k}))x_k^* \qquad (11\text{A}.1)$$

Define the function $Z_k(x, x_k, d_k, i_k) = [U_k(x, x_k, d_k, i_k) - (1 + \rho)]d_k$. To simplify notation, we will avoid recalling Z_k's arguments if this creates no ambiguity. A glance at (11.8) shows that Z_k is continuous if G's atom at $1 + r(x)$ remains in C_k^1, that is, if (11A.1) is satisfied. If $i_k = \rho$, then $C_k^2 = \emptyset$, $\bar{S}_k^2 = 0$ and $1 - P_k^1 = P_k^3$. Thus, if $i_k = \rho$,

$$Z_k = (1 - P_k^1)(1 + \rho)(e_k - x_k^*) + cx_k^*\bar{S}_k^3$$

$$= \int_{C_k^3} [(1 + \rho)(e_k - x_k^*) + cx_k^*s]\, dG$$

Since $(1 + \rho)(e_k - x_k^*) + x_k^*s \leq 0$ for all $s \in C_k^3$ and $c < 1$, if $i_k = \rho$, the above expression shows that $Z_k \leq 0$ and that $Z_k < 0$ if $P_k^3 > 0$.

Let $i^{\max}$ be such that (11A.1) holds as an equality, that is,

$$i^{\max} = \rho + \frac{1}{d_k^*}((1 + r(x_k^* + x_{-k}))x_k^* + (1 + \rho)(e_k - x_k^*)) > \rho$$

To simplify notation, denote $G^- \equiv \lim_{s \to (1+r(x))^-} G(s; x)$. If $i_k = i^{\max}$, then $P_k^1 = 1 - G^-$, and using (11.8), $Z_k(i^{\max}) = (1 - G^-)(i^{\max} - \rho)d_k^* + G^-(1 + \rho)(e_k - x_k^*) + x_k^*\bar{S}_k^2 + cx_k^*\bar{S}_k^3$. Substituting the definition of $i^{\max}$ and rearranging terms yields

$$Z_k(i^{\max}) = (1 - G^-)(1 + r(x_k^* + x_{-k}))x_k^*$$

$$+ (1 + \rho)(e_k - x_k^*) + x_k^*\bar{S}_k^2 + cx_k^*\bar{S}_k^3$$

Since $\Psi_k(x_k^* + x_{-k}, x_k^*) > 0$ and $\bar{S}(x) = \bar{S}_k^1 + \bar{S}_k^2 + \bar{S}_k^3$, then $(1 + \rho) \times (e_k - x_k^*) + x_k^*\bar{S}_k^2 + cx_k^*\bar{S}_k^3 > -x_k^*\bar{S}_k^1$. Thus, $Z_k(i^{\max}) > (1 - G^-)(1 + r(x_k^* + x_{-k}))x_k^* - x_k^*\bar{S}_k^1$. But, at $i_k = i^{\max}$, $\bar{S}_k^1 = (1 - G^-)(1 + r(x_k^* + x_{-k}))$, therefore, $Z_k(i^{\max}) > 0$. The existence of $i_k^* \in [\rho, i^{\max}]$ such that $Z_k(x_k^* + x_{-k}, x_k^*, d_k^*, i_k^*) = 0$ is guaranteed by an application of the Intermediate Value Theorem to the continuous function Z_k on the interval $[\rho, i^{\max}]$. It has been proved that there exists a candidate (x_k^*, d_k^*, i_k^*) satisfying the requirements of points (a), (b) and (c) in (ii).

We now show that (x_k^*, d_k^*, i_k^*) is an optimal solution of program (I). Define

$$\Gamma = \{(x_k, d_k, i_k) | x_k \geq 0, d_k \geq 0, i_k \geq \rho, e_k + d_k - x_k \geq 0, Z_k(\cdot) \geq 0\}$$

Clearly, (x_k^*, d_k^*, i_k^*) belongs to Γ with $Z_k = 0$. Recall that $\Pi_k = \Psi_k - Z_k$ since $Z_k = (U_k - (1 + \rho))d_k$. We have:

$$\max_{(x_k, d_k, i_k) \in \Gamma} \Pi_k \leq \max_{(x_k, d_k, i_k) \in \Gamma} \Psi_k - \min_{(x_k, d_k, i_k) \in \Gamma} Z_k \leq \max_{x_k \geq 0} \Psi_k$$

showing that (x_k^*, d_k^*, i_k^*) is an optimal solution of program (I).

Moreover, $P_k^1 > 0$, given that $P_k^1 = 0$ implies $\Pi_k = 0$ (see (11.9)). This proves point (i).

Conversely, let $(x_k^{**}, d_k^{**}, i_k^{**})$ be an optimal solution of program (I). The optimal solution $(x_k^{**}, d_k^{**}, i_k^{**})$ necessarily satisfies (11A.1). Assume the contrary, then $P_k^1 = 0$ and $\Pi_k = 0$. But choosing $x_k = d_k = 0$ yields $\Pi_k = e_k(1 + \rho) > 0$, a contradiction.

It is easy to show that Π_k is a strictly decreasing function of i_k if $d_k > 0$. Since Ψ_k does not depend on i_k, Z_k is a strictly increasing function of i_k if $d_k > 0$, and it has been shown above that for all admissible x_k, d_k, there exists i_k such that (1.1) and $Z_k = 0$ hold simultaneously. Any optimal solution of program (I) therefore necessarily satisfies $Z_k = 0$. Since Π_k and Ψ_k coincide on the set $\Gamma \cap \{Z_k = 0\}$, it follows that x_k^{**} maximises Ψ_k, showing that $(x_k^{**}, d_k^{**}, i_k^{**})$ meets the requirements of points (a), (b) and (c) in (ii). This completes the proof of point (ii).   ■

A.2   Proof of proposition 4

Point (i) is proved first. If $P_k^1 = 1$, then $P_k^2 = P_k^3 = 0$ and (11.8) easily shows that $(U_k - (1 + \rho))d_k = (i_k - \rho)d_k = 0$. Conversely, if $(i_k - \rho)d_k = 0$, then, either $i_k = \rho$ or $d_k = 0$. If $i_k = \rho$, then $C_k^2 = \emptyset$ and $P_k^2 = 0$. From (11.8), it is readily seen that

$$0 = (U_k - (1 + \rho))d_k = \int_{C_k^3} [(1 + \rho)(e_k - x_k) + cx_k s] \, dG$$

In the above expression, the integrand is necessarily negative. Thus, $P_k^3 > 0$ would imply $(U_k - (1 + \rho))d_k < 0$, a contradiction. If $d_k = 0$, then $C_k^2 = \emptyset$ and the same line of reasoning yields $P_k^3 = 0$. This shows that $P_k^1 = 1$.

To prove point (*ii*), remark first that point (*i*) trivially implies that if $P_k^3 > 0$, then $(i_k - \rho)d_k > 0$. Conversely, assume $(i_k - \rho)d_k > 0$. Using point (*i*) again, $P_k^2 > 0$ or $P_k^3 > 0$. Assume that $P_k^3 = 0$, then,

$$(U_k - (1 + \rho))d_k = P_k^1(i_k - \rho)d_k + \int_{C_k^2} [(1 + \rho)(e_k - x_k) + x_k s]\, dG$$

Since $\Pi_k > 0$, then $P_k^1 > 0$ (see (11.9)). In addition, the integrand of the above expression is non-negative on C_k^2. Therefore, $(U_k - (1 + \rho))d_k > 0$, a contradiction showing that $P_k^3 > 0$. ∎

A.3   An example in which $\bar{S}(x)$ is linear

We give here the details of the derivation of the limiting case considered in section 6 of the chapter. In all that follows, we assume assumptions A1′, A2′ and A3.

Under these assumptions, $\pi(\theta, r) = q \max\{0, \kappa + \theta - 1 - r\} + (1 - q) \max\{0, \theta - r\}$. Define the bounds $r_0 = \theta_0 - ((1 + \rho)f/(1 - q))$ and $r_1 = \theta_1 - ((1 + \rho)f/(1 - q))$. Under A2′, one shows that $r_0 = r^{\min}$ and $r_1 = r^{\max}$. To see this, note first that $r > r_1$ is equivalent to $(1 - q)(\theta_1 - r) < (1 + \rho)f$. Second, $r > r_1$ implies $\kappa + \theta_1 - 1 - r < \kappa - 1 + ((1 + \rho)f/(1 - q)) < -(\theta_1 - \theta_0) < 0$, where the next to last inequality follows from assumption A2′. A consequence of the above inequalities is now that $r > r_1$ implies $\pi(\theta, r) = (1 - q)\max\{0, \theta - r\} < (1 + \rho)f$, which in turn implies that the set of loan applicants is empty.

Next, $r < r_0$ is equivalent to $(1 - q)(\theta_0 - r) > (1 + \rho)f$, which implies $\pi(\theta, r) > (1 + \rho)f$ for all $\theta \in [\theta_0, \theta_1]$ and thus that the set of loan applicants is equal to $[\theta_0, \theta_1]$.

Finally, using assumption A2′, it is easy to check that $\kappa + \theta - 1 - r < 0$ for all $\theta \in [\theta_0, \theta_1]$ and all $r \in [r_0, r_1]$. If this is the case, $\pi(\theta, r) = (1 - q) \times \max\{0, \theta - r\}$, so that the set of firms applying for a loan is $\{\theta \in [\theta_0, \theta_1] | (1 - q)(\theta - r) \geq (1 + \rho)f\}$, and that $\hat{\theta}(r) = r + ((1 + \rho)f/(1 - q))$. This proves that $r^{\min} = r_0$ and $r^{\max} = r_1$.

Since θ is uniformly distributed, $A(r) = (\theta_1 - \hat{\theta}(r))/(\theta_1 - \theta_0)$. By the same token, in the 'bad state' of nature ω_0,

$$\sigma(\omega_0, r) = \frac{1}{\theta_1 - \hat{\theta}(r)} \int_{\hat{\theta}(r)}^{\theta_1} \min\{1 + r, \kappa + \theta\}\, d\theta$$

and since $\min\{1 + r, \kappa + \theta\} = \kappa + \theta$ for all $r \in [r^{\min}, r^{\max}]$, simple computations show that $\sigma(\omega_0, r) = \kappa + \frac{1}{2}(\theta_1 + \hat{\theta}(r))$.

In the 'good' state of nature ω_1,

$$\sigma(\omega_1, r) = \frac{1}{\theta_1 - \hat{\theta}(r)} \int_{\hat{\theta}(r)}^{\theta_1} \min\{1 + r, 1 + \theta\}\, d\theta$$

and since under the integral sign, $\theta \geq \hat{\theta}(r) \geq r$, clearly, $\min\{1 + r, 1 + \theta\} = 1 + r$. Thus, $\sigma(\omega_1, r) = (1 + r)$.

Inversion of $A(r)$ yields $1 + r(x) = \alpha_1 - \beta_1 x$, where to simplify notation, $\alpha_1 = 1 + \theta_1 - ((1 + \rho)f/(1 - q))$, $\beta_1 = (\theta_1 - \theta_0)$. By definition, $\tilde{S}(\omega_1, x) = 1 + r(x)$. Simple computations then show that $\tilde{S}(\omega_0, x) = \alpha_0 - \beta_0 x$, where $\alpha_0 = \kappa + \theta_1$ and $\beta_0 = \beta_1/2$. It is finally easy to check that

$$\bar{S}(x) = [q\alpha_0 + (1 - q)\alpha_1] - [q\beta_0 + (1 - q)\beta_1]x$$

In this example, the expected average return on loans $\bar{S}(x)$ is linear with respect to x.

A.4   Proof of proposition 5

Clearly, bank k can always obtain more than 0 by choosing $x_k = 0$. Thus, $P_k^1 > 0$, and the set of possible values of P_k^1 can be restricted to $\{1 - q, 1\}$. Since in addition $S^{\min}$ belongs either to C_k^1, C_k^2 or to C_k^3 (see the definitions in section 4), we know that necessarily, P_k^2, $P_k^3 \in \{0, q\}$ and that $P_k^2 + P_k^3 \in \{0, q\}$. Define $Z_k = [U_k - (1 + \rho)]d_k$.

The safe case is characterised by $P_k^1 = 1$ and thus $\bar{S}_k^1 = \bar{S}(x)$. Bank k's profit thus writes $\Pi_k^1 = (1 + \rho)e_k + x_k[\bar{S}(x) - (1 + \rho)] + (\rho - i_k)d_k$, and $Z_k = (i_k - \rho)d_k$. In the safe case, bank k will always have an incentive to set $(i_k - \rho)d_k = 0$ and the depositor's individual rationality constraint is therefore always binding. Substituting $Z_k = 0$ in Π_k^1 trivially yields the expression

$$\Psi_k^1 = (1 + \rho)e_k + x_k[\bar{S}(x) - (1 + \rho)] \tag{11A.2}$$

The risky case is characterised by $P_k^1 = (1 - q)$ and either $P_k^2 = q$ or $P_k^3 = q$. In this case, bank k's profit writes $\Pi_k^c = (1 - q)\{(1 + \rho)e_k + x_k[1 + r(x) - (1 + \rho)] + (\rho - i_k)d_k\}$, and Z_k writes $Z_k = (1 - q)(i_k - \rho)d_k + q(1 + \rho)(e_k - x_k) + x_k\bar{S}_k^2 + cx_k\bar{S}_k^3$. The subcase in which $P_k^2 = q$ is dominated by the safe case. More precisely, in this subcase, $\bar{S}_k^3 = 0$, but Π_k^c is decreasing with respect to i_k, while Z_k increases with i_k. Setting $i_k = \rho$, the bank would be perfectly safe – that is, $P_k^1 = 1$ and $P_k^2 = 0$, and earn greater profits than if $P_k^2 > 0$. We thus neglect this subcase without loss of generality.

Assume now that $P_k^3 = q$ in the risky case. Then, $\bar{S}_k^2 = 0$. For the same reasons as before, the bank will choose (i_k, d_k) so as to meet the participation constraint. It is easy to check that this can always be done. Substituting Z_k in Π_k^c with $\bar{S}_k^2 = 0$ and $\bar{S}_k^3 = qS^{min}(x)$ yields the following expression of profit:

$$\Psi_k^c = (1 + \rho)e_k + x_k[\bar{S}(x) - (1 + \rho)] - (1 - c)qx_k S^{min}(x)$$

(11A.3)

Expressions (11A.2) and (11A.3) can be rewritten as the concave functions (11.13) and (11.14) (see pp. 250–1). Bank k's objective is expressed as (11.13) if x_k is safe and as (11.14) if x_k is risky. Since the set of safe strategies is closed – i.e. $[0, \bar{A}_k]$, a maximum of Ψ_k always exists. It is equal either to the maximum of Ψ_k^c, or to $\bar{A}_k$ or to the maximum of Ψ_k^1. This completes the proof of point (*i*). The above reasoning shows that point (*ii*) is also true, since the depositors' participation constraint is binding in the two relevant cases.   ■

A.5   Proof of proposition 7

Equation (11.17) has a unique solution $x_*^c = [\alpha_q^c - (1 + \rho)][(n + 1)\beta_q^c]^{-1}$. To be a Nash equilibrium, x_*^c must also satisfy $\bar{A}_k[(n - 1)x_*^c, e] \leq B_k^c[(n - 1)x_*^c]$, to ensure that a safe strategy does not yield greater profits. Since $\bar{A}_k$ is one to one as a function of e, there exists a unique value, denoted e_1, such that $\bar{A}_k[(n - 1)x_*^c, e_1] = B_k^c[(n - 1)x_*^c]$. This proves that for all $e \leq e_1$, x_*^c is an equilibrium.

Equation (11.18) has a unique positive root, the expression of which is given by

$$\bar{x}_* = \bar{A}^*(e) = \frac{1}{2n\beta_0}\left(-[(1 + \rho) - \alpha_0]\right.$$
$$\left. + \sqrt{[(1 + \rho) - \alpha_0]^2 + 4n\beta_0(1 + \rho)e}\right)$$

Remark that $\bar{A}^*(e)$ is a non-negative, strictly increasing function of e which tends towards infinity with e. In addition, $\bar{A}^*(0) = 0$. It follows that $\bar{A}^*(e)$ is one to one. But $\bar{x}_*$ is an equilibrium if it is a best response to $(n - 1)\bar{x}_*$, that is, only if

$$\bar{x}_* \leq Q_k^1[(n - 1)\bar{x}_*]$$

(11A.4)

$$\bar{x}_* \geq B_k^c[(n - 1)\bar{x}_*]$$

(11A.5)

It is easy to show that inequality (11A.4) is equivalent to $\bar{x}_* \leq x_*^1$, where x_*^1 is the solution of (11.19) (see below). Since $\bar{A}^*(e)$ is one to one, there exists a unique value e_2 such that $\bar{A}^*(e_2) = x_*^1$. It follows that a safe equilibrium exists only if $e \leq e_2$.

Inequality (11A.5) yields a lower bound on e for the existence of safe equilibria. Since B_k^c is decreasing, it crosses the diagonal only once. More precisely, let $\tilde{x}$ be the unique solution of $\tilde{x} = B_k^c[(n-1)\tilde{x}]$. Define then e_3 as the unique value of equity such that $\bar{A}^*(e_3) = \tilde{x}$. Clearly, inequality (11A.5) is satisfied for all $e \geq e_3$. We can therefore conclude that $\bar{x}_*$ is an equilibrium if and only if $e_3 \leq e \leq e_2$.

Equation (11.19) has a unique solution $x_*^1 = [(n+1)\beta_q]^{-1}[\alpha_q - (1+\rho)]$. To be a Nash equilibrium, x_*^1 must also satisfy $x_*^1 \leq \bar{A}_k[(n-1)x_*^1, e]$. For the same reasons as before, there exists a unique threshold e_s such that $x_*^1 = \bar{A}_k[(n-1)x_*^1, e_s]$. Remark that the latter equation is by definition equivalent to $\bar{A}^*(e_s) = x_*^1$. Recalling the definition of e_2 given above, it then follows that $e_s = e_2$. We conclude that x_*^1 is an equilibrium if and only if $e \geq e_2$.

To summarise the above discussion, we have shown the existence of three equity thresholds, e_1, e_2 and e_3 which determine symmetric equilibrium types.

It is straightforward to check that x_*^c is an increasing function of c, and thus $x_*^c < x_*^1$, if and only if $(1-q)(2\alpha_0 - \alpha_1) + (1+\rho) > 0$. Since $\alpha_0 < 1 + \rho < \alpha_1$, x_*^c is an increasing function of c if $3\alpha_0 > \alpha_1$. Using the properties of $\bar{A}_k$ and B_k^c, the definitions of the thresholds, and $x_*^c < x_*^1$, the following string of inequalities is true: $\bar{A}_k[(n-1)x_*^c, e_1] = B_k^c[(n-1)x_*^c] < Q_k^c[(n-1)x_*^c] = x_*^c < x_*^1 = \bar{A}_k[(n-1)x_*^1, e_2] < \bar{A}_k[(n-1)x_*^c, e_2]$. Since $\bar{A}_k$ increases with e, it follows that $e_1 < e_2$.

Now, assume that $\tilde{x} \geq x_*^c$. Then, since B_k^c is decreasing,

$$\tilde{x} = B_k^c[(n-1)\tilde{x}] \leq B_k^c[(n-1)x_*^c] < Q_k^c[(n-1)x_*^c] = x_*^c$$

a contradiction. Therefore, $\tilde{x} < x_*^c < x_*^1$. Finally, $\bar{A}^*(e_3) = \tilde{x} < x_*^1 = \bar{A}^*(e_2)$, and since $\bar{A}^*(e)$ is increasing, $e_3 < e_2$. ∎

Bibliography

Bernanke, B. and A. Blinder (1988) Credit, money, and aggregate demand, *American Economic Review*, 78, pp. 435–9

Bernanke, B. and C. Lown (1991) The credit crunch, *Brookings Papers on Economic Activity*, 2, pp. 205–47

Bester, H. (1995) A bargaining model of financial intermediation, *European Economic Review*, 39, pp. 211–28

Bolton, P. and X. Freixas (1994) Direct bond financing, financial intermediation and investment: an incomplete contract perspective, Brussels: ECARE, mimeo

Boyd J.H. and E.C. Prescott (1986) Financial intermediary coalitions, *Journal of Economic Theory*, 38, pp. 211–32

Bulow, J., J. Geanakoplos and P. Klemperer (1985) Multimarket oligopoly: strategic substitutes and complements, *Journal of Political Economy*, 93, pp. 488–511

Calomiris, C. and C. Kahn (1991) The role of demandable debt in structuring optimal banking arrangements, *American Economic Review*, 81, pp. 497–513

Chiappori, P.A., D. Perez-Castrillo and T. Verdier (1995) Spatial competition in the banking system: localization, cross-subsidies and the regulation of interest rates, *European Economic Review*, 39, pp. 889–918

de Palma, A. and R.J. Gary-Bobo (1994) Credit crunch in a model of the banking industry, *Discussion Paper*, Université de Cergy-Pontoise

Dermine, J., D. Neven and J.-F. Thisse (1991) Towards an equilibrium model of the mutual funds industry, *Journal of Banking and Finance*, 15, pp. 485–99

Dewatripont, M. and J. Tirole (1993) *La reglementation prudentielle des banques*, Editions Payot Lausanne: English translation, *The Prudential Regulation of Banks*, Cambridge, Mass: MIT Press

Diamond, D. (1984) Financial intermediation and delegated monitoring, *Review of Economic Studies*, 51, pp. 393–414

Diamond, D. and P. Dybvig (1983) Bank runs, liquidity and deposit insurance, *Journal of Political Economy*, 91, pp. 401–19

Donaldson, R.G. (1993) Financing banking crises: lessons from the panic of 1907, *Journal of Monetary Economics*, 31, pp. 69–95

Fama, E. (1980) Banking in the theory of Finance, *Journal of Monetary Economics*, 6, pp. 39–57

Gehrig, T. (1996) Natural oligopoly and customer networks in intermediated markets, *International Journal of Industrial Organization*, 14, pp. 101–18

Gehrig T. and M. Jackson (1994) Bid–ask spreads with indirect competition among specialists, *WWZ Discussion Paper*, 9419, Universität Basel

Goodhart, C.A.E. (1993) Can we improve the structure of financial systems?, *European Economic Review*, 37, pp. 269–91

Hellwig, M. (1994) Liquidity Provision, banking, and the allocation of interest rate risk, *European Economic Review*, 38, pp. 1363–89

Jacklin, C. and S. Bhattacharya (1988) Distinguishing panics and information-based bank runs: welfare and policy implications, *Journal of Political Economy*, 96, pp. 568–92

Kareken, J.H. and N. Wallace (1978) Deposit insurance and bank regulation: a partial equilibrium exposition, *Journal of Business*, 51, pp. 413–38

Klein, M. (1971) A theory of the banking firm, *Journal of Money, Credit, and Banking*, 3, pp. 205–18

Lucas, D.J. and R.L. McDonald (1992) Bank financing and investment decisions with asymmetric information about loan quality, *Rand Journal of Economics*, 23, pp. 86–105

Matutes, C. and A.J. Padilla (1994) Shared ATM networks and banking competition, *European Economic Review*, 38, pp. 1113–38

Matutes, C. and X. Vives (1994) Imperfect competition, risk-taking, and regulation in banking, *Discussion Paper*, Institut d'Anàlisi Econòmica, Barcelona: CSIC

Monti, M. (1972) Deposit, credit, and interest rate determination under alternative banking objectives, in G.P. Szego and K. Shell (eds.), *Mathematical Methods in Investment and Finance*, Amsterdam: North-Holland

Phlips, L. (1983) *The Economics of Price Discrimination*, Cambridge: Cambridge University Press

    (1996) On the detection of collusion and predation, *European Economic Review*, 40(3–5), pp. 495–510

Postlewaite, A. and X. Vives (1987) Bank runs as an equilibrium phenomenon, *Journal of Political Economy*, 95, pp. 485–91

Repullo, R. (1990) A model of imperfect competition in banking, Madrid: Bank of Spain, mimeo

Repullo, R. and J. Suarez (1994) Entrepreneurial moral hazard and bank monitoring: a model of financial intermediation, *Discussion Paper*, Madrid: CEMFI

Rochet, J.-C. (1992a) Capital requirements and the behaviour of commercial banks, *European Economic Review*, 36, pp. 1137–70

    (1992b) Concurrence imparfaite et strategie bancaire, *Revue Economique*, 43, pp. 261–75

Rochet J.-C. and J. Tirole (1996) Interbank lending and systemic risk, *Journal of Money, Credit, and Banking*, 28, pp. 733–62

Schmidt-Mohr, U. and J. M. Villas-Boas (1993) Oligopoly with asymmetric information: the case of credit markets, Berkeley: University of California, mimeo

Smith, B.D. (1984) Private information, deposit interest rates, and the stability of the banking system, *Journal of Monetary Economics*, 14, pp. 293–317

von Thadden, E.-L. (1995) Long-term contracts, short-term investment and monitoring, *Review of Economic Studies*, 62, pp. 557–75

Yanelle, M.O. (1988) On the theory of intermediation, PhD dissertation, University of Bonn

    (1995) Price competition among intermediaries: the role of the strategy space, *Discussion Paper*, 9503, Paris: DELTA

Yosha, O. (1994) Diversification and competition: financial intermediation in a large Cournot–Walras economy, Brown University, mimeo

12 How the adoption of a new technology is affected by the interaction between labour and product markets

Xavier Wauthy and Yves Zenou

1 Introduction

It is commonly observed that firms in a given industry often use different technologies. Many explanations can be given such as the history of each firm, the existence of patents and licences or differences in skilled labour availability. These differences are often considered as exogenous in the industrial organisation literature although, at some point, they must result from firms' decisions. What should be clear, however, is that the use of different technologies directly affects the degree of competition in a given industry. In particular, equilibrium concentration is likely to reflect technological asymmetries so that the fact that some firms persist in using less efficient technologies could be viewed as a way to alleviate competition.

It has been argued that the adoption of different technologies may reflect strategic considerations. For example, in a completely symmetric environment, Mills and Smith (1996) show that the implications of technological choices at the product-competition stage may induce firms to choose different technologies. They consider a two-stage game in which firms pre-commit to technological choices in the first stage and compete in quantities in the second. They define particular technologies as specific combinations of fixed costs and constant marginal costs, a low marginal cost being associated with a larger fixed cost. In this context, once a firm has chosen the low-marginal-cost technology, the other firm may be better off choosing the high-marginal-cost technology and save on fixed costs. This leads to heterogeneous technological choices, and thus to a higher industry concentration in equilibrium. As argued by these authors, anti-trust policy tends to view conducts that increase industry concentration with suspicion but it turns out that in their model this conduct is precisely the one which induces the larger welfare.

In the present chapter, we also consider *a duopoly set-up in which technologies choices are made in a strategic context*. Firms are homogeneous *ex ante* and face the same opportunities in the adoption of a new technology. More precisely, we assume that an innovation process has been perfected and is freely available to all firms. In this context, firms must choose whether or not they adopt this new technology. However, we introduce labour market elements as a major determinant of technological choices.

To be more specific, we show that when firms take into account the effect of technological choices on labour market equilibrium, they can be led to make different choices, even though they face a completely symmetric opportunity set. Thus, we underline *the role of labour markets as a (possibly) major determinant of firms' strategical technological choices*. At a broader level, it can also be viewed as an attempt to model the interaction between product and labour markets in oligopolistic industries. This consideration has been widely neglected in the literature (with some important exceptions, such as Horn and Wolinsky, 1988; Ulph and Ulph, 1994; Gabszewicz and Turrini, 2000). This is somewhat paradoxical in view of the huge literature emphasising various forms of pre-commitments (in terms of products' characteristics, capacity levels, . . .) as major strategic weapons aimed at relaxing product market competition. In this respect, labour is just one of these inputs over which pre-commitment is possible, if not natural. Typically, as soon as the functioning of labour markets entails some form of rigidity, there is room for some strategic behaviour aimed at relaxing competition in the product market. Taking explicit account of the strategic implications of labour market structures may well be part of the way towards this 'better understanding of how collusion works and what antitrust authorities should do – and can do – about it' advocated by Louis Phlips.[1]

The main intuition that underlies our chapter can be summarised as follows. An innovation process is often viewed as a cost-reducing innovation. The importance of the innovation is thus summarised by the *exogenous* marginal cost differential it leads to. Here, we adopt a slightly different view by stipulating that a process innovation consists in a more efficient technology in the sense that it increases the marginal productivity of labour. Note, then, that a higher marginal productivity of labour does not imply a lower marginal cost of production since labour market conditions may change owing to technological change. This is especially likely to happen since the adoption of a new technology may involve an adjustment of workers' skills. Reflecting this argument, we assume that workers must acquire a specific training when they work in the innovative

---

[1] Phlips (1995, p. 1).

firm. In other words, the adoption of the process innovation involves a specific training cost. This training cost will in turn lead to the emergence of a dual labour market structure in which the primary sector consists of innovative firms demanding high-skilled workers and the secondary one of standard firms with low-skilled workers. The adoption of the new technology by one firm at least thus affects the structure of the labour market. In order to model workers' behaviour in this context, we assume that the workforce is heterogeneous in its ability to acquire the specific training required in the primary sector. Workers' heterogeneity is central for the analysis to follow. Within this framework, the firm's problem is summarised as follows: in order to take advantage of the new technology, the firm must attract workers in the primary sector – i.e. induce some workers to bear (part of) the training cost; this is obviously achieved through higher wages. The labour market thus generates a negative externality that influences the choice of adopting the new technology. In a very simple framework of Cournot competition, we show that an innovation process which increases labour productivity may yield the three following potential subgame perfect equilibria (hereafter, SPEs) outcomes: no firm adopts the new technology; only one firm does it; both of them adopt it. In other words, the conditions prevailing in the labour market may affect the adoption of a new technology in an industry and generate heterogeneous technological choices.

The chapter is organised as follows. In section 2, we present the model. The Cournot subgames are discussed in section 3 and SPEs are characterised in section 4. In section 5, we discuss our results and section 6 draws some final conclusions.

2 The model

The firm

We consider the market for an *homogeneous product* whose inverse demand is given by $p = 1 - q$. Two firms are competing imperfectly in the product market. They choose quantities in order to maximise their profits in a non-cooperative way. Two technologies are available: the standard one, labelled S and the new one, labelled N. We assume that once technologies are adopted by firms, they use labour as their sole variable input.

Technology S yields a constant marginal productivity of labour which is normalised to 1 for simplicity. It does not require any training period to work in the firm that adopts S.[2] The new technology N is more efficient and

---

[2] Indeed, 'adopting' S basically amounts to sticking to the old technology for which workers are already adequately trained.

therefore exhibits a constant marginal productivity of labour equal to $a > 1$. However, it requires training costs that are exogenously shared between workers and firms (g is the fraction borne by workers).

In this context, we consider a *two-stage game* in which firms precommit to technological choices in the first stage and compete '*à la* Cournot' in the second stage.

The workforce

In order to model workers' behaviour, we adopt a framework inspired by the address models developed in product differentiation theories. Workers are endowed with one indivisible unit of labour and are all *heterogeneous*. Indeed, they all differ in their ability of acquiring skills and are uniformly distributed in a (compact) interval $[0, L]$ where L is arbitrarily large; $x \in [0, L]$ denotes the type of worker by measuring his unit training cost. The density in the interval $[0, L]$ is 1. Workers decide to work in the firm that offers the highest *net* wage.

The labour market

As stated in the introduction, there is a *dual labour market structure with heterogeneous workers*. The *secondary sector* is defined by firms that adopt the standard technology S which does not require training costs. We assume that in this sector the labour market is competitive and we denote by v the market-clearing wage. At this wage, a worker is indifferent between working in the secondary sector and being unemployed. In the context of an homogeneous workforce, this sector is typically viewed as a waiting sector since workers are always better off in the primary one (Burda, 1988; Saint-Paul, 1996). When the labour force is heterogeneous, this is not always true because of the training costs required in the primary sector (Wauthy and Zenou, 1997). The *primary sector* is composed of firms that adopt the new technology which entails a specific training cost. Without loss of generality we normalise it to a units. As stated above, we assume that the training cost is exogenously shared between firms and workers (g being the fraction borne by workers). When a firm adopts the new technology N there is a new labour market for specific skills since primary firms must set a wage above v to induce individuals to work there. We assume that the net wage associated with a skill acquisition of a units is defined by $w - gxa$ for a worker of type x. The reservation wage of a worker of type x for such a job is therefore equal to $v + gax$.

It should be clear by now that our view of the labour market is inspired by address models of vertical differentiation. The primary and secondary jobs are vertically differentiated in the sense that at equal wages, all workers would prefer to allocate their labour unit in the secondary sector in order to save on training costs. Moreover, workers differ in their willingness to work in the primary sector, depending on their defining attribute, as reflected in the distribution of reservation wages.

In both markets the wage is set non-strategically so as to clear the market.[3] In the primary sector, labour supply for a wage level w is given by the set of workers of types x for which $w - gxa \geq v$. We may thus express the labour supply in the primary market as follows:

$$L^S = \frac{w - v}{g \cdot a} \tag{12.1}$$

The labour demand in the same market is given by the aggregate demand of firms which depends on production decisions. By denoting the (aggregate) labour demand by L^D, the equilibrium wage in the primary sector is given by:

$$w = v + g \cdot a \cdot L^D \tag{12.2}$$

We are now able to characterise the firm's training cost under technology N. Consider first the case when only one firm is active in the primary sector and demands L^D workers. Given that the wage is chosen so as to equate supply and demand, the set of workers who supply their labour unit consists of workers of types $x \in [0, L^D]$. The total training cost borne by the firm is equal to:

$$TC^{NS} = \int_0^{L^D} a(1 - g)x\,dx = \frac{a(1 - g)}{2}(L^D)^2 \tag{12.3a}$$

Consider now the case when both firms adopt the new technology. We assume that workers are allocated randomly to jobs. In this case, the training cost is:

$$TC^{NN} = \frac{a(1 - g)}{2}(L_1^D + L_2^D)L_1^D \tag{12.3b}$$

Observe that when firms bear all the training cost – i.e. $g = 0$ – no dual labour market structure emerges because there is an asymmetry between workers and firms. Indeed, workers are indifferent between the two types of jobs at wage v but firms are not indifferent to the workers' type since the training cost increases with x. We must assume in this case that firms are able to identify workers' type in order to select only the most able ones.

---

[3] The role of this assumption will be discussed later. Notice, however, that strategic wage-setting in the primary market will dramatically affect firms' incentives.

Notice, however, that sharing the training cost leads to the workers' self-selection, thereby dispensing with the need of the firm to screen them.

3   The second stage: Cournot subgames

It follows from section 2 that adopting the new technology N in the first stage has two main implications for competition in the second: it allows the firm to benefit from a higher marginal product and it changes the firm's cost structure. Indeed, since the wage in the primary sector must rise in order to attract more (and thus less able) workers, the wage bill and the part of the training cost borne by the firm are now both marginally increasing with the output level. In other words, *choosing N in the first stage yields an increasing marginal cost in the second stage.* Furthermore, the choice of S implies a lower marginal product of labour but a constant marginal cost since no training cost is required, allowing firms to hire workers from the secondary labour market at wage v. Consequently, when considering the adoption of technology N, *firms face a trade-off between marginal product of labour and costs' structure.* Observe that the rival's choice exerts a negative externality since the wage pressure is greater when the two firms are active in the primary sector, thereby increasing marginal cost levels.

As usual, to study the technological choice by firms, we solve the two-stage game by backward induction. Let us thus start with the Cournot subgames.

There are three possible Cournot subgames depending on whether one, two or none of the firms has chosen the technology N. Since marginal productivity of labour is constant, we can express output as a direct function of labour input. If we denote by l_i the labour input in firm i, we can summarise firms' payoffs in the second stage as follows.

Subgame (S, S):   *both firms choose the standard technology.*
We have a standard symmetric Cournot game with constant marginal cost. Therefore, the two firms face the following payoff function:

$$\pi_i = l_i(1 - l_i - l_j) - v l_i \qquad i, j = 1, 2$$

Firms' best replies are symmetric and given by:

$$l_i = \frac{1 - v - l_j}{2} \qquad i = 1, 2$$

and it is easily checked that the Nash equilibrium quantity is equal to:

$$l_1^{SS} = l_2^{SS} = \frac{1 - v}{3} \tag{12.4}$$

with payoffs

$$\pi_1^{SS} = \pi_2^{SS} = \left(\frac{1-v}{3}\right)^2 \tag{12.5}$$

Subgame (N, S):   *one firm chooses the standard technology and the other the new one.*

By convention let firm 1 choose the new technology N and firm 2 the standard one S. Using (12.2) and (12.3a), we obtain the following payoffs:

$$\pi_1 = al_1(1 - al_1 - l_2) - (v + agl_1)l_1 - \frac{a}{2}(1 - g)(l_1)^2$$

$$\pi_2 = l_2(1 - al_1 - l_2) - vl_2$$

The best replies are therefore given by:

$$l_1 = \frac{a - v - al_2}{a(2a + g + 1)}, \qquad l_2 = \frac{1 - v - l_1}{2}$$

and the Nash equilibrium labour demands are equal to:

$$l_1^{NS} = \frac{a(1 + v) - 2v}{a(3a + 2g + 2)}, \qquad l_2^{NS} = \frac{1 + a(1 - 2v) - g(1 - v)}{3a + 2g + 2} \tag{12.6}$$

The payoffs functions are:

$$\pi_1^{NS} = \left(\frac{1 + 2a + g}{2a}\right)\left[\frac{a(1 + v) - 2v}{3a + 2g + 2}\right]^2 \tag{12.7a}$$

$$\pi_2^{NS} = \left[\frac{1 + a(1 - 2v) - g(1 - v)}{3a + 2g + 2}\right]^2 \tag{12.7b}$$

Subgame (N, N):   *both firms choose the new technology.*

Using (12.2) and (12.3b) we characterise firms' symmetric payoffs as follows:

$$\pi_i = al_i(1 - al_i - al_j) - [v + ag(l_i + l_j)]l_i - \frac{a}{2}(1 - g)(l_i + l_j)l_i$$

$$i, j = 1, 2$$

Firms' best replies are symmetric and given by:

$$l_i = \frac{2(a - v) - a(2a + g + 1)l_j}{2a(2a + g + 1)}$$

Table 12.1   *The second-stage payoff matrix*

	N	S
N	(π_1^{NN}, π_2^{NN})	(π_1^{NS}, π_2^{NS})
S	(π_1^{SN}, π_2^{SN})	(π_1^{SS}, π_2^{SS})

The Nash equilibrium quantities and profit are respectively equal to:

$$l_1^{NN} = l_2^{NN} = \frac{2(a - v)}{3a(2a + g + 1)} \tag{12.8}$$

$$\pi_1^{NN} = \pi_2^{NN} = \frac{2}{a}\left[\frac{a - v}{3(2a + g + 1)}\right]^2 \tag{12.9}$$

By symmetry $\pi_i^{NS} = \pi_i^{SN}$, $i = 1, 2$ and table 12.1 thus summarises the Cournot equilibrium payoffs in the four possible subgames.

The following comments are in order here. First, the main implication of technological choices in the Cournot game is captured by their effects on marginal costs for a firm choosing N. They are given by the following expressions in subgames (N, S), (N, N), respectively:[4]

$$mc_1(NS) = \frac{v + (1 + g)\, q_1}{a} \tag{12.10}$$

$$mc_i(NN) = \frac{v}{a} + \frac{1 + g}{2a}q_j + \frac{1 + g}{a}q_i \qquad i, j = 1, 2 \tag{12.11}$$

Observe that the slope of the marginal cost does not depend on whether one or two firms uses the technology, but the value of the intercept does. *This is the externality coming from the labour market.* Inspection of (12.10) and (12.11) reveals that adopting the new technology implies an increasing marginal cost, however training costs are shared between the firms and the workers. Note that the larger the part of the training cost borne by the workers the steeper the marginal cost. This might seem surprising at first glance since a higher g lowers the part of training cost borne by the firm but since workers' training costs increase, a higher wage is required at the margin to attract an additional worker. We thus observe a (negative) training cost effect and a (positive) wage-bill effect. Since we have assumed

---

[4] Remember that in subgame (N, S) by convention firm 1 chooses the new technology N and firm 2 the standard one S.

that firms were not allowed to discriminate in gross wages, it is quite intuitive to understand that this second effect dominates the first.[5]

Second, the (N, S) subgame deserves special attention. Indeed, since only firm 1 has adopted the new technology, *the two firms compete in quantities under different cost structures*. Therefore we cannot ensure *a priori* that both firms will be active in equilibrium. It could indeed happen that N is a drastic innovation. In the present setting, a 'drastic innovation' is defined as an innovation such that only firm N is active in equilibrium, enjoying the associated monopoly profits. Computations indicate that the condition for a non-drastic innovation is that:

$$a(1 - 2v) + 1 + g(1 - v) > 0$$

Therefore, whenever $v \leq 1/2$ the condition for a non-drastic innovation is automatically fulfilled. When $v > 1/2$, the condition is:

$$1 < a < \frac{1 + g(1 - v)}{2v - 1}$$

Thus, for a large enough, the S firm is pulled out of the industry. Restricting our analysis to non-drastic innovations and thus assuming that $v \leq 1/2$ in the sequel, it is interesting to compare output and profit levels in equilibrium. Straightforward computations indicate that $q_1^* > q_2^*$ if and only if:

$$a > \frac{1 + g + v(2 + g)}{3v} > 1$$

In other words, in order for the N firm to produce more than the S firm in equilibrium, a must be high enough. Therefore, for relatively low values of a the N firm is dominated at the Cournot equilibrium. Correspondingly, it is possible to show (numerically) that in the asymmetric Cournot game, a must be large enough in order to ensure that the N firm captures higher profits than the S one in equilibrium. However, the larger g, the more likely it is that the adoption of the new technology N generates competitive advantage. These results are quite intuitive. Indeed, since firms face different cost structures – i.e. firm 1 faces a marginal cost equal to $(v + (1 + g) q_1)/a$ while firm 2's marginal cost is v, firm 1 benefits from a marginal cost advantage only for relatively low output levels – i.e. for $q_1 < v(a - 1)/(1 + g)$. This explains why a technology which

---

[5] Observe from (12.9) that when both firms adopt the new technology, their payoffs depend negatively on g. Therefore, in our example, firms could be inclined to bear all the training cost.

increases labour productivity is not necessarily more profitable. The labour market parameters are thus crucial here. We summarise our findings in proposition 1.

Proposition 1:   When adoption involves a specific training cost, adopting the new technology does not imply competitive advantage in equilibrium.

4   Technological choices

Before we study the first stage of our game, it is useful to consider the extreme case in which the new technology does not require specific training cost – i.e. the labour cost is invariably given by v. Since we have assumed that the technology N is freely available, it is clear that both firms will always choose technology N in a subgame perfect equilibrium (SPE). In other words, as long as the adoption of the technology does not affect the labour market, both firms adopt it. However, we will show now that the existence of a specific training cost in the primary sector may lead to heterogeneous technological choices.

Let us now analyse the first stage in which firms choose the type of technology (strategies N, or S). The payoffs matrix of this game is derived from the equilibrium of the different subgames solved in section 3 and summarised by table 12.1. In order to characterise the equilibrium[6] in the first-stage of the game, we characterise firms' best replies and concentrate on non-drastic innovations. It is indeed obvious that if the innovation is drastic, both firms will adopt it. Using table 12.1, the problem can be summarised as follows:

- If firm j chooses the technology S, the best reply for firm i is S if and only if:

$$\left(\frac{1-v}{3}\right)^2 \geq \left(\frac{1+2a+g}{2a}\right)\left[\frac{a(1+v)-2v}{3a+2g+2}\right]^2 \tag{12.12}$$

- If firm j chooses the technology N, the best reply for firm i is N if and only if

$$\frac{2}{a}\left[\frac{a-v}{3(2a+g+1)}\right]^2 \geq \left[\frac{1+a(1-2v)-g(1-v)}{3a+2g+2}\right]^2 \tag{12.13}$$

Observe that (12.12) is a polynomial expression of degree 3 whose analytical solution turns out to be quite messy. Equation (12.13) is a

---

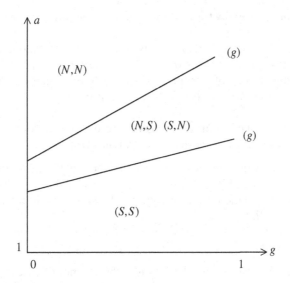

Figure 12.1   A representative partition of the (a, g) space according to the nature of SPE

polynomial expression of degree 5 for which no analytical solution can be found. We have therefore performed numerical computations using the *Mathematica* Software in order to solve the problem. Observe, however, that all rational functions entering in both equations are well defined continuous functions in the relevant parameters' constellations – i.e. for $a > 1$, $v < 1$ and $g \in [0, 1]$. We can therefore rely on the results of our numerical computations.[7]

For any given value of the market-clearing wage $v \leq 1/2$, we have identified two functions, $\gamma(g)$ and $\delta(g)$ which characterise the solution in a of (12.12) and (12.13), respectively. Figure 12.1 summarises the results of our numerical computations by plotting the functions $\gamma(g)$ and $\delta(g)$ for some fixed level of v.

- When $a < \gamma(g)$, S is a best reply against S
- When $a > \delta(g)$, N is a best reply against N
- When $a \in [\gamma(g), \delta(g)]$, N is a best reply against S and S is a best reply against N.

It follows that for $a \in [1, \gamma(g)]$, (S, S) is the unique SPE. When $a \in [\gamma(g), \delta(g)]$, we have two SPEs involving only one firm adopting the

---

[7] Under the assumption that $v \leq 1/2$, these functions are in fact monotone in the relevant domain of $a > 1$ and $g \in [0, 1]$.

new technology. Finally for $a > \delta(g)$, we have a unique SPE in which both firms adopt the new technology.

Note that the interval $[\gamma(g), \delta(g)]$ is never empty. Therefore, we always end up with a partition of the (a, g) space into three regions, each of them corresponding to one of our three possible SPE outcomes. Computations also indicate that $\delta(g) - \gamma(g)$ is increasing in g.

Proposition 2:   We obtain the following result that does not depend on the way firms and workers share the training cost.

- When the productivity gain is small, none of the firm adopts technology N in an SPE
- When the productivity gain is large, the two firms adopt technology N in an SPE
- For intermediate values of the productivity gain, one firm only adopts technology N.

Proposition 2 establishes that, even in the absence of patent protection or licence fees, a process innovation may not be adopted by all firms within a given industry. This may thus explain endogenously technological heterogeneity. This result proceeds first from the idea that the adoption of a new technology tends to carry with it an adjustment of the labour force: the matching between skills' requirements associated with the innovation and skill availability in the labour market becomes central. It is indeed obvious that a technology whose skill requirements are much above existing standards in the labour market is not very likely to be adopted, simply because the training costs involved would be too high. This provides a first and direct link between labour markets and technology adoption. However, it hardly explains heterogeneous choices by the firms. This is where strategic considerations comes into play. Indeed, in an oligopolistic industry, the attractiveness of an innovation process will depend on rivals' choices. In the present analysis, the labour market exerts a negative externality. Indeed, once a firm has chosen the new technology, this technology becomes less attractive to the other because of a labour cost effect. Once a firm has adopted the new technology, it may be optimal to the other firm to choose S because it would otherwise imply a higher pressure in the primary labour market, thereby pushing wages and thus production costs up. Clearly, the rise in marginal productivity of labour has to be large enough in order to sustain a symmetric (N, N) equilibrium – i.e. to overcome the negative externality. Moreover, since quantities are strategic substitutes, choosing technology S may allow the firm to benefit from the less aggressive behaviour of the N firm, which is facing increasing marginal cost. This argument is best illustrated by the fact that in an asymmetric equilibrium, the S firm may be the dominant one. It also follows that if firms were to choose technologies in sequence – i.e. in a Stackelberg-like framework – the first-mover advantage could take the form of a non-adoption.

Clearly, our result bears some resemblance to that of Mills and Smith (1996) since they also conclude with heterogeneous choices of technologies as possible equilibrium outcomes. However, one major difference has to be underlined. In their paper, the relative attractiveness of the different technologies depends exclusively on their influence for the competition in the product market since associated costs are exogenously given. In the present analysis, the relative attractiveness of the new technology is endogenous to the firms' choices owing to the explicit treatment of the labour market.

5 Discussion

In section 4, we have shown by means of an example that, when firms take into account the effects of technological progress on labour market equilibrium, they could be led to choose different technologies although they face *ex ante* a completely symmetric opportunity set. Admittedly, the model we have considered relies on very specific assumptions. It is therefore important to evaluate the robustness of our conclusions in more general settings.

Let us first discuss the relevance of training costs as the central argument governing labour market behaviour. Although this seems quite natural in a context of new technologies, it should be clear that a similar argument can apply to any context in which technological choices are associated with specific, thin, labour markets. Indeed, what is basically required for our result is a finitely elastic labour supply, so that a firm faces an increasing marginal cost. Second, the training sequence we consider is rather special. Indeed, in our static framework, it is implicitly assumed that training and production are taking place simultaneously. It is perhaps more intuitive to assume that production takes place after some training period. In this case, adopting the new technology will amount to bearing first a training cost, which depends on the number of workers hired and can be viewed as a sunk cost afterwards, and facing a constant marginal cost of production corresponding to the wage level. Note, then, that this does not preclude the existence of heterogeneous choices. Indeed, the labour market still exerts a negative externality since the level of the (fixed) training cost depends on the aggregate labour demand and thus on rivals' choices. More fundamentally, this would affect the conditions of competition in the second stage. Indeed, the numbers of workers trained will determine the production capacities in the Cournot game, so that product competition takes place under limited production capacities.

Another limitation of the model is that the wage in the primary sector is set according to a Walrasian mechanism. Since at most two firms operate in this market, it seems natural to consider that these firms enjoy some market power. Doing this would raise very serious technical problems – in particular, the existence of an equilibrium in wages may be highly problematic, especially when both firms are active in the primary market. When the two firms are active in the primary market, a Bertrand-like competition is likely to be observed. Since workers maximise net wages and firms require identical training, a slight differential is sufficient for one firm to capture all workers – or, more precisely, to enjoy the possibility of choosing among the entire set of applicants at this wage. Firms could therefore enter in a upper-bidding process. It is clear, however, that defining a wage equilibrium in this case is quite problematic. Indeed, wages determine the labour supply addressed to each firm, and thereby production capacities. A game where firms choose wages and quantities simultaneously would face first a definition problem – indeed, the strategies in the quantity game would be contingent on the wage schedule, since this would determine maximal outputs. Let us assume then that firms set wages and quantities sequentially. This amounts to considering a two-stage game in which firms name wages, hire workers and train them in the first stage and compete in quantities in the second. Let us assume that firms cannot fire workers in the second period. Thus, all costs are borne in the first stage and are irrelevant in the second. Characterising an SPE of this game is not easy. An outcome of the first stage consists in a vector of wages and labour force for each firm. Any such outcome defines a very simple game at the second stage where firms are Cournot competitors facing a limited production capacity. Unfortunately, the first stage of the game is not so simple. Recall that workers allocate their labour unit by comparing net wages. If wages are equal they are indifferent between the two firms, otherwise they apply to the high-wage firm. However, it is not obvious that this firm should hire all applicants so that some applicants can be rationed and may be willing to accept a position in the low-wage firm. Choosing a wage slightly above the rival's, allows a firm – say, firm 1 – to capture the whole labour supply in the primary market. Either firm 1 hires all applicants, which implies that production capacity of firm 2 is zero in the Cournot game, or firm 1 hires only part of the applicants and obviously the one exhibiting the lowest training costs. Note, then, that increasing the wage above the other's has two implications. First it allows the firm to pre-empt the market completely, but it also allows the firm to select among the applicants the most able ones, in which case firm 2's output is determined by the residual supply addressed to her after firm 1 has hired all the workers it wants. A wage increase may in fact therefore, result in a lower cost. Thus, although it seems intuitive that an equilibrium should involve equal wages, the existence of such an equilibrium is not guaranteed. Consider an equilibrium candidate with equal wages set at a level which determines the aggregate labour supply required for producing the symmetric Cournot equilibrium outputs. Raising the wage slightly above the other's is clearly profitable simply because it allows the firm to benefit from lower cost associated with the possibility of choosing the most able applicants.

In view of the preceding remarks, it is worth discussing alternative frameworks for modelling product market competition. In this respect our results largely depend on the assumption that firms set quantities instead of prices. Indeed, in the present framework, the adoption of the new technology yields increasing marginal costs, and it is well known that the existence of a pure strategy equilibrium in prices is problematic in this case. Note that if firms were to hire workers before price competition takes place, a similar problem would arise since firms would then face limited production capacities as a function of their labour force. What makes the problem serious is that if on the one hand a pure strategy equilibrium does not exist, on the other payoffs associated with a mixed strategy equilibrium will be above the Bertrand ones. Thus, firms would be inclined to adopt the new technology because the resulting changes in the labour market translate into quantitative restrictions in the product market. Firms have a clear incentive to adopt the new technology, since it has the desirable implication of relaxing price competition. More generally, under price competition, firms could be tempted to use the labour market strategically, in order to achieve more collusive outcomes. Technological choices could be viewed as commitments to particular cost functions (see Vives, 1986). These choices are then governed by their strategic implications for product market competition and equilibrium outcomes are likely to be viewed as less competitive.

6   Concluding remarks

In this chapter, we have considered an example where the structure of the labour market affects firms' technological choices. The adoption of a new technology involves an adjustment of workers' skills which essentially translates into an increasing marginal cost. The labour market entails a negative externality because a firm's incentive to adopt the new technology depends on the shape of the resulting cost function, which in turn depends on the other firms' choices. In this context, firms may be led to choose different technologies in equilibrium – i.e. in equilibrium not all firms adopt the new technology. The present chapter can be viewed as a modest attempt to introduce labour market components in the analysis of oligopolistic industries. In this respect, we have shown that the structure of the labour market may have very important implications: in particular, it directly affects the degree of competition in the product market. Even though we have stressed that generalisations should not be expected to be easy, we believe that this topic deserves to be investigated further.

Bibliography

Bénassy, J.P. (1989) Market size and substitutability in imperfect competition: a Bertrand–Edgeworth–Chamberlin model, *Review of Economic Studies*, 56, pp. 217–34

Burda, M. (1988) Wait unemployment, *Economic Policy*, 7, pp. 393–425

Gabszewicz, J. and A. Turrini (2000) Workers' skills, product quality and industry equilibrium, *International Journal of Industrial Organization*, 18, pp. 575–93

Horn, H. and A. Wolinsky (1988) Bilateral monopolies and incentives for merger, *Rand Journal of Economics*, 19, pp. 408–19

Mills, D.E. and W. Smith (1996) It pays to be different: endogenous heterogeneity of firms in an oligopoly, *International Journal of Industrial Organization*, 14, pp. 317–29

Phlips, L. (1995) *Competition Policy: a Game-Theoretic Perspective*, Cambridge: Cambridge University Press

Reinganum, J. (1989) The timing of innovation: research, development, and diffusion, chapter 14 in R. Schmalensee and R.D. Willig (eds.), *Handbook of Industrial Organization*, 1, Amsterdam: North-Holland, pp. 849–908

Saint-Paul, E. (1996) *Dual Labor Markets: A Macroeconomic Perspective*, Cambridge, Mass.: MIT Press

Vives, X. (1986) Commitment, flexibility and market outcomes, *International Journal of Industrial Organization*, 4, pp. 217–29

Wauthy, X. and Y. Zenou (1997) Dual labor markets, efficiency wages and labour heterogeneity, *CORE Discussion Paper*, 9772

Ulph A.M. and D.T. Ulph (1994) Labor markets and innovation: *ex post* bargaining, *European Economic Review*, 38, pp. 195–210

Index

288   **Index**

Printed in the United States
By Bookmasters